HOURS WITH THE MYSTICS

VOL. I.

And yet, as Angels, in some brighter dreams,
  Call to the soul, when man doth sleep;
So some strange thoughts transcend our wonted themes,
  And into glory peep.

HENRY VAUGHAN.

HOURS WITH THE MYSTICS

A Contribution to the History of Religious Opinion

By ROBERT ALFRED VAUGHAN, B.A.

THIRD EDITION

TWO VOLUMES—VOL. I.

Anchora Spei

STRAHAN & COMPANY LIMITED
34 PATERNOSTER ROW, LONDON

Ballantyne Press
BALLANTYNE AND HANSON, EDINBURGH
CHANDOS STREET, LONDON

PREFACE TO THE THIRD EDITION.

———

THE work which is now again published was the result of too many years' steady application, and has served too great an intellectual use in the special department of thought of which it treats, to be allowed to fall into oblivion. Certainly the reading which the author thought it necessary to accomplish before he presented his conclusions to the public was vast and varied. That the fruit of his labours was commensurate may be gathered from the honest admiration which has been expressed by men knowing what hard study really means. The first edition of the 'Hours with the Mystics' appeared in 1856; the second was, to a great extent, revised by the author, but it did not appear until after his death. It was edited by his father, though most of the work of correction and verification was done by the author's widow.

There is no intention of writing a memoir here. That has already been done. But it has been suggested that it might be interesting to trace how Mysticism gradually became the author's favourite study. To do that it may be well to give a very short sketch of his literary career.

From the time he was quite a child he had the fixed

idea that he must be a literary man. In his twenty-first year (1844) he published a volume of poems, entitled ' The Witch of Endor, and other Poems.' The poetry in this little volume—long since out of print—was held to give promise of genius. It was, of course, the production of youth, and in after years the author was fully conscious of its defects. But even though some critics (and none could be a harder critic of his own work than himself) might point out an ' overcrowding of metaphor' and a ' want of clearness,' others could instance evidences of 'high poetical capability' and 'happy versification. But at the time it was thought desirable that the young poet should turn his attention to prose composition with the same earnestness. With that object his father proposed to him the study of the writings of Origen, with a view to an article on the subject in the *British Quarterly Review*. When just twenty-two the author finished this task, his first solid contribution to the literature of the day. The article showed signs of diligence and patient research in gaining a thorough knowledge of the opinions of the great thinker with whom it dealt. ' It is nobly done,' Judge Talfourd wrote. ' If there is some exuberance of ornament in the setting forth of his (Origen's) brilliant theories, it is only akin to the irregular greatness and the Asiatic splendour of the mind that conceived them.' And the words of the late Sir James Stephen were not less flattering : 'If I had been told that the writer of it (the article) was a grandfather, I should have wondered only that the old man had retained so much spirit and been able to combine it with a maturity of judgment so well becoming his years.' We believe it is no presumption to say that the article has not ceased to be useful to those who wish to gain an idea of the character of one whose name has often been the subject of bitter wordy war between Christian men.

In 1846, a dramatic piece by Alfred Vaughan, entitled 'Edwin and Elgiva,' appeared in the *London University Magazine*. The subject was one of a most sensational character, and was treated accordingly. Dunstan and his companions are painted in very black colours, and any doubts as to the reality of the cruelties alleged to have been practised on the unhappy Queen are not entertained. Two poems, the ' Masque of Antony' and 'Disenchantment,' though not published until later, were written about the same date.

At this time, the author was attending the theological course at Lancashire Independent College, of which his father was the president. Having completed his term of residence there, he went over to Halle in order to spend a year in a German University, before entering upon any fixed pastoral work. There he had a good opportunity of studying the state of German religious thought. The following extract from his journal shows the effect produced on his mind :—' If I am spared to return, I will preach more of what is called the Gospel than I did before. *The talk about adapting religion to the times which is prevalent here, even among the religious, appears to me a miserable mistake. It never needed adapting so much as when the apostles preached it, but they made no such effort.*' It was, too, while studying German speculations that the author adopted the system of philosophy, distinct alike from sceptical and mystical, which is apparent in this his chief work.

It is, we believe, impossible for an earnest mind to go through life without periods of sad and painful doubt. The author was no exception to this rule, and while at Halle he seems to have suffered bitterly. But he knew the one refuge for the doubting heart, and turned to it. In the 'Dream of Philo,' written at this time and published in the volumes of 'Essays and Remains,' we see some reflection of his own feelings, and the following verses which we venture to quote must, we think, strike a responsive chord in many a heart yearning for peace amidst the turmoil of the world :——

> Not a pathway in life's forest,
>   Not a pathway on life's sea ;
> Who doth heed me, who doth lead me,
>   Ah, woe is me !
>
> Vain the planting and the training,
>   For life's tree on every side
> Ever launches useless branches,
>   Springs not high but spreadeth wide.
>
> Ah, my days go not together
>   In an earnest solemn train,
> But go straying for their playing,
>   Or are by each other slain.
>
> Listen, listen, thou forgettest
>   Thou art one of many more ;
> All this ranging and this changing
>   Has been law to man of yore.
>
> And thou canst not in life's city
>   Rule thy course as in a cell
> There are others, all thy brothers,
>   Who have work to do as well.

Some events that mar thy purpose
　　May light *them* upon their way;
Our sun-shining in declining
　　Gives earth's other side the day.

Every star is drawn and draweth
　　Mid the orbits of its peers;
And the blending thus unending
　　Makes the music of the spheres.

If thou doest one work only,
　　In that one work thou wilt fail;
Use thou many ropes if any
　　For the shifting of thy sail.

Then will scarce a wind be stirring
　　But thy canvas it shall fill;
Not the near way as thou thoughtest,
But through tempest as thou oughtest,
Though not straightly, not less greatly,
　　Thou shalt win the haven still.

These verses have been called 'Alfred Vaughan's Psalm of Life.' The lessons taught may be an encouragement to others, as they have been to the author's son, in times of trial and disappointment.

But it must not be supposed that at this time the author's thoughts were all devoted to painful doubts and yearnings. He determined while in Germany to unite the labours of a literary man to the work of a pastor. His first plan was to take special periods of Church History and lay them before his readers in the form of dramas. He thus describes his idea:—'I shall commence the series with Savonarola. I think it will not be necessary to pay regard to chronological order in the order of composition. I may afterwards take up Chrysostom, per-

haps Hildebrand, endeavouring in all not merely to
develop the character of the principal personage, but to
give an exact picture of the religious and political spirit
of the times. They must be dramas on the principles
of *King John* or *Henry IV.*, rather than those of *Hamlet*
or *Macbeth.*' With this scheme his father did not
entirely agree, and the consequence was a considerable
correspondence. Dr. Vaughan never doubted the genius
of his son, or that something definite would come of
his literary tastes, but he appears to have thought that
the dramatic form was not a good way in which to
bring the result of genuine hard work before the public.
As it happened, none of these dramas saw the light,
though the plan of the 'Hours with the Mystics' shows
the strong attachment the author felt for that kind of
writing, and it also shows the way in which he could
overcome any difficulties arising from its peculiarities.
The notion of gentlemen discussing the Mystics, over
their wine and walnuts, or in the garden with the ladies
in the twilight of a summer evening, has had to encounter the sneers of some harsh critics, but we cannot
help thinking that advantage is gained by the device
of these conversations, because the talking by various
speakers affords an easy opportunity of glancing over
many varying theories upon any subject at the same time,
while the essayist would find it difficult to keep his line
of argument clear, and at the same moment state the
divergent lines of thought necessary for the right understanding of the position generally.

The author began definite ministerial work at Bath
in 1848. The thoroughness with which he performed
his pastoral duties did not give him much time for

literary work. The articles written during his stay in that city were those on Schleiermacher and Savonarola. The materials for both essays were collected while at Halle. When writing to inform his father of the completion of the first of the articles, he refers to the Mystics in the following way :—

'I shall not begin to write another article at once. But I should like to fix on one to have more-or-less in view. There are three subjects on which I should like to write some time or other—(1) Savonarola, for which I have much material; (2) on Mysticism, tracing it in the East, in the Greek Church, in the German Mystics of the 14th century, in the French Mystics, and lastly in those most recent; (3) Leo the Great and his stirring times. I should like to do the Savonarola next. But I should also like to know what you think on these subjects, or on any other you would perhaps like better. The first and third would consist largely of interesting narrative. The second would be rather less popular but more novel.'

The 'second' subject was worked up into the two volumes now republished. As it gradually became his favourite study, he felt that the field was expanding before him, and that it would be necessary, if he did justice to his theme, to treat it at a greater length than could be allowed to a magazine article. In the *British Quarterly Review* articles appeared on 'Madame Guyon,' and 'The Mystics and the Reformers,' which were simply the first results of his reading for the great work. It was at Birmingham that most of this writing was done : while there he was an indefatigable student. 'There,' says a writer in the *Eclectic Review*, Nov. 1861,

p. 508, 'he made himself familiar with many languages
—the old German, the Spanish, even the Dutch,
adding these to the Italian, French, Latin, and
Greek in the classical and later forms, and all as
preparations to the History of Mysticism to which
he had pledged himself.   The Mystics had thrown
a spell upon him.   Seldom have they wrought their
charms without seducing to their bewildering self-
abandonment. . . . . In the case of Alfred Vaughan
it was not so ; he continued faithful to the high duties
of life.   He trod the sphere of action and compelled
the ghostly band he visited, or who visited him, to pay
tribute to the highest religious teaching of Christian
truth and life.'   But the body would not keep pace with
his mind.   In 1855 he was obliged to resign his pastoral
charge at Birmingham, and from that time he devoted
himself entirely to literature.   He wrote several articles
and criticisms, chiefly in the *British Quarterly* amongst
these, one on Kingsley's 'Hypatia,' which we believe was
much appreciated by the future Canon of Westminster.
An article on ' Art and History ' appeared in *Fraser's
Magazine* about the same time.   And now we reach
the first publication of his greater achievement, the
'Hours with the Mystics.'   In August, 1855, the printing
of the original edition began, and was completed in the
February of the following year.   The author lived long
enough afterwards to witness its success, and then
swiftly came the end.   In October, 1857, Alfred Vaughan
passed away into another world where he has doubtless found many of those on whose characters he
loved to muse.   We will not attempt any analysis
of *his* character, but we cannot resist the impulse

to insert one loving tribute to his memory, which appeared in a Birmingham paper (*Aris' Gazette,* Nov. 27th, 1857). 'It has seemed fit to the All-Wise Disposer of events to withdraw from this world one of its holiest and most gifted inhabitants, one who, had his life been prolonged, bade fair to have taken rank among its brightest lights and most distinguished ornaments. . . . . The strength and sweetness, so happily blended in his character, were apparent in his preaching ; he was tender enough for the most womanly heart, he was intellectual enough for the most masculine mind. As a writer he had already attained considerable reputation, and promised to become one of the chief luminaries of the age. As a Christian, he was sound in faith, benignant in spirit, and most holy in life; a delighter in the doctrine of God, his Saviour, and an eminent adorner of that doctrine.'

Before venturing on any remarks upon the subject-matter of the book itself, we may be allowed to make a slight reference to opinions expressed upon it at the time of its publication. In *Fraser's Magazine* for September, 1856, there was a long review by Canon Kingsley. In this article weak points are shown and sometimes the criticisms are rather severe ; but there was too much real sympathy between the two men (though they never knew each other personally) for the reviewer not fully to appreciate the good qualities in the work before him. Now that Charles Kingsley's name is such a household word in England, no apology is needed for quoting two passages from the above-mentioned essay. ' There is not a page,' it says in one place, 'nor a paragraph in which there is not something worth recollecting, and often reflections very wise and weighty indeed, which show that whether or not Mr. Vaughan has thoroughly grasped the subject of Mysticism, he has grasped and made part of his own mind and heart many things far more practically important than Mysticism, or any other form of thought; and no one ought to rise up from the perusal of his book without finding himself, if not a better, at least a more thoughtful man, and perhaps a humbler one also, as he learns how many more struggles and doubts, discoveries, sorrows and joys, the human race has passed through, than are contained in his own private experience.' In another place, while pointing out various improvements which he would like to see in another edition, Mr. Kingsley adds, 'But whether our hope be fulfilled or not, a useful and honourable future is before the man who could write such a book as this is in spite of all defects.' The reviewer adds later in a reprint of this essay, 'Mr. Vaughan's death does not, I think, render it necessary for me to alter any of the opinions expressed here, and least of all that in the last sentence, fulfilled now more perfectly than I could have foreseen.'

With the mention of Charles Kingsley's name we are reminded of others of the same school of thought, and therefore the following comparison in an article in the *Eclectic Review* (November, 1861) may prove interesting. The reader must judge of its truth. 'While Robertson of Brighton,' says the reviewer, 'was preaching his sermons, and Archer Butler was preparing his Lectures on Philosophy, Alfred Vaughan about the same age, but younger than either, was accumulating material for, and putting into shape, the "Hours with the Mystics."

He died within a year or two of their departure, and still nearer to the period of youth than those extraordinary men. His name suggests their names to the mind —all victims to the fatal thirty-four and thirty-seven. He had not the wonderful touch of Robertson's "vanished hand"; he had not the tenacity of muscle and fibre of Archer Butler; but he combined many of the characteristics of both, and added that which gave individuality to his genius. He had not the fine subtle sense of insight possessed by Robertson ; he had not the rapid and comprehensive power of Butler. They again had not his large and generous culture.' More of such favourable criticisms and kindly words from men of learning might be quoted, but we forbear. The task of referring to such sentiments is not unnaturally attractive to the son of such a man ; but it is simply desired to put forward this book once again on its own merits, in the hope that there are still many who will rightly appreciate the labour and genius to which it bears witness.

About the work itself it will be necessary to say only a few words.

When the 'Hours with the Mystics' first appeared it traversed ground which was to a great extent untrodden, at any rate in England. Mysticism, though a favourite study of the author, was not then, and can scarcely be said to be now, a popular subject. A matter-of-fact age puts such ideas on one side, as something too weak for serious consideration. The majority indeed have but a very hazy notion as to what Mysticism is ; they only have an idea that something is meant which is very inferior, and they pass it by. Well has Mr. Maurice said that such terms (Mediæval Phil. p. 143) 'are the cold formal generalisations of a late period, commenting on men with which it has no sympathy.' In the minds of thoughtful men the name of mystic points to a special and recognisable tendency, and the history given in this book shows that the same tendency has been working in the world for ages ;—Hindus and Persians, Neoplatonists and Schoolmen, Anabaptists and Swedenborgians, have all felt its force. The main principle of all their doctrine was the necessity of a closer union with the Deity. Among Christians,—with whom we are chiefly concerned,— this close connection, it was thought, could only be gained after passing through stages of illumination and purification ; and progress in the way of perfection was to be made not by labour and study, but by solitude. and asceticism. In these volumes this doctrine is exhibited ; especially we trace the influence which the pseudo-Dionysius had in the fourth century ; how, under his guidance, these ideas spread in the East, and thence to the West ; the position taken up by Mystics against the Schoolmen, and the condition of Mysticism at the time of the Reformation. These topics are interesting, and to the questions which must be raised in connection with them in every thoughtful mind, it is hoped that the reader will find satisfactory answers in the following pages.

It will be seen that the field over which the reader is taken by the author is very large. It is believed that though there have been during recent years various contributions made to the literature on this subject, no writer has attempted to take in all the various phases which are pictured in this book. In German Mystics some writers have found a congenial theme ; others have taught us more about the mysterious religions of the East. It is, we think, to be regretted that more attention has not been paid to the Mystics of the Scholastic period. The position held by Hugo of S. Victor and his followers was by no means insignificant. As a mystic, Hugo showed that it was possible to combine contemplation with common sense and learning. In an age when Scholasticism was submitting religion to cold and exact logic, it was like turning from some dusty road into a quiet grass-grown lane, to hear of devout contemplation leading up to perfect holiness and spiritual knowledge. Most of us are ready to agree with these men when they maintain that there are mysteries of Divine Truth which cannot be analysed by the understanding, but which can be embraced by thoughtful and reverent contemplation. So long as the use of both learning and devotion was admitted, we are able to sympathise with them. But it is a truism to say that the tendency of any movement is to go to extremes. The Mystics of this period appear to have recoiled horror-struck from what seemed to them rationalistic or materialistic ideas. In that, they might be right enough. But starting from the true standpoint that there are mysteries in the Infinite which we finite creatures cannot fathom with our finite minds, they proceeded to the extreme of putting devotion before knowledge. Next, they thought there was nothing to which they could not attain by devout yearning, even to absorption into the Deity. The logical conclusion of these theories tended to pantheism : those who discarded logic

yielded to fanaticism. Into that error fell most of the
disciples of the great Scholastic Mystics. And has not
the like occurred elsewhere in history? Putting religion
out of the question, Wycliffe may have been a socialist,
but he was far behind his followers. But as such a falling
away on the part of the disciple cannot justly
take from the character of the master, so we would
still say a word for Hugo of S. Victor. A man whose
aim in life was the knowledge of God, and who worked
for that end with courage and diligence, is not a
character to be neglected. ' His name,' says Mr. Maurice
(Mediæval Phil. p. 148), 'has been less remembered in
later times than it deserves, because it has been overshadowed by those of other men who met some of the
tastes of the age more successfully, though their actual
power was not greater than his, perhaps not equal to it.'

In Hugo of S. Victor and his predecessors, Bernard
and Anselm, we see the combination of Scholasticism
and Mysticism. To some extent they were able to
keep a middle course. They would not allow their
reason to run riot over sacred mysteries, and their firm
hold on the articles of the Catholic faith prevented them
from sinking into vague pantheism.

Among the Mystics of Germany who come next
in the hasty survey we are here attempting, there does
not appear to have been so much steadiness. We do
not mean to say that the Scholastic Mystics were
perfect; they were not free from exaggerations, but
their extravagances appear to us less dangerous than were
those of the old German Mystics. The names of the
leading German Mystics are more familiar to most people
than are any others. Who has not heard of Tauler?

What the influence of his teaching was is shown in the following pages. He may be exonerated from all charge of pantheism, as may, also, be Ruysbroek and Suso ; but it is very doubtful whether the writings left by Eckart acquit him of all connection with these errors. He has been claimed as orthodox by churchmen, and as a pantheist by many pantheists ; and extracts can be quoted from his works in support of either theory. Eckart's position was difficult. The general temper of the world at the time was restless ; the errors and abuses of the Church drove earnest men to look within. They turned their attention to personal holiness, to the neglect of the fact that they had any duties towards the Christian brotherhood at large. To urge his hearers to a closer union with God was a noble subject for a preacher. But must it not be confessed that Eckart had gone too far when he could utter such words as these, 'a truly divine man has been so made one with God that henceforth he does not think of God or look for God outside himself ?' His teaching certainly approached often towards the brink of the abyss of pantheism, and as Archbishop Trench says (Med. Ch. Hist., p. 348), 'sometimes it does not stop short of the brink.'

Between these two schools, the Scholastic and the German, many comparisons may be made. The effect of them on the Catholic Church as it then existed was very different : the teaching of Anselm and Bernard was calculated to strengthen the Church, while that of the later school was not. Anselm and his friends were aware of the necessity for personal holiness, but they were always willing for their disciples to climb the road to perfection

by the help of the means of grace held out in the Church,
as well as by devout contemplation.   The Germans, on
the contrary, felt there was something wrong with the
existing ecclesiastical arrangements, and through indifference to them drew their disciples away from many practices which were then accounted necessary to salvation.
By this disregard for rites and ceremonies, and by their
use of the German language in their teaching, they paved
the way for the Reformers, and that is a great claim on
our respect.   At the same time, we cannot help thinking
their hazy ideas rather chilling.   Surely the highest
point in the history of Mysticism had been reached and
passed when the struggle to make reason and imagination
work together gave way to mere ecstatic rhapsody.

Quietism is discussed in the second volume at considerable length; the familiar names of Madame Guyon, Bossuet
and Fénélon are brought before us.   The story is a sad
one.   There may be some who think that Madame Guyon
was not worthy of the friendship of such a saint as
Fénléon,——that must be a matter of opinion; but on
one point all will agree, the conduct of Bossuet under
the circumstances was not very creditable.   Those who
have a high opinion of the piety of Bossuet will confess
that he does not appear in the narrative to advantage,
even though they may not be able to agree with all the
statements the author of this work makes about the
Bishop of Meaux.   Fénélon was tender, gentle, loving,
and Bossuet was firm, stern, and strict, but they both did
their best to serve God in their relative positions, and
He, whose servants they were, will judge them.

Glancing, then, through the entire length of this
history, we see that the great principle which appears to

have actuated all Mystics was a desire for union with God. This they tried to cultivate by seclusion and asceticism. They neglected social duties and fled away into monasteries and deserts; and sometimes their practical life was not equal in holiness to the reported spirituality of their ecstasies. Their excesses of mortification appear almost ludicrous when they themselves alone are concerned, but when their mad conduct is seen affecting others our feelings grow stronger. But let us speak gently of such eccentricities. These good people, for good they certainly were, could not appreciate the fact that God was in the busy town as well as in the lonely desert. They heard no voice within them urging them to treat a beggar kindly for the sake of the Son of God. Some of them were very charitable, but what was the nature of their charity? Was it not simply done for their own advantage? Did they really think of charity as an act done to God, not meritorious, but as being an offering to their Heavenly Father of His own? It is to be feared that that was not the general idea. The more extravagant Mystics appear really to have been horribly selfish. They had yet to learn that the closer union for which they longed is not attained by efforts to 'faire son salut,' or by sitting still in the comfortable assurance of an imputed righteousness. Then it must be remembered that all these frantic efforts or dreamy ecstasies were made with a view to union with God. And this 'union' was of a novel kind—in many cases there was a notion of an absorption into the Deity, together with other ideas which clearly involved erroneous views of God. It was the old story of carrying one particular article of faith or pious opinion to extremes, and this to the disregard, more or less complete, of all else. The same thing had happened before in the history of the Christian Church. It is not for us to lay down a definition of what is true union with God; but we may say that the fellowship which all true believers enjoy with the Father through the Son was not enough for the Mystic. He struggled and panted for more. How each one succeeded or failed the individual reader of the work must judge, and decide for himself.

Before going further, it may be well to refer to an attack which was made on the author for his treatment of mediæval saints and of the stories connected with them. Obviously, a man who sympathises with an emotional form of religion would not be inclined to confine these enthusiasts within such narrow limits as would one of a colder temperament. This may explain the feelings of the critics in question. There can be little doubt that the ascetic and the nun, with their mortifications and trances, had not for the author much attraction. Even the style in which the book was written may have led him to write too lightly on some details of this period; but if such were the case, he knew, as well as any critic, that these people were trying to do their duty, even if they failed. The ascetic who thought he had no duty in the world, and therefore ran away and refused to 'fight a battle for the Lord,' and the ' hysterical sister,' are rather subjects for pity than for jest; and contrary as all the author's convictions may have been to asceticism, he would rather have wept over their strange acts and mad fancies than scoffed at them. We feel convinced that any harsh remarks should be taken as referring to the system which brought its victims into such a condition, and not to the victims themselves. Though disapproving of the system, the author would never have withheld his admiration from any individual act of self-sacrifice, when it was done from a right motive and was the offering of a loving heart.

The fact that this book is again published by request is a sign that the author's labours have been appreciated and that his name is not forgotten. 'Some men,' he once wrote in a letter, 'who have died young, have lived far longer than others who have outpassed their three-score years and ten. Life consists not in the abundance of things a man possesseth, nor in the abundance of things a man doeth, but in the abundance of thoughts he thinks leading toward some special result in this world or the next.' So, again, he writes in his diary, ' Reputation—consider it, soul of mine, not as an end, but as a means of sowing right thoughts and feelings among thy fellows. Strive towards power over the thoughts of men—power that may be solemnly used in God's sight as being a faithful steward for His glory. Have I a brain that must be busy, a will in this direction which—with all my vacillation elsewhere—has been and is unconquerable ? Let me pray to use it with reverent lowliness of heart as a talent committed to me, fearing to misuse it, to allow any corner of the estate to be waste, or any wain of the harvest to fall into the enemy's hand.'

If it now be asked, what are the uses of this book, we may answer that it has proved helpful as a history of religious thought. Further, it is hoped that it has been, and still will be, useful on account of the moral lessons to be drawn from the historical facts.

It may also be used as showing how necessary it is
to associate Christianity with our daily lives ; how desirable it is that preachers should avoid confining their
hearers' attention to their own individual souls. And then
it further teaches that, while we take religion into the
world, we may learn also to value more the privileges of
quiet and retired communion with God. In these practical
modern days the idea of contemplation appears out of
place ; and yet it was our Divine Master who said, ' Come
apart into a desert place and rest awhile.' Perhaps the
world would have been better if the hermits had paid
more attention to the little word '*awhile*.' But the
bustle of the present day is just as likely to make us
forget the injunction altogether.

The book's republication now seems to have a special
opportuneness, for in much of the more spiritual progress going on around us there is a good deal of
Mysticism. As in times past men sought refuge in
devout contemplation from Materialism, so now a horror
of Rationalism and a sense of injustice are likely to
drive many to the same extreme. Whether or not there
has been any undue extravagance developed as yet, it is
not for us to decide. But this history will show how easy
and possible it is to carry a good principle beyond its
proper limits.

Before concluding, one further personal word must be
permitted. No preface to this book, however short,
would be complete without at least a reference to her
who helped the author in his labours as only a good
wife can, and who has taught his son to love God and
reverence his father's memory as only a good mother

can. To her, the reappearance of this work causes a ray of light amidst a life darkened by much trouble and suffering.

It need scarcely be added that the writer of these words esteems it an honour to be in any way connected with his father's labours. What the loss of such a father has been to him cannot be described in words. The following remarks of a clerical friend of the author may partly express the writer's present feelings : 'He is gone, young in years—but for him we may not lament the dispensation—since assuredly he was not only mature in intellect but rich in grace. I delight to think of him as one of that "blessed company," the Church above—to the perfect love and friendship of some members of which I love to look forward, if by God's grace I may be found worthy to attain to it.'

This book never had any public dedication. It was the work of the best years of a life offered to God. What was not done for the first edition will not be done now ; but let these few lines of the author's son be an offering to the glory of God—to the memory of his father—to the self-devotion of his mother.

In one of the author's poems is the following verse which is strangely appropriate at this place:—

> Let us toil on—the work we leave behind us,
>   Though incomplete, God's hand will yet embalm,
> And use it some way ; and the news will find us
>   In heaven above, and sweeten endless calm.

WYCLIFFE VAUGHAN.

LITTLEMORE, NEAR OXFORD,
  November, 1879.

PREFACE TO THE FIRST EDITION.

THE subject of the present work is one which will generally be thought to need some words of explanation, if not of apology. Mysticism is almost everywhere synonymous with what is most visionary in religion and most obscure in speculation. But a *history* of Mysticism—old visions and old obscurities—who is bold enough to expect a hearing for that? Is the hopeful present, struggling toward clear intelligence, to pause and hear how, some hundreds of years ago, men made themselves elaborately unintelligible? Is our straining after action and achievement to be relaxed while you relate the way in which Mystics reduced themselves to utter inactivity? While we are rejoicing in escape from superstitious twilight, is it well to recall from Limbo the phantasms of forgotten dreamers, and to people our sunshine with ghostly shadows? And since Mysticism is confessedly more or less a mistake, were it not better to point out to us, if you can, a something true and wise, rather than offer us your portrait of an exaggeration and a folly?

Such are some of the questions which it will be natural to ask. The answer is at hand. First of all, Mysticism, though an error, has been associated, for the most part, with a measure of truth so considerable, that its good has greatly outweighed its evil. On this ground alone, its history should be judged of interest. For we grow more hopeful and more charitable as we mark how small a leaven of truth may prove an antidote to error, and how often the genuine fervour of the spirit has all but made good the failures of the intellect.

In the religious history of almost every age and country, we meet with a certain class of minds, impatient of mere ceremonial forms and technical distinctions, who have pleaded the cause of the heart against prescription, and yielded themselves to the most vehement impulses of the soul, in its longing to escape from the sign to the thing signified—from the human to the divine. The story of such an ambition, with its disasters and its glories, will not be deemed, by any thoughtful mind, less worthy of record than the career of a conqueror. Through all the changes of doctrine and the long conflict of creeds, it is interesting to trace the unconscious unity of mystical temperaments in every communion. It can scarcely be without some profit that we essay to gather together and arrange this company of ardent natures ; to account for their harmony and their differences, to ascertain the extent of their influence for good and evil, to point out their errors, and to estimate even dreams impossible to cold or meaner spirits.

These Mystics have been men of like passions and in like perplexities with many of ourselves. Within them and without them were temptations, mysteries, aspirations like our own. A change of names, or an interval of time, does not free us from liability to mistakes in their direction, or to worse, it may be, in a direction opposite. To distinguish between the genuine and the spurious in their opinion or their life, is to erect a guide-post on the very road we have ourselves to tread. It is no idle or pedantic curiosity which would try these spirits by their fruits, and see what mischief and what blessing grew out of their misconceptions and their truth. We learn a lesson for ourselves, as we mark how some of these Mystics found God within them after vainly seeking Him without— hearkened happily to that witness for Him which speaks in our conscience, affections, and desires ; and, recognising love by love, finally rejoiced in a faith which was rather the life of their heart than the conclusion of their logic. We learn a lesson for ourselves, as we see one class among them forsaking common duties for the feverish exaltation of a romantic saintship, and another persisting in their conceited rejection of the light without, till they have turned into darkness their light within.

But the interest attaching to Mysticism is by no means merely historic. It is active under various forms in our own time. It will certainly play its part in the future. The earlier portion of this work is occupied, it must be confessed, with modes of thought and life extremely remote from anything with which we are now familiar. But only by such inquiry into those bygone speculations could the character and influence of Christian Mysticism be duly estimated, or even accounted for. Those preliminaries once past, the reader will find himself in contact with opinions and events less removed from present experience.

The attempt to exhibit the history of a certain phase of religious life through the irregular medium of fiction, dialogue, and essay, may appear to some a plan too fanciful for so grave a theme. But it must be remembered, that any treatment of such a subject which precluded a genial exercise of the imagination would be necessarily inadequate, and probably unjust. The method adopted appeared also best calculated to afford variety and relief to topics unlikely in themselves to attract general interest. The notes which are appended have been made more copious than was at first designed, in order that no confusion may be possible between fact and fiction, and that every statement of importance might be sustained by its due authority. It is hoped that, in this way, the work may render its service, not only to those who deem secondary information quite sufficient on such subjects, but also to the scholar, who will thus be readily enabled to test for himself my conclusions, and who will possess, in the extracts given, a kind of anthology from the writings of the leading Mystics. To those familiar with such inquiries it may perhaps be scarcely necessary to state that I have in no instance allowed myself to cite as an authority any passage which I have not myself examined, with its context, in the place to which I refer. In the *Chronicle of Adolf Arnstein* the minimum of invention has been employed, and no historical personage there introduced utters any remark bearing upon Mysticism for which ample warrant cannot be brought forward. Wherever, in the conversations at Ashfield, any material difference of opinion is expressed by the speakers, Atherton may be understood as setting forth what we ourselves deem the truth of the matter. Some passages in these volumes, and the substance of the chapters on Quietism, have made their appearance previously in the pages of one of our quarterly periodicals.

It should be borne in mind that my design does not require of me that I should give an account of all who are anywhere known to have entertained mystical speculation, or given themselves to mystical practice. I have endeavoured to portray and estimate those who have made epochs in the history of Mysticism, those who are fair representatives of its stages or transitions, those whose enthusiasm has been signally benign or notoriously baneful. I have either mentioned by name only, or passed by in silence, the followers or mere imitators of such men, and those Mystics also whose obscure vagaries neither produced any important result nor present any remarkable phænomena. Only by resolute omission on this principle has it been possible to preserve in any measure that historical perspective so essential to the truth of such delineations.

The fact that the ground I traverse lies almost wholly unoccupied, might be pleaded on behalf of my undertaking. The history of Mysticism has been but incidentally touched by English writers. Germany possesses many monographs of unequal value on detached parts of the subject. Only recently has a complete account of Christian Mysticism appeared, at all on a level with the latest results of historical inquiry.* This laborious compilation presents the dry bones of doctrinal opinion, carefully separated from actual life—a grave

---

* *Die Christliche Mystik.* Von Dr. Ludwig Noack. Königsberg.

defect in any branch of ecclesiastical history, absolutely
fatal to intelligibility and readableness in this. If we
except the researches of the Germans into their own
mediæval Mysticism, it may be truly said that the little
done in England has been better done than the much
in Germany. The Mysticism of the Neo-Platonists has
found a powerful painter in Mr. Kingsley. The Mysticism
of Bernard meets with a wise and kindly critic in Sir
James Stephen.

If, then, the subject of this book be neither insignificant in itself, nor exhausted by the labours of
others, my enterprise at least is not unworthy, however
questionable its success.

THE AUTHOR.

February 1st, 1856.

PREFACE TO THE SECOND EDITION.

THIS work has been some time out of print. It
was my hope that the Second Edition might
have been brought within a single volume. But that
has not been practicable.

The present edition has been revised by the Author,
and some fifty pages of new matter have been introduced. This new matter will be found mainly in
the Sixth Chapter of the Sixth Book. In that enlarged treatment of the topic of "German Mysticism in
the Fourteenth Century" the reader will meet with a

slight recurrence of former trains of thought, which the Author might have been inclined to suppress, but with which I have not deemed it well to intermeddle. It will be seen that the design of the supplementary matter is, in part, as a reply to criticisms which seemed to call for some such explanation ; and, in part, that points touched upon elsewhere might be given with more fulness.

To see this Second Edition through the press has been the work of one whose intelligent sympathy and patient effort assisted and encouraged the Author, in many ways, in the prosecution of his studies, and who now finds the solace of her loneliness in treasuring up the products of his mind, and in cherishing the dear ones he has left to her wise love and oversight.

If Mysticism be often a dream, it is commonly a dream in the right direction. Its history presents one of the most significant chapters in the story of humanity.

ROBERT VAUGHAN.

September 7th, 1860.

CONTENTS OF VOL. I.

———◆———

BOOK I.—INTRODUCTION.

CHAPTER I.

CHAPTER II.

CHAPTER III.

CHAPTER IV.

CHAPTER V.

BOOK IV.—MYSTICISM IN THE GREEK CHURCH.

CHAPTER I.

CHAPTER II.

BOOK V.—MYSTICISM IN THE LATIN CHURCH.

CHAPTER I.

CHAPTER II.

BOOK VI.—GERMAN MYSTICISM IN THE FOURTEENTH CENTURY.

CHAPTER I.

BOOK THE FIRST

INTRODUCTION

CHAPTER I.

Wie fruchtbar ist der kleinste Kreis,
Wenn man ihn wohl zu pflegen weiss.[1]

GOETHE.

IT was on the evening of a November day that three friends sat about their after-dinner table, chatting over their wine and walnuts, while the fire with its huge log crackled and sparkled, and the wind without moaned about the corners of the house.

Everyone is aware that authors have in their studies an unlimited supply of rings of Gyges, coats of darkness, tarn-caps, and other means of invisibility,—that they have the key to every house, and can hear and see words and actions the most remote. Come with me, then, kindly reader, and let us look and listen unseen ; we have free leave ; and you must know these gentlemen better.

First of all, the host. See him leaning back in his chair, and looking into the fire, one hand unconsciously smoothing with restless thumb and finger the taper stem of his wineglass, the other playing with the ears of a favourite dog. He appears about thirty years of age, is tall, but loses something of his real height by a student's stoop about the shoulders. Those decided almost shaggy eyebrows he has would lead you to expect quick, piercing eyes,—the eyes of the observant man of action. But now that he looks towards us, you see instead eyes of hazel, large, slow-rolling, often dreamy in their gaze,—such for size and lustre as Homer gives to ox-eyed Juno. The mouth, too,

[1] How fruitful may the smallest circle grow,
If we the secret of its culture know.

and the nose are delicately cut. Their outline indicates taste rather than energy. Yet that massive jaw, again, gives promise of quiet power,—betokens a strength of that sort, most probably, which can persevere in a course once chosen with indomitable steadiness, but is not an agile combative force, inventive in assaults and rejoicing in adventurous leadership. Men of his species resemble fountains, whose water-column a sudden gust of wind may drive aslant, or scatter in spray across the lawn, but—the violence once past—they play upward as truly and as strong as ever.

Perhaps it is a pity that this Henry Atherton is so rich as he is,—owns his Ashfield House, with its goodly grounds, and has never been forced into active professional life, with its rough collisions and straining anxieties. Abundance of leisure is a trial to which few men are equal. Gray was in the right when he said that something more of genius than common was required to teach a man how to employ himself. My friend became early his own task-master, and labours harder from choice than many from necessity. To high attainment as a classical scholar he has added a critical acquaintance with the literature and the leading languages of modern Europe. Upstairs is a noble library, rich especially in historical authorities, and there Atherton works, investigating now one historic question, now another, endeavouring out of old, yellow-faced annals to seize the precious passages which suggest the life of a time, and recording the result of all in piles of manuscript.

How often have I and Gower—that youngest of the three, on the other side, with the moustache—urged him to write a book. But he waits, and, with his fastidiousness, will always wait, I am afraid, till he has practically solved this problem ;— given a subject in remote history, for which not ten of your friends care a straw ; required such a treatment of it as shall at once be relished by the many and accredited as standard by the few. So, thinking it useless to write what scarcely anyone will read, and despairing of being ever erudite and popular at the same time, he is content to enquire and to accumulate in most happy obscurity. Doubtless the world groans under its many books, yet it misses some good ones that would assuredly be written if able men with the ambition were oftener possessed of the time required, or if able men with the time were oftener possessed of the ambition.

You ask me, 'Who is this Gower?'

An artist. Atherton met with him at Rome, where he was tracing classic sites, and Gower worshipping the old masters. Their pathway chanced on one or two occasions to coincide, and by little and little they grew fast friends. They travelled through Germany together on their way home, and found their friendship robust enough to survive the landing on our British shore. Unquestionably the pictured Vatican, sunny Forum, brown Campagna, garlanded baths of Caracalla, with quaint, ingenious Nuremberg, and haunted Hartz, made common memories for both. But this was not all. Atherton had found the young painter in a sentimental fever. He raved about Shelley; he was full of adoration for the flimsiest abstractions —enamoured of impersonations the most impalpable; he discoursed in high strain on the dedication of life as a Hymn to Intellectual Beauty. The question of questions with him concerned not Truth or Fable, but the Beautiful or the Not-Beautiful. Whatever charmed his taste was from Ormuzd, the Good: whatever revolted it, from Ahriman, the Evil; and so the universe was summarily parted. He fancied he was making art religious, while, in fact, he made religion a mere branch of art,—and that branch, of all others, the most open to individual caprice.

From these wanderings Atherton reclaimed him, wisely, and therefore almost insensibly. Gower never forgot the service.

In his admiration for Atherton, when fully conscious of it, he little suspected that he, too, had conferred a benefit in his turn. Atherton had looked too much within, as Gower too exclusively without. A certain imaginative, even poetical element, dormant in the mind of the former, was resuscitated by this friendship.

Gower rejoices in the distressingly novelish Christian name of Lionel. Why will parents give names to their offspring which are sure to entail ridicule during the most susceptible period of existence ? No sooner did young Lionel enter school, with that delicate red-and-white complexion, and long curling hair, than he was nicknamed Nelly. But he fought his way stoutly till he won a title from the first part of his name rather than the last, and in school traditions figures still as Lion, royally grim and noble. That open countenance and high forehead, with the deep piercing eyes set rather far apart, constitute not merely a promising physiognomy for the artist, they bear faithful witness to mental power and frankness of character, to practical sagacity and force. In one respect only can he be charged with asserting in his person his professional pretensions,—his hair is parted in the middle, falling in natural waves on either side ; long enough, as your eye tells you, for grace ; too short for affectation.

One quality in Gower I have always especially liked,—his universality. Not that he sets up for Encyclopædism ; on the contrary, he laments more than he need the scantiness of his knowledge and his want of time for its enlargement. What I mean is that with every kind of enquiry, every province of culture, he seems to have intuitively the readiest sympathy. Though his notion of the particular art or science may be only cursory and general, his imagination puts him in some way in the place of its exclusive devotees, and he enters into their feelings till their utmost worship appears scarcely excessive to him. I have heard such votaries pour out unreservedly into his ear, as into that of a brother enthusiast, all those delightful details of adventure, of hope and fear, of research and of conjecture, which make the very life of the most minute or the most arid pursuits, and which books impart to us so rarely. And all this (making the world to him such a wide one) without taking aught from his allegiance to painting. Already have his genius and his diligence achieved success—you will find his pictures realizing high prices—and that snug little box of his, only ten minutes' walk from Ashfield, is furnished much too handsomely to accord with the popular idea of what must be the residence of a young artist, five-and-twenty, but newly started in his profession, and with all his 'expectations' gathered up within his brush.

'The third member of the trio, Mr. Author, has not certainly the personal advantages of our friend Gower. I suppose you expect me to say 'our' now, if only as a compliment. Yet stay —a very expressive face, with a genial hearty look about it ;— there! now he is smiling, that rather clumsy mouth is quite pleasant ; but he lets too much beard grow for my taste.'

Bearded Willoughby, O Reader, is a literary man, a confirmed bachelor, they say ; and encrusted with some roughnesses and oddities which conceal from the eyes of strangers his real warmth of heart and delicacy of feeling. His parents destined him for the Church from those tender years wherein the only vocation manifest is that which summons boyhood to peg-top and jam tart. When the time drew near in which he should have taken orders, Willoughby went up to London, brimful of eager philanthropy, of religious doubts, and of literary ambition, to become one of the High-priests of Letters. His first work was a novel to illustrate the mission of the literary Priesthood, a topsy-turvy affair, but dashingly clever—by the way, you can scarcely offend him more than to mention it now ;—with this book he succeeded in producing a sensation, and the barrier thus passed, his pen has found full employment ever since. He has now abandoned the extravagances of hero-worship, and I have even heard him intimate a doubt as to whether 'able editors' were, after all, the great, divinely-accre-dited hierophants of the species.

At present Willoughby is occupied, as time allows, with a philosophical romance, in which are to be embodied his views of society as it is and as it should be. This desperate enter-prise is quite a secret ; even Atherton and Gower know nothing of it ; so you will not mention it, if you please, to more than half-a-dozen of your most intimate friends.

Willoughby was first introduced to Atherton as the author of some articles in favour of certain social reforms in which the latter had deeply interested himself. So remarkable were these papers for breadth, discrimination, and vivacity of style, that the admiring Atherton could not rest till he had made the acquaintance of the writer. The new combatant awakened general attention, and Frank Willoughby was on the point of becoming a lion. But his conversational powers were incon-siderable. His best thoughts ran with his ink from the point of the pen. So Atherton, with little difficulty, carried him off from the lion-hunters.

The three friends were agreed that the crowning locality of all for any mortal was a residence a few miles from town, with congenial neighbours close at hand,—a house or two where one might drop in for an evening at any time. As was their theory so was their practice, and the two younger men are often to be found in the evening at Atherton's, sometimes in the library with him, sometimes in the drawing-room, with the additional enjoyment afforded by the society of his fair young wife and her sister.

But while I have been Boswellizing to you about the past history of these friends of mine, you cannot have heard a word they have been saying. Now I will be quiet,—let us listen.

CHAPTER II.

Philosophy itself
Smacks of the age it lives in, nor is true
Save by the apposition of the present.
And truths of olden time, though truths they be,
And living through all time eternal truths,
Yet want the seas'ning and applying hand
Which Nature sends successive.   Else the need
Of wisdom should wear out and wisdom cease,
Since needless wisdom were not to be wise.

EDWIN THE FAIR.

ATHERTON. A pleasant little knot to set us, Gower,— to determine the conditions of your art.

WILLOUGHBY. And after dinner, too, of all times.

GOWER. Why not ? If the picture-critics would only write their verdicts after dinner, many a poor victim would find his dinner prospects brighter.   This is the genial hour ; the very time to discuss æsthetics, where geniality is everything.

WILLOUGHBY. Do you remember that passage in one of our old plays (I think it was in Lamb I saw it), where the crazed father asks all sorts of impossible things from the painter.   He wants him to make the tree shriek on which his murdered son hangs ghastly in the moonlight.

GOWER. Salvator has plenty of them, splintered with shrieking.

WILLOUGHBY. But this man's frenzy demands more yet :— make me cry, make me mad, make me well again, and in the end leave me in a trance,—and so forth.

ATHERTON. Fortunate painter—a picture gallery ordered in a breath !

WILLOUGHBY. By no means.   Now does this request, when you come to think of it, so enormously violate the conditions of the art? Seriously, I should state the matter thus :—The artist is limited to a moment only, and yet is the greater artist in proportion as he can not only adequately occupy, but even transcend that moment.

GOWER. I agree with you. Painting reaches its highest aim when it carries us beyond painting ; when it is not merely itself a creation, but makes the spectator creative, and prompts him with the antecedents and the consequents of the represented action.

ATHERTON. But all are not equal to the reception of such suggestions.

GOWER. And so, with unsusceptible minds, we must be satisfied if they praise us for our imitation merely.

WILLOUGHBY. Yet even they will derive more pleasure, though unable to account for it, from works of this higher order. Those, assuredly, are the masterpieces of art, in any branch, which are, as it were, triumphal arches that lead us out into the domain of some sister art. When poetry pourtrays with the painter,—

GOWER. My favourite, Spenser, to wit.—

WILLOUGHBY. When painting sings its story with the minstrel, and when music paints and sings with both, they are at their height. Take music, for instance. What scenes does some fine overture suggest, even when you know nothing of its design, as you close your eyes and yield to its influence. The events, or the reading of the previous day, the incidents of history or romance, are wrought up with glorious transfigurations, and you are in the land of dreams at once. Some of them rise before me at this moment, vivid as ever :—now I see the fair damosels of the olden time on their palfreys, prancing on the sward beside a castle gate, while silver trumpets blow ; then, as the music changes, I hear cries far off on forlorn and haunted moors ; now it is the sea, and there sets the sun, red, through the ribs of a wrecked hull, that cross it like skeleton giant bars. There is one passage in the overture to Fra Diavolo, during which I always emerge, through ocean caves, in some silken palace of the east, where the music rises and rains in the fountains, and ethereally palpitates in their wavering rainbows. But dream-scenery of this sort is familiar to most persons at such times.

GOWER. I have often revelled in it.

WILLOUGHBY. And what is true for so many with regard to music, may sometimes be realized on seeing pictures.

ATHERTON. Only, I think, in a way still more accidental and arbitrary. An instance, however, of the thing you mention did happen to me last week. I had been reading a German writer on mysticism, searching, after many disappointments, for a satisfactory definition of it. Page after page of metaphysical verbiage did I wade through in vain. At last, what swarms of labouring words had left as obscure as ever, a picture seemed to disclose to me in a moment. I saw that evening, at a friend's house, a painting which revealed to me, as I imagined, the very spirit of mysticism in a figure; it was a visible emblem or hieroglyph of that mysterious religious affection.

WILLOUGHBY. Your own subjectivity forged both lock and key together, I suspect.

GOWER. What in the world did the piece represent?

ATHERTON. I will describe it as well as I can. It was the interior of a Spanish cathedral. The most prominent object in the foreground below was the mighty foot of a staircase, with a balustrade of exceeding richness, which, in its ascent, crosses and recrosses the picture till its highest flight is lost in darkness, —for on that side the cathedral is built against a hill. A half-light slanted down—a sunbeam through the vast misty space —from a window without the range of the picture. At various stages of the mounting stairway figures on pillars, bearing escutcheons, saints and kings in fretted niches, and painted shapes of gules and azure from the lofty window in the east, looked down on those who were ascending, some in brightness, some in shadow. At the foot of the stairs were two couchant griffins of stone, with expanded spiny wings, arched necks fluted with horny armour, and open threatening jaws.

GOWER. Now for the interpretation of your parable in stone.

ATHERTON. It represented to me the mystic's progress—my mind was full of that—his initiation, his ascent, his consummation in self-loss. First of all the aspirant, whether he seeks superhuman knowledge or superhuman love, is confronted at the outset by terrible shapes—the Dwellers of the Threshold, whether the cruelty of asceticism, the temptations of the adversary, or the phantoms of his own feverish brain. This fiery baptism manfully endured, he begins to mount through alternate glooms and illuminations; now catching a light from some source beyond the grosser organs of ordinary men, again in darkness and barren drought of soul. The saintly memories of adepts and of heroes in these mystic labours are the faithful witnesses that cheer him at each stage, whose far glories beacon him from their place of high degree as he rises step by step. Are not those first trials fairly symbolized by my griffins, those vicissitudes of the soul by such light and shadow, and those exalted spectators by the statues of my stairway and the shining ones of my oriel window? Then for the climax. The aim of the mystic, if of the most abstract contemplative type, is to lose himself in the Divine Dark[1]—to escape from everything definite, everything palpable, everything human, into the Infinite Ful-

---

[1] The writer, who goes by the name of Dionysius Areopagita, teaches that the highest spiritual truth is revealed only to those ' who have transcended every ascent of every holy height, and have left behind all divine lights and sounds and heavenly discoursings, and have passed into that Darkness where He really is (as saith the Scripture) who is above all things.'—*De Mysticâ Theologiâ,* cap. i. § 3.

ness; which is, at the same time, the 'intense inane.' The profoundest obscurity is his highest glory; he culminates in darkness; for is not the deathlike midnight slumber of the sense, he will ask us, the wakeful noonday of the spirit? So, as I looked on the picture, I seemed to lose sight of him where the summit of the stair was lost among the shadows crouched under the roof of that strange structure.

GOWER. I perceive the analogy. I owe you thanks for enabling me to attach at least some definite idea to the word mysticism. I confess I have generally used the term mystical to designate anything fantastically unintelligible, without giving to it any distinct significance.

WILLOUGHBY. I have always been partial to the mystics, I must say. They appear to me to have been the conservators of the poetry and heart of religion, especially in opposition to the dry prose and formalism of the schoolmen.

ATHERTON. So they really were in great measure. They did good service, many of them, in their day—their very errors often such as were possible only to great souls. Still their notions concerning special revelation and immediate intuition of God were grievous mistakes.

WILLOUGHBY. Yet without the ardour imparted by such doctrines, they might have lacked the strength requisite to withstand misconceptions far more mischievous.

ATHERTON. Very likely. We should have more mercy on the one-sidedness of men, if we reflected oftener that the evil we condemn may be in fact keeping out some much greater evil on the other side.

WILLOUGHBY. I think one may learn a great deal from such erratic or morbid kinds of religion. Almost all we are in a position to say, concerning spiritual influence, consists of negatives —and what that influence is *not* we can best gather from these abnormal phases of the mind. Certainly an impartial estimate of the good and of the evil wrought by eminent mystics, would prove a very instructive occupation; it would be a trying of the spirits by their fruits.

GOWER. And all the more useful as the mistakes of mysticism, whatever they may be, are mistakes concerning questions which we all feel it so important to have rightly answered; committed, too, by men of like passions with ourselves, so that what was danger to them may be danger also to some of us, in an altered form.

ATHERTON. Unquestionably. Rationalism overrates reason, formalism action, and mysticism feeling—hence the common attributes of the last, heat and obscurity. But a tendency to excess in each of these three directions must exist in every age among the cognate varieties of mind. You remember how Pindar frequently introduces into an ode two opposite mythical personages, such as a Pelops or a Tantalus, an Ixion or a Perseus, one of whom shall resemble the great man addressed by the poet in his worse, the other in his better characteristics; that thus he may be at once encouraged and deterred. Deeper lessons than were drawn for Hiero from the characters of the heroic age may be learnt by us from the religious struggles of the past. It would be impossible to study the position of the old mystics without being warned and stimulated by a weakness and a strength to which our nature corresponds;—unless, indeed, the enquiry were conducted unsympathizingly; with cold hearts, as far from the faith of the mystics as from their follies.

GOWER. If we are likely to learn in this way from such an investigation, suppose we agree to set about it, and at once.

ATHERTON. With all my heart. I have gone a little way in this direction alone; I should be very glad to have company upon the road.

WILLOUGHBY. An arduous task, when you come to look it

in the face,—to determine that narrow line between the genuine ardour of the Christian and the overwrought fervours of the mystical devotee,—to enter into the philosophy of such a question ; and that with a terminology so misleading and so defective as the best at our service. It will be like shaping the second hand of a watch with a pair of shears, I promise you. We shall find continually tracts of ground belonging to one of the rival territories of True and False inlaid upon the regions of the other, like those patches from a distant shire that lie in the middle of some of our counties. Many of the words we must employ to designate a certain cast of mind or opinion are taken from some accidental feature or transitory circumstance,—express no real characteristic of the idea in question. They indicate our ignorance, like the castles with large flags, blazoned with the arms of sovereigns, which the old monkish geographers set down in their maps of Europe to stand instead of the rivers, towns, and mountains of an unknown interior.

ATHERTON. True enough ; but we must do the best we can. We should never enter on any investigation a little beneath the surface of things if we consider all the difficulties so gravely. Besides, we are not going to be so ponderously philosophical about the matter. The facts themselves will be our best teachers, as they arise, and as we arrange them when they accumulate.

History fairly questioned is no Sphinx. She tells us what kind of teaching has been fruitful in blessing to humanity, and why ; and what has been a mere boastful promise or powerless formula. She is the true test of every system, and the safeguard of her disciples from theoretical or practical extravagance. Were her large lessons learned, from how many foolish hopes and fears would they save men ! We should not then see a fanatical confidence placed in pet theories for the summary expulsion of all superstition, wrongfulness, and ill-will,—theories whose prototypes failed ages back : neither would good Christian folk be so frightened as some of them are at the seemingly novel exhibitions of unbelief in our time.

WILLOUGHBY. A great gain—to be above both panic and presumption. I have never heartily given myself to a historic study without realizing some such twofold advantage. It animated and it humbled me. How minute my power ; but how momentous to *me* its conscientious exercise ! I will hunt this mystical game with you, or any other, right willingly ; all the more so, if we can keep true to a historic rather than theoretical treatment of the subject.

GOWER. As to practical details, then :—I propose that we have no rules.

WILLOUGHBY. Certainly not ; away with formalities ; let us be Thelemites, and do as we like. We can take up this topic as a bye-work, to furnish us with some consecutive pursuit in those intervals of time we are so apt to waste. We can meet—never mind at what intervals, from a week to three months—and throw into the common stock of conversation our several reading on the questions in hand.

ATHERTON. Or one of us may take up some individual or period ; write down his thoughts : and we will assemble then to hear and talk the matter over.

GOWER. Very good. And if Mrs. Atherton and Miss Merivale will sometimes deign to honour our evenings with their society, our happiness will be complete.

This mention of the ladies reminds our friends of the time, and they are breaking up to join them.

The essays and dialogues which follow have their origin in the conversation to which we have just listened.

CHAPTER III.

If we entertain the inward man in the purgative and illuminative way, that is, in actions of repentance, virtue, and precise duty, that is the surest way of uniting us to God, whilst it is done by faith and obedience ; and that also is love ; and in these peace and safety dwell. And after we have done our work, it is not discretion in a servant to hasten to his meal, and snatch at the refreshment of visions, unions, and abstractions ; but first we must gird ourselves, and wait upon the master, and not sit down ourselves, till we all be called at the great supper of the Lamb.—JEREMY TAYLOR.

SO, we are to be etymological to-night,' exclaimed Gower, as he stepped forward to join Willoughby in his inspection of a great folio which Atherton had laid open on a reading desk, ready to entertain his friends.

'What says Suidas about our word mysticism?'

WILLOUGHBY. I see the old lexicographer derives the original word from the root *mu*, to close : the secret rites and lessons of the Greek mysteries were things about which the mouth was to be closed.[1]

GOWER. We have the very same syllable in our language for the same thing—only improved in expressiveness by the addition of another letter,—we say, ' to be *mum*.'

ATHERTON. Well, this settles one whole class of significations at once. The term mystical may be applied in this sense to any secret language or ritual which is understood only by the initiated. In this way the philosophers borrowed the word figuratively from the priests, and applied it to their inner esoteric

---

[1] On the word μύησις Suidas says, Εἴρηται δὲ παρὰ τὸ τὰ μυστήρια καὶ ἀπόρρητα τελεῖσθαι· ἢ διὰ τὸ μυόντας τὰς αἰσθήσεις καὶ ἐπέκεινα σωματικῆς φαντασίας γενομένους, τὰς θείας εἰσδέχεσθαι ἐλλάμψεις.

Suicer also cites Hesychius : *Etym. Mag.*—Μύστης, παρὰ τὸ μύω, τὸ καμμύω. μύοντες γὰρ τὰς αἰσθήσεις καὶ ἔξω τῶν σαρκικῶν φροντίδων γινόμενοι, οὕτω τὰς θείας ἀναλάμψεις ἐδέχοντο.

doctrines.   The disciple admitted to these was a philosophical 'myst,' or mystic.

WILLOUGHBY. The next step is very obvious.   The family of words relating to mystery, initiation, &c., are adopted into the ecclesiastical phraseology of the early Christian world,—not in the modified use of them occasionally observable in St. Paul, but with their old Pagan significance.

GOWER. So that the exclusive and aristocratic spirit of Greek culture re-appears in Christianity?

ATHERTON. Just so.   Thus you see the church doors shutting out the catechumens from beholding 'the mystery' (as they came to call the Eucharist, *par excellence*) quite as rigidly as the brazen gates of Eleusis excluded the profane many.   You hear Theodoret and Ambrose speaking freely before the uninitiated on moral subjects, but concerning the rites they deemed of mysterious, almost magical efficacy, they will deliver only obscure utterances to such auditors ; their language is purposely dark and figurative,—suggestive to the initiated, unintelligible to the neophyte.   How often on approaching the subject of the sacrament, does Chrysostom stop short in his sermon, and break off abruptly with the formula,—' the initiated will understand what I mean.'   So Christianity, corrupted by Gentile philosophy, has in like manner its privileged and its inferior order of votaries,—becomes a respecter of persons, with arbitrary distinction makes two kinds of religion out of one, and begins to nourish with fatal treachery its doctrine of reserve.[2]

WILLOUGHBY. But Suidas has here, I perceive, a second meaning in store for us.   This latter, I suspect, is most to our purpose,—it is simply an extension of the former.   He refers the word to the practice of closing as completely as possible

[2] See Bingham, *Antiq. of the Christian Church*, vol. ix. pp. 96-105. Clement of Alexandria abounds in examples of the application to Christian doctrine of the phraseology in use concerning the heathen mysteries ;— *e.g. Protrept.* cap. xii. § 120.

every avenue of perception by the senses, for the purpose of withdrawing the mind from everything external into itself, so as to fit it (raised above every sensuous representation) for receiving divine illumination immediately from above.

GOWER. Platonic abstraction, in fact.

ATHERTON. So it seems.   The Neo-Platonist was accustomed to call every other branch of science the 'lesser mysteries:' this inward contemplation, the climax of Platonism, is the *great* mystery, the inmost, highest initiation.   Withdraw into thyself, he will say, and the adytum of thine own soul will reveal to thee profounder secrets than the cave of Mithras.   So that his *mysticus* is emphatically the enclosed, self-withdrawn, introverted man.[3]   This is an initiation which does not merely, like that of Isis or of Ceres, close the lips in silence, but the eye, the ear, every faculty of perception, in inward contemplation or in the ecstatic abstraction of the trance.

WILLOUGHBY. So then it is an effort man is to make—in harmony with the matter-hating principles of this school—to strip off the material and sensuous integuments of his being, and to reduce himself to a purely spiritual element.   And in thus ignoring the follies and the phantasms of Appearance—as they call the actual world—the worshipper of pure Being believed himself to enjoy at least a transitory oneness with the object of his adoration?

ATHERTON. So Plotinus would say, if not Plato.   And now we come to the transmission of the idea and the expression to the Church.   A writer, going by the name of Dionysius

---

[3] Both Plotinus and Proclus speak of the highest revelation concerning divine things as vouchsafed to the soul which withdraws into itself, and, dead to all that is external, ' gazes with closed eyes' (μύσασαν).   See Tholuck's *Blüthensammlung aus der Morgenlandischen Mystik; Einleitung,*

§ 1, p. 6.   Dr. Tholuck is the only German writer I have seen who throws light on the word in question by accurately investigating its etymology and successive meanings; and I readily acknowledge my debt to his suggestions on this point.

the Areopagite, ferries this shade over into the darkness visible of the ecclesiastical world in the fifth century. The system of mystical theology introduced by him was eminently adapted to the monastic and hierarchical tendencies of the time. His '*Mystic*' is not merely a sacred personage, acquainted with the doctrines and participator in the rites called mysteries, but one also who (exactly after the Neo-Platonist pattern) by mortifying the body, closing the senses to everything external, and ignoring every 'intellectual apprehension,'[4] attains in passivity a divine union, and in ignorance a wisdom transcending all knowledge.

GOWER. Prepared to say, I suppose, with one of old George Chapman's characters—

> I'll build all inward—not a light shall ope
> The common out-way.—
> I'll therefore live in dark ; and all my light,
> Like ancient temples, let in at my top.

WILLOUGHBY. Not much light either. The mystic, as such, was not to *know* anything about the Infinite, he was 'to gaze with closed eyes,' passively to receive impressions, lost in the silent, boundless 'Dark' of the Divine Subsistence.

[4] Dionysius thus describes the mystical adept who has reached the summit of union :—'Then is he delivered from all seeing and being seen, and passes into the truly mystical darkness of ignorance, where he excludes all intellectual apprehensions (τὰς γνωστικὰς ἀντιλήψεις), and abides in the utterly Impalpable and Invisible ; being wholly His who is above all, with no other dependence, either on himself or any other ; and is made one, as to his nobler part, with the utterly Unknown, by the cessation of all knowing ; and at the same time, in that very knowing nothing, he knows what transcends the mind of man.'— *De Mysticâ Theologiâ*, cap. i. p. 710. *S. Dion. Areop. Opp.* Paris, 1644. So again he exhorts Timothy 'by assiduous practice in mystical contemplations to abandon the senses and all operations of the intellect ; all objects of sense and all objects of thought, all things non-existent and existent (αἰσθητὰ =οὐκ ὄντα, νοητὰ=ὄντα), and ignorantly to strive upwards towards Union as close as possible with Him who is above all essence and knowledge :—inasmuch as by a pure, free, and absolute separation (ἐκστάσει) of himself from all things, he will be exalted (stripped and freed from everything) to the superessential radiance of the divine darkness.'—p. 708.

About the words rendered 'intellectual apprehensions' commentators differ. The context, the antithesis, and the parallel passage in the earlier part of the chapter, justify us in understanding them in their strict sense, as conveying the idea of cessation from all mental action whatsoever.

ATHERTON. This, then, is our result. The philosophical perfection of Alexandria and the monastic perfection of Byzantium belong to the same species. Philosophers and monks alike employ the word mysticism and its cognate terms as involving the idea, not merely of initiation into something hidden, but, beyond this, of an internal manifestation of the Divine to the intuition or in the feeling of the secluded soul. It is in this last and narrower sense, therefore, that the word is to be understood when we speak of mystical death, mystical illumination, mystical union with God, and, in fact, throughout the phraseology of what is specially termed *Theologia Mystica.*[5]

GOWER. I have often been struck by the surprising variety in the forms of thought and the modes of action in which mysticism has manifested itself among different nations and at different periods. This arises, I should think, from its residing in so central a province of the mind—the feeling. It has been incorporated in theism, atheism, and pantheism. It has given men gods at every step, and it has denied all deity except self. It has appeared in the loftiest speculation and in the grossest idolatry. It has been associated with the wildest licence and with the most pitiless asceticism. It has driven men out into action, it has dissolved them in ecstasy, it has frozen them to torpor.

ATHERTON. Hence the difficulty of definition. I have seen none which quite satisfies me. Some include only a particular phase of it, while others so define its province as to stigmatise as mystical every kind of religiousness which rises above the zero of rationalism.

WILLOUGHBY. The Germans have two words for mysticism— *mystik* and *mysticismus.* The former they use in a favourable, the latter in an unfavourable, sense.—

GOWER. Just as we say piety and pietism, or rationality and

[5] See Note, p. 23.

rationalism; keeping the first of each pair for the use, the second for the abuse. A convenience, don't you think?

ATHERTON. If the adjective were distinguishable like the nouns—but it is not; and to have a distinction in the primitive and not in the derivative word is always confusing. But we shall keep to the usage of our own language. I suppose we shall all be agreed in employing the word mysticism in the unfavourable signification, as equivalent generally to *spirituality diseased,* grown unnatural, fantastic, and the like.

GOWER. At the same time admitting the true worth of many mystics, and the real good and truth of which such errors are the exaggeration or caricature.

ATHERTON. I think we may say thus much generally—that mysticism, whether in religion or philosophy, is that form of error which mistakes for a divine manifestation the operations of a merely human faculty.

WILLOUGHBY. There you define, at any rate, the characteristic misconception of the mystics.

GOWER. And include, if I mistake not, enthusiasts, with their visions; pretended prophets, with their claim of inspiration; wonder-workers, trusting to the divine power resident in their theurgic formulas; and the philosophers who believe themselves organs of the world-soul, and their systems an evolution of Deity.

ATHERTON. Yes, so far; but I do not profess to give any definition altogether adequate. Speaking of *Christian* mysticism, I should describe it generally as the exaggeration of that aspect of Christianity which is presented to us by St. John.

GOWER. That answer provokes another question. How should you characterize John's peculiar presentation of the Gospel?

ATHERTON. I refer chiefly to that admixture of the contemplative temperament and the ardent, by which he is personally distinguished,—the opposition so manifest in his epistles to all religion of mere speculative opinion or outward usage,—the concentration of Christianity, as it were, upon the inward life derived from union with Christ. This would seem to be the province of Christian truth especially occupied by the beloved disciple, and this is the province which mysticism has in so many ways usurped.

GOWER. Truly that unction from the Holy One, of which John speaks, has found some strange claimants !

WILLOUGHBY. Thus much I think is evident from our enquiry —that mysticism, true to its derivation as denoting a *hidden* know-ledge, faculty, or life (the exclusive privilege of sage, adept, or recluse), presents itself, in all its phases, as more or less the religion of internal as opposed to external revelation,—of heated feeling, sickly sentiment, or lawless imagination, as opposed to that reasonable belief in which the intellect and the heart, the inward witness and the outward, are alike engaged.

NOTE TO PAGE 21.

Numerous definitions of ‘Mystical Theology’ are supplied by Roman Catholic divines who have written on the subject. With all of them the terms denote the religion of the heart as distinguished from speculation, scholasticism, or ritualism ; and, moreover, those higher experiences of the divine life associ-ated, in their belief, with extraordinary gifts and miraculous powers. Such definitions will accordingly comprehend the theopathetic and theurgic forms of mysticism, but must necessarily exclude the theosophic. Many of them might serve as definitions of genuine religion. These mystical experiences have been always coveted and admired in the Romish Church ; and those, therefore, who write concerning them employ the word mysticism in a highly favourable sense. That excess of subjectivity—those visionary raptures and supernatural exaltations, which we regard as the symptoms of spiritual disease, are, in the eyes of these writers, the choice rewards of sufferings and of aspirations the most intense,—they are the vision of God and things celestial enjoyed by the pure in heart,—the dazzling glories wherewith God has crowned the heads of a chosen few, whose example shall give light to all the world.

Two or three specimens will suffice. Gerson gives the two following defini-tions of the *Theologia Mystica :*—‘ Est animi extensio in Deum per amoris desiderium.’ And again : ‘ Est motio anagogica in Deum per purum et fervidum amorem.’ Elsewhere he is more metaphorical, describing it as the theology which teaches men to escape from the stormy sea of sensuous desires to the safe harbour of Eternity, and shows them how to attain that love which snatches them away to the Beloved, unites them with Him, and secures them rest in Him. Dionysius the Carthusian (associating evidently *mystica* and *mysteriosa*) says,—'Est autem mystica Theologia secretissima mentis cum Deo locutio.' John à Jesu Maria calls it, 'cœlestis quædam Dei notitia per unionem voluntatis Deo adhærentis elicita, vel lumine cœlitus immisso producta.' This mystical theology, observes the Carthusian Dionysius, farther, (commentating on the Areopagite), is no science, properly so called ; even regarded as an act, it is simply the concentration (defixio) of the mind on God—admiration of his majesty—a suspension of the mind in the boundless and eternal light—a most fervid, most peaceful, transforming gaze on Deity, &c.

All alike contrast the mystical with the scholastic and the symbolical theo-logy. The points of dissimilarity are thus summed up by Cardinal Bona :—'Per scholasticam discit homo recte uti intelligibilibus, per symbolicam sensi-bilibus, per hanc (mysticam) rapitur ad supermentales excessus. Scientiæ humanæ in valle phantasiæ discuntur, hæc in apice mentis. Illæ multis egent discursibus, et erroribus subjectæ sunt : hæc unico et simplici verbo docetur et discitur, et est mere supernaturalis tam in substantiâ quam in modo procedendi.' — *Via Compendii ad Deum*, cap. iii. 1-3.

The definition given by Corderius in his introduction to the mystical theology of Dionysius is modelled on the mysticism of John de la Cruz :—'Theologia Mystica est sapientia experimentalis, Dei affectiva, divinitus infusa, quæ mentem ab omni inordinatione puram, per actus supernaturales fidei, spei, et charitatis, cum Deo intime conjungit.'—*Isagoge*, cap. ii.

The most negative definition of all is that given by Pachymeres, the Greek paraphrast of Dionysius, who has evidently caught his master's mantle, or cloak of darkness. 'Mystical theology is not perception or discourse, not a movement of the mind, not an operation, not a habit, nothing that any other power we may possess will bring to us ; but if, in absolute immobility of mind we are illumined concerning it, we shall know that it is beyond everything cognizable by the mind of man.'—*Dion. Opp.* vol. i. p. 722.

In one place the explanations of Corderius give us to understand that the mysticism he extols does at least open a door to theosophy itself, *i.e.* to inspired science. He declares that the mystical theologian not only has revealed to him the hidden sense of Scripture, but that he can understand and pierce the mysteries of any natural science whatsoever, in a way quite different from that possible to other men—in short, by a kind of special revelation.—*Isagoge*, cap. iv.

The reader will gather the most adequate notion of what is meant, or thought to be meant, by mystical theology from the description given by Ludovic Blosius, a high authority on matters mystical, in his *Institutio Spiritualis*. Corderius cites him at length, as 'sublimissimus rerum mysticarum interpres.'

Happy, he exclaims, is that soul which steadfastly follows after purity of heart and holy introversion, renouncing utterly all private affection, all self-will, all self-interest. Such a soul deserves to approach nearer and ever nearer to God. Then at length, when its higher powers have been elevated, purified, and furnished forth by divine grace, it attains to unity and nudity of spirit—to a pure love above representation—to that simplicity of thought which is devoid of all thinkings. Now, therefore, since it hath become receptive of the sur-passing and ineffable grace of God, it is led to that living fountain which flows from everlasting, and doth refresh the minds of the saints unto the full and in over-measure. Now do the powers of the soul shine as the stars, and she herself is fit to contemplate the abyss of Divinity with a serene, a simple, and a jubilant intuition, free from imagination and from the smallest admixture of the intellect. Accordingly, when she lovingly turns herself absolutely unto God, the incomprehensible light shines into her depths, and that radiance blinds the eye of reason and understanding. But the simple eye of the soul itself remains open—that is *thought*, pure, naked, uniform, and raised above the understanding.

Moreover, when the natural light of reason is blinded by so bright a glory, the soul takes cognizance of nothing in time, but is raised above time and space, and assumes as it were a certain attribute of eternity. For the soul which has abandoned symbols and earthly distinctions and processes of thought, now learns experimentally that God far transcends all images—corporeal, spiritual, or divine, and that whatsoever the reason can apprehend, whatsoever can be said or written concerning God, whatsoever can be predicated of Him by words, must manifestly be infinitely remote from the reality of the divine subsistence which is unnameable. The soul knows not, therefore, what that God is she feels. Hence, by a foreknowledge which is exercised without knowledge, she rests in the nude, the simple, the unknown God, who alone is to be loved. For the light is called *dark*, from its excessive brightness. In this darkness the soul receives the hidden word which God utters in the inward silence and secret recess of the mind. This word she receives, and doth happily experience the bond of mystical union. For when, by means of love, she hath transcended reason and all symbols, and is carried away above herself (a favour God alone can procure her), straightway she flows away from herself and flows forth into God (*a se defluens profluit in Deum*), and then is God her peace and her enjoyment. Rightly doth she sing, in such a transport, ' I will both lay me down in peace and sleep.' The loving soul flows down, I say, falls away from herself, and, reduced as it were to nothing, melts and glides away altogether into the abyss of eternal love. There, dead to herself, she lives in God, knowing nothing, perceiving nothing, except the love she tastes. For she loses herself in that vastest solitude and darkness of Divinity : but thus to lose is in fact to find herself. There, putting off whatsoever is human, and putting on whatever is divine, she is transformed and transmuted into God, as iron in a furnace takes the form of fire and is transmuted into fire. Nevertheless, the essence of the soul thus deified remains, as the glowing iron does not cease to be iron. . . .

The soul, thus bathed in the essence of God, liquefied by the consuming fire of love, and united to Him without medium, doth, by wise ignorance and by the inmost touch of love, more clearly know God than do our fleshly eyes discern the visible sun. . . .

Though God doth sometimes manifest himself unto the perfect soul in most sublime and wondrous wise, yet he doth not reveal himself *as he is* in his own ineffable glory, but as it is possible for him to be seen in this life.—*Isagoge Cord.* cap. vii.

CHAPTER IV.

The desire of the moth for the star,
Of the night for the morrow,
The devotion to something afar
From the sphere of our sorrow.
SHELLEY.

WILLOUGHBY. Here's another definition for you :—
Mysticism is *the romance of religion.* What do you say?

GOWER. True to the spirit—not scientific, I fear.

WILLOUGHBY. Science be banished! Is not the history of mysticism bright with stories of dazzling spiritual enterprise, sombre with tragedies of the soul, stored with records of the achievements and the woes of martyrdom and saintship? Has it not reconciled, as by enchantment, the most opposite extremes of theory and practice? See it, in theory, verging repeatedly on pantheism, ego-theism, nihilism. See it, in practice, producing some of the most glorious examples of humility, benevolence, and untiring self-devotion. Has it not commanded, with its indescribable fascination, the most powerful natures and the most feeble—minds lofty with a noble disdain of life, or low with a weak disgust of it? If the self-torture it enacts seems hideous to our sobriety, what an attraction in its reward! It lays waste the soul with purgatorial pains—but it is to leave nothing there on which any fire may kindle after death. What a promise!—a perfect sanctification, a divine calm, fruition of heaven while yet upon the earth!

ATHERTON. Go on, Willoughby, I like your enthusiasm. Think of its adventures, too.

WILLOUGHBY. Aye, its adventures — both persecuted and canonized by kings and pontiffs ; one age enrolling the mystic among the saints, another committing him to the inquisitor's torch, or entombing him in the Bastille. And the principle indestructible after all—some minds always who must be religious mystically or not at all.

ATHERTON. I thought we might this evening enquire into the causes which tend continually to reproduce this religious phenomenon. You have suggested some already. Certain states of society have always fostered it. There have been times when all the real religion existing in a country appears to have been confined to its mystics.

WILLOUGHBY. In such an hour, how mysticism rises and does its deeds of spiritual chivalry——

GOWER. Alas! Quixotic enough, sometimes.

WILLOUGHBY. How conspicuous, then, grows this inward devotion !—even the secular historian is compelled to say a word about it——

ATHERTON. And a sorry, superficial verdict he gives, too often.

WILLOUGHBY. How loud its protest against literalism, formality, scholasticism, human ordinances! what a strenuous reaction against the corruptions of priestcraft !

ATHERTON. But, on the other side, Willoughby—and here comes the pathetic part of its romance—mysticism is heard discoursing concerning things unutterable. It speaks, as one in a dream, of the third heaven, and of celestial experiences, and revelations fitter for angels than for men. Its stammering utterance, confused with excess of rapture labouring with emotions too huge or abstractions too subtle for words, becomes utterly unintelligible. Then it is misrepresented : falls a victim to reaction in its turn ; the delirium is dieted by persecution, and it is consigned once more to secrecy and silence.

GOWER. There, good night, and pleasant dreams to it !

WILLOUGHBY. It spins still in its sleep its mingled tissue of good and evil.

ATHERTON. A mixture truly. We must not blindly praise it in our hatred of formalism. We must not vaguely condemn it in our horror of extravagance.

GOWER. What you have both been saying indicates at once three of the causes we are in search of,—indeed, the three chief ones, as I suppose : first of all, the reaction you speak of against the frigid formality of religious torpor ; then, heart-weariness, the languishing longing for repose, the charm of mysticism for the selfish or the weak ; and, last, the desire, so strong in some minds, to pierce the barriers that hide from man the unseen world—the charm of mysticism for the ardent and the strong.

ATHERTON. That shrinking from conflict, that passionate yearning after inaccessible rest, how universal is it ; what wistful utterance it has found in every nation and every age ; how it subdues us all, at times, and sinks us into languor.

WILLOUGHBY. Want of patience lies at the root—who was it said that he should have all eternity to rest in ?

ATHERTON. Think how the traditions of every people have embellished with their utmost wealth of imagination some hidden spot upon the surface of the earth, which they have pourtrayed as secluded from all the tumult and the pain of time— a serene Eden—an ever-sunny Tempe—a vale of Avalon—a place beyond the sterner laws and rougher visitations of the common world—a fastness of perpetual calm, before which the tempests may blow their challenging horns in vain—they can win no entrance. Such, to the fancy of the Middle Age, was the famous temple of the Sangreal, with its dome of sapphire, its six-and-thirty towers, its crystal crosses, and its hangings of green samite, guarded by its knights girded by impenetrable forest, glittering on the onyx summit of Mount Salvage, for

ever invisible to every eye impure, inaccessible to every failing
or faithless heart. Such, to the Hindoo, was the Cridavana
meadow, among the heights of Mount Sitanta, full of flowers,
of the song of birds, the hum of bees—'languishing winds and
murmuring falls of waters.' Such was the secret mountain
Kinkadulle, celebrated by Olaus Magnus, which stood in a
region now covered only by moss or snow, but luxuriant once,
in less degenerate days, with the spontaneous growth of every
pleasant bough and goodly fruit. What places like these have
been to the popular mind, even such a refuge for the Ideal
from the pursuit of the Actual—that the attainment of Ecstasy,
the height of Contemplation, the bliss of Union, has been for
the mystic.

GOWER. So those spiritual Lotos-eaters will only

> ———— hearken what the inner spirit sings,
> There is no joy but calm ;

or, in their 'fugitive and cloistered virtue,' as Milton calls
it, say,

> ———— let us live and lie reclined
> On the hills like gods together, careless of mankind.

ATHERTON. Some ; not all, however. Neither should we
suppose that even those who have sunk to such a state——

WILLOUGHBY. They would say—risen—

ATHERTON. Be it by sinking or rising, they have not been
brought to that pass without a conflict. From life's battle-field
to the hospital of the hermitage has been but a step for a multitude of minds. Hiding themselves wounded from the victor
(for the enemy they could not conquer shall not see and mock
their sufferings), they call in the aid of an imaginative religion-
ism to people their solitude with its glories. The Prometheus
chained to his rock is comforted if the sea nymphs rise from
the deep to visit him, and Ocean on his hippogriff draws near.
And thus, let the gliding fancies of a life of dreams, and Ima-

gination, the monarch of all their main of thought, visit the sorrow of these recluses, and they think they can forget the ravages of that evil which so vexed them once. Hence the mysticism of the visionary. He learns to crave ecstasies and revelations as at once his solace and his pride.

GOWER. Is it not likely, too, that some of these mystics, in seasons of mental distress of which we have no record, tried Nature as a resource, and found her wanting? Such a disappointment would make that ascetic theory which repudiates the seen and actual, plausible and even welcome to them. After demanding of the natural world what it has not to bestow, they would hurry to the opposite extreme, and deny it any healing influence whatever. Go out into the woods and valleys, when your heart is rather harassed than bruised, and when you suffer from vexation more than grief. Then the trees all hold out their arms to you to relieve you of the burthen of your heavy thoughts ; and the streams under the trees glance at you as they run by, and will carry away your trouble along with the fallen leaves; and the sweet-breathing air will draw it off together with the silver multitudes of the dew. But let it be with anguish or remorse in your heart that you go forth into Nature, and instead of your speaking her language, you make her speak yours. Your distress is then infused through all things, and clothes all things, and Nature only echoes, and seems to authenticate, your self-loathing or your hopelessness. Then you find the device of your sorrow on the argent shield of the moon, and see all the trees of the field weeping and wringing their hands with you, while the hills, seated at your side in sackcloth, look down upon you prostrate, and reprove you like the comforters of Job.

ATHERTON. Doubtless, many of these stricken spirits suffered such disappointment at some early period of their history. Failure was inevitable, and the disease was heightened. How

Coleridge felt this when he says so mournfully in his Ode to Dejection,—

> It were a vain endeavour
> Though I should gaze for ever
> On that green light that lingers in the west :
> I may not hope from outward forms to win
> The passion and the life whose fountains are within.

WILLOUGHBY. The feeling of the other class we spoke of—the men of bolder temperament—has been this : 'I am a king and yet a captive ; submit I cannot ; I care not to dream ; I must in some way act.'

GOWER. And, like Rasselas, a prince and yet a prisoner in the narrow valley, such a man, in his impatience, takes counsel of a philosopher, who promises to construct a pair of wings wherewith he shall overfly the summits that frown around him. The mystagogue is a philosopher such as Rasselas found, with a promise as large and a result as vain.

ATHERTON. Hence the mysticism of the theurgist, who will pass the bounds of the dreaded spirit world ; will dare all its horrors to seize one of its thrones ; and aspires—a Manfred or a Zanoni—to lord it among the powers of the air.

WILLOUGHBY. And of the mysticism of the theosophist, too, whose science is an imagined inspiration, who writes about plants and minerals under a divine afflatus, and who will give you from the resources of his special revelation an explanation of every mystery.

GOWER. The explanation, unhappily, the greatest mystery of all.

ATHERTON. Curiously enough, the Bible has been made to support mysticism by an interpretation, at one time too fanciful, at another too literal.

WILLOUGHBY. We may call it, perhaps, the innocent cause of mysticism with one class, its victim with another : the one, running into mysticism because they wrongly interpreted the

Bible; the other interpreting it wrongly because they were mystics. The mystical interpreters of school and cloister belong to the latter order, and many a Covenanter and godly trooper of the Commonwealth to the former.

GOWER. Not an unlikely result with the zealous Ironside—his reading limited to his English Bible and a few savoury treatises of divinity—pouring over the warlike story of ancient Israel, and identifying himself with the subjects of miraculous intervention, divine behest, and prophetic dream. How glorious would those days appear to such a man, when angels went and came among men; when, in the midst of his husbandry or handicraft, the servant of the Lord might be called aside to see some 'great sight:' when the fire dropped sudden down from heaven on the accepted altar, like a drop spilt from the lip of an angel's fiery vial full of odours; when the Spirit of the Lord moved men at times, as Samson was moved in the camp of Dan, between Zorah and Eshtaol; and when the Lord sent men hither and thither by an inward impulse, as Elijah was sent from Gilgal to Bethel, and from Bethel back to Jericho, and from Jericho on to Jordan. Imagination would reproduce those marvels in the world within, though miracles could no longer cross his path in the world without. He would believe that to him also words were given to speak, and deeds to do; and that, whether in the house, the council, or the field, he was the Spirit's chosen instrument and messenger.

ATHERTON. This is the practical and active kind of mysticism so prevalent in that age of religious wars, the seventeenth century.

WILLOUGHBY. The monks took the opposite course. While the Parliamentarian soldier was often seen endeavouring to adapt his life to a mistaken application of the Bible, the ascetic endeavoured to adapt the Bible to his mistaken life.

GOWER. The New Testament not authorising the austerities of a Macarius or a Maximus, tradition must be called in——

WILLOUGHBY. And side by side with tradition, mystical interpretation. The Bible, it was pretended, must not be understood as always meaning what it seems to mean.

ATHERTON. It then becomes the favourite employment of the monk to detect this hidden meaning, and to make Scripture render to tradition the same service which the mask rendered to the ancient actor, not only disguising the face, but making the words go farther. To be thus busied was to secure two advantages at once; he had occupation for his leisure, and an answer for his adversaries.

CHAPTER V.

Oh ! contemplation palls upon the spirit,
Like the chill silence of an autumn sun :
While action, like the roaring south-west wind,
Sweeps, laden with elixirs, with rich draughts
Quickening the wombed earth.
    Guta.   And yet what bliss,
When, dying in the darkness of God's light,
The soul can pierce these blinding webs of nature,
And float up to the nothing, which is all things—
The ground of being, where self-forgetful silence
Is emptiness,—emptiness fulness,—fulness God,—
Till we touch Him, and, like a snow-flake, melt
Upon his light-sphere's keen circumference !
THE SAINT'S TRAGEDY.

GOWER. Thanks, if you please, not reproaches. I was calling help for you, I was summoning the fay to your assistance, to determine the best possible order of your mystics.

WILLOUGHBY. The fay ?

GOWER. The fay. Down with you in that arm-chair, and sit quietly. Know that I was this morning reading Andersen's Märchen—all about Ole-Luk-Oie, his ways and works—the queer little elf. Upstairs he creeps, in houses where children are, softly, softly, in the dusk of the evening, with what do you think under his arm?—two umbrellas, one plain, the other covered with gay colours and quaint figures. He makes the eyes of the children heavy, and when they are put to bed, holds over the heads of the good children the painted umbrella, which causes them to dream the sweetest and most wonderful dreams imaginable ; but over the naughty children he holds the other, and they do not dream at all. Now, thought I, let me emulate the profundity of a German critic. Is this to be treated as a

simple child's tale? Far from it. There is a depth of philosophic meaning in it. Have not the mystics been mostly
childlike natures? Have not their lives been full of dreams,
manifold and strange—and they therefore, if any, especial
favourites of Ole-Luk-Oie? They have accounted their dreams
their pride and their reward. They have looked on the sobriety
of dreamlessness as the appropriate deprivation of privilege
consequent on carnality and ignorance; in other words, the
non-dreamers have been with them the naughty children. To
learn life's lessons well is, according to them, to enjoy as a
recompence the faculty of seeing visions and of dreaming dreams.
Here then is the *idea* of mysticism. You have its myth, its
legend. Ole-Luk-Oie is its presiding genius. Now, Atherton,
if you could but get hold of his umbrella, the segments of that
silken hemisphere, with its painted constellations, would give
you your divisions in a twinkling. That was why I wanted
him. But I do not see him letting himself down the bellrope,
or hear his tap at the door. I am afraid we must set to work
without him.

WILLOUGHBY. So be it. A local or historical classification
of the mystics is out of the question. I scarcely think you can
find a metaphysical one that will bear the test of application
and be practically serviceable. Then the division some adopt,
of heterodox and orthodox, saves trouble indeed, but it is so
arbitrary. The Church of Rome, from whom many of these
mystics called heretical, dared to differ, is no church at all in the
true sense, and assuredly no standard of orthodoxy. In addition to this I have a nervous antipathy to the terms themselves;
for, as I have a liking for becoming the champion of any cause
which appears to be borne down by numbers, I find my friends
who are somewhat heterodox, frequently charging me with what
is called orthodoxy, and those again who are orthodox as often
suspecting me of heterodoxy.

ATHERTON. Hear my proposed division. There are three kinds of mysticism, *theopathetic, theosophic,* and *theurgic.* The first of these three classes I will subdivide, if needful, into *transitive* and *intransitive.*

GOWER. Your alliteration is grateful to my ear ; I hope you have not strained a point to secure us the luxury.

ATHERTON. Not a hair's breadth, I assure you.

WILLOUGHBY. Etymologically such a division has the advantage of showing that all the forms of mysticism are developments of the *religious* sentiment ; that in all its varieties the relationship, real or imaginary, which mysticism sustains to the Divine, is its primary element ;—that its widely differing aspects are all phases it presents in its eccentric orbit about the central luminary of the Infinite.

GOWER. Your theopathetic mysticism must include a very wide range. By the term theopathetic you denote, of course, that mysticism which resigns itself, in a passivity more or less absolute, to an imagined divine manifestation. Now, one man may regard himself as overshadowed, another as impelled by Deity. One mystic of this order may do nothing, another may display an unceasing activity. Whether he believes himself a mirror in whose quiescence the Divinity 'glasses himself ;' or, as it were, a leaf, driven by the mighty rushing wind of the Spirit, and thus the tongue by which the Spirit speaks, the organ by which God works—the principle of passivity is the same.

ATHERTON. Hence my subdivision of this class of mystics into those whose mysticism assumes a transitive character, and those with whom mysticism consists principally in contemplation, in Quietism, in negation, and so is properly called intransitive.

WILLOUGHBY. Yet some of those whose mysticism has been pre-eminently negative, who have hated the very name of speculation, and placed perfection in repose and mystical death, have mingled much in active life. They appear to defy our arrangement.

ATHERTON. It is only in appearance. They have shrunk from carrying out their theory to its logical consequences. Their activity has been a bye-work. The diversities of character observable in the mysticism which is essentially intransitive arise, not from a difference in the principle at the root, but from varieties of natural temperament, of external circumstances, and from the dissimilar nature or proportion of the foreign elements incorporated.

GOWER. It is clear that we must be guided by the rule rather than the exception, and determine, according to the predominant element in the mysticism of individuals, the position to be assigned them. If we were to classify only those who were perfectly consistent with themselves, we could include scarcely half-a-dozen names, and those, by the way, the least rational of all, for the most thorough-going are the madmen.

ATHERTON. The mysticism of St. Bernard, for example, in spite of his preaching, his travels, his diplomacy, is altogether contemplative—the intransitive mysticism of the cloister. His active labours were a work apart.

GOWER. Such men have been serviceable as members of society in proportion to their inconsistency as devotees of mysticism. A heavy charge this against their principle.

WILLOUGHBY. In the intransitive division of the theopathetic mysticism you will have three such names as Suso, Ruysbrook, Molinos, and all the Quietists, whether French or Indian.

ATHERTON. And in the transitive theopathy all turbulent prophets and crazy fanatics. This species of mysticism usurps the will more than the emotional part of our nature. The subject of it suffers under the Divine, as he believes, but the result of the manifestation is not confined to himself, it passes on to his fellows.

GOWER. If you believe Plato in the Ion, you must range here all the poets, for they sing well, he tells us, only as they are carried out of themselves by a divine madness, and mastered by an influence which their verse communicates to others in succession.

WILLOUGHBY. We must admit here also, according to ancient superstition, the Pythoness on her tripod, and the Sibyl in her cave at Cumæ, as she struggles beneath the might of the god :—

> Phœbi nondum patiens immanis in antro
> Bacchatur vates, magnum si pectore possit
> Excussisse Deum : tanto magis ille fatigat
> Os rabidum, fera corda domans, fingitque premendo.

ATHERTON. I have no objection. According to Virgil's description, the poor Sibyl has earned painfully enough a place within the pale of mysticism. But those with whom we have more especially to do in this province are enthusiasts such as Tanchelm, who appeared in the twelfth century, and announced himself as the residence of Deity ; as Gichtel, who believed himself appointed to expiate by his prayers and penance the sins of all mankind ; or as Kuhlmann, who traversed Europe, the imagined head of the Fifth monarchy, summoning kings and nobles to submission.

GOWER. Some of these cases we may dismiss in a summary manner. The poor brainsick creatures were cast on evil times indeed. What we should now call derangement was then exalted into heresy, and honoured with martyrdom. We should have taken care that Kuhlmann was sent to an asylum, but the Russian patriarch burned him, poor fellow.

ATHERTON. We must not forget, however, that this species of mysticism has sometimes been found associated with the announcement of vital truths Look at George Fox and the early Quakers

WILLOUGHBY. And I would refer also to this class some of the milder forms of mysticism, in which it is seen rather as a single morbid element than as a principle avowed and carried out. Jung Stilling is an instance of what I mean. You see him, fervent, earnest, and yet weak; without forethought, without perseverance; vain and irresolute, he changes his course incessantly, seeing in every variation of feeling and of circumstance a special revelation of the Divine will.

ATHERTON. Add to this modification a kindred error, the doctrine of a '*particular faith*' in prayer, so much in vogue in Cromwell's court at Whitehall. Howe boldly preached against it before the Protector himself.

WILLOUGHBY. Now, Atherton, for your second division, theosophic mysticism. Whom do you call theosophists?

ATHERTON. Among the Germans I find mysticism generally called theosophy when applied to natural science. Too narrow a use of the word, I think. We should have in that case scarcely any theosophy in Europe till after the Reformation. The word itself was first employed by the school of Porphyry. The Neo-Platonist would say that the priest might have his traditional *discourse* concerning God (theology), but he alone, with his intuition, the highest *wisdom* concerning him.

GOWER. I can't say that I have any clear conception attached to the word.

ATHERTON. You want examples? Take Plotinus and Behmen.

GOWER. What a conjunction!

ATHERTON. Not so far apart as may appear. Their difference is one of application more than of principle. Had Plotinus thought a metal or a plant worth his attention, he would have maintained that concerning that, even as concerning the infinite, all truth lay stored within the recesses of his own mind. But of course he only cared about ideas. Mystical philosophy is really a contradiction in terms, is it not?

GOWER. Granted, since philosophy must build only upon reason.

ATHERTON. Very good. Then when philosophy falls into mysticism I give it another name, and call it theosophy. And, on the other side, I call mysticism, trying to be philosophical, theosophy likewise. That is all.

WILLOUGHBY. So that the theosophist is one who gives you a theory of God, or of the works of God, which has not reason, but an inspiration of his own for its basis.

ATHERTON. Yes; he either believes, with Swedenborg and Behmen, that a special revelation has unfolded to him the mystery of the divine dispensations here or hereafter—laid bare the hidden processes of nature, or the secrets of the other world ; or else, with Plotinus and Schelling, he believes that his intuitions of those things are infallible because divine— subject and object being identical,—all truth being within him. Thus, while the mystic of the theopathetic species is content to contemplate, to feel, or to act, suffering under Deity in his sublime passivity, the mysticism I term theosophic aspires to know and believes itself in possession of a certain super- natural divine faculty for that purpose.

GOWER. You talk of mysticism trying to be philosophical ; it does then sometimes seek to justify itself at the bar of reason ?

ATHERTON. I should think so—often : at one time trying to refute the charge of madness and prove itself throughout rational and sober; at another, using the appeal to reason up to a certain point and as far as serves its purpose, and then disdainfully mocking at demands for proof, and towering above argument, with the pretence of divine illumination.

WILLOUGHBY. Some of these mystics, talking of reason as they do, remind me of Lysander at the feet of Helena, protest- ing (with the magic juice scarce dry upon his eyelids) that the decision of his spell-bound faculties is the deliberate exercise of manly judgment—

> The mind of man is by his reason swayed,
> And *reason* says you are the worthier maid.

GOWER. Now you come to Shakspeare, I must cap your quotation with another : I fit those mystics Atherton speaks of as using reason up to a certain point and then having done with it, with a motto from the *Winter's Tale*—much at their service. They answer, with young enamoured Florizel, when Reason, like a grave Camillo, bids them ' be advised'—

> I am ; and by my fancy : if my reason
> Will thereto be obedient, I have reason ;
> If not, my senses better pleased with madness
> Do bid it welcome.

ATHERTON. To classify the mystics adequately, we should have a terminology of dreams rich as that of Homer, and distinguish, as he does, the dream-image of complete illusion from the half-conscious dream between sleeping and waking ;—ὄναρ from ὕπαρ. How unanimous, by the way, would the mystics be in deriving ὄνειρον from ὄνειαρ—*dream* from *enjoyment*.

WILLOUGHBY. To return from the poets to business ; was not all the science of the Middle Age theosophic rather than philosophic ? Both to mystical schoolmen and scholastic mystics the Bible was a book of symbols and propositions, from which all the knowable was somehow to be deduced.

ATHERTON. Most certainly. The mystical interpretation of Scripture was their measuring-reed for the temple of the universe. The difference, however, between them and Behmen would be this—that, while both essayed to read the book of nature by the light of grace, Behmen claimed a special revelation, a divine mission for unfolding these mysteries in a new fashion ; schoolmen, like Richard of St. Victor, professed to do so only by the supernatural aid of the Spirit illuminating the data afforded by the Church. And again, Behmen differs from

Schelling and modern theosophy in studying nature through the medium of an external revelation mystically understood, while they interpret it by the unwritten inward revelation of Intellectual Intuition. I speak only of the difference of principle, not of result. But no one will dispute that nearly every scientific enquiry of the Middle Age was conducted on mystical principles, whether as regarded our source of knowing or its method.

WILLOUGHBY. And what wonder? Does not Milton remind us that Julian's edict, forbidding Christians the study of heathen learning, drove the two Apollinarii to ' coin all the seven liberal sciences' out of the Bible? The jealous tyranny of the Papacy virtually perpetuated the persecution of the Apostate. Every lamp must be filled with church oil. Every kind of knowledge must exist only as a decoration of the ecclesiastical structure. Every science must lay its foundation on theology. See a monument attesting this, a type of the times, in the cathedral of Chartres, covered with thousands of statues and symbols, representing all the history, astronomy, and physics of the age—a sacred encyclopædia transferred from the pages of Vincent of Beauvais to the enduring stone, so to bid all men see in the Church a Mirror of the Universe—a *speculum universale.* Who can be surprised that by the aid of that facile expedient, mystical interpretation, many a work of mortal brain should have been bound and lettered as ' HOLY BIBLE,' or that research should have simulated worship, as some Cantab, pressed for time, may study a problem at morning chapel?

ATHERTON. What interminable lengths of the fine-spun, gay-coloured ribbons of allegory and metaphor has the mountebank ingenuity of that mystical interpretation drawn out of the mouth of Holy Writ!

GOWER. And made religion a toy—a tassel on the silken purse of the spendthrift Fancy.

WILLOUGHBY. Granting, Atherton, your general position that the undue inference of the objective from the subjective produces mysticism, what are we to say of a man like Descartes, for example? You will not surely condemn him as a mystic.

ATHERTON. Certainly, not altogether; reason holds its own with him—is not swept away by the hallucinations of sentiment, or feeling, or special revelation; but none of our powers act quite singly—*nemo omnibus horis sapit*—a mystical element crops out here and there. I think he carried too far the application of a principle based, in great part at least, on truth. In his inference of the objective from the subjective, I think he was so far right that our ability to conceive of a Supreme Perfection affords a strong presumption that such a God must exist. It is not to be supposed that the conception can transcend the reality. His argument from within is a potent auxiliary of the argument from without, if not by itself so all-sufficient as he supposes. There are, too, I think, certain necessary truths which, by the constitution of our mind, we cannot conceive as possibly other than they are, when once presented to us from without. But we surely should not on this account be justified in saying with the mystic Bernard, that each soul contains an infallible copy of the ideas in the Divine Mind, so that the pure in heart, in proportion as they have cleansed the internal mirror, must in knowing themselves, know also God. It must be no less an exaggeration of the truth to say, with the philosopher Descartes, that certain notions of the laws of Nature are impressed upon our minds, so that we may, after reflecting upon them, discover the secrets of the universe. On the strength of this principle he undertakes to determine exactly how long a time it must have required to reduce chaos to order. The effort made by Descartes to insulate himself completely from the external world and the results of experience, was cer-

tainly similar in mode, though very different in its object, from
the endeavours after absolute self-seclusion made by many of
the mystics. The former sought to detect by abstraction the
laws of mind ; the latter, to attain the vision of God.

GOWER. There is much more of mysticism discernible in
some of the systems which have followed in the path opened
by Descartes. What can be more favourable than Schelling's
Identity principle to the error which confounds, rather than
allies, physics and metaphysics, science and theology ?

ATHERTON. Behmen himself is no whit more fantastical in
this way than Oken and Franz Baader.

GOWER. These theosophies, old and new, with their self-
evolved inexplicable explanations of everything, remind me of
the Frenchman's play-bill announcing an exhibition of the Universal Judgment by means of three thousand five hundred
puppets. The countless marionette figures in the brain of the
theosophist—Elements, Forms, Tinctures, Mothers of Nature,
Fountain-spirits, Planetary Potencies, &c., are made to shift
and gesticulate unceasingly, through all possible permutations
and combinations, and the operator has cried 'Walk in !' so
long and loudly, that he actually believes, while pulling the
wires in his metaphysical darkness, that the great universe is
being turned and twitched after the same manner as his painted
dolls.

WILLOUGHBY. I must put in a word for men like Paracelsus
and Cornelius Agrippa. They helped science out of the hands
of Aristotle, baptized and spoiled by monks. Europe, newly-
wakened, follows in search of truth, as the princess in the fairy-
tale her lover, changed into a white dove ; now and then, at
weary intervals, a feather is dropped to give a clue ; these aspi-
rants caught once and again a little of the precious snowy
down, though often filling their hands with mere dirt, and
wounding them among the briars. Forgive them their signa-

tures, their basilisks and homunculi, and all their restless, wrathful arrogance, for the sake of that indomitable hardihood which did life-long battle, single-handed, against enthroned prescription.

ATHERTON. With all my heart. How venial the error of their mysticism (with an aim, at least, so worthy), compared with that of the enervating Romanist theopathy whose 'holy vegetation' the Reformers so rudely disturbed. On the eve of the Reformation you see hapless Christianity, after vanquishing so many powerful enemies, about to die by the hand of ascetic inventions and superstitions, imaginary sins and imaginary virtues,—the shadowy phantoms of monastic darkness; like the legendary hero Wolf-Dietrich, who, after so many victories over flesh-and-blood antagonists, perishes at last in a night-battle with ghosts.

GOWER. The later mystical saints of the Romish calendar seem to me to exhibit what one may call the degenerate chivalry of religion, rather than its romance. How superior is Bernard to John of the Cross! It is easy to see how, in a rough age of fist-law, the laws of chivalry may inculcate courtesy and ennoble courage. But when afterwards an age of treaties and diplomacy comes in—when no Charles the Bold can be a match for the Italian policy of a Louis XI.—then these laws sink down into a mere fantastic code of honour. For the manly gallantry of Ivanhoe we have the euphuism of a Sir Piercie Shafton. And so a religious enthusiasm, scarcely too fervent for a really noble enterprise (could it only find one), gives birth, when debarred from the air of action and turned back upon itself, to the dreamy extravagances of the recluse, and the morbid ethical punctilios of the Director.

WILLOUGHBY. The only further question is about your third division, Atherton,—theurgic mysticism. We may let the Rabbinical Solomon—mastering the archdæmon Aschmedai and all his host by the divine potency of the Schemhamporasch engraven on his ring, chaining at his will the colossal powers of the air by the tremendous name of Metatron,—stand as an example of theurgy.

GOWER. And Iamblichus, summoning Souls, Heroes, and the Principalities of the upper sphere, by prayer and incense and awful mutterings of adjuration.

ATHERTON. All very good ; but hear me a moment. I would use the term theurgic to characterize the mysticism which claims supernatural powers generally,—works marvels, not like the black art, by help from beneath, but as white magic, by the virtue of talisman or cross, demi-god, angel, or saint. Thus theurgic mysticism is not content, like the theopathetic, with either feeling or proselytising ; nor, like the theosophic, with knowing ; but it must open for itself a converse with the world of spirits, and win as its prerogative the power of miracle. This broad use of the word makes prominent the fact that a common principle of devotional enchantment lies at the root of all the pretences, both of heathen and of Christian miracle-mongers. The celestial hierarchy of Dionysius and the benign dæmons of Proclus, the powers invoked by Pagan or by Christian theurgy, by Platonist, by Cabbalist, or by saint, alike reward the success-ful aspirant with supernatural endowments ; and so far Apol-lonius of Tyana and Peter of Alcantara, Asclepigenia and St. Theresa, must occupy as religious magicians the same province. The error is in either case the same—a divine efficacy is attri-buted to rites and formulas, sprinklings or fumigations, relics or incantations, of mortal manufacture.

WILLOUGHBY. It is not difficult to understand how, after a time, both the species of mysticism we have been discussing may pass over into this one. It is the dream of the mystic that he can elaborate from the depth of his own nature the whole pro-mised land of religious truth, and perceive (by special revelation) rising from within, all its green pastures and still waters,—somewhat as Pindar describes the sun beholding the Isle of Rhodes emerging from the bottom of the ocean, new-born, yet perfect, in all the beauty of glade and fountain, of grassy upland and silver tarn, of marble crag and overhanging wood, sparkling from the brine as after a summer shower. But alas, how tardily arises this new world of inner wonders! It must be accelerated—drawn up by some strong compelling charm. The doctrine of passivity becomes impossible to some temperaments beyond a certain pass. The enjoyments of the vision or the rapture are too few and far between—could they but be produced at will! Whether the mystic seeks the triumph of superhuman knowledge or that intoxication of the feeling which is to translate him to the upper world, after a while he craves a sign. Theurgy is the art which brings it. Its appearance is the symptom of failing faith, whether in philosophy or religion. Its glory is the phosphorescence of decay.

ATHERTON. Generally, I think it is; though it prevailed in the age of the Reformation—borrowed, however, I admit, on the revival of letters, from an age of decline.

BOOK THE SECOND

———◆———

EARLY ORIENTAL MYSTICISM

CHAPTER I.

> From worldly cares himselfe he did esloyne,
> And greatly shunned manly exercise ;
> From everie worke he chalenged essoyne,
> For contemplation sake : yet otherwise
> His life he led in lawlesse riotise ;
> By which he grew to grievous maladie :
> For in his lustlesse limbs through evill guise,
> A shaking fever raignd continually ;
> Such one was Idlenesse, first of this company.
>
> Spenser.

HAVING free access to the Commonplace Book of my friend Atherton, I now extract therefrom a few notes, written after reading Wilkins' translation of the Bagvat-Gita. This episode in a heroic poem of ancient India is considered the best exponent of early oriental mysticism. I give these remarks just as I find them, brief and rough-hewn, but not, I think, hasty.

Observations on Indian mysticism, à propos of the Bagvat-Gita.

This poem consists of a dialogue between the god Crishna and the hero Arjoun. Crishna, though wearing a human form, speaks throughout as Deity. Arjoun is a young chieftain whom he befriends. A great civil war is raging, and the piece opens on the eve of battle. Crishna is driving the chariot of Arjoun, and they are between the lines of the opposing armies. On either side the war-shells are heard to sound—shells to which the Indian warriors gave names as did the paladins of Christendom to their swords. The battle will presently join, but Arjoun appears listless and sad. He looks on either army ;

in the ranks of each he sees preceptors whom he has been taught to revere, and relatives whom he loves. He knows not for which party to desire a bloody victory : so he lays his bow aside and sits down in the chariot. Crishna remonstrates, reminds him that his hesitation will be attributed to cowardice, and that such scruples are, moreover, most unreasonable. He should learn to act without any regard whatever to the consequences of his actions. At this point commence the instructions of the god concerning faith and practice.

So Arjoun must learn to disregard the consequences of his actions. I find here not a 'holy indifference,' as with the French Quietists, but an indifference which is unholy. The *sainte indifférence* of the west essayed to rise above self, to welcome happiness or misery alike as the will of Supreme Love. The odious indifference of these orientals inculcates the supremacy of selfishness as the wisdom of a god. A steep toil, that apathy towards ourselves ; a *facilis descensus*, this apathy toward others. One Quietist will scarcely hold out his hand to receive heaven : another will not raise a finger to succour his fellow.

Mysticism, then, is born armed completely with its worst extravagances. An innocent childhood it never had ; for in its very cradle this Hercules destroys, as deadly serpents, Reason and Morality. Crishna, it appears, can invest the actions of his favourites with such divineness that nothing they do is wrong. For the mystical adept of Hindooism the distinction between good and evil is obliterated as often as he pleases. Beyond this point mysticism the most perverted cannot go ; since such emancipation from moral law is in practice the worst aim of the worst men. The mysticism of a man who declares himself the Holy Ghost constitutes a stage more startling but less guilty ; for responsibility ends where insanity begins.

The orientals know little of a system of forces. They carry a single idea to its consequences. The dark issue of the self-

deifying tendency is exhibited among them on a large scale,—
the degrees of the enormity are registered and made portentously
apparent as by the movement of a huge hand upon its dial.
Western mysticism, checked by many better influences, has
rarely made so patent the inherent evil even of its most mischievous forms. The European, mystic though he be, will
occasionally pause to qualify, and is often willing to allow some
scope to facts and principles alien or hostile to a favourite idea.

It should not be forgotten that the doctrine of metempsychosis
is largely answerable for Crishna's cold-blooded maxim. He
tells Arjoun that the soul puts on many bodies, as many
garments, remaining itself unharmed: the death of so many
of his countrymen—a mere transition, therefore—need not
distress him.

CHAPTER II.

Quel diable de jargon entends-je ici ?   Voici bien du haut style.
MOLIÈRE.

M YSTICISM has no genealogy.   It is no tradition conveyed across frontiers or down the course of generations
as a ready-made commodity.   It is a state of thinking and
feeling, to which minds of a certain temperament are liable at
any time or place, in occident and orient, whether Romanist
or Protestant, Jew, Turk, or Infidel.   It is more or less determined by the positive religion with which it is connected.   But
though conditioned by circumstance or education, its appearance is ever the spontaneous product of a certain crisis in
individual or social history.

A merely imitative mysticism, as exemplied by some Trac-
tarian ecclesiastics, is an artificial expedient, welcome to ambitious minds as an engine, to the frivolous as a devotional
diversion, to the weak and servile as a softly-cushioned yoke.

Were mysticism a transmitted principle we should be able to
trace it through successive translations to a form which might
be termed primitive.   We might mark and throw off, as we
ascended, the accretions with which it has been invested, till
we reached its origin—the simple idea of mysticism, new-born.
The mysticism of India, the earliest we can find, shows us that
nothing of this sort is possible.   That set of principles which
we repeatedly encounter, variously combined, throughout the
history of mysticism, exhibits itself in the Bagvat-Gita almost
complete.   The same round of notions, occurring to minds of

similar make under similar circumstances, is common to mystics in ancient India and in modern Christendom. The development of these fundamental ideas is naturally more elevated and benign under the influence of Christianity.

Summarily, I would say, this Hindoo mysticism—

(1.) Lays claim to disinterested love, as opposed to a mercenary religion;

(2.) Reacts against the ceremonial prescription and pedantic literalism of the Vedas;

(3.) Identifies, in its pantheism, subject and object, worshipper and worshipped;

(4.) Aims at ultimate absorption in the Infinite;

(5.) Inculcates, as the way to this dissolution, absolute passivity, withdrawal into the inmost self, cessation of all the powers,—giving recipes for procuring this beatific torpor or trance;

(6.) Believes that eternity may thus be realized in time;

(7.) Has its mythical miraculous pretentions, *i.e.*, its theurgic department;

(8.) And, finally, advises the learner in this kind of religion to submit himself implicitly to a spiritual guide,—his Guru.

With regard to (1), it is to be observed that the disinterestedness of the worship enjoined by Crishna is by no means absolute, as Madame Guyon endeavoured to render hers. The mere ritualist, buying prosperity by temple-gifts, will realise, says Crishna, only a partial enjoyment of heaven. Arjoun, too, is encouraged by the prospect of a recompence, for he is to aspire to far higher things. 'Men who are endowed with true wisdom are unmindful of good or evil in this world,—wise men who have abandoned all thought of the fruit which is produced from their actions are freed from the chains of birth, and go to the regions of eternal happiness.'

In some hands such doctrine might rise above the popular morality; in most it would be so interpreted as to sink below even that ignoble standard.

(3.) 'God,' saith Crishna, 'is the gift of charity; God is the offering; God is in the fire of the altar; by God is the sacrifice performed; and God is to be obtained by him who maketh God alone the object of his works.' Again, 'I am moisture in the water, light in the sun and moon, . . . human nature in mankind, . . . the understanding of the wise, the glory of the proud, the strength of the strong,' &c.

(4.) This eternal absorption in Brahm is supposed to be in some way consistent with personality, since Crishna promises Arjoun enjoyment. The mystic of the Bagvat-Gita seeks at once the highest aim of the Hindoo religion, the attainment of such a state that when he dies he shall not be born again into any form on earth. Future birth is the Hindoo hell and purgatory. So with Buddhism, and its Nirwana.

But the final absorption which goes by the name of Nirwana among the Buddhists is described in terms which can only mean annihilation. According to the Buddhists all sentient existence has within it one spiritual element, homogeneous in the animal and the man,—Thought, which is a divine substance. This 'Thought' exists in its highest degree in man, the summit of creation, and from the best among men it lapses directly out of a particular existence into the universal. Thus the mind of man is divine, but most divine when nearest nothing. Hence the monastic asceticism, inertia, trance, of this kindred oriental superstition. (*See* Spence Hardy's *Eastern Monachism.*)

(5.) 'Divine wisdom is said to be confirmed when a man can restrain his faculties from their wonted use, as the tortoise draws in his limbs.'

The devotees who make it their principal aim to realise the

emancipation of the spirit supposed to take place in trance, are called Yogis.

'The Yogi constantly exerciseth the spirit in private. He is recluse, of a subdued mind and spirit, free from hope and free from perception. He planteth his own seat firmly on a spot that is undefiled, neither too high nor too low, and sitteth upon the sacred grass which is called Koos, covered with a skin and a cloth. There he whose business is the restraining of his passions should sit, with his mind fixed on one object alone ; in the exercise of his devotion for the purification of his soul, keeping his head, his neck, and body steady, without motion ; his eyes fixed on the point of his nose, looking at no other place around.'

The monks of Mount Athos, whose mysticism was also of this most degraded type, substituted, as a gazing-point, the navel for the nose.

Ward, in describing the Yogi practice, tells us that at the latest stage the eyes also are closed, while the fingers and even bandages are employed to obstruct almost completely the avenues of respiration. Then the soul is said to be united to the energy of the body ; both mount, and are as it were con-centrated in the skull ; whence the spirit escapes by the basilar suture, and, the body having been thus aban-doned, the incorporeal nature is reunited for a season to the Supreme.[1]

---

[1] See Wilkins' *Bagvat-Gita*, pp. 63-65. *Ward*, ii. 180. Also, *Asiatic Researches*, vol. xvii. pp. 169-313, con-taining an account of these Yogis, by Horace Hayman Wilson. One sect, we are told, have a way of contempla-ting Vishnu in miniature, by imagining the god in their heart, about the size of an open hand, and so adoring him from top to toe. In this gross concep-tion of an indwelling deity these Hin-doos do indeed exceed St. Theresa, who after swallowing the wafer con-ceives of Christ as prisoner in her in-wards, and, making her heart a doll's-house, calls it a temple. But beyond her, and beyond the Indians, too, in sensuousness, are the Romanist stories of those saints in whom it is declared that a *post-mortem* examination has disclosed the figure of Christ, or the insignia of his passion, miraculously modelled in the chambers of the heart.

Stupifying drugs were doubtless employed to assist in inducing this state of insensibility.

Chrishna teaches that 'the wisely devout' walk in the night
of time when all things rest, and sleep in the day of time
when all things wake. In other words, the escape from
sense is a flight from illusion into the undeceiving condition
of trance. So the Code of Menu pronounces the waking
state one of deceptive appearances—a life among mere
phantasmata ; that of sleep a little nearer reality ; while
that of ecstasy, or trance, presents the truth—reveals a
new world, and enables the inner eye (which opens as
the outer one is closed) to discern the inmost reality of
things.

These are pretensions which mysticism has often repeated.
This notion underlies the theory and practice of spiritual clair-
voyance.

(6.) 'The learned behold him (Deity) alike in the reverend
Brahmin perfected in knowledge ; in the ox and in the
elephant ; in the dog, and in him who eateth the flesh of dogs.
Those whose minds are fixed on this equality gain eternity even
in this world' (transcend the limitation of time).

(7.) The following passage, given by Ward, exhibits at once
the nature of the miraculous powers ascribed to the highest
class of devotees, and the utter lawlessness arrogated by these
'god-intoxicated' men :—

' He (the Yogi) will hear celestial sounds, the songs and
conversation of celestial choirs. He will have the perception
of their touch in their passage through the air. He is able to
trace the progress of intellect through the senses, and the path
of the animal spirit through the nerves. He is able to enter a
dead or a living body by the path of the senses, and in this
body to act as though it were his own.

' He who in the body hath obtained liberation is of no caste, of no sect, of no order; attends to no duties, adheres to no shastras, to no formulas, to no works of merit; he is beyond the reach of speech; he remains at a distance from all secular concerns; he has renounced the love and the knowledge of sensible objects; he is glorious as the autumnal sky; he flatters none, he honours none; he is not worshipped, he worships none; whether he practises and follows the customs of his country or not, this is his character.'

In the fourteenth century, mystics were to be found among the lower orders, whose ignorance and sloth carried negation almost as far as this. They pretended to imitate the divine immutability by absolute inaction. The dregs and refuse of mysticism along the Rhine are equal in quality to its most ambitious produce on the banks of the Ganges.

(8.) The Guru is paralleled by the Pir of the Sufis, the Confessor of the Middle Age, and the Directeur of modern France.[2]

A mysticism which rests ultimately on the doctrine that the human soul is of one substance with God, is fain to fall down and worship at the feet of a man. Such directorship is, of course, no essential part of mysticism—is, in fact, an inconsistency; but, though no member, or genuine outgrowth, it is an entozoon lamentably prevalent. The mystic, after all his pains to reduce himself to absolute passivity, becomes not theopathetic, but *anthropopathetic*—suffers, not under God, but man.

---

[2] *Asiatic Researches, loc. cit.* The worshipped principle of Hindooism is not love, but power. Certain objects are adored as containing divine energy. The Guru is a representative and vehicle of divine power—a Godful man, and accordingly the most imperious of task-masters. The prodigies of asceticism, so abundant in Indian fable, had commonly for their object the attainment of superhuman powers. Thus Taraki, according to the Siva Puran, stood a hundred years on tip-toe, lived a hundred years on air, a hundred on fire, &c. for this purpose.—Notes to *Curse of Kehama*, p. 237.

The following passage, cited by Ward, exhibits the subjective idealism of these Hindoos in its most daring absurdity. 'Let every one meditate upon himself; let him be the worshipper and the worship. Whatever you see is but yourself, and father and mother are nonentities; you are the infant and the old man, the wise man and the fool, the male and the female; it is you who are drowned in the stream—you who pass over ; you are the sensualist and the ascetic, the sick man and the strong ; in short, whatsoever you see, that is you, as bubbles, surf, and billows are all but water.'

Now, there is an obvious resemblance between this idealism and that of Fichte. The Indian and the German both ignore the notions formed from mere sensible experience ; both dwell apart from experience, in a world fashioned for themselves out of 'pure thought ;' both identify thought and being, subject and object. But here the likeness ends. The points of contrast are obvious. The Hindoo accepts as profoundest wisdom what would be an unfair caricature of the system of Fichte. The idealism of the Oriental is dreamy and passive ; it dissolves his individuality ; it makes him a particle, wrought now into this, now into that, in the ever-shifting phantasmagoria of the universe ; he has been, he may be, he, therefore, in a sense is, anything and everything. Fichte's philosophy, on the contrary, rests altogether on the intense activity— on the autocracy of the Ego, which posits, or creates, the Non-Ego.' He says, ' The activity and passivity of the Ego are one and the same. For in as far as it does *not* posit a something in itself, it posits that something in the Non-Ego. Again, the activity and passivity of the Non-Ego are one and the same. In as far as the Non-Ego works upon the Ego, and will absorb a something in it, the Ego posits that very thing in the Non-Ego.' (*Grundlage der gesammten Wissenschaftslehre*, § 3. *Sämmtliche Werke*, v. i. p. 177.) Action is all in all with him. God he calls 'a pure Action (*reines Handeln*), the life and principle of a supersensuous order of the world—just as I am a pure Action, as a link in that order. (*Gerichtliche Verantwortung gegen die Anklage des Atheismus*, *Werke*, v. p. 261.) Charged with denying personality to God, Fichte replies that he only denied him that conditioned personality which belongs to ourselves— a denial, I suppose, in which we should all agree. The only God in his system which is not an uninfluential abstraction is manifestly the Ego—that is dilated to a colossal height, and deified. Pre-eminently anti-mystical as was the natural temperament of Fichte, here he opens a door to the characteristic misconception of mysticism—the investiture of our own notions and our own will with a divine authority or glory. He would say, ' The man of genius *does* think divine thoughts. But the man who is unintelligible, who, in the very same province of pure thought as that occupied by the true philosopher, thinks only at random and incoherently ; *he* is mistaken, I grant, in arrogating inspiration—*him* I call a mystic.' But of unintelligibility or incoherence what is to be the test,—who is to be the judge? In this anarchy of gods, numerous as thinkers, one deity must have as much divine right as another. There can be no appeal to experience, which all confessedly abandon ; no appeal to facts, which each Ego creates after its own fashion for itself.

BOOK THE THIRD

——◆——

THE MYSTICISM OF THE NEO-PLATONISTS

CHAPTER I.

—— a man is not as God,
But then most godlike being most a man.

TENNYSON.

KATE. What a formidable bundle of papers, Henry.

ATHERTON. Don't be alarmed, I shall not read all this to you; only three Neo-Platonist letters I have discovered.

MRS. ATHERTON. We were talking just before you came in, Mr. Willoughby, about Mr. Crossley's sermon yesterday morning.

WILLOUGHBY. Ah, the Tabernacle in the Wilderness; did you not think his remarks on the use and abuse of symbolism in general very good? Brief, too, and suggestive; just what such portions of a sermon should be.

ATHERTON. He overtook me on my walk this morning, and I alluded to the subject. He said he had been dipping into Philo last week, and that suggested his topic. I told him I had paid that respectable old gentleman a visit or two lately, and we amused ourselves with some of his fancies. Think of the seven branches of the candlestick being the seven planets —the four colours employed, the four elements—the forecourt symbolizing the visible, the two sanctuaries the ideal world— and so on.

GOWER. At this rate the furniture in one of Hoffmann's tales cannot be more alive with spirit than Philo's temple apparatus. An ingenious trifler, was he not?

ATHERTON. Something better, I should say.

GOWER. Not, surely, when his great characteristic is an unsurpassed facility for allegorical interpretation. Is not mystical exegesis an invariable symptom of religious dilettantism?

ATHERTON. With the successors and imitators—yes; not with the more earnest originals,—such names as Philo, Origen, Swedenborg.

GOWER. But, at any rate, if this spiritualizing mania be Philo's great claim to distinction, head a list of mystical commentators with him, and pass on to some one better.

ATHERTON. He need not detain us long. For our enquiry he has importance chiefly as in a sort the intellectual father of Neo-Platonism—the first meeting-place of the waters of the eastern and the western theosophies. This is his great object—to combine the authoritative monotheism of his Hebrew Scriptures with the speculation of Plato.

GOWER. Absurd attempt!—to interpret the full, clear utterance of Moses, who has found, by the hesitant and conflicting conjectures of Plato, who merely seeks.

WILLOUGHBY. Yet a very natural mistake for a Jew at Alexandria, reared in Greek culture, fascinated by the dazzling abstractions of Greek philosophy. He belonged less to Jerusalem, after all, than to Athens.

ATHERTON. There lies the secret. Philo was proud of his saintly ancestry, yet to his eye the virtues of the Old Testament worthy wore a rude and homely air beside the refinement of the Grecian sage. The good man of Moses and the philosopher of Philo represent two very different ideals. With the former the moral, with the latter the merely intellectual, predominates. So the Hebrew faith takes with Philo the exclusive Gentile type,—despises the body, is horrified by matter, tends to substitute abstraction for personality, turns away, I fear, from the publican and the sinner.

GOWER. So, then, Platonism in Philo does for Judaism what

it was soon to do for Christianity,—substitutes an ultra-human standard—an ascetic, unnatural, passively-gazing contemplation —an ambitious, would-be-disembodied intellectualism, for the all-embracing activities of common Christian life, so lowly, yet so great.

WILLOUGHBY. Yet Alexandrian Platonism was the gainer by Philo's accommodation. Judaism enfeebled could yet impart strength to heathendom. The infusion enabled the Neo-Plato-nists to walk with a firmer step in the religious province ; their philosophy assumed an aspect more decisively devout. Nume-nius learns of Philo, and Plotinus of Numenius, and the ecstasy of Plotinus is the development of Philo's intuition.

GOWER. Let me sum up ; and forgive an antithesis. Philo's great mistake lay in supposing that the religion of philosophy was necessarily the philosophy of religion. But we have forgotten your letter, Atherton.

ATHERTON. Here is the precious document—a letter written by Philo from Alexandria, evidently just after his journey to Rome. (*Reads.*)

PHILO TO HEPHÆSTION.

I am beginning to recover myself, after all the anxiety and peril of our embassy to Caligula. Nothing shall tempt me to visit Rome again so long as this Emperor lives. Our divine Plato is doubly dear after so long an absence. Only an im-perative sense of duty to my countrymen could again induce me to take so prominent a part in their public affairs. Except when our religion or our trade is concerned, the government has always found us more docile than either the Greeks or the Egyptians, and we enjoy accordingly large privileges. Yet when I saw the ill turn our cause took at Rome, I could not but sigh for another Julius Cæsar.

I am sorry to find you saying that you are not likely to visit

Alexandria again.   This restless, wicked city can present but few attractions, I grant, to a lover of philosophic quiet.   But I cannot commend the extreme to which I see so many hastening.   A passion for ascetic seclusion is becoming daily more prevalent among the devout and the thoughtful, whether Jew or Gentile.   Yet surely the attempt to combine contemplation and action should not be so soon abandoned.   A man ought at least to have evinced some competency for the discharge of the social duties before he abandons them for the divine.   First the less, then the greater.

I have tried the life of the recluse.   Solitude brings no escape from spiritual danger.   If it closes some avenues of temptation, there are few in whose case it does not open more.   Yet the Therapeutæ, a sect similar to the Essenes, with whom you are acquainted, number many among them whose lives are truly exemplary.   Their cells are scattered about the region bordering on the farther shore of the Lake Mareotis.   The members of either sex live a single and ascetic life, spending their time in fasting and contemplation, in prayer or reading.   They believe themselves favoured with divine illumination—an inner light.   They assemble on the Sabbath for worship, and listen to mystical discourses on the traditionary lore which they say has been handed down in secret among themselves.   They also celebrate solemn dances and processions, of a mystic significance, by moonlight on the shore of the great mere.   Sometimes, on an occasion of public rejoicing, the margin of the lake on our side will be lit with a fiery chain of illuminations, and galleys, hung with lights, row to and fro with strains of music sounding over the broad water.   Then the Therapeutæ are all hidden in their little hermitages, and these sights and sounds of the world they have abandoned, make them withdraw into themselves and pray.

Their principle at least is true.   The soul which is occupied with things above, and is initiated into the mysteries of the Lord, cannot but account the body evil, and even hostile. The soul of man is divine, and his highest wisdom is to become as much as possible a stranger to the body with its embarrassing appetites. God has breathed into man from heaven a portion of his own divinity. That which is divine is invisible. It may be extended, but it is incapable of separation. Consider how vast is the range of our thought over the past and the future, the heavens and the earth. This alliance with an upper world, of which we are conscious, would be impossible, were not the soul of man an indivisible portion of that divine and blessed Spirit (εἰ μὴ τῆς θείας καὶ εὐδαίμονος ψυχῆς ἐκείνης ἀπόσπασμα ἦν οὐ διαιρετόν). Contemplation of the Divine Essence is the noblest exercise of man; it is the only means of attaining to the highest truth and virtue, and therein to behold God is the consummation of our happiness here.

The confusion of tongues at the building of the tower of Babel should teach us this lesson. The heaven those vain builders sought to reach, signifies symbolically the mind, where dwell divine powers. Their futile attempt represents the presumption of those who place sense above intelligence—who think that they can storm the Intelligible by the Sensible. The structure which such impiety would raise is overthrown by spiritual tranquillity. In calm retirement and contemplation we are taught that we know like only by like, and that the foreign and lower world of the sensuous and the practical may not intrude into the lofty region of divine illumination.

I have written a small treatise on the Contemplative Life, giving an account of the Therapeutæ. If you will neither visit me nor them, I will have a copy of it made, and send you.[1] Farewell.

---

[1] Philo gives an account of the Therapeutæ referred to in the letter, in his treatise *De Vitâ Contemplativâ.*

Passages corresponding with those contained in the letter contributed by Atherton, concerning the enmity of

GOWER. How mistaken is Philo in maintaining that the senses cannot aid us in our ascent towards the supersensuous; —as though the maltreatment of the body, the vassal, by the soul, the suzerain, were at once the means and the proof of mastery over it. Duly care for the body, and the thankful creature will not forget its place, and when you wish to meditate, will disturb you by no obtrusive hint of its presence. I find that I can rise above it only by attention to its just claims. If I violate its rights I am sued by it in the high court of nature, and cast with costs.

MRS. ATHERTON. And certainly our most favoured moments of ascent into the ideal world have their origin usually in some suggestion that has reached us through the senses. I remember a little song of Uhland's called *The Passing Minstrel*—a brief parable of melody, like so many of his pieces,—which, as I understood it, was designed to illustrate this very truth. The poet falls asleep on a ' hill of blossoms' near the road, and his soul flutters away in dream to the golden land of Fable. He wakes, as one fallen from the clouds, and sees the minstrel with his harp, who has just passed by, and playing as he goes, is lost to sight among the trees. ' Was it he,' the poet asks, ' that sang into my soul those dreams of wonder?' Another might inform the fancy with another meaning, according to the mood of the hour. It appeared to me an emblem of the way in which we are often indebted to a sunset or a landscape, to a strain of music or a suddenly-remembered verse, for a voyage into a world of

---

the flesh and the divine nature of the soul, are to be found in the works of Philo, *Sacr. Leg. Alleg.* lib. iii. p. 101 (ed. Mangey) ; lib. ii. p. 64 ; *De eo quod det. potiori insid. soleat,* pp. 192, 208.

Philo's interpretation of the scriptural account concerning Babel is contained in the *De Confus. Linguarum,* p. 424. His exposition of Gen. i. 9,

illustrates the same principle, *Sacr. Leg. Alleg.* lib. i. p. 54 ; so of Gen. xxxvii. 12 ; *De eo quod pot.* p. 192.

Eusebius shows us how Eleazar and Aristobulus must have prepared the way for Philo in this attempt to harmonize Judaism with the letters and philosophy of Greece. *Præp. Evang.* lib. viii. 9, 10.

vision of our own, where we cease altogether to be aware of the external cause which first transported us thither.

ATHERTON. That must always be true of imagination. But Platonism discards the visible instead of mounting by it. Considered morally, too, this asceticism sins so grievously. It misuses the iron of the will, given us to forge implements withal for life's husbandry, to fashion of it a bolt for a voluntary prison. At Alexandria, doubtless, Sin was imperious in her shamelessness, at the theatre and at the mart, in the hall of judgment and in the house of feasting, but there was suffering as well as sin among the crowds of that great city, with all their ignorance and care and want, and to have done a something to lessen the suffering would have prepared the way for lessening the sin.

CHAPTER II.

La philosophie n'est pas philosophie si elle ne touche à l'abîme ; mais elle cesse d'être philosophie si elle y tombe.—COUSIN.

GOWER. I hope you are ready, Atherton, to illumine my darkness concerning Neo-Platonism, by taking up that individual instance you were speaking of last Monday.

ATHERTON. I have something ready to inflict ; so prepare to listen stoutly. (*Reads.*)

Plato pronounces Love the child of Poverty and Plenty—the Alexandrian philosophy was the offspring of Reverence and Ambition. It combined an adoring homage to the departed genius of the age of Pericles with a passionate, credulous craving after a supernatural elevation. Its literary tastes and religious wants were alike imperative and irreconcilable. In obedience to the former, it disdained Christianity ; impelled by the latter, it travestied Plato. But for that proud servility which fettered it to a glorious past, it might have recognised in Christianity the only satisfaction of its higher longings. Rejecting that, it could only establish a philosophic church on the foundation of Plato's school, and, forsaking while it professed to expound him, embrace the hallucinations of intuition and of ecstasy, till it finally vanishes at Athens amid the incense and the hocus-pocus of theurgic incantation. As it degenerates, it presses more audaciously forward through the veil of the unseen. It must see visions, dream dreams, work spells, and call down deities, demi-gods, and dæmons from their dwellings in

the upper air.   The Alexandrians were eclectics, because such
reverence taught them to look back; mystics, because such
ambition urged them to look up.   They restore philosophy,
after all its weary wanderings, to the place of its birth; and, in
its second childhood, it is cradled in the arms of those old
poetic faiths of the past, from which, in the pride of its youth,
it broke away.

The mental history of the founder best illustrates the origin
of the school.   Plotinus, in A.D. 233, commences the study of
philosophy in Alexandria, at the age of twenty-eight.   His
mental powers are of the concentrative rather than the comprehensive order.   Impatient of negation, he has commenced an
earnest search after some truth which, however abstract, shall
yet be positive.   He pores over the Dialogues of Plato and the
Metaphysics of Aristotle, day and night.   To promote the
growth of his 'soul-wings,' as Plato counsels, he practises
austerities his master would never have sanctioned.   He
attempts to live what he learns to call the 'angelic life;' the
'life of the disembodied in the body.'   He reads with admiration the life of Apollonius of Tyana, by Philostratus, which has
recently appeared.   He can probably credit most of the marvels
recorded of that strange thaumaturgist, who, two hundred
years ago, had appeared—a revived Pythagoras, to dazzle
nation after nation through which he passed, with prophecy
and miracle; who had travelled to the Indus and the Ganges,
and brought back the supernatural powers of Magi and Gymno-
sophists, and who was said to have displayed to the world
once more the various knowledge, the majestic sanctity, and
the superhuman attributes, of the sage of Crotona.   This portraiture of a philosophical hierophant—a union of the philosopher and the priest in an inspired hero, fires the imagination
of Plotinus.   In the New-Pythagoreanism of which Apollonius was a representative, Orientalism and Platonism were

alike embraced.[1]   Perhaps the thought occurs thus early to
Plotinus—could I travel eastward I might drink myself at
those fountain-heads of tradition whence Pythagoras and Plato
drew so much of their wisdom.   Certain it is, that, with this
purpose, he accompanied, several years subsequently, the disastrous expedition of Gordian against the Parthians, and narrowly
escaped with life.

At Alexandria, Plotinus doubtless hears from orientals there
some fragments of the ancient eastern theosophy—doctrines
concerning the principle of evil, the gradual development of the
Divine Essence, and creation by intermediate agencies, none of
which he finds in his Plato.   He cannot be altogether a
stranger to the lofty theism which Philo marred, while he
attempted to refine, by the help of his 'Attic Moses.'   He
observes a tendency on the part of philosophy to fall back upon
the sanctions of religion, and on the part of the religions of the
day to mingle in a Deism or a Pantheism which might claim
the sanctions of philosophy.   The signs of a growing toleration
or indifferentism meet him on every side.   Rome has long
been a Pantheon for all nations, and gods and provinces together have found in the capitol at once their Olympus and
their metropolis.   He cannot walk the streets of Alexandria
without perceiving that the very architecture tells of an alliance
between the religious art of Egypt and of Greece.   All, except
Jews and Christians, join in the worship of Serapis.[2]   Was not

---

[1] The testimony of Cicero and Iamblichus may be received as indicating
truly the similarity of spirit between
Pythagoras and Plato,—their common
endeavour to escape the sensuous, and
to realize in contemplative abstraction
that tranquillity, superior to desire and
passion, which assimilated men to
gods.   The principles of both de-
generated, in the hands of their latest
followers, into the mysteries of a
theurgic freemasonry.   The scattered

Pythagoreans were, many of them,
incorporated in the Orphic associa-
tions, and their descendants were those
itinerant vendors of expiations and of
charms—the ἀγύρται of whom Plato
speaks (*Repub.* ii. p. 70)—the Grecian
prototypes of Chaucer's Pardonere.
Similarly, in the days of Iamblichus,
the charlatans glorified themselves as
the offspring of Plato.

[2] Clement of Alexandria gives a full
account of the various stories respect-

the very substance of which the statue of that god was made, an amalgam?—fit symbol of the syncretism which paid him homage. Once Serapis had guarded the shores of the Euxine, now he is the patron of Alexandria, and in him the attributes of Zeus and of Osiris, of Apis and of Pluto, are adored alike by East and West. Men are learning to overlook the external differences of name and ritual, and to reduce all religions to one general sentiment of worship. For now more than fifty years, every educated man has laughed, with Lucian's satire in his hand, at the gods of the popular superstition. A century before Lucian, Plutarch had shown that some of the doctrines of the barbarians were not irreconcilable with the philosophy in which he gloried as a Greek. Plutarch had been followed by Apuleius, a practical eclectic, a learner in every school, an initiate in every temple, at once sceptical and credulous, a sophist and a devotee.

Plotinus looks around him, and inquires what philosophy is doing in the midst of influences such as these. Peripateticism exists but in slumber under the dry scholarship of Adrastus and Alexander of Aphrodisium, the commentators of the last century.[3] The New Academy and the Stoics attract youth still, but they are neither of them a philosophy so much as a system of ethics. Speculation has given place to morals. Philosophy is taken up as a branch of literature, as an elegant recreation, as a theme for oratorical display. Plotinus is persuaded that

---

ing this idol, *Protrept.* c. iv. p. 42 (ed. Potter) ; moreover an etymology and legend to match, *Strom.* lib. i. p. 383.

Certain sorts of wood and metal were supposed peculiarly appropriate to certain deities. The art of the theurgist consisted partly in ascertaining the virtues of such substances ; and it was supposed that statues constructed of a particular combination of materials, correspondent with the tastes and attributes of the deity represented,

possessed a mysterious influence attracting the Power in question, and inducing him to take up his residence within the image. Iamblichus lays down this principle of sympathy in the treatise *De Mysteriis*, v. 23, p. 139 (ed. Gale, 1678). Kircher furnishes a description of this statue of Serapis, *Œdip. Ægypt.* i. 139.

[3] See *Histoire de l'Ecole d'Alexandrie*, par M. Jules Simon, tom. i. p. 99.

philosophy should be worship—speculation, a search after God —no amusement, but a prayer.   Scepticism is strong in proportion to the defect or weakness of everything positive around it.   The influence of Ænesidemus, who, two centuries ago, proclaimed universal doubt, is still felt in Alexandria.   But his scepticism would break up the foundations of morality.   What is to be done?   Plotinus sees those who are true to speculation surrendering ethics, and those who hold to morality abandoning speculation.

In his perplexity, a friend takes him to hear Ammonius Saccas.   He finds him a powerful, broad-shouldered man, as he might naturally be who not long before was to be seen any day in the sultry streets of Alexandria, a porter, wiping his brow under his burden.   Ammonius is speaking of the reconciliation that might be effected between Plato and Aristotle.   This eclecticism it is which has given him fame.   At another time it might have brought on him only derision; now there is an age ready to give the attempt an enthusiastic welcome.

'What,' he cries, kindling with his theme, 'did Plato leave behind him, what Aristotle, when Greece and philosophy had waned together?   The first, a chattering crew of sophists : the second, the lifeless dogmatism of the sensationalist.   The self-styled followers of Plato were not brave enough either to believe or to deny.   The successors of the Stagyrite did little more than reiterate their denial of the Platonic doctrine of ideas. Between them morality was sinking fast.   Then an effort was made for its revival.   The attempt at least was good.   It sprang out of a just sense of a deep defect.   Without morality, what is philosophy worth?   But these ethics must rest on speculation for their basis.   The Epicureans and the Stoics, I say, came forward to supply that moral want.   Each said, we will be practical, intelligible, utilitarian.   One school, with its hard lesson of fate and self-denial; the other, with its easier doctrine of pleasure, more or less refined, were rivals in their profession of ability to teach men how to live. In each there was a certain truth, but I will honour neither with the name of a philosophy. They have confined themselves to mere ethical application—they are willing, both of them, to let first principles lie unstirred. Can scepticism fail to take advantage of this? While they wrangle, both are disbelieved. But, sirs, can we abide in scepticism?—it is death. You ask me what I recommend? I say, travel back across the past. Out of the whole of that by-gone and yet undying world of thought, construct a system greater than any of the sundered parts. Repudiate these partial scholars in the name of their masters. Leave them to their disputes, pass over their systems, already tottering for lack of a foundation, and be it yours to show how their teachers join hands far above them. In such a spirit of reverent enthusiasm you may attain a higher unity, you mount in speculation, and from that height ordain all noble actions for your lower life. So you become untrue neither to experience nor to reason, and the genius of eclecticism will combine, yea, shall I say it, will surpass while it embraces, all the ancient triumphs of philosophy!'[4]

Such was the teaching which attracted Longinus, Herennius, and Origen (not the Father). It makes an epoch in the life of Plotinus. He desires now no other instructor, and is preparing to become himself a leader in the pathway Ammonius has pointed out. He is convinced that Platonism, exalted into an enthusiastic illuminism, and gathering about itself all the scattered truth upon the field of history,—Platonism, mystical and catholic, can alone preserve men from the abyss of scepticism. One of the old traditions of Finland relates how a mother once found her son torn into a thousand fragments at the bottom of the River of Death. She gathered the scattered members to

[4] See Note, p. 82.

her bosom, and rocking to and fro, sang a magic song, which
made him whole again, and restored the departed life.   Such a
spell the Alexandrian philosophy sought to work—thus to
recover and re-unite the relics of antique truth, dispersed and
drowned by time.

Plotinus occupied himself only with the most abstract questions concerning knowledge and being.   Detail and method—
all the stitching and clipping of eclecticism, he bequeathed as
the handicraft of his successors.   His fundamental principle is
the old *petitio principii* of idealism.   Truth, according to him,
is not the agreement of our apprehension of an external object
with the object itself—it is rather the agreement of the mind
with itself.   The objects we contemplate and that which contemplates, are identical for the philosopher.   Both are thought;
only like can know like; all truth is within us.   By reducing
the soul to its most abstract simplicity, we subtilise it so that
it expands into the infinite.   In such a state we transcend our
finite selves, and are one with the infinite ; this is the privileged
condition of ecstasy.   These blissful intervals, but too evanescent
and too rare, were regarded as the reward of philosophic asceticism—the seasons of refreshing, which were to make amends for
all the stoical austerities of the steep ascent towards the abstraction of the primal unity.

Thus the Neo-Platonists became ascetics and enthusiasts :
Plato was neither.   Where Plato acknowledges the services of
the earliest philosophers—the imperfect utterances of the world's
first thoughts,—Neo-Platonism (in its later period, at least)
undertakes to detect, not the similarity merely, but the identity
between Pythagoras and Plato, and even to exhibit the Platonism of Orpheus and of Hermes.   Where Plato is hesitant or
obscure, Neo-Platonism inserts a meaning of its own, and is
confident that such, and no other, was the master's mind.
Where Plato indulges in a fancy, or hazards a bold assertion,

Neo-Platonism, ignoring the doubts Plato may himself express elsewhere, spins it out into a theory, or bows to it as an infallible revelation.[5] Where Plato has the doctrine of Reminiscence, Neo-Platonism has the doctrine of Ecstasy. In the Reminiscence of Plato, the ideas the mind perceives are without it. Here there is no mysticism, only the mistake incidental to metaphysicians generally, of giving an actual existence to mere mental abstractions. In Ecstasy, the ideas perceived are within the mind. The mystic, according to Plotinus, contemplates the divine perfections in himself; and, in the ecstatic state, individuality (which is so much imperfection), memory, time, space, phenomenal contradictions, and logical distinctions, all vanish. It is not until the rapture is past, and the mind, held in this strange solution, is, as it were, precipitated on reality, that memory is again employed. Plotinus would say that Reminiscence could impart only inferior knowledge, because it implies separation between the subject and the object. Ecstasy is superior—is absolute, being the realization of their identity. True to this doctrine of absorption, the Pantheism of Plotinus teaches him to maintain, alike with the Oriental mystic at one extreme of time, and with the Hegelian at the other, that our individual existence is but phenomenal and transitory. Plotinus, accordingly, does not banish reason, he only subordinates it to ecstasy where the Absolute is in question.[6] It is not till the last that he calls in supernatural aid. The wizard king builds his tower of speculation by the hands of human workmen till he reaches the top story, and then summons his genii to fashion the battlements of adamant, and crown them with starry fire.

GOWER. Thanks. These Neo-Platonists are evidently no mere dreamers. They are erudite and critical, they study and

[5] See *Jules Simon*, ii. pp. 626, &c.   [6] See Note to Chap. III. p. 92.

they reason, they are logicians as well as poets ; they are not
mystics till they have first been rationalists, and they have
recourse at last to mysticism only to carry them whither they
find reason cannot mount.

ATHERTON. Now, I have a letter by Plotinus. It is without a date, but from internal evidence must have been written
about A.D. 260.

PLOTINUS TO FLACCUS.

I applaud your devotion to philosophy ; I rejoice to hear
that your soul has set sail, like the returning Ulysses, for its
native land—that glorious, that only real country—the world of
unseen truth.   To follow philosophy, the senator Rogatianus,
one of the noblest of my disciples, gave up the other day all
but the whole of his patrimony, set free his slaves, and surrendered all the honours of his station.

Tidings have reached us that Valerian has been defeated,
and is now in the hands of Sapor.   The threats of Franks and
Allemanni, of Goths and Persians, are alike terrible by turns
to our degenerate Rome.   In days like these, crowded with
incessant calamities, the inducements to a life of contemplation
are more than ever strong.   Even my quiet existence seems
now to grow somewhat sensible of the advance of years.   Age
alone I am unable to debar from my retirement.   I am weary
already of this prison-house, the body, and calmly await the
day when the divine nature within me shall be set free from
matter.

The Egyptian priests used to tell me that a single touch with
the wing of their holy bird could charm the crocodile into
torpor ; it is not thus speedily, my dear friend, that the pinions
of your soul will have power to still the untamed body.   The
creature will yield only to watchful, strenuous constancy of
habit.   Purify your soul from all undue hope and fear about

earthly things, mortify the body, deny self,—affections as well as appetites, and the inner eye will begin to exercise its clear and solemn vision.

You ask me to tell you how we know, and what is our criterion of certainty. To write is always irksome to me. But for the continual solicitations of Porphyry, I should not have left a line to survive me. For your own sake and for your father's, my reluctance shall be overcome.

External objects present us only with appearances. Concerning them, therefore, we may be said to possess opinion rather than knowledge. The distinctions in the actual world of appearance are of import only to ordinary and practical men. Our question lies with the ideal reality that exists behind appearance. How does the mind perceive these ideas? Are they without us, and is the reason, like sensation, occupied with objects external to itself? What certainty could we then have, what assurance that our perception was infallible? The object perceived would be a something different from the mind perceiving it. We should have then an image instead of reality. It would be monstrous to believe for a moment that the mind was unable to perceive ideal truth exactly as it is, and that we had not certainty and real knowledge concerning the world of intelligence. It follows, therefore, that this region of truth is not to be investigated as a thing external to us, and so only imperfectly known. It is *within* us. Here the objects we contemplate and that which contemplates are identical,— both are thought. The subject cannot surely *know* an object different from itself. The world of ideas lies within our intelligence. Truth, therefore, is not the agreement of our apprehension of an external object with the object itself. It is the agreement of the mind with itself. Consciousness, therefore, is the sole basis of certainty. The mind is its own witness. Reason sees in itself that which is above itself as its source;

and again, that which is below itself as still itself once more.

Knowledge has three degrees—Opinion, Science, Illumination. The means or instrument of the first is sense; of the second, dialectic; of the third, intuition. To the last I subordinate reason. It is absolute knowledge founded on the identity of the mind knowing with the object known.[7]

There is a raying out of all orders of existence, an external emanation from the ineffable One (πρόοδος). There is again a returning impulse, drawing all upwards and inwards towards the centre from whence all came (ἐπιστροφή). Love, as Plato in the *Banquet* beautifully says, is the child of Poverty and Plenty.[8] In the amorous quest of the soul after the Good, lies the painful sense of fall and deprivation. But that Love is blessing, is salvation, is our guardian genius; without it the centrifugal law would overpower us, and sweep our souls out far from their source toward the cold extremities of the Material and the Manifold. The wise man recognises the idea of the Good within him. This he develops by withdrawal into the Holy Place of his own soul. He who does not understand how the soul contains the Beautiful within itself, seeks to realize beauty without, by laborious production. His aim should rather be to concentrate and simplify, and so to expand his

---

[7] The statements made in this and the preceding paragraph, and the reasons adduced by Plotinus in support of them, will be found in the fifth Ennead, lib. v. c. 1. He assumes at once that the mind must be, from its very nature, the standard of certitude. He asks (p. 519) Πῶς γὰρ ἂν ἔτι νοῦς, ἀνοηταίνων εἴη; δεῖ ἄρα αὐτὸν ἀεὶ εἰδέναι καὶ μὴ δ'ἂν ἐπιλαθέσθαί ποτε. He urges that if Intelligibles were without the mind it could possess but images of them; its knowledge, thus mediate, would be imperfect, p. 521. Truth consists in the harmony of the mind with itself. Καὶ γὰρ αὖ, οὕτως οὐδ' ἀποδείξεως δεῖ, οὐδὲ πίστεως ὅτι οὕτως

αὐτὸς γὰρ οὕτως. καὶ ἐναργῆς αὐτὸς αὑτῷ. καὶ εἴ τι πρὸ αὐτοῦ, ὅτι ἐξ αὐτοῦ. καὶ εἴ τι μετ' ἐκεῖνο, ὅτι αὐτός. καὶ οὐδεὶς πιστότερος αὐτῷ περὶ αὐτοῦ. καὶ ὅτι, ἐκεῖ τοῦτο, καὶ ὄντως. ὥστε καὶ ἡ ὄντως ἀλήθεια, οὐ συμφωνοῦσα ἄλλῳ, ἀλλ' ἑαυτῇ. καὶ οὐδὲν παρ' αὐτὴν ἄλλο λέγει καὶ ἔστι. καὶ ὅ ἐστι τοῦτο καὶ λέγει, p. 522.

[8] *Enn.* iii. lib. v. capp. 2 & 7. There the gardens of Jove, and Porus, with his plenty, are said to be allegorical representations of the intellectual food of a soul nourished and delighted by the truths of Reason. Poverty, again, with its sense of need, is the source of intellectual desire. Comp. Plato, *Symp.* p. 429 (*Bekk*).

being; instead of going out into the Manifold, to forsake it for the One, and so to float upwards towards the divine fount of being whose stream flows within him.

You ask, how can we know the Infinite?[9] I answer, not by reason. It is the office of reason to distinguish and define. The Infinite, therefore, cannot be ranked among its objects. You can only apprehend the Infinite by a faculty superior to reason, by entering into a state in which you are your finite self no longer, in which the Divine Essence is communicated to you. This is Ecstasy. It is the liberation of your mind from its finite consciousness. Like only can apprehend like; when you thus cease to be finite, you become one with the Infinite. In the reduction of your soul to its simplest self ($\ddot{a}\pi\lambda\omega\sigma\iota\varsigma$), its divine essence, you realize this Union, this Identity ($\ddot{\epsilon}\nu\omega\sigma\iota\nu$).

But this sublime condition is not of permanent duration. It is only now and then that we can enjoy this elevation (mercifully made possible for us) above the limits of the body and the world. I myself have realized it but three times as yet, and Porphyry hitherto not once. All that tends to purify and elevate the mind will assist you in this attainment, and facilitate the approach and the recurrence of these happy intervals. There are, then, different roads by which this end may be reached. The love of beauty which exalts the poet; that devotion to the One and that ascent of science which makes the ambition of the philosopher; and that love and those prayers by which some devout and ardent soul tends in its moral purity towards perfection. These are the great highways conducting to that height above the actual and the particular, where we stand in the immediate presence of the Infinite, who shines out as from the deeps of the soul.[10]

[9] See Note 2, p. 82.   [10] *Enn.* i. lib. 3, c. 1.

NOTE TO PAGE 75.

This imaginary fragment from Ammonius Saccas is, I believe, true to what seems fairly inferred concerning his teaching. See *Brucker*, ii. p. 211 ; and *Jules Simon*, i. 205 ; ii. 668.

Plotinus appears to have been indebted to Numenius even more than to Ammonius or Potamon for some of the ideas peculiar to his system. The modicum of information concerning Numenius which Eusebius has handed down shows that this Platonist anticipated the characteristic doctrine of Neo-Platonism concerning the Divine Being. Like the Neo-Platonist, he pursued philosophical inquiry in a religious spirit, imploring, as Plotinus does, divine illumination. He endeavoured to harmonize Pythagoras and Plato, to elucidate and confirm the opinions of both by the religious dog-mas of the Egyptians, the Magi, and the Brahmins, and, like many of the Christian Fathers, he believed that Plato stood indebted to the Hebrew as well as to the Egyptian theology for much of his wisdom. He was pressed by the same great difficulty which weighed upon Plotinus. How could the immutable One create the Manifold without self-degradation ? He solved it in a manner substantially the same. His answer is—by means of a hypostatic emanation. He posits in the Divine Nature three principles in a descending scale. His order of existence is as follows :—

I. *God*, the Absolute.

II. *The Demiurge ;* he is the Artificer, in a sense, the imitator of the former. He contemplates matter, his eye ordains and upholds it, yet he is himself separate from it, since matter contains a concupiscent principle,—is fluctuating, and philosophically non-existent. The Demiurge is the ἀρχὴ γενέσεως, and good ; for goodness is the original principle of Being. The second Hypostasis, engaged in the contemplation of matter, does not attain the serene self-contemplation of the First.

III. *Substance* or Essence, of a twofold character, corresponding to the two former.

The Universe is a copy of this third Principle.

This not very intelligible theory, which of course increases instead of les-sening the perplexity in which the Platonists were involved, though differing in detail from that of Plotinus, proceeds on the same principle ;—the expedient, namely, of appending to the One certain subordinate hypostases to fill the gap between it and the Manifold. (See, on his opinions, *Euseb. Præp. Evang.* lib. viii. p. 411 (ed. Viger) ; lib. xi. c. 18, p. 537 ; capp. 21, 22, and lib. xv. c. 17.

NOTE TO PAGE 81.

Plotinus and his successors are the model of the Pseudo-Dionysius in his language concerning the Deity. Of his abstract primal principle neither being nor life can be predicated ; he is above being and above life. *Enn.* iii. lib. 8, c. 9. But man by simplifying his nature to the utmost possible extent may become lost in this Unity. In *Enn.* v. lib. 5, c. 8, the mind of the contemplative philosopher is described as illumined with a divine light. He cannot tell whence it comes, or whither it goes. It is rather he himself who approaches or withdraws. He must not pursue it (οὐ χρὴ διώκειν) but abide (a true Quietist) in patient waiting, as one looking for the rising of the sun out of the ocean. The soul, blind to all beside, gazes intently on the ideal vision of the Beautiful, and is glorified as it contemplates it—ἐκεῖ ἑαυτὸν πᾶς τρέπων καὶ διδοὺς, στὰς δὲ καὶ οἷον πληρωθεὶς μένους, εἶδε μὲν τὰ πρῶτα καλλίω γενόμενον ἑαυτὸν, καὶ ἐπιστίλβοντα ὡς ἐγγὺς ὄντος αὐτοῦ.

But this is only a preliminary stage of exaltation. The Absolute, or the

One, has no parts ; all things partake of him, nothing possesses him ; to see impartially is an impossibility, a contradiction,—if we imagine we recognise a portion he is far from us yet,—to see him mediately (δι' ἑτέρων) is to behold his traces, not himself. Ὅταν μὲν ὁρᾷς ὅλον βλέπε. But, asks Plotinus, is not seeing him wholly identity with him ? cap. 10.

The mystical aspirant is directed therefore to leave the glorified image of himself, radiant with the transforming effulgence of Beauty, to escape from his individual self by withdrawing into his own unity, wherein he becomes identified with the Infinite One—εἰς ἓν αὐτῷ ἐλθὼν, καὶ μήκετι σχίσας, ἐν ὁμοῦ πάντα ἐστὶ μετ' ἐκείνου τοῦ θεοῦ, ἀψοφητὶ παρόντος. Retreating into the inmost recesses of his own being, he there ἔχει πᾶν, καὶ ἀφεὶς τὴν αἴσθησιν εἰς τ' οὐπίσω, τοῦ ἑτέρος εἶναι φόβῳ, εἷς ἐστίν ἐκεῖ. No language could more clearly express the doctrine of identity—the object seen and the subject seeing are one. Plotinus triumphantly asks— πῶς οὖν ἔσται τίς ἐν καλῷ, μὴ ὁρμῶν αὐτό; ἢ ὁρῶν αὐτὸ ὡς ἕτερον, οὐδέπω ἐν καλῷ· γενόμενος δὲ αὐτὸ, οὕτω μάλιστα ἐν καλῷ· εἰ οὖν ὄρασις τοῦ ἔξω, ὄρασιν μὲν οὐ δεῖ εἶναι, ἢ οὕτως ὡς ταὐτὸν τῷ ὁρατῷ. *Ibid.* pp. 552-3.

CHAPTER III.

Lume è lassù che visibile face
Lo creatore a quella creatura
Che solo in lui vedere ha la sua pace.[1]
                                        DANTE.

MRS. ATHERTON. I confess I cannot understand what that state of mind can be which Plotinus calls ecstasy in the letter you read us last night, and about which most of your mystical fraternity talk so mysteriously.

KATE. I think I shall have myself mesmerised some day to form an idea.

WILLOUGHBY. I suppose the mystic, by remaining for many hours (enfeebled, perhaps, by fast and vigil), absolutely motionless, ceasing to think of anything—except that he *thinks* he is successful in thinking of nothing, and staring pertinaciously at vacancy, throws himself at last into a kind of trance. In this state he may perceive, even when the eyes are closed, some luminous appearance, perhaps the result of pressure on the optic nerve—I am not anatomist enough to explain ; and if his mind be strongly imaginative, or labouring with the ground-swell of recent excitement, this light may shape itself into archetype, dæmon, or what not. In any case, the more distinct the object seen, the more manifestly is it the projection of his own mind—a Brocken-phantom, the enlarged shadow of himself moving on some shifting tapestry of mist.

KATE. Like the woodman described by Coleridge as beholding with such awe an appearance of the kind, when he

[1] There is above a light which makes visible the Creator to that creature who finds his peace only in the vision of Him.

Sees full before him gliding without tread
An image with a glory round its head,
This shade he worships for its golden hues,
And *makes* (not knowing) that which he pursues.

ATHERTON. Such has been the god of many a mystic. He will soar above means, experience, history, external revelation, and ends by mistaking a hazy reflex of his own image for Deity.

GOWER. But we must not forget that, according to Plotinus, all sense of personality is lost during ecstasy, and he would regard any light or form whatever (presented to what one may call his cerebral vision) as a sign that the trance was yet incomplete. He yearns to escape from everything that can be distinguished, bounded, or depicted, into the illimitable inane.

ATHERTON. Very true. And it is this extreme of negation and abstraction for which Plotinus is remarkable, that makes it alone worth our while to talk so much about him. His philosophy and that of his successors, mistaken for Platonism, was to corrupt the Christian Church. For hundreds of years there will be a succession of prelates, priests, or monks, in whose eyes the frigid refinements of Plotinus will be practically, though not confessedly, regarded as representing God far more worthily than the grand simplicity and the forcible figurativeness of Scripture language. For the Christian's God will be substituted that sublime cypher devised by Plotinus—that blank something, of which you cannot say that it exists, for it is above existence.

Stop a moment—let me tell my beads, and try to count off the doctrines we shall meet with again and again in those forms of Christian mysticism where the Neo-Platonist element prevails—the germs of all lie in Plotinus.

There is, first of all, the principle of negation ; that all so-called manifestations and revelations of God do in fact veil him ; that no affirmative can be predicated of him, because he is above all our positive conceptions; that all symbols, figures, media, partial representations, must be utterly abandoned because, as finite, they fall infinitely short of the Infinite.

Here we are sunk below humanity—our knowledge consists in ignorance—our vision in darkness.

The next step raises us in an instant from this degrading limitation up to Deity—'sets our feet in a large room,' as the later mystics phrased it—even in infinity, and identifies us for a time with God.

Since the partial finite way of knowing God is so worthless, to know him truly we must escape from the finite, from all processes, all media, from the very gifts of God to God himself, and know him immediately, completely, in the infinite way— by receiving, or being received into, him directly.

To attain this identity, in which, during a brief space of rapture at least, the subject and object, the knower and the known, are one and the same, we must withdraw into our inmost selves, into that simple oneness of our own essence which by its very rarity is susceptible of blending with that supreme attenuation called the Divine Essence. So doing, we await in passivity the glory, the embrace of Union. Hence the inmost is the highest—introversion is ascension, and *introrsum ascendere* the watchword of all mystics. God is found within, at once radiating from the depths of the soul, and absorbing it as the husk of personality drops away.

WILLOUGHBY. And so the means and faculties God has given us for knowing him are to lie unused.

ATHERTON. Certainly; night must fall on reason, imagination, memory—on our real powers—that an imaginary power may awake. This is what the mystics call the absorption of the powers in God, leaving active within us nothing natural, in order that God may be substituted for ourselves, and all operations within be supernatural, and even divine.

GOWER. Then mysticism is a spiritual art whereby the possible is forsaken for the impossible—the knowable for the unknowable.

WILLOUGHBY. Or a contrivance, say, for reaching Divinity which realizes only torpor.

GOWER. A sorry sight this misdirection and disappointment of spiritual aspiration. Does it not remind you of that ever-suggestive legend of Psyche—how she has to carry the box of celestial beauty to Venus, and by the way covets some of this loveliness for herself. She lifts the lid, and there steals out a soporific vapour, throwing her into a deep slumber on the edge of a dizzy precipice. There she lies entranced till Eros comes to waken and to rescue her.

ATHERTON. I should grow very tiresome if I were now to attempt to indicate the likeness and the difference between ancient and modern speculation on these questions, and where I think the error lies, and why. But you must bear with me, Kate, if I hang some dry remarks on what you said just now.

KATE. I am sure I—

ATHERTON. You quoted Coleridge a minute since. He first, and after him Carlyle, familiarized England with the German distinction between reason and understanding. In fact, what the Epicureans and the Stoics were to Plotinus in his day, that were Priestley and Paley to Coleridge. The spiritualist is the sworn foe of your rationalist and pleasures-of-virtue man. Romance must loathe utilitarianism, enthusiasm scorn expediency. Hence the reaction which gives us Schelling as the Plotinus of Berlin, and Coleridge as the Schelling of Highgate. The understanding had been over-tasked—set to work unanimated and unaided by the conscience and the heart. The result was pitiable—lifeless orthodoxy and sneering scepticism. Christianity was elaborately defended on its external evidences ; the internal evidence of its own nature overlooked.

What was needful at such a juncture? Surely that *both* should be employed in healthful alliance—the understanding and the conscience—the faculty which distinguishes and judges, and the faculty which presides over our moral nature, deciding about right and wrong.   These are adequate to recognise the claims of Revelation.   The intellectual faculty can deal with the historic evidence, the moral can pronounce concerning the tendency of the book, righteous or unrighteous.   In those features of it unexplained and inexplicable to the understanding, if we repose on faith, we do so on grounds which the understanding shows to be sound.   Hence the reception given to Christianity is altogether reasonable.

But no such moderate ground as this would satisfy the ardour which essayed reform ; the understanding, because it could not do everything—could not be the whole mind, but only a part— because it was proved unequal to accomplish alone the work of all our faculties together, was summarily cashiered.   We must have for religion a new, a higher faculty.   Instead of reinforcing the old power, a novel nomenclature is devised which seems to endow man with a loftier attribute.   This faculty is the intuition of Plotinus, the *Intellectuelle Anschauung* of Schelling ; the Intuitive Reason, Source of Ideas and Absolute Truths, the Organ of Philosophy and Theology, as Coleridge styles it.   It is a direct beholding, which, according to Plotinus, rises in some moments of exaltation to ecstasy.   It is, according to Schelling, a realization of the identity of subject and object in the individual, which blends him with that identity of subject and object called God ; so that, carried out of himself, he does, in a manner, think divine thoughts—views all things from their highest point of view—mind and matter from the centre of their identity.[2] He becomes recipient, according to Emerson, of the Soul of the world.   He loses, according to Coleridge, the particular in

[2] See Schelling's *System des Tran-scendentalen Idealismus,* pp. 19-23 (Tübingen, 1800), and Chalybæus, *Hist. Entw. d. Spec. Phil.* p. 244.

the universal reason; finds that ideas appear within him from an internal source supplied by the Logos or Eternal Word of God—an infallible utterance from the divine original of man's highest nature.[3]

WILLOUGHBY. One aim in all—to escape the surface varieties of our individual (or more properly dividual) being, and penetrate to the universal truth—the absolute certainty everywhere the same :—a shaft-sinking operation—a descent into our original selves—digging down, in one case from a garden, in another from a waste, here from the heart of a town, there from a meadow, but all the miners are to find at the bottom a common ground—the primæval granite—the basis of the eternal truth-pillars. This I take to be the object of the self-simplification Plotinus inculcates—to get beneath the finite superficial accretions of our nature.

ATHERTON. And what comes of it after all? After denuding ourselves of all results of experience, conditioned distinctions, &c., we are landed in a void, we find only hollow silence, if we may accept a whisper or two, saying that ingratitude, treachery, fraud, and similar crimes, are very wrong.

GOWER. And even these dictates are those of our moral sense, not of an intellectual power of insight. For surely to call conscience practical Reason, as Kant does, is only to confound our moral and intellectual nature together.

ATHERTON. Very well, then. Seclude and simplify yourself thoroughly, and you do not find data within you equal to your need—equal to show you what God is, has done, should do, &c.

WILLOUGHBY. But all these intuitionalists profess to evolve from their depths very much more than those simplest ethical perceptions.

ATHERTON. By carrying down with them into those depths

---

[3] *Aids to Reflection,* pp. 225, 249. The reader is referred to a discriminating criticism of this doctrine in the *British Quarterly Review,* No. xxxvii.

the results of the understanding, of experience, of external culture, and then bringing them up to light again as though they
had newly emerged from the recesses of the Infinite.   This
intuitional metal, in its native state, is mere fluent, formless
quicksilver ; to make it definite and serviceable you must fix it
by an alloy ; but then, alas ! it is *pure* Reason no longer, and,
so far from being universal truth, receives a countless variety of
shapes, according to the temperament, culture, or philosophic
party, of the individual thinker.   So that, in the end, the result
is merely a dogmatical investiture of a man's own notions with
a sort of divine authority.   You dispute with Schelling, and he
waves you away as a profane and intuitionless laic.   What is
this but the sacerdotalism of the philosopher?   The fanatical
mystic who believes himself called on to enforce the fantasies
of his special revelation upon other men, does not more utterly
contemn argument than does the theosophist, when he bids you
kick your understanding back into its kennel, and hearken in
reverend awe to *his* intuitions.

WILLOUGHBY. Telling you, too, that if your inward witness
does not agree with his, you are, philosophically speaking, in
the gall of bitterness and the bond of iniquity.

ATHERTON. You are catching the approved style of expression
so much in vogue with our modern religious infidelity.   This is
the artifice—to be scriptural in phrase, and anti-scriptural in
sense : to parade the secret symbols of Christianity in the van
of that motley army which marches to assail it.

GOWER. The expedient reminds me of the device of Cam-
byses, who, when he drew out his forces against the Egyptians,
placed a row of ibises in front of his line, and the Egyptians, it
is said, suffered defeat rather than discharge an arrow which
might wound the birds they worshipped.

WILLOUGHBY. To go back to Plotinus.[4]   That doctrine of

4 See Note, p. 92.

the Epistrophe—the return of all intelligence by a law of nature to the divine centre—must inevitably be associated with the unhealthy morality always attendant on pantheism. It is an organic process godward, ending in loss of personal existence, no moral or spiritual elevation.

GOWER. His abstract Unity has no character, only negation of all conceivable attributes—so will and character can have no place in his theory of assimilation to God. Self-culture is self-reduction. What a plan of the universe !—all intelligence magnetically drawn to the Centre, like the ships to the Mountain of the Loadstone in the *Arabian Nights*—as they approach, the nails which hold them together are withdrawn, they fall apart, and all the fabric is dissolved.

WILLOUGHBY. It is curious to observe how rapidly the mind gives way under the unnatural strain of this super-essential abstraction, and indemnifies itself by imaginative and fantastical excesses for the attempt to sojourn in an atmosphere so rare. At first, ecstasy is an indescribable state—any form or voice would mar and materialize it. The vague boundlessness of this exaltation, in which the soul swoons away, is not to be hinted at by the highest utterance of mortal speech. But a degenerate age or a lower order of mind demands the detail and imagery of a more tangible marvel. The demand creates supply, and the mystic, deceiver or deceived, or both, begins to furnish forth for himself and others a full itinerary of those regions in the unseen world which he has scanned or traversed in his moments of elevation. He describes the starred baldrics and meteor-swords of the aërial panoply ; tells what forlorn shapes have been seen standing dark against a far depth of brightness, like stricken pines on a sunset horizon ; what angelic forms, in gracious companies, alight about the haunts of men, thwarting the evil and opening pathways for the good ; what genii tend what mortals, and under what astral influences they work weal or woe ; what beings of the middle air crowd in embattled rows the mountain side, or fill some vast amphitheatre of silent and inaccessible snow,—how some encamp in the valley, under the pennons of the summer lightning, and others find a tented field where the slow wind unrolls the exhalations along the marsh, and builds a billowy canopy of vapours : all is largely told,—what ethereal heraldry marshals with its blazon the thrones and dominions of the unseen realm ; what giant powers and principalities darken with long shadow, or illumine with a winged wake of glory, the forms of following myriads,—their ranks and races, wars and destiny, as minutely registered as the annals of some neighbour province, as confidently recounted as though the seer had nightly slipped his bonds of flesh, and mingled in their council or their battle.

ATHERTON. A true portraiture. Observe how this mysticism pretends to raise man above self into the universal, and issues in giving us only what is personal. It presents us, after all, only with the creations of the fancy, the phenomena of the sensibility peculiar to the individual,—that finite, personal idiosyncrasy which is so despised. Its philosophy of the universe subsides into a morbid psychology. Man is persuaded that he is to traverse the realms of fire and air, where the intelligible essences and archetypes of all things dwell ; and, like the Knight of La Mancha, he never stirs in reality from the little grass-plot of individual temperament on which his wondrous wooden horse stands still. This theosophy professes to make man divine, and it fails at last to keep him even rational. It prevents his becoming what he might be, while it promises to make him what he never can become.

NOTE TO PAGE 90.

M. Simon has shown, with much acuteness, in what way the exigencies of the system of Plotinus compelled him to have recourse to a new faculty, distinct from reason.

Plotinus perceived that Plato had not been true to the consequences of his own dialectics. When he had reached the summit of his logical abstraction,—had passed through definition after definition, each more intangible than the last, on his way upward towards the One, he arrived at last at a God who was above Being itself. From this result he shrank, and so ceased to be consistent. How could such a God be a God of Providence, such a shadow of a shade a creator? Plato was not prepared, like Plotinus, to soar so completely above experience and the practical as to accept the utmost consequences of his logical process. So, that his God might be still the God of Providence, he retained him within the sphere of reason, gave him Being, Thought, Power, and called him the Demiurge. When Plotinus, like a true eclectic, carried still farther his survey of what history afforded him, he found Aristotle postulating a Deity so restricted by his own abstraction and immutability as to render it impossible to associate with his nature the idea of superintendence. It was feared that to represent God as the God of Creation and of Providence would be to dualize him. And yet the world did exist. How were the serene and remote Unity demanded by logic, and that activity and contact with matter no less imperatively demanded for God by experience, to be reconciled with each other? It is scarcely necessary to observe that there was no real difficulty. The whole problem was the result of the notion, so universal, concerning the evil of matter, and of the wrong answer given by ancient philosophy to the vexed question—Does the Supreme work τῷ εἶναι, or τῷ βούλεσθαι? Philosophy maintained the former; the Christian Church the latter. To remove this obstacle which philosophy had itself constructed, Plotinus proposed his theory of these hypostases, in the Divine Nature. Above and beyond a God such as that of Plato, he places another like that of Aristotle, and above him a simple Unity, like the God of the Eleatics. The last was the ultimatum of the process of logical simplification—a something above being. But the hypothesis was destitute of proof—it was, in fact, contrary to reason. Plotinus must therefore either surrender his theory or bid farewell to reason. He chose the latter course. He does not deny the important services of reason, but he professes to transcend its limits. He calls in mysticism to substantiate, by the doctrines of Illumination and Identity, his imaginary God. He affirms a God beyond reason, and then a faculty beyond reason to discern that God withal.

This attempt to solve the problem in question is of course a failure. It is still more open than the system of Plato to Aristotle's objection, that it resembled the expedient of an arithmetician who should endeavour to simplify a calculation he found perplexing by taking still higher figures. Plotinus does not explain what he means by a Hypostasis. If the Hypostases in his Trinity have reality, the ideal unity he is so anxious to preserve in the Divine Nature is after all destroyed. If they have not, the gap between the One and the Manifold is still without a bridge, and the difficulty they are introduced to remove remains in effect where it was. If this hypothesis had made no part of the system of Plotinus, the great occasion for the doctrine of Ecstasy and the most powerful internal inducement to mysticism would have been wanting. The philosopher escapes from his labyrinth by borrowing the wings of the mystic.—See *Jules Simon*, tom. i. pp. 63, 84 ; ii. 462.

CHAPTER IV.

Stargaze. 'Tis drawn, I assure you, from the aphorisms of the old Chaldeans, Zoroaster the first and greatest magician, Mercurius Trismegistus, the later Ptolemy, and the everlasting prognosticator, old Erra Pater.—MASSINGER.

WILLOUGHBY. We have now about done, I suppose, with the theosophic branch of the Neo-Platonist school; with its latest leaders it degenerates into theurgic mysticism.

KATE. I hope it is going to degenerate into something one can understand.

GOWER. The great metaphysician, Plotinus, is off the stage, that is some comfort for you, Miss Merivale. Magic is less wearisome than metaphysics.

ATHERTON. The change is marked, indeed. Plotinus, wrapt in his proud abstraction, cared little for fame. His listening disciples were his world. Porphyry entered his school fresh from the study of Aristotle. At first the daring opponent of the master, he soon became the most devoted of his scholars. With a temperament more active and practical than that of Plotinus, with more various ability and far more facility in adaptation, with an erudition equal to his fidelity, blameless in his life, pre-eminent in the loftiness and purity of his ethics, he was well fitted to do all that could be done towards securing for the doctrines he had espoused that reputation and that wider influence to which Plotinus was so indifferent. His aim was twofold. He engaged in a conflict hand to hand with two antagonists at once, by both of whom he was eventually

vanquished.   He commenced an assault on Christianity without, and he endeavoured to check the progress of superstitious
usage within the pale of Paganism.   But Christianity could
not be repulsed, and heathendom would not be reformed.   In
vain did he attempt to substitute a single philosophical religion
which should be universal, for the manifold and popular Polytheism of the day.   Christian truth repelled his attack on the
one side, and idolatrous superstition carried his defences on the
other.

WILLOUGHBY.   A more false position could scarcely have been
assumed.   Men like Porphyry constituted themselves the
defenders of a Paganism which did but partially acknowledge
their advocacy.   Often suspected by the Emperors, they were
still oftener maligned and persecuted by the jealousy of the
priests.   They were the unaccredited champions of Paganism,
for they sought to refine while they conserved it.   They defended it, not as zealots, but as men of letters.[1]   They defended
it because the old faith could boast of great names and great
achievements in speculation, literature, and art, and because
the new appeared novel and barbarian in its origin, and
humiliating in its claims.   They wrote, they lectured, they disputed, in favour of the temple and against the church, because
they dreamed of the days of Pericles under the yoke of the
Empire : not because they worshipped idols, but because they
worshipped Plato.

MRS. ATHERTON.   And must not that very attempt, noticed
just now, to recognise all religions, have been as fatal to them
as the causes you mention ?

ATHERTON.   Certainly.   Mankind does not require a revelation to give them a religion, but to give them one which shall
be altogether true.   These Neo-Platonists were confronted by
a religion intolerant of all others.   They attempted, by keeping

---

[1] *J. Simon*, i. 154 ; ii. 173.

open house in their eclectic Pantheon, to excel where they thought their antagonist deficient. They failed to see in that benign intolerance of falsehood, which stood out as so strange a characteristic in the Christian faith, one of the credentials of its divine origin. No theory of the universe manufactured by a school can be a gospel to man's soul. They forgot that lip-homage paid to all religions is the virtual denial of each.

GOWER. Strange position, indeed, maintaining as their car-dinal doctrine the unity and immutability of the divine nature, and entering the lists as conservators of polytheism; teaching the most abstract and defending the most gross conceptions of deity; exclaiming against vice, and solicitous to preserve all the incentives to it which swarm in every heathen mythology. Of a truth, no clean thing could be brought out of that unclean,—the new cloth would not mend the old garment. Men know that they *ought* to worship; the question is, Whom? and How?

WILLOUGHBY. Then, again, their attempt to combine religion and philosophy robbed the last of its only principle, the first of its only power. The religions lost in the process what sanctity and authoritativeness they had to lose, while speculation aban-doned all scientific precision, and deserted its sole consistent basis in the reason. This endeavour to philosophise superstition could only issue in the paradoxical product of a philosophy without reason, and a superstition without faith. To make philosophy superstitious was not difficult, and they did that; but they could not—do what they would—make superstition philosophical.

ATHERTON. Add, too, that Greek philosophy, which had always repelled the people, possessed no power to seclude them from the Christianity that sought them out. In vain did it borrow from Christianity a new refinement, and receive some rays of light from the very foe which fronted it——

WILLOUGHBY. As is very visible in the higher moral tone of Porphyry's *Treatise on Abstinence.*

ATHERTON. The struggles of heathendom to escape its doom only the more display its weakness and the justice of the sentence.

GOWER. Like the man in the *Gesta Romanorum,* who came to the gate where every humpbacked, one-eyed, scald-headed passenger had to pay a penny for each infirmity : they were going only to demand toll for his hunch, but he resisted, and in the struggle was discovered to be amenable for every deformity and disease upon the table. So, no doubt, it must always be with systems, states, men, and dogs, that won't know when they have had their day. The scuffle makes sad work with the patched clothes, false teeth, wig, and cosmetics.

ATHERTON. Life is sweet.

As to Porphyry it was doubtless his more practical temperament that led him to modify the doctrine of Plotinus concerning ecstasy. With Porphyry the mind does not lose, in that state of exaltation, its consciousness of personality. He calls it a dream in which the soul, dead to the world, rises to an activity that partakes of the divine. It is an elevation above reason, above action, above liberty, and yet no annihilation, but an ennobling restoration or transformation of the individual nature.[2]

GOWER. One of Porphyry's notions about the spirits of the air, of which you told me in our walk yesterday, quite haunted me afterwards. It contains a germ of poetry.

KATE. By all means let us have it.

GOWER. Our philosopher believed in a certain order of evil genii who took pleasure in hunting wild beasts,—dæmons, whom men worshipped by the title of Artemis and other names, falsely attributing their cruelty to the calm and guiltless gods,

[2] *J. Simon*, liv. iii. chap. 4.

who can never delight in blood. Some of these natures hunted another prey. They were said to chase souls that had escaped from the fetters of a body, and to force them to re-enter some fleshly prison once more. How I wish we could see a design of this by David Scott! Imagine the soul that has just leaped out of the door of that dungeon of ignorance and pain, the body, as Porphyry would term it, fluttering in its new freedom in the sunshine among the tree-tops, over wild and town—all the fields of air its pleasure-ground for an exulting career on its upward way to join the journeying intelligences in their cars above. But it sees afar off, high in mid-air, a troop of dark shapes; they seem to approach, to grow out of the airy recesses of the distance—they come down the white precipices of the piled clouds, over the long slant of some vapour promontory—forms invisible to man, and, with them, spectre-hounds, whose baying spirits alone can hear. As they approach, the soul recognises its enemies. In a moment it is flying away, away, and after it they sweep—pursuers and pursued, shapes so ethereal that the galleries of the ant are not shaken as hunters and quarry glide into the earth, and not a foam-bell is broken or brushed from the wave when they emerge upon the sea, and with many a winding and double mount the air. At last hemmed in, the soul is forced—spite of that desperate sidelong dart which had all but eluded them—down into a body, the frame of a beggar's babe or of a slave's; and, like some struggling bird, drawn with beating wings beneath the water, it sinks into the clay it must animate through many a miserable year to come.

WILLOUGHBY. I wish you would paint it for us yourself. You might represent, close by that battle of the spirits, a bird singing on a bough, a labourer looking down, with his foot upon his spade, and peasants dancing in their 'sunburnt mirth' and jollity—wholly unconscious, interrupted neither in toil nor pleasure by the conflict close at hand. It might read as a satire on the too common indifference of men to the spiritual realities which are about them every hour.

MRS. ATHERTON. The picture would be as mysterious as an Emblem by Albert Durer.

GOWER. It is that suggestiveness I so admire in the Germans. For the sake of it I can often pardon their fantastic extravagances, their incongruous combinations, their frequent want of grace and symmetry.

ATHERTON. So can I, when an author occupies a province in which such indirectness or irony, such irregularity, confusion, or paradox, are admissible. Take, as a comprehensive example, Jean Paul. But in philosophy it is abominable. There, where transparent order should preside, to find that under the thick and spreading verbiage meaning is often lacking, and, with all the boastful and fire-new nomenclature, if found, is old and common,—that the language is commonly but an array of what one calls

> Rich windows that exclude the light,
> And passages that lead to nothing ;—

This puts me out of all patience.

GOWER. The fault you object to reminds me of some Flemish landscape-pieces I have seen ; there are trees, so full of grand life, they seem with their outstretched arms to menace the clouds, and as though, if they smote with their many hundred hands, they could beat away the storm instead of being bowed by it ; and underneath these great ones of the forest, which should shadow nothing less than a woodland council of Titans or a group of recumbent gods, the painter places only a rustic with a cow or two, an old horse, a beggar, or some other most every-day of figures.

MRS. ATHERTON. And you mean that the German words are large-looking as the trees, and the ideas worn and ordinary as the figures ? What will Mr. Willoughby say to that ?

ATHERTON. I think Willoughby will agree with me that it is high time that we should go back to our theurgic mysticism and Iamblichus. Here is a letter of his :—

IAMBLICHUS TO AGATHOCLES.

I assure you, my friend, that the efforts of Porphyry, of whom you appear disposed to think so highly, will be altogether in vain. He is not the true philosopher you imagine. He grows cold and sceptical with years. He shrinks with a timid incredulity from reaping in that field of supernatural attainment which theurgy has first opened, and now continually enlarges and enriches. Theurgy, be sure of it, is the grand, I may say, the sole path to the exaltation we covet. It is the heaven-given organum, in the hands of the wise and holy, for obtaining happiness, knowledge, power.

The pomp of emperors becomes as nothing in comparison with the glory that surrounds the hierophant. The priest is a prophet full of deity. The subordinate powers of the upper world are at his bidding, for it is not a man, but a god who speaks the words of power. Such a man lives no longer the life common to other men. He has exchanged the human life for the divine. His nature is the instrument and vehicle of Deity, who fills and impels him (ὄργανον τοῖς ἐπιπνέουσι θεοῖς.) Men of this order do not employ, in the elevation they experience, the waking senses as do others (οὔτε κατ᾽ αἴσθησιν ἐνεργοῦσιν οὔτε ἐγρηγόρασι). They have no purpose of their own, no mastery over themselves. They speak wisdom they do not understand, and their faculties, absorbed in a divine power, become the utterance of a superior will.

Often, at the moment of inspiration, or when the afflatus has subsided, a fiery Appearance is seen,—the entering or departing Power. Those who are skilled in this wisdom can tell by the character of this glory the rank of the divinity who has seized for the time the reins of the mystic's soul, and guides it as he will. Sometimes the body of the man subject to this influence is violently agitated, sometimes it is rigid and motionless. In some instances sweet music is heard, in others, discordant and fearful sounds. The person of the subject has been known to dilate and tower to a superhuman height; in other cases, it has been lifted up into the air. Frequently, not merely the ordinary exercise of reason, but sensation and animal life would appear to have been suspended; and the subject of the afflatus has not felt the application of fire, has been pierced with spits, cut with knives, and been sensible of no pain. Yea, often, the more the body and the mind have been alike enfeebled by vigil and by fasts, the more ignorant or mentally imbecile a youth may be who is brought under this influence, the more freely and unmixedly will the divine power be made manifest. So clearly are these wonders the work, not of human skill or wisdom, but of supernatural agency! Characteristics such as these I have mentioned, are the marks of the true inspiration.

Now, there are, O Agathocles, four great orders of spiritual existence,—Gods, Dæmons, Heroes or Demi-gods, and Souls. You will naturally be desirous to learn how the apparition of a God or a Dæmon is distinguished from those of Angels, Principalities, or Souls. Know, then, that their appearance to man corresponds to their nature, and that they always manifest themselves to those who invoke them in a manner consonant with their rank in the hierarchy of spiritual natures. The appearances of Gods are uniform (μονοειδῆ), those of Dæmons various (ποικίλα). The Gods shine with a benign aspect. When a God manifests himself, he frequently appears to hide sun or moon, and seems as he descends too vast for earth to contain. Archangels are at once awful and mild; Angels yet more gracious; Dæmons terrible. Below the four leading classes I have mentioned are placed the malignant Dæmons, the Anti-gods (ἀντιθέους).

Each spiritual order has gifts of its own to bestow on the

initiated who evoke them.   The Gods confer health of body, power and purity of mind, and, in short, elevate and restore our natures to their proper principles.   Angels and Archangels have   at   their   command   only   subordinate   bestowments. Dæmons, however, are hostile to the aspirant,—afflict both body and mind, and hinder our escape from the sensuous. Principalities, who govern the sublunary elements, confer temporal advantages.   Those of a lower rank, who preside over matter (ύλικά), display their bounty in material gifts.   Souls that are pure are, like Angels, salutary in their influence.   Their appearance encourages the soul in its upward efforts.   Heroes stimulate to great actions.   All these powers depend, in a descending chain, each species on that immediately above it. Good Dæmons are seen surrounded by the emblems of blessing, Dæmons who execute judgment appear with the instruments of punishment.

There is nothing unworthy of belief in what you have been told concerning the sacred sleep, and divination by dreams.   I explain it thus :—

The soul has a twofold life, a lower and a higher.   In sleep that soul is freed from the constraint of the body, and enters, as one emancipated, on its divine life of intelligence.   Then, as the noble faculty which beholds the objects that truly are—the objects in the world of intelligence—stirs within, and awakens to its power, who can be surprised that the mind, which contains in itself the principles of all that happens, should, in this its state of liberation, discern the future in those antecedent principles which will make that future what it is to be?   The nobler part of the soul is thus united by abstraction to higher natures, and becomes a participant in the wisdom and foreknowledge of the Gods.

Recorded examples of this are numerous and well authenticated ; instances occur, too, every day.   Numbers of sick, by

sleeping in the temple of Æsculapius, have had their cure re-
vealed to them in dreams vouchsafed by the god.   Would not
Alexander's army have perished but for a dream in which
Dionysus pointed out the means of safety?   Was not the siege of
Aphutis raised through a dream sent by Jupiter Ammon to Lysan-
der?   The night-time of the body is the day-time of the soul.

What I have now said—with little method, I confess—sets
before you but a portion of the prerogatives in which the
initiated glory.   There is much behind for which words are
too poor.   I have written enough, I am sure, to kindle your
ambition, to bid you banish doubt, and persevere in the
aspirations which so possessed you when I saw you last.[3]
Farewell.

GOWER. That explanation of prophetic dreams and the
temple sleep is very curious and characteristic.   No doubt the
common phenomena of mesmerism may have been among
the sacred secrets preserved by the priests of Egypt and of
Greece.

KATE. The preference for young and weakly persons, who
would possess an organization more susceptible of such influences, makes it look very likely.

ATHERTON. Observe how completely the theurgic element,
with Iamblichus, supersedes the theosophic.   In the process of
time the philosophical principles on which the system of
Plotinus rested are virtually surrendered, little by little, while
divination and evocations are practised with increasing credu-
lity, and made the foundation of the most arrogant pretensions.
Plotinus declared the possibility of an absolute identification
of the divine with the human nature.   Here was the broadest
basis for mysticism possible.   Porphyry retired from this position, took up narrower ground, and qualified the great mystical

[3] See Note, p. 106.

principle of his master.   He contended that in the union which takes place in ecstasy, we still retain the consciousness of personality.   Iamblichus, the most superstitious of all in practice, diminished the real principle of mysticism still farther in theory. He denied that man has a faculty inaccessible to passion, and eternally active.[4]

WILLOUGHBY. And so the metaphysics and the marvels of mysticism stand in an inverse ratio to each other.   But it is not unnatural that as the mystic, from one cause or another, gives up those exaggerated notions of the powers of man and those mistaken views of the relationship between man and God, which went together to make up a mystical system of philosophy, he should endeavour to indemnify himself by the evocations of theurgy, so as to secure, if possible, through a supernatural channel, what speculation had unsuccessfully attempted.

ATHERTON. True ; but in this case I should invert the order, and say that as the promise of theurgy exercised an attraction of growing strength on an order of mind less fitted for speculation, such temperaments would readily drop the speculative principle of mysticism in their eagerness to grasp the illusive prize—apparently so practical—which a commerce with superior natures held out.

WILLOUGHBY. And so the intellectual ambition and the poetical spirit, so lofty in Plotinus, subside, among the followers of Iamblichus, into the doggrel of the necromancer's charm.

GOWER. Much such a descent as the glory of Virgil has suffered, whose tomb at Pausilipo is now regarded by the populace of degenerate Naples less with the reverence due to the poet than with the awe which arises from the legendary repute of the mediæval magician.

ATHERTON. So the idealism of strong minds becomes super-

[4] *Jules Simon*, ii. 218.

stition in the weak.   In the very shrine where culture paid its homage to art or science, feebleness and ignorance, in an age of decline, set up the image-worship of the merely marvellous.

MRS. ATHERTON. I think you mentioned only one other of these worthies.

ATHERTON. Proclus.   He is the last great name among the Neo-Platonists.   He was the most eclectic of them all, perhaps because the most learned and the most systematic.   He elaborated the trinity of Plotinus into a succession of impalpable Triads, and surpassed Iamblichus in his devotion to the practice of theurgy.   Proclus was content to develop the school in that direction which Iamblichus—(successful from his very faults)—had already given it.   With Proclus, theurgy was the art which gives man the magical passwords that carry him through barrier after barrier, dividing species from species of the upper existences, till, at the summit of the hierarchy, he arrives at the highest.   According to him, God is the Non-Being who is above all being.   He is apprehended only by negation. When we are raised out of our weakness, and on a level with God, it seems as though reason were silenced, for then we are above reason.   We become intoxicated with God, we are inspired as by the nectar of Olympus.   He teaches philosophy as the best preparation for Quietism.   For the scientific enquirer, toiling in his research, Proclus has a God to tell of, supreme, almighty, the world-maker and governor of Plato. For him who has passed through this labour, a God known only by ecstasy—a God who is the repose he gives—a God of whom the more you deny the more do you affirm.

WILLOUGHBY. And this is all !   After years of austerity and toil, Proclus—the scholar, stored with the opinions of the past, surrounded by the admiration of the present—the astronomer, the geometrician, the philosopher,—learned in the lore of

symbols and of oracles, in the rapt utterances of Orpheus and
of Zoroaster—an adept in the ritual of invocations among
every people in the world—he, at the close, pronounces Quietism
the consummation of the whole, and an unreasoning contemplation, an ecstasy which casts off as an incumbrance all the
knowledge so painfully acquired, the bourne of all the journey.

MRS. ATHERTON. As though it were the highest glory of
man, forgetting all that his enquiry has achieved, hidden away
from the world,—to gaze at vacancy, inactive and infantine;—
to be like some peasant's child left in its cradle for a while in
the furrow of a field, shut in by the little mound of earth on
either side, and having but the blue æther above, dazzling and
void. at which to look up with smiles of witless wonder.

NOTE TO PAGE 103.

Iamblichus de Mysteriis, sect. x. cc. 1, 4, 6; iii. 4, 8, 6, 24; i. 5, 6;
ii. 3; iii. 31; ii. 4, 6, 7; iii. 1, 3. These passages, in the order given, will
be found to correspond with the opinions expressed in the letter as those of
Iamblichus.

The genuineness of the treatise *De Mysteriis* has been called in question,
but its antiquity is undoubted. It differs only in one or two very trivial
statements from the doctrines of Iamblichus as ascertained from other sources,
and is admitted by all to be the production, if not of Iamblichus himself, of
one of his disciples, probably writing under his direction. *Jules Simon*, ii. 219.

For the opinions ascribed to Porphyry in this letter, see his *Epistola ad
Anebonem*, passim. He there proposes a series of difficult questions, and displays that sceptical disposition, especially concerning the pretensions of Theurgy,
which so much scandalized Iamblichus. The *De Mysteriis* is an elaborate reply
to that epistle, under the name of Abammon.

In several passages of the *De Mysteriis* (ii. 11; v. 1, 2, 3, 7; vi. 6) Iamblichus
displays much anxiety lest his zeal for Theurgy should lead him to maintain
any position inconsistent with the reverence due to the gods. He was closely
pressed on this weak point by the objections of Porphyry. (*Ep. ad Anebon.*
5, 6.) His explanation in reply is, that the deities are not in reality drawn
down by the mere human will of the Theurgist, but that man is raised to a
participation in the power of the gods. The approximation is real, but the
apparent descent of divinity is in fact the ascent of humanity. By his long
course of preparation, by his knowledge of rites and symbols, of potent hymns,
and of the mysterious virtues of certain herbs and minerals, the Theurgist is
supposed to rise at last to the rank of an associate with celestial powers; their
knowledge and their will become his, and he controls inferior natures with the
authority of the gods themselves.

Iamblichus supposes, moreover, that there is an order of powers in the world,
irrational and undiscerning, who are altogether at the bidding of man when
by threats or conjurations he chooses to compel them. *De Myst.* vi. 5.

BOOK THE FOURTH

———◆———

MYSTICISM IN THE GREEK CHURCH

CHAPTER I.

'Questi ordini di su tutti s'ammirano
E di giù vincon si che verso Iddio
Tutti tirati sono e tutti tirano.
    E Dionisio con tanto disio
A contemplar questi ordini si mise,
Che li nomò e distinse com' io.[1]
                                    DANTE.

KATE. I have been looking at the pictures in Mrs. Jameson's *Sacred and Legendary Art*, of those strange creatures, the hermit saints—the Fathers of the desert. Only see this one, what a mane and claws! The two lions digging the grave there are own brothers to the holy men themselves.

ATHERTON. Yet they claimed powers as much above humanity as, to look at them, you would think them beneath it.

GOWER. Religious Nebuchadnezzars.

WILLOUGHBY. No shavelings, at any rate, like the smooth-faced sanctities of the later calendar.

ATHERTON. You will find among these anchorites almost all the wonder-working pretensions of mediæval mysticism in full development, thus early;—the discernment of spirits, gift of prophecy, miraculous powers of various kinds, ecstasy, exorcism, &c. &c. I should take St. Antony as a fair specimen of the whole class.[2]

---

[1] All these orders gaze admiring upward, and exert an influence downward (each on that immediately beneath it), so that they all together reciprocally draw and are drawn toward God. Dionysius gave himself with such zeal to the contemplation of them that he named and distinguished them as I have done.

[2] *Athanasii Opp. Vita S. Antonii.* The vision alluded to is related p. 498.

MRS. ATHERTON. Look, here is his picture ; there he stands, with crutch and bell and pig.

ATHERTON. The bell denotes his power over evil spirits, and the pig the vanquished dæmon of sensuality. In his life, by Athanasius, there is a full account of his battle with many dæmons in the shape of lions, bulls, and bears. He passed twenty years in an old castle which he found full of serpents. The power of the saint expelled those unpleasant aborigines. That nose, you see there, was supposed to possess the faculty of detecting by its miraculous keenness of scent the proximity of an evil spirit. There is an odour of iniquity, you must know, as well as an odour of sanctity. This disposition to literalize metaphors gave currency to the monkish stories of after times concerning the refreshing fragrance found to arise from the remains of disinterred saints. In fact, the materialization of the spiritual, or what passes for such, is the characteristic principle of the theurgic mysticism within the Roman Catholic Church. St. Antony, on one occasion, sees his own soul, separated from the body, carried through the air.

GOWER. A striking instance, I should say, of the objectivity of the subject.

ATHERTON. One of his visions is not without grandeur. The brethren had been questioning him one day concerning the state of departed spirits. The following night he heard a voice saying, ' Antony, get up ; go out and look !' He obeyed, and saw a gigantic figure, whose head was in the clouds, and whose outstretched arms extended far across the sky. Many souls were fluttering in the air, and endeavouring, as they found opportunity, to fly upward past this dreadful being. Numbers of them he seized in the attempt, and dashed back upon the earth. Some escaped him and exulted above, while he raged at their success. Thus sorrowing and rejoicing were mingled together, as some were defeated and others triumphant.

This, he was given to understand, was the rise and fall of souls.

WILLOUGHBY. That picture would be really Dantesque, if only a little more definite. Macarius is another great name, too, among these Christian ascetics and theurgists—the one who retired to the deserts of Nitria in the fourth century.

ATHERTON. He is not only famous for his measure of the supernatural powers ascribed to his brethren, but his homilies have been appealed to by modern theopathetic mystics as an authority for Quietism. He teaches perfectionist doctrine, certainly, but I do not think his words will bear the construction Poiret and others would give them. He was at least innocent of the *sainte indifférence*.[3]

MRS. ATHERTON. You said we were to discuss Dionysius the Areopagite this evening.

KATE. Pray introduce me first. I know nothing about him.

ATHERTON. No one does know who really wrote the books which passed under that name. It is generally admitted that the forgery could not have been committed earlier than the middle of the fifth century, probably somewhat later. So all I can tell you is, that somewhere or other (it is not unlikely at Constantinople, but there is no certainty), about the time when Theodoric was master of Italy—when the Vandal swarms had not yet been expelled from northern Africa—while Constantinople was in uproar between the greens and the blues, and rival ecclesiastics headed city riots with a rabble of monks, artizans, and bandit soldiery at their heels—while orthodoxy was grappling with the Monophysite and Eutychian heresies on

---

[3] Poiret, *Bibliotheca Mysticorum*, p. 95. Macarius gives great prominence to the doctrine of Union—describes the streaming in of the Hypostatic Light—how the spiritual nature is all-pervaded by the glory, and even the body is not so gross as to be impenetrable by the divine radiance. Some centuries later we find the monks of Mount Athos professing to discern this supernatural effulgence illuminating their stomachs. Gass, *Die Mystik des N. Cabasilas*, p. 56.

either hand, and the religious world was rocking still with the groundswell that followed those stormy synods in which Palestine and Alexandria, Asia and Constantinople, from opposite quarters, gathered their strength against each other —a monk or priest was busy, in his quiet solitude, with the fabrication of sundry treatises and letters which were to find their way into the Church under the all-but apostolic auspices of that convert made by the Apostle of the Gentiles when he spoke on Mars Hill. The writings would seem to have been first appealed to as genuine in the year 533. As heretics cited them, their authority was disputed at the outset; but being found favourable to the growing claims of the hierarchy, and likely to be useful, they were soon recognised and employed accordingly.[4]

WILLOUGHBY. Proclus could not have been long dead, and his reputation must have been still at its height, when this anonymous—let us call him Dionysius at once—was writing his Platonized theology.

ATHERTON. With the divines of Byzantium Proclus represented the grand old world of Greek thought. Even those who wrote against him as a heathen betray the influence he exercised on their doctrines. The object of Dionysius evidently was to accommodate the theosophy of Proclus to Christianity. Another aim, not less conspicuous, was to strengthen all the pretensions of the priesthood, and to invest with a new traditionary sanction the ascetic virtues of the cloister.

---

[4] In the year 533 the books of Dionysius were cited by the Severians, and their genuineness called in question by the bishop because neither Athanasius nor Cyril had made any allusion to them. *Acta Concil. Hard.* ii. p. 1159.

CHAPTER II.

They that pretend to these heights call them the secrets of the kingdom ; but they are such which no man can describe ; such which God hath not revealed in the publication of the Gospel ; such for the acquiring of which there are no means prescribed, and to which no man is obliged, and which are not in any man's power to obtain ; nor such which it is lawful to pray for or desire ; nor concerning which we shall ever be called to account.—JEREMY TAYLOR.

'I HAVE here,' said Atherton on the next evening, 'some notes on the doctrine of this pretended Areopagite—a short summary ; shall I read it ?'

'By all means.'

So the following abstract was listened to—and with creditable patience.[1]

(1.) All things have emanated from God, and the end of all is return to God. Such return—deification, he calls it—is the consummation of the creature, that God may finally be all in all. A process of evolution, a centrifugal movement in the Divine Nature, is substituted in reality for creation. The antithesis of this is the centripetal process, or movement of involu-

---

[1] For the passages authenticating this account, see *Dion. Areop. Opp.* as follows :—

(1.) *De Div. Nom.* c. iv. § 1 ; v. 3, 6, 8 ; vi. 2, 3 ; i. 1. *De Eccl. Hier.* i. 3.

(2.) *De Cœl. Hier.* i. 2, 3 ; v. 3, 4 ; vii. *De Eccl. Hier.* i. 1 ; x. 3. The resemblance of this whole process to the Pröodos and Epistrophe of Plotimus is sufficiently obvious.

(3.) *De Div. Nom.* iv. 20, p. 488. The chase after evil runs through sections 24-34. He sums up in one place thus :—' In a word, good springs from the sole and complete cause, but evil from many and partial defects. God knows the evil as good, and with him the causes of things evil are beneficent powers.' Proclus seeks escape from the hopeless difficulty in precisely the same way.

Concerning the *Via negativa* and *affirmativa*, see *De Div. Nom.* i. 1, 5, 4 ; *De Cœl. Hier.* xv. ; and *De Myst. Theol.* i. 2, 3.

(4.) *Ibid.* Also, *Fb. ad. Dorotheum De Myst. Theol.* iii. pp. 714, 721.

tion, which draws all existence towards the point of the Divine centre. The degree of real existence possessed by any being is the amount of God in that being—for God is the existence in all things. Yet He himself cannot be said to exist, for he is above existence. The more or less of God which the various creatures possess is determined by the proximity of their order to the centre.

(2.) The chain of being in the upper and invisible world, through which the Divine Power diffuses itself in successive gradations, he calls the Celestial Hierarchy. The Ecclesiastical Hierarchy is a corresponding series in the visible world. The orders of Angelic natures and of priestly functionaries correspond to each other. The highest rank of the former receive illumination immediately from God. The lowest of the heavenly imparts divine light to the highest of the earthly hierarchy. Each order strives perpetually to approximate to that immediately above itself, from which it receives the transmitted influence ; so that all, as Dante describes it, draw and are drawn, and tend in common towards the centre—God.

The three triads of angelic existences, to whom answer the ranks of the terrestrial hierarchy, betrays the influence of Proclus, whose hierarchy of ideas corresponds, in a similar manner, to his hierarchy of hypostases.

GOWER. The system reminds one of those old pictures which are divided into two compartments, the upper occupied by angels and cherubs on the clouds, and the lower by human beings on the earth, gazing devoutly upward at their celestial benefactors.

ATHERTON. The work of Christ is thrown into the background to make room for the Church. The Saviour answers, with Dionysius, rather to the Logos of the Platonist than to the Son of God revealed in Scripture. He is allowed to be, as incarnate, the founder of the Ecclesiastical Hierarchy ; but, as such, he is removed from men by the long chain of priestly orders, and is less the Redeemer, than remotely the Illuminator, of the species.

Purification, illumination, perfection,—the three great stages of ascent to God (which plays so important a part in almost every succeeding attempt to systematise mysticism) are mystically represented by the three sacraments, — Baptism, the Eucharist, and Unction. The Church is the great Mystagogue : its liturgy and offices a profound and elaborate system of symbolism.

(3.) The Greek theory, with its inadequate conception of the nature of sin, compels Dionysius virtually to deny the existence of evil. Everything that exists is good, the more existence the more goodness, so that evil is a coming short of existence. He hunts sin boldly from place to place throughout the universe, and drives it at last into the obscurity of the limbo he contrives for it, where it lies among things unreal.

All that exists he regards as a symbolical manifestation of the super-existent. What we call creation is the divine allegory. In nature, in Scripture, in tradition, God is revealed only in figure. This sacred imagery should be studied, but in such study we are still far from any adequate cognizance of the Divine Nature. God is above all negation and affirmation : in Him such contraries are at once identified and transcended. But by negation we approach most nearly to a true apprehension of what He is.

Negation and affirmation, accordingly, constitute the two opposed and yet simultaneous methods he lays down for the knowledge of the Infinite. These two paths, the *Via Negativa* (or Apophatica) and the *Via Affirmativa* (or Cataphatica) constitute the foundation of his mysticism. They are distinguished and elaborated in every part of his writings. The positive is the descending process. In the path downward from God, through inferior existences, the Divine Being may be said to have many names ;—the negative method is one of ascent ; in that, God is regarded as nameless, the inscrutable Anonymous. The symbolical or visible is thus opposed, in the Platonist style, to the mystical or ideal. To assert anything concerning a God who is above all affirmation is to speak in figure, to veil him. The more you deny concerning Him, the more of such veils do you remove. He compares the negative method of speaking concerning the Supreme to the operation of the sculptor, who strikes off fragment after fragment of the marble, and progresses by diminution.

(4.) Our highest knowledge of God, therefore, is said to consist in mystic ignorance. In omni-nescience we approach Omniscience. This Path of Negation is the highway of mysticism. It is by refraining from any exercise of the intellect or of the imagination—by self-simplification, by withdrawal into the inmost, the divine essence of our nature—that we surpass the ordinary condition of humanity, and are united in ecstasy with God. Dionysius does not insist so much on Union as the later mystics, but he believes, at all events, that the eminent saint may attain on earth an indescribable condition of soul—an elevation far transcending the reach of our natural faculties—an approach towards the beatific vision of those who are supposed to gaze directly on the Divine Essence in heaven. His disciple is perpetually exhorted to aspire to this climax of abstraction—above sight, and thought, and feeling, as to the highest aim of man.

WILLOUGHBY. What contradictions are here ! With one breath he extols ineffable ignorance as the only wisdom ; with the next he pretends to elucidate the Trinity, and reads you off a muster-roll of the heavenly hierarchies.

GOWER. And are not these, supplemented by the hierarchy of ecclesiastics, his real objects of worship ? No man could make an actual God of that super-essential ultimatum, that blank Next-to-Nothingness which the last Neo-Platonists imagined as their Supreme. Proclus could not; Dionysius could not. What then? A reaction comes, which, after refining polytheism to an impalpable unity, restores men to polytheism once more. Up mounts speculation, rocket-like : men watch it, a single soaring star with its train of fire, and, at the height, it breaks into a scattering shower of many-coloured sparks. From that Abstraction of which nothing can be predicated, nothing can be expected. The figment above being is above benignity. So the objects of invocation are gods, demigods, dæmons, heroes ; or, when baptized, cherubim, seraphim, thrones, dominions, powers, archangels, angels, saints ; in either case, whether at Athens or at Constantinople, the excessive subtilisation of the One contributes toward the worship of the Manifold.

ATHERTON. The theology of the Neo-Platonists was always in the first instance a mere matter of logic. It so happened that they confounded Universals with causes. The miserable consequence is clear. The Highest becomes with them, as he is with Dionysius, merely the most comprehensive, the universal idea, which includes the world, as genus includes species.[2]

MRS. ATHERTON. The divinity of this old Father must be a bleak affair indeed—Christianity frozen out.

GOWER. I picture him to myself as entering with his philosophy into the theological structure of that day, like Winter into the cathedral of the woods (which an autumn of decline has begun to harm already) ;—what life yet lingers, he takes away,—he untwines the garlands from the pillars of the trees,

---

[2] See Meier, '*Dionysii Areop. et Mysticorum sœculi* xiv. *doctrinœ inter se comparantur.*' He remarks justly 'causæ ad Causatum relationem cum relatione generis ad speciem confudit' p 13.

extinguishes the many twinkling lights the sunshine hung wavering in the foliage, silences all sounds of singing, and fills the darkened aisles and dome with a coldly-descending mist, whose silence is extolled as above the power of utterance, —its blinding, chill obscureness lauded as clearer than the intelligence and warmer than the fervour of a simple and scriptural devotion.

ATHERTON. You have described my experience in reading him, though I must say he suggested nothing to me about your cathedral of the woods, &c. His verbose and turgid style, too, is destitute of all genuine feeling.[3] He piles epithet on epithet, throws superlative on superlative, hyperbole on hyperbole, and it is but log upon log,—he puts no fire under, neither does any come from elsewhere. He quotes Scripture—as might be expected—in the worst style, both of the schoolman and the mystic. Fragments are torn from their connexion, and carried away to suffer the most arbitrary interpretation, and strew his pages that they may appear to illustrate or justify his theory.

GOWER. How forlorn do those texts of Scripture look that you discern scattered over the works of such writers, so manifestly transported from a region of vitality and warmth to an expanse of barrenness. They make the context look still more sterile, and while they say there must be life *somewhere*, seem to affirm, no less emphatically, that it is not in the neighbourhood about them. They remind me of those leaves from the chestnut and the birch I once observed upon a glacier. There they lay, foreign manifestly to the treeless world in which they were found ; the ice appeared to have shrunk from them, and they from the ice ; each isolated leaf had made itself a cup-like cavity, a tiny open sarcophagus of crystal, in which it

---

[3] The *hyper* and the *a* privative are in constant requisition with Dionysius. He cannot suffer any ordinary epithet to go alone, and many of his adjectives march pompously, attended by a *hyper* on one side, and a superlative termination on the other.

had lain, perhaps for several winters. Doubtless, a tempest, which had been vexing some pleasant valley far down beneath, and tearing at its trees, must have whirled them up thither. Yet the very presence of the captives reproached the poverty of the Snow-King who detained them, testifying as they did to a genial clime elsewhere, whose products that ice-world could no more put forth, than can such frozen speculations as this of Dionysius, the ripening 'fruits of the Spirit.'

WILLOUGHBY. His lurking fatalism and his pantheism were forgiven him, no doubt, on consideration of his services to priestly assumption. He descends from his most cloudy abstraction to assert the mysterious significance and divine potency of all the minutiæ of the ecclesiastical apparatus and the sacerdotal etiquette. What a reputation these writings had throughout the middle age!

ATHERTON. Dionysius is the mythical hero of mysticism. You find traces of him everywhere. Go almost where you will through the writings of the mediæval mystics, into their depths of nihilism, up their heights of rapture or of speculation, through their over-growth of fancy, you find his authority cited, his words employed, his opinions more or less fully transmitted, somewhat as the traveller in the Pyrenees discerns the fame of the heroic Roland still preserved in the names and in the legends of the rock, the valley, or the flower. Passages from the Areopagite were culled, as their warrant and their insignia, by the priestly ambassadors of mysticism, with as much care and reverence as the sacred verbenæ that grew within the enclosure of the Capitoline by the Feciales of Rome.

MRS. ATHERTON. 'Oh, sweet Fancy, let her loose,' as Keats says. I think my husband has been learning in Mr. Gower's school. How far he went to fetch that simile!

GOWER. Perhaps he has my excuse in this case, that he could not help it.

WILLOUGHBY. Or he may at once boldly put in the plea of Sterne, who in one place lays claim to the gratitude of his readers for having voyaged to fetch a metaphor all the way to the Guinea coast and back.

ATHERTON. It contributed greatly to the influence of the Areopagite that he became confounded with the Dionysius, or St. Denys, who was adopted as the patron-saint of France.

KATE. A singular fortune, indeed : so that he was two other people besides himself ;—like Mrs. Malaprop's Cerberus, three gentlemen at once.

GOWER. I think we have spent time enough upon him. Grievously do I pity the miserable monks his commentators, whose minds, submerged in the *mare tenebrosum* of the cloister, had to pass a term of years in the mazy arborescence of his verbiage,—like so many insects within their cells in the branches of a great coral.[4]

ATHERTON. Don't throw away so much good compassion, I dare say it kept them out of mischief.

WILLOUGHBY. I cannot get that wretched abstraction out of my head which the Neo-Platonists call deity. How such a notion must have dislocated all their ethics from head to foot ! The merest anthropomorphism had been better ;—yes, Homer and Hesiod are truer, after all.

ATHERTON. I grant the gravity of the mischief. But we must not be too hard on this ecclesiastical Neo-Platonism. It does but follow Aristotle here. You remember he considers the possession of virtues as quite out of the question in the case of the gods.

GOWER. Is it possible? Why, that is as though a man should lame himself to run the faster. Here is a search after

---

[4] The later Greek theology modified the most objectionable parts of the Dionysian doctrine, while continuing to reverence him as a Father. See Ullmann's *Nicholas von Methone.*

God, in which, at starting, all moral qualities are removed from him; so that the testimony of conscience cannot count for anything;—the inward directory is sealed; the clue burnt. Truly the world by wisdom knew not God!

WILLOUGHBY. This unquestionably is the fatal error of Greek speculation—the subordination of morals to the intellectual refinements of an ultra-human spiritualism. Even with Numenius you have to go down the scale to a subordinate god or hypostasis before you arrive at a deity who condescends to be *good*.

GOWER. How much 'salt' there must still have been in the mediæval Christianity to survive, as far as it did, the reception of these old ethical mistakes into the very heart of its doctrine!

ATHERTON. Aristotle reasons thus: how can the gods exhibit fortitude, who have nothing to fear—justice and honesty, without a business—temperance, without passions? Such insignificant things as moral actions are beneath them. They do not toil, as men. They do not sleep, like Endymion, 'on the Latmian hill.' What remains? They lead a life of contemplation;—in contemplative energy lies their blessedness.[5] So the contemplative sage who *energises* directly toward the central Mind—the intellectual source and ultimatum, is the true imitator of the divine perfections.

GOWER. Transfer this principle to Christianity, and the monk becomes immediately the highest style of man.

WILLOUGHBY. And you have a double morality at once: heroic or superhuman virtues, the graces of contemplation for the saintly few,—glorious in proportion to their uselessness; and ordinary virtues for the many,—social, serviceable, and secondary.

ATHERTON. Not that the schoolman would release his saint altogether from the obligations of ordinary morality; but he

[5] Aristot. *Eth. Nic.* lib. x. c. 8.—See Note, Page 123.

would say, this ordinary morality does not fit the contemplatist for heaven—it is but a preliminary exercise—a means to an end, and that end, the transcendence of everything creaturely, a superhuman exaltation, the ceasing from his labours, and swooning as it were into the divine repose.

WILLOUGHBY. Then I must put in a word for our mystics. It is not they who corrupted Christian morals by devising this divorce between the virtues of daily life and certain other virtues which are *un*human, anti-terrestrial, hypercreaturely—forgive the word—they drive us hard for language. They found the separation already accomplished ; they only tilled with ardour the plot of ground freely allotted them by the Church.

ATHERTON. Just so ; in this doctrine of moral dualism—the prolific mother of mystics—Aquinas is as far gone as Bernard.

GOWER. The mention of Bernard's name makes one impatient to get away from the Greek Church, westward.

ATHERTON. We may say farewell to Byzantium now. That Greek Church never grew beyond what it was in the eighth and ninth centuries.

GOWER. I have always imagined it a dwarf, watching a Nibelungen hoard, which after all never enriches anybody. Nothing but that tedious counting, and keeping tidy, and standing sentinel, for ages.

ATHERTON. See what good a little fighting does. The Greek Church had its scholastic element—witness John of Damascus ; it had its mystical—as we have seen ; but neither the one nor the other was ever developed to such vigour as to assert itself against its rival, and struggle for mastery. In the West the two principles have their battles, their armistices, their reconciliations, and both are the better. In the East they are coupled amicably in the leash of antiquity, and dare not so much as snarl.

WILLOUGHBY. I suppose the mysticism of the Greek Church

was more objective, as the Germans would say,—dependent on its sacramental media and long trains of angelic and human functionaries, handing down illumination; that of the West, subjective.

ATHERTON. That will be generally true. The eastern mysticism creeps under the sacerdotal vestments, is never known to quit the precincts of church and cloister, clings close to the dalmatica, and lives on whiffs of frankincense. The western is often to be found far from candle, book, and bell, venturing to worship without a priest.

In short, as Gower would antithetically say, the mystic of the East is always a slave, the mystic of the West often a rebel; Symbolism is the badge of the one, Individualism the watchword of the other.

GOWER. How spiteful you are to-night, Atherton. I propose that we break up, and hear nothing more you may have to say.

———

NOTE TO PAGE 121.

Aristotle extols contemplation, because it does not require means and opportunity, as do the social virtues, generosity, courage, &c. Plotinus lays still more stress on his distinction between the mere political virtues—which constitute simply a preparatory, purifying process, and the superior, or exemplary—those divine attainments whereby man is united with God. Aquinas adopts this classification, and distinguishes the virtues as *exemplares, purgatoriæ* and *politicæ*. He even goes so far as to give to each of the cardinal virtues a contemplative and ascetic turn; designating Prudence, in its highest exercise, as contempt for all things worldly; Temperance is abstraction from the sensuous; Fortitude, courage in sustaining ourselves in the aerial regions of contemplation, remote from the objects of sense; Justice, the absolute surrender of the spirit to this law of its aspiration. He argues that, as man's highest blessedness is a beatitude surpassing the limits of human nature, he can be prepared for it only by having added to that nature certain principles from the divine;—such principles are the theological or superhuman virtues, Faith, Hope, and Charity. See Münscher's *Dogmengeschichte,* 2 Abth. 2 Absch. § 136.
In consequence of the separation thus established between the human and the divine, we shall find the mystics of the fourteenth century representing regeneration almost as a process of dehumanization, and as the substitution of a divine nature for the human in the subject of grace. No theologians could have been further removed from Pelagianism; few more forgetful than these ardent contemplatists that divine influence is vouchsafed, not to obliterate and

supersede our natural capacities by some almost miraculous faculty, but to restore and elevate man's nature, to realise its lost possibilities, and to consecrate it wholly, in body and soul—not in spirit, merely—to the service of God.

With one voice both schoolmen and mystics would reason thus :—' Is not heaven the extreme opposite of this clouded, vexed, and sensuous life? Then we approach its blessedness most nearly by a life the most contrary possible to the secular,—by contemplation, by withdrawment, by total abstraction from sense,'

This is one view of our best preparation for the heavenly world. At the opposite pole stands Behmen's doctrine, far less dangerous, and to be preferred if we must have an extreme, *viz.*, that the believer is virtually in the heavenly state already—that eternity should be to us as time, and time as eternity.

Between these two stands the scriptural teaching. St. Paul does not attempt to persuade himself that earth is heaven, that faith is sight, that hope is fruition. He groans here, being burdened; he longs to have done with shortcoming and with conflict ; to enter on the vision face to face, on the unhindered service of the state of glory. But he does not deem it the best preparation for heaven to mimic upon earth an imaginary celestial repose,—he will rather labour to-day his utmost at the work to-day may bring,—he will fight the good fight, he will finish his course, and then receive the crown.

BOOK THE SIXTH

———◆———

GERMAN MYSTICISM IN THE FOURTEENTH CENTURY

CHAPTER I.

Look up, my Ethel!
When on the glances of the upturned eye
The plumed thoughts take travel, and ascend
Through the unfathomable purple mansions,
Threading the golden fires, and ever climbing
As if 'twere homewards winging—at such time
The native soul, distrammelled of dim earth,
Doth know herself immortal, and sits light
Upon her temporal perch.

VIOLENZIA.

THE winter had now broken up his encampment, and was already in full retreat. With the approach of spring the mystical conversations of our friends entered on the period of the Middle Ages. The lengthening mornings found Atherton early at his desk, sipping a solitary and preliminary cup of coffee, and reading or writing. Willoughby felt his invention quickened by the season, and a new elasticity pervade him. His romance advanced with fewer hindrances from that cross-grained dissatisfaction which used so frequently to disfigure his manuscript with the thorny scratches and interlineations of an insatiable correction.

Gower, too, could enter once more on the enjoyment of his favourite walk before breakfast. In wandering through the dewy meadows, in 'the slanting sunlight of the dawn,' he felt, as we all must, that there is truth in what the chorus of mystics have ever said or sung about the inadequacy of words to express the surmise and aspiration of the soul. In a morning solitude there seems to lie about our fields of thought an aerial wealth too plenteous to be completely gathered into the granary of language.

O who would mar the season with dull speech,
That must tie up our visionary meanings
And subtle individual apprehensions
Into the common tongue of every man?
And of the swift and scarce detected visitants
Of our illusive thoughts seek to make prisoners,
And only grasp their garments.

It is one of the pleasant pastimes of the spring to watch day by day the various ways in which the trees express, by a physiognomy and gesture of their own, their expectation of the summer. Look at those young and delicate ones, alive with impatience to the tip of every one of the thousand sprays that tremble distinct against the sky, swaying uneasily to and fro in the sharp morning breeze. They seem longing to slip their rooted hold upon the earth, and float away to embrace their bridegroom sun in the air. And see those veterans—what a gnarled, imperturbable gravity in those elder citizens of park or wood: they are used to it; let the day bring new weatherstains or new buds, they can bide their time. And are they not already wrapped, many of them, in hood and habit of dark glossy ivy—woodland senatorial fur—they can afford to wait. Here, look, close beside us, the eyes of the buds are even now peeping through the black lattice of the boughs, and those amber-coloured clouds overhead are looking them promises of kindly showers as they sail by. What is that sparkling on yonder hill? Only the windows of a house with eastern aspect: the sun lights his beacon-fire regularly there, to signal to his children down in the hollow that he is coming, though they cannot see him yet, and will roll away the cloud from the valley mouth, and make the place of their night-sepulchre glorious with his shining raiment.

Amidst these delights of nature, and the occupation of his art, Gower thought sometimes of the mystics who enjoy such things so little. He had even promised to write a short paper on the mystical schoolmen of St. Victor, Hugo and Richard, and was himself surprised to find how soon he warmed to the subject—with what zest he sought for glimpses of cloister-life in the twelfth and thirteenth centuries.

When next our friends met in the library, Gower expressed his hearty and unceremonious satisfaction at their having done, as he hoped, with that 'old bore,' Dionysius Areopagita. By none was the sentiment echoed with more fervour than by Atherton, whose conscience perhaps smote him for some dry reading he had inflicted on his auditors. But he made no apology, that Gower might not think he took his remark to himself, and return him a compliment.

WILLOUGHBY. To see how this world goes round! Only think of Proclus having his revenge after all,—he and his fellows ruling from their urns when dead the Christianity which banished them while living.

ATHERTON. Not altogether satisfactory, either, could he have looked in upon the world, and seen the use to which they put him. It was true that, under the name of Dionysius, his ideas were reverenced and expounded by generations of dreaming monks,—that under that name he contributed largely to those influences which kept stagnant the religious world of the East for some nine hundred years. But it was also true that his thoughts were thus conserved only to serve the purpose of his ancient enemies; so that he assisted to confer omnipotence on those Christian priests whom he had cursed daily in his heart while lecturing, sacrificing, and conjuring at Athens.

GOWER. Again I say, let us turn from the stereotyped Greek Church to the West,—I want to hear about St. Bernard.

ATHERTON. Presently. Let us try and apprehend clearly the way in which Neo-Platonism influenced mediæval Europe.

WILLOUGHBY. A trifling preliminary! Atherton means us to stay here all night. You may as well resign yourself, Gower.

ATHERTON. Never fear; I only want to look about me, and see where we are just now. Suppose ourselves sent back to the Middle Age—what will be our notion of Platonism? We can't read a line of Greek. We see Plato only through Plotinus, conserved by Augustine, handed down by Apuleius and Boethius. We reverence Aristotle, but we care only for his dialectics. We only assimilate from antiquity what seems to fall within the province of the Church. Plato appears to us surrounded by that religious halo with which Neo-Platonism invested philosophy when it grew so devotional. We take Augustine's word for it that Plotinus really enunciated the long-hidden esoteric doctrine of Plato. The reverent, ascetic, ecstatic Platonism of Alexandria seems to us so like Christianity, that we are almost ready to believe Plato a sort of harbinger for Christ. We are devoted Realists; and Realism and Asceticism make the common ground of Platonist and Christian. If scholastic in our tendencies, Aristotle may be oftener on our lips; if mystical, Plato; but we overlook their differences. We believe, on Neo-Platonist authority, that the two great ones were not the adversaries which had been supposed. Aristotle is in the forecourt, and through study of him we pass into that inner shrine where the rapt Plato (all but a monk in our eyes) is supposed to exemplify the contemplative life.

Dionysius in the East, then, is soporific. Mysticism, there, has nothing to do save drowsily to label all the Church gear with symbolic meanings of wondrous smallness.

Dionysius in the West has come into a young world where vigorous minds have been long accustomed to do battle on the grandest questions; grace and free-will—how they work together; sin and redemption—what they really are; faith and reason—what may be their limits.

GOWER. Compare those great controversies with that miserable Monophysite and Monothelite dispute for which one can never get up an interest. How much we owe still to that large-souled Augustine.[1]

ATHERTON. Well, for this very reason, they might worship Dionysius as a patron saint to their hearts' content at St. Denis, but he could never be in France the master mystagogue they made him at Byzantium. His name, and some elements in his system, became indeed an authority and rallying point for the mystical tendency of the West, but the system as a whole was never appropriated. He was reverentially dismembered, and so mixed up with doctrines and questions foreign to him, by a different order of minds, with another culture, and often with another purpose, that I would defy his ghost to recognise his own legacy to the Church.

GOWER. Good Hugo of St. Victor, in his *Commentary on the Hierarchies*, does certainly wonderfully soften down the pantheism of his original. Dionysius comes out from under his hands almost rational, quite a decent Christian.

ATHERTON. And before Hugo, if you remember, John Scotus Erigena translated him, and elaborated on his basis a daring system of his own, pantheistic I fear, but a marvel of intellectual power—at least two or three centuries in advance of his age. And these ideas of Erigena's, apparently forgotten, filter through, and reappear once more at Paris in the free-thinking philosophy of such men as David of Dinant and Amalric of Bena.[2]

WILLOUGHBY. Strange enough : so that, could Dionysius have returned to the world in the thirteenth century, he, the worshipper of the priesthood, would have found sundry of his own principles in a new livery, doing service in the ranks of the laity against the clergy, and strengthening the hands of that succession of heretics so long a thorn in the side of the corrupt hierarchy of France.

[1] See Note 1, p. 146.   [2] See Note 2, p. 146.

ATHERTON. In Germany, a century later, many of the mystics put Platonist doctrine to a similar use. In fact, I think we may say generally that the Neo-Platonist element, which acted as a mortal opiate in the East, became a vivifying principle in the West. There the Alexandrian doctrine of Emanation was abandoned, its pantheism nullified or rejected, but its allegorical interpretation, its exaltation, true or false, of the spirit above the letter,—all this was retained, and Platonism and mysticism together created a party in the Church the sworn foes of mere scholastic quibbling, of an arid and lifeless orthodoxy, and at last of the more glaring abuses which had grown up with ecclesiastical pretension.

GOWER. Now for Bernard. I see the name there on that open page of your note-book. Read away—no excuses.

ATHERTON. Some old notes. But before I read them, look at this rough plan of the valley of Clairvaux, with its famous abbey. I made it after reading the *Descriptio Monasterii Claræ-Vallensis*, inserted in the Benedictine edition of Bernard's works. It will assist us to realize the locality in which this great church-father of the twelfth century passed most of his days. It was once called the Valley of Wormwood—was the ill-omened covert of banditti; Bernard and his monks come clearing and chanting, praying and planting; and lo! the absinthial reputation vanishes—the valley smiles—is called, and made, Clairvaux, or Brightdale.

KATE. Transformed, in short, into 'a serious paradise,' as Mr. Thackeray would say.

ATHERTON. Yes, you puss. Here, you see, I have marked two ranges of hills which, parting company, enclose the broad sweep of our Brightdale, or Fairvalley. Where the hills are nearest together you see the one eminence covered with vines, the other with fruit trees; and on the sides and tops dusky groups of monks have had many a hard day's work, getting rid of brambles and underwood, chopping and binding faggots, and preparing either slope to yield them wherewithal to drink, from the right hand, and to eat, from the left. Not far from this entrance to the valley stands the huge pile of the abbey itself, with its towers and crosses, its loop-hole windows and numerous outbuildings. That is the river Aube (Alba) running down between the heights; here, you see, is a winding channel the monks have dug, that a branch of it may flow in under the convent walls. Good river! how hard it works for them. No sooner under the archway than it turns the great wheel that grinds their corn, fills their caldarium, toils in the tannery, sets the fulling-mill agoing. Hark to the hollow booming sound, and the regular tramp, tramp of those giant wooden feet; and there, at last, out rushes the stream at the other side of the building, all in a fume, as if it had been ground itself into so much snowy foam. On this other side, you see it cross, and join the main course of its river again. Proceeding now along the valley, with your back to the monastery, you pass through the groves of the orchard, watered by crossing runnels from the river, overlooked by the infirmary windows—a delightful spot for contemplative invalids. Then you enter the great meadow —what a busy scene in hay-making time, all the monks out there, helped by the additional hands of *donati* and *conductitii*, and the country folk from all the region round about,—they have been working since sunrise, and will work till vespers; when the belfry sounds for prayers at the fourth hour after sunrise, they will sing their psalms in the open air to save time, and doubtless dine there too—a monastic pic-nic. On one side of the meadow is a small lake, well stored with fish. See some of the brethren angling on its bank, where those osiers have been planted to preserve the margin; and two others have put off in a boat and are throwing their net, with edifying talk at whiles perhaps, on the parallel simplicity of fish and sinners.

At the extremity of the meadow are two large farm-houses, one on each side the river ; you might mistake them for monasteries from their size and structure, but for the ploughs and yokes of oxen you see about.

MRS. ATHERTON. Thank you; so much for the place ; and the man—his personal appearance—is anything known about that ?'

ATHERTON. You must imagine him somewhat above the middle height, very thin, with a clear, transparent, red-and-white complexion ; always retaining some colour on his hollow cheeks ; his hair light ; his beard inclining to red—in his later years, mixed with white ; his whole aspect noble and persuasive, and when he speaks under excitement losing every trace of physical feebleness in the lofty transformation of a benign enthusiasm.[3]

Now I shall trouble you with some of my remarks, on his mysticism principally. You will conceive what a world of business he must have had upon his shoulders, even when at home at Clairvaux, and acting as simple abbot ; so much detail to attend to,—so many difficulties to smooth, and quarrels to settle, and people to advise, in connexion with his own numerous charge and throughout all the surrounding neighbourhood ; while to all this was added the care of so many infant monasteries, springing up at the rate of about four a year, in every part of Europe, founded on the pattern of Clairvaux, and looking to him for counsel and for men. I scarcely need remind you how struggling Christendom sent incessant monks and priests, couriers and men-at-arms, to knock and blow horn at the gate of Clairvaux Abbey ; for Bernard, and none but he, must come out and fight that audacious Abelard ; Bernard must decide between rival Popes, and cross the Alps time after time to quiet tossing Italy ; Bernard alone is the hope of fugitive Pope and trembling

[3] *Vita,* ii. cap. v.

Church; he only can win back turbulent nobles, alienated people, recreant priests, when Arnold of Brescia is in arms at Rome, and when Catharists, Petrobrusians, Waldenses, and heretics of every shade, threaten the hierarchy on either side the Alps; and at the preaching of Bernard the Christian world pours out to meet the disaster of a new crusade.

GOWER. And accomplishing a work like this with that emaciated, wretchedly dyspeptic frame of his !—first of all exerting his extraordinary will to the utmost to unbuild his body ; and then putting forth the same self-control to make the ruins do the work of a sound structure.

ATHERTON. Could we have seen him at home at Clairvaux, after one of those famous Italian journeys, no look or word would have betrayed a taint of spiritual pride, though every rank in church and state united to do him honour—though great cities would have made him almost by force their spiritual king—though the blessings of the people and the plaudits of the council followed the steps of the peacemaker—and though, in the belief of all, a dazzling chain of miracles had made his pathway glorious.   We should have found him in the kitchen, rebuking by his example some monk who grumbled at having to wash the pots and pans ; on the hill-side, cutting his tale and bearing his burthen with the meanest novice ; or seen him oiling his own boots, as they say the arch-tempter did one day ; we should have interrupted him in the midst of his tender counsel to some distressed soul of his cloistered flock, or just as he had sat down to write a sermon on a passage in Canticles against the next church-festival.[4]   But now to my notes. (*Atherton reads.*)

[4] See the account of his diet, and of the feebleness and sickness consequent on his austerities, by the same biographer (Alanus), *Vita*, ii. cap. x., in the Paris reprint of 1839, from the Benedictine edition of Bernard, tom. ii. p. 2426.   John Eremita describes the devil's visit to Bernard, 'ut ungeret sandalia sua secundum consuetudinem,' and relates the rebuke of the proud monk who would not wash the *scutellæ* in the kitchen. — *Vita*, iv. p. 2508.

In considering the religious position of Bernard, I find it not at all remarkable that he should have been a mystic,—very remarkable that he should not have been much more the mystic than he was. This moderation may be attributed partly to his constant habit of searching the Scriptures—studying them devotionally for himself, unencumbered with the commentaries reverenced by tradition.[5] Rigid exemplar and zealous propagator of monasticism as he was, these hours with the Bible proved a corrective not unblessed, and imparted even to the devotion of the cloister a healthier tone. Add to this his excellent natural judgment, and the combination, in his case, of the active with the contemplative life. He knew the world and men; he stood with his fellows in the breach, and the shock of conflict spoiled him for a dreamer. The distractions over which he expended so much complaint were his best friends. They were a hindrance in the way to the monastic ideal of virtue—a help toward the Christian. They prevented his attaining that pitch of uselessness to which the conventual life aspires, and brought him down a little nearer to the meaner level of apostolic labour. They made him the worse monk, and by so much the better man.

With Bernard the monastic life is the one thing needful. He began life by drawing after him into the convent all his kindred; sweeping them one by one from the high seas of the world with the irresistible vortex of his own religious fervour. His incessant cry for Europe is—Better monasteries, and more of them. Let these ecclesiastical castles multiply; let them cover and command the land, well garrisoned with men of God, and then, despite all heresy and schism, theocracy will flourish, the earth shall yield her increase, and all people praise the Lord. Who so wise as Bernard to win souls for Christ—that is to say, recruits for the cloister? With what

[5] *Vita*, ii. cap. x. 32.

eloquence he paints the raptures of contemplation, the vanity
and sin of earthly ambition or of earthly love! Wherever
in his travels Bernard may have preached, there, presently,
exultant monks must open wide their doors to admit new
converts. Wherever he goes he bereaves mothers of their
children, the aged of their last solace and last support;
praising those the most who leave most misery behind them.
How sternly does he rebuke those Rachels who mourn and
will not be comforted for children dead to them for ever!
What vitriol does he pour into the wounds when he asks if
they will drag their son down to perdition with themselves
by resisting the vocation of heaven! whether it was not
enough that they brought him forth sinful to a world of sin,
and will they now, in their insane affection, cast him into the
fires of hell?[6] Yet Bernard is not hard-hearted by nature.
He can pity this disgraceful weakness of the flesh. He makes
such amends as superstition may. I will be a father to him,
he says. Alas! cold comfort. You, their hearts will answer,
whose flocks are countless, would nothing content you but
our ewe lamb? Perhaps some cloister will be, for them too,
the last resource of their desolation. They will fly for ease in
their pain to the system which caused it. Bernard hopes so.
So inhuman is the humanity of asceticism; cruel its tender
mercies; thus does it depopulate the world of its best in
order to improve it.

To measure, then, the greatness of Bernard, let me clearly
apprehend the main purpose of his life. It was even this
convent-founding, convent-ruling business. This is his proper
praise, that, though devoted body and soul, to a system so
false, he himself should have retained and practised so much
of truth.

The task of history is a process of selection. The farther

[6] *Epp.* cx., cxi.

we recede from a period, the more do we eliminate of what interests us no longer.   A few leading events stand clearly out as characteristic of the time, and about them all our details are clustered.   But when dealing with an individual, or with the private life of any age, the method must be reversed, and we must encumber ourselves again with all the cast-off baggage that strews the wayside of time's march.

So with Bernard.   The Abelard controversy, the schism, the quarrels of pope and emperor, the crusade, are seen by us —who know what happened afterwards—in their true importance.   These facts make the epoch, and throw all else into shade.   But we could not so have viewed them in the press and confusion of the times that saw them born.   Bernard and his monks were not always thinking of Abelard or Anaclet, of Arnold of Brescia, Roger of Sicily, or Lothaire.   In the great conflicts which these names recal to our minds, Bernard bore his manful part as a means to an end.   Many a sleepless night must they have cost him, many a journey full of anxiety and hardship, many an agonizing prayer, on the eve of a crisis calling for all his skill and all his courage.   But these were difficulties which he was summoned to encounter on his road to the great object of his life—the establishment of ecclesiastical supremacy by means of the conventual institute.   The quarrels within the Church, and between the Church and the State, must be in some sort settled before his panacea could be applied to the sick body of the time.   In the midst of such controversies a host of minor matters would demand his care, —to him of scarcely less moment, to us indifferent.   There would be the drawing out of convent charters and convent rules, the securing of land, of money, of armed protection for the rapidly increasing family of monasteries ; election of abbots and of bishops ; guidance of the same in perplexity ; holding of synods and councils, with the business thereto pertaining ; delinquencies and spiritual distresses of individuals ; jealous squabbles to be soothed between his Cistercian order and them of Clugny ; suppression of clerical luxury and repression of lay encroachment, &c. &c. Thus the year 1118 would be memorable to Bernard and his monks, not so much because in it Gelasius ascended the chair of St. Peter, and the Emperor Henry gave him a rival, or even because then the order of Knights Templars took its rise, so much as from their joy and labour about the founding of two new monasteries,—because that year saw the establishment of the first daughter of Clairvaux, the Abbey of Fontaines, in the diocese of Chalons ; and of a sister, Fontenay, beside the Yonne ;—the one a growth northward, among the dull plains of Champagne, with their lazy streams and monotonous poplars ; the other a southern colony, among the luscious slopes of vine-clad Burgundy.[7]

Bernard had his wish. He made Clairvaux the cynosure of all contemplative eyes. For any one who could exist at all as a monk, with any satisfaction to himself, that was the place above all others. Brother Godfrey, sent out to be first abbot of Fontenay,—as soon as he has set all things in order there, returns, only too gladly, from that rich and lovely region, to re-enter his old cell, to walk around, delightedly revisiting the well-remembered spots among the trees or by the waterside, marking how the fields and gardens have come on, and relating to the eager brethren (for even Bernard's monks have curiosity) all that befel him in his work. He would sooner be third prior at Clairvaux than abbot of Fontenay. So, too, with brother Humbert, commissioned in like manner to regulate Igny Abbey (fourth daughter of Clairvaux). He soon comes back, weary of the labour and sick for home, to look on the Aube once more, to hear the old mills go drumming and

[7] *Chronologia Bernardina, Opp.* tom. i. p. 83.

droning, with that monotony of muffled sound—the associate of his pious reveries—often heard in his dreams when far away; to set his feet on the very same flagstone in the choir where he used to stand, and to be happy. But Bernard, though away in Italy, toiling in the matter of the schism, gets to hear of his return, and finds time to send him across the Alps a letter of rebuke for this criminal self-pleasing, whose terrible sharpness must have darkened the poor man's meditations for many a day.[8]

Bernard had farther the satisfaction of improving and extending monasticism to the utmost; of sewing together, with tolerable success, the rended vesture of the papacy; of suppressing a more popular and more scriptural Christianity, for the benefit of his despotic order; of quenching for a time, by the extinction of Abelard, the spirit of free inquiry; and of seeing his ascetic and superhuman ideal of religion everywhere accepted as the genuine type of Christian virtue.

At the same time the principles advocated by Bernard were deprived, in his hands, of their most noxious elements. His sincere piety, his large heart, his excellent judgment, always qualify, and seem sometimes to redeem, his errors. But the well-earned glory and the influence of a name achieved by an ardour and a toil almost passing human measure, were thrown into the wrong scale. The mischiefs latent in the teaching of Bernard become ruinously apparent in those who entered into his labours. His successes proved eventually the disasters of Christendom. One of the best of men made plain the way for some of the worst. Bernard, while a covert for the fugitive pontiff, hunted out by insurgent people or by wrathful emperor, would yet impose some rational limitations on the papal authority.[9] But the chair upheld by Bernard was to be filled by an Innocent III., whose merciless arrogance should know no

<hr/>

[8] *Epist.* cxli.   [9] *De Consideratione*, IV. iii. 7, and II. vi. 11. pp. 1028 and 1060.

bounds. Bernard pleaded nobly for the Jews, decimated in the crusading fury.[10] Yet the atrocities of Dominic were but the enkindling of fuel which Bernard had amassed. Disciple of tradition as he was, he would allow the intellect its range ; zealous as he might be for monastic rule, the spontaneous inner life of devotion was with him the end—all else the means. Ere long, the end was completely forgotten in the means. In succeeding centuries, the Church of Rome retained what life it could by repeating incessantly the remedy of Bernard. As corruption grew flagrant, new orders were devised. Bernard saw not, nor those who followed in his steps, that the evil lay, not in the defect or abuse of vows and rules, but in the introduction of vows and rules at all,—that these unnatural restraints must always produce unnatural excesses.

What is true concerning the kind of religious impulse imparted to Europe by the great endeavour of Bernard's life is no less so as regards the character of his mysticism.

In the theology of Bernard reason has a place, but not the right one. His error in this respect is the primary source of that mystical bias so conspicuous in his religious teaching. Like Anselm, he bids you believe first, and understand, if possible, afterwards. He is not prepared to admit the great truth that if Reason yields to Faith, and assigns itself anywhere a limit, it must be on grounds satisfactory to Reason. To any measure of Anselm's remarkable speculative ability, Bernard could lay no claim. He was at home only in the province of practical religion. But to enquiries and reasonings such as those in which Anselm delighted, he was ready to award, not blame, but admiration. Faith, with Bernard, receives the treasure of divine truth, as it were, wrapped up (*involutum*) ; Understanding may afterwards cautiously unfold the envelope, and peep at the prize, but may never examine the contents first,

---

[10] *Epist.* ccclxv. to the Archbishop of Mayence, against the fanatic Rudolph.

to determine whether it shall be received or not.[11] If the chase be so dear to that mighty hunter, Intellect, he shall have his sport, on certain conditions. Let him admit that the Church has caught and killed the quarry of truth, and brought it to his door. That granted, he may, if he will, cry boot and saddle, ride out to see where the game broke cover, or gallop with hounds, and halloo over hill and dale, pursuing an imaginary object, and learning how truth *might* have been run down. Great, accordingly, was Bernard's horror when he beheld Abelard throwing open to discussion the dogmas of the Church; when he saw the alacrity with which such questions were taken up all over France, and learnt that not the scholars of Paris merely, but an ignorant and stripling laity were discussing every day, at street corners, in hall, in cottage, the mysteries of the Trinity and the Immaculate Conception. Faith, he cried, believes; does not discuss; Abelard holds God in suspicion, and will not believe even Him without reason given.[12] At the same time, the *credo ut intelligam* of Bernard is no indolent or constrained reception of a formula. Faith is the divine persuasion of the pure in heart and life. Bernard would grant that different minds will apprehend the same truth in different aspects; that an absolute uniformity is impossible. But when faith is made to depend so entirely on the state of the heart, such concessions are soon withdrawn. A difference in opinion from the acknowledged standard of piety is regarded as a sure sign of a depraved heart. A divine illumination as to doctrine

---

[11] He thus distinguishes Faith, Intellection, and Opinion :—Fides est voluntaria quædam et certa prælibatio necdum propalatæ veritatis. Intellectus est rei cujuscunque invisibilis certa et manifesta notitia. Opinio est quasi pro vero habere aliquid ; quod falsum esse nescias. . . . . . Quid igitur distat (fides) ab intellectu? Nempe quod etsi non habet incertum non magis quam intellectus, habet tamen involucrum, quod non intellectus. . . . . . Nil autem malumus scire, quam quæ fide jam scimus. Nil supererit ad beatitudinem, cum quæ jam certa sunt nobis, erunt æque et nuda.—*De Consideratione*, V. 4, p. 1075.

[12] See Note, p. 149.

is assumed for those whose practical holiness caused them to shine as lights in the Church.[13]

Thus, on the elementary question of faith, the mystical tendency of Bernard is apparent; the subjective and even the merely emotional element assumes undue prominence; and a way is opened for the error incident to all mysticism—the unwarrantable identification of our own thoughts with the mind of God. But if, in his starting-point, Bernard be a mystic, much more so is he in the goal he strains every power to reach.

The design of Christianity is, in his idea, not to sanctify and elevate all our powers, to raise us to our truest manhood, accomplishing in every excellence all our faculties both of mind and body, but to teach us to nullify our corporeal part, to seclude ourselves, by abstraction, from its demands, and to raise us, while on earth, to a super-human exaltation above the flesh, —a vision and a glory approaching that of the angelic state. Thus he commences his analysis of meditation by describing the felicity of angels. They have not to study the Creator in his works, slowly ascending by the media of sense. They behold all things in the Word—more perfect there, by far, than in themselves. Their knowledge is immediate—a direct intuition of the primal ideas of things in the mind of the Creator. To such measure of this immediate intuition as mortals may attain he exhorts the devout mind to aspire. They do well who piously employ their senses among the things of sense for the divine glory and the good of others. Happier yet are they who, with a true philosophy, survey and explore things visible, that they may rise through them to a knowledge of the Invisible. But most of all does he extol the state of those who, not by gradual stages of ascent, but by a sudden rapture, are elevated at times, like St. Paul, to the immediate vision of heavenly things.

[13] See Note, p. 149.

Such favoured ones are adepts in the third and highest species of meditation. Totally withdrawn into themselves, they are not only, like other good men, dead to the body and the world, and raised above the grosser hindrances of sense, but even beyond those images and similitudes drawn from visible objects which colour and obscure our ordinary conceptions of spiritual truths.[14]

But if, so far, Bernard betrays the mystic, in this ambition to transcend humanity and to anticipate the sight and fruition of the celestial state, let him have full credit for the moderation which preserved him from going farther. Compared with that of many subsequent mystics, the mysticism of Bernard is sobriety itself. From the practical vice of mysticism in his Church,—its tendency to supersede by extraordinary attainments the humbler and more arduous Christian virtues— Bernard was as free as any one could be in those times. Against the self-indulgence which would sacrifice every active external obligation to a life of contemplative sloth he protested all his days, by word and by example. He is equally removed from the pantheistic extreme of Eckart and the imaginative extravagances of St. Theresa. His doctrine of Union with God does not surrender our personality or substitute God for the soul in man. When he has occasion to speak, with much hesitation and genuine humility, of the highest point of his own experience, he has no wonderful visions to relate. The visit of the Saviour to his soul was unattended by visible glory, by voices, tastes, or odours ; it vindicated its reality only by the joy which possessed him, and the new facility with which he brought forth the practical fruits of the Spirit.[15] He prays God for peace and joy and charity to all men, and leaves other exaltations of devotion to apostles and apostolic men,—'the high hills to the harts and the climbing goats.' The fourth

[14] See Note 1, p. 150.   [15] See Note 2, p. 150.

and highest stage of love in his scale,—that transformation and utter self-loss in which we love ourselves only for the sake of God, he believes unattainable in this life,—certainly beyond his own reach. To the mystical death, self-annihilation, and holy indifference of the Quietists, he is altogether a stranger.[16]

It is worth while at least to skim and dip among his sermons on the Canticles. The *Song of Solomon* is a trying book for a man like Bernard, and those expositions do contain much sad stuff, interspersed, however, with many fine reaches of thought and passages of consummate eloquence. Mystical interpretation runs riot. Everything is symbolized. Metaphors are elaborated into allegories, similitudes broken up into divers branches, and about each ramification a new set of fancies clustered. The sensuous imagery borrowed from love and wine—the kisses, bedchambers, and winecellars of the soul, remind us at every page of that luscious poetry in which the Persian Sufis are said to veil the aspirations of the spirit of man after its Maker. Yet, with all the faults of a taste so vicious there is no affectation, no sentimentality, nothing intentionally profane. It was with Bernard a duty and a delight to draw as much meaning as possible from the sacred text, by the aid of an inexhaustible fancy and an inventive ingenuity in that way, which only Swedenborg has surpassed. Even in his letters on comparatively ordinary topics, he always gives a certain largeness to his subject by his lofty imaginative style of handling it. He seldom confines himself to the simple point in hand, but starts off to fetch for it adornments, illustrations, or sanctions from quarters the most remote, or heights the most awful. Always

---

[16] Sane in hoc gradu (tertio) diu statur : et nescio si a quoquam hominum quartus in hac vita perfecte apprehenditur, ut se scilicet diligat homo tantum propter Deum. Asserant hoc si qui experti sunt : mihi, fateor, impossibile videtur.—*De diligendo Deo*, xv. and *Epist.* xi. 8. And, again, in the same treatise (vii. 17),—Non enim sine præmio diligitur Deus, etsi absque præmii intuitu diligendus sit. . . . . Verus amor se ipso contentus est. Habet præmium, sed id quod amatur.

in earnest, yet always the rhetorician, he seems to write as though viewing, not the subject itself, but some vast reflection of it projected on the sky. In those sermons on *Solomon's Song,* it is generally rather the glowing and unseemly diction, than the thought, we have to blame. With such allowance, it is not difficult to discern, under that luxuriance of flowers and weeds, many a sentiment true and dear to the Christian heart in every age.

Bernard appears to have believed himself invested on some occasions with miraculous powers. So far he has a place in the province of theurgic mysticism. Perhaps the worst thing of this sort to be laid to his charge is his going so far as he did towards endorsing the prophecies of the Abbess Hildegard.[17]

[17] See Note, p. 151.

─────────

NOTE TO PAGE 131.

The writings of Augustine handed Neo-Platonism down to posterity as the original and esoteric doctrine of the first followers of Plato. He enumerates the causes which led, in his opinion, to the negative position assumed by the Academics, and to the concealment of their real opinions. He describes Plotinus as a resuscitated Plato. *Contra Academ.* iii. 17-20.

He commends Porphyry for his measure of scepticism as regards Theurgy, and bestows more than due praise on the doctrine of Illumination held by Plotinus, for its similarity to the Christian truth concerning divine grace. *De Civitate Dei,* x. 10; x. 2.

He gives a scale of the spiritual degrees of ascent to God, formed after the Platonist model (the ἐπαναβαθμοὶ of the Symposium), and so furnished a precedent for all the attempts of a similar kind in which scholastic mysticism delighted to exercise its ingenuity. *De Quantitate Animæ,* c. 35.

He enumerates three kinds of perception,—corporeal, intellectual (*scientia*) and spiritual (*sapientia*); and in describing the last uses the words *introrsum ascendere* (*De Trin.* xii. 15; and comp. *De Lib. Arbit.* ii. 12). But this phrase does not appear to have carried, with Augustine, the sense it bore when gladly adopted by mystical divines of the thirteenth and fourteenth centuries. He says elsewhere that man, like the prodigal, must come to himself before he can arise and go to his Father, (*Retract.* i. 8.) Here what the wanderer finds within is the voice of conscience, and in this sense it is quite true that the step inward is a step upward. But it is not true that the inmost is the highest in the sense that man is able by abstraction and introspection to discover within himself a light which shall supersede, or supplement, or even supply the place of external Revelation.

NOTE TO PAGE 131.

JOHN SCOTUS ERIGENA.—This remarkable man began to teach in the 'School of the Palace,' under Charles the Bald, about the middle of the ninth century. He translated Dionysius, took part in the Gottschalk controversy, and, at last, when persecuted for the freedom of his opinions, found a refuge with Alfred the Great.

Erigena idolizes Dionysius and his commentator Maximus. He believes in their hierarchies, their divine Dark, and supreme Nothing. He declares, with them, that God is the essence of all things. *Ipse namque omnium essentia est qui solus vere est, ut ait Dionysius Areopagita. Esse,* inquit, *omnium est Superesse Divinitatis.—De Div. Nat.* i. 3, p. 443, (*Jo. Scoti Opp.* Paris, 1853.)

But though much of the language is retained, the doctrine of Dionysius has assumed a form altogether new in the brain of the Scotchman. The phraseology of the emanation theory is, henceforth, only metaphor. What men call creation is, with Erigena, a necessary and eternal self-unfolding (*analysis*, he calls it) of the divine nature. As all things are now God, self-unfolded, so, in the final restitution, all things will be resolved into God, self-withdrawn. Not the mind of man merely, as the Greek thought, but matter and all creatures will be reduced to their primordial causes, and God be manifested as all in all. *De Div. Nat.* i. 72. Postremo universalis creatura Creatori adunabitur, et erit in ipso et cum ipso unum. Et hic est finis omnium visibilium et invisibilium, quoniam omnia visibilia in intelligibilia, et intelligibilia in ipsum Deum transibunt, mirabili et ineffabili adunatione, non autem, ut sæpe diximus, essentiarum aut substantiarum confusione aut interitu—v. 20, p. 894. In this restitution, the elect are united to God with a degree of intimacy peculiar to themselves—v. 39. The agent of this restoration, both for beings above and below mankind, is the Incarnate Word —v. 25, p. 913. Erigena regards our incarceration in the body, and the distinction of sex, as the consequence of sin. He abandons the idea of a sensuous hell. What is termed the fire of hell is with him a principle of law to which both the good and evil are subject, which wickedness assimilates and makes a torment ; goodness a blessing. So, he says, the light is grateful to the sound eye, painful to the diseased ; and the food which is welcome to health is loathed by sickness. *De Prædestinatione,* cap. xvii. p. 428. This idea, in which there lies assuredly an element of truth, became a favourite one with the mystics, and re-appears in many varieties of mysticism. Erigena, farther, anticipates Kant in regarding time and space as mere modes of conception peculiar to our present state. He himself is much more rationalist than mystic (except in the fanciful interpretations of Scripture to which he is compelled to resort) ; but his system was developed, three centuries later, into an extreme and revolutionary mysticism.

The combination of Platonism and Christianity, so often attempted, abandoned, and renewed, assumes five distinct phases.

I. In the East, with Dionysius ; dualistic, with real and ideal worlds apart, removing man far from God by an intervening chain of hierarchic emanations.

II. In the West, with Scotus Erigena ; abandoning emanation for ever, and taking up instead the idea to which the Germans give the name of *Immanence.* God regarded more as the inner life and vital *substratum* of the universe, than as radiating it from a far-off point of abstraction.

III. In the thirteenth century, at Paris, with Amalric of Bena and David of Dinant. They pronounce God the material, essential cause of all things,—not the *efficient* cause merely. The Platonic identification of the *veile* and the *esse* in God. David and his sect blend with their pantheism the doctrine that under the coming new dispensation—that of the Holy Ghost—all believers are to regard themselves as incarnations of God, and to dispense (as men filled with the Spirit) with all sacraments and external rites. They carry the spiritualizing tendency of Erigena to a monstrous extreme, claim special revelation, declare the real resurrection accomplished in themselves, and that they are already in heaven, which they regard as a state and not a place. They maintain that the good are sufficiently rewarded and the bad adequately punished by the blessedness or the privation they inwardly experience in time,—in short, that retribution is complete on this side the grave, and heavy woes, accordingly, will visit corrupt Christendom. The practical extravagance of this pantheism was repeated, in the fourteenth century, by fanatical mystics among the lower orders.

IV. With Eckart, who reminds us of Plotinus. The 'Intuition' of Plotinus is Eckart's 'Spark of the Soul,' the power whereby we can transcend the sensible, the manifold, the temporal, and merge ourselves in the changeless One. At the height of this attainment, the mystic of Plotinus and the mystic of Eckart find the same God,—that is, the same blank abstraction, above being and above attributes. But with Plotinus such escape from finite consciousness is possible only in certain favoured intervals of ecstasy. Eckart, however (whose very pantheism is the exaggeration of a Christian truth beyond the range of Plotinus), will have man realize habitually his oneness with the Infinite. According to him, if a man by self-abandonment attains this consciousness, God has realized Himself within him—has brought forth his Son— has evolved his Spirit. Such a man's knowledge of God is God's knowledge of Himself. For all spirit is one. To distinguish between the divine ground of the soul and the Divinity is to disintegrate the indivisible Universal Spirit—is to be far from God—is to stand on the lower ground of finite misconception, within the limits of transitory Appearance. The true child of God 'breaks through' such distinction to the 'Oneness.' Thus, creation and redemption are resolved into a necessary process—the evolution and involution of Godhead. Yet this form of mediæval pantheism appears to advantage when we compare it with that of ancient or of modern times. The pantheism of the Greek took refuge in apathy from Fate. The pantheism of the present day is a plea for self-will. But that of Eckart is half redeemed by a sublime disinterestedness, a confiding abnegation of all choice or preference, which betrays the presence of a measure of Christian element altogether inconsistent with the basis of his philosophy.

V. With Tauler and the 'German Theology.' This is the best, indisputably, of all the forms assumed by the combination in question. The Platonism is practically absorbed in the Christianity. Tauler speaks of the ideal existence of the soul in God—of the loss of our nameless Ground in the unknown Godhead, and we find language in the *Theologia Germanica* concerning God as the substance of all things—concerning the partial and the Perfect, the manifold and the One, which might be pantheistically construed. But such interpretation would be most unfair, and is contradicted by the whole tenour both of the sermons and the treatise. An apprehension of the nature of sin so searching and profound as that in the 'Theology,' is impossible to pantheism. Luther could see therein only most Christian theism. These mystics still employed some of the terms transmitted by a revered philosophy. Tauler cites with deference the names of Dionysius, Proclus, and Plotinus. This mysticism clothes its thought with fragments from the old philosopher's cloak—but the heart and body belong to the school of Christ. With Dionysius, and even with Erigena, man seems to need but a process of approximation to the divine subsistence—a rise in the scale of being by becoming *quantitatively* rather than *qualitatively* more. With the German mystics he must be altogether unmade and born anew. To shift from one degree of illumination to another somewhat higher, is nothing in their eyes, for the need lies not in the understanding, but in heart and will. According to them, man must stand virtually in heaven or hell—be God's or the devil's. The Father of our spirits is not relegated from men by ecclesiastical or angelic functionaries, but nearer to every one, clerk or lay, gentle or simple, than he is to himself. So the exclusiveness and the frigid intellectualism so characteristic of the ancient ethnic philosophy, has vanished from the Teutonic mysticism. Plato helps rather than harms by giving a vantage ground and defence to the more true and subjective, as opposed to a merely institutional Christianity.

Both Eckart and the *Theologia Germanica* would have man 'break through' and transcend 'distinction.' But it is true, with slight exception, that the distinctions Eckart would escape are natural ; those which the 'Theology' would surpass, for the most part artificial. The asceticism of both is excessive. The self-reduction of Eckart is, however, more metaphysical than moral ; that of the 'Theology' moral essentially. Both would say, the soul of the regenerate man is one with God—cannot be separated from Him. But only Eckart would say, such soul is not *distinct* from God. Both would essay to pass from the Nature to the Being of God—from his manifested Existence to his Essence, and they both declare that our nature has its being in the divine. But such assertion, with Tauler and the *Theologia Germanica*, by no means deifies man. It is but the Platonic expression of a great Christian doctrine—the real Fatherhood of God.

NOTE TO PAGE 142.

Itaque tum per totam fere Galliam in civitatibus, vicis, et castellis, a scholaribus, non solum intra scholas, sed etiam triviatim ; nec a litteratis, aut provectis tantum, sed a pueris et simplicibus, aut certe stultis, de sancta Trinitate, quæ Deus est, disputaretur, &c.—*Epist.* 337, and comp. *Epist.* 332. Bernard at first refused to encounter Abelard, not simply because from his inexperience in such combats he was little fitted to cope with that dialectic Goliath—a man of war from his youth—but because such discussions were in themselves, he thought, an indignity to the faith.—*Epist.* 189. Abelard he denounces as wrong, not only in his heretical results, but in principle,—Cum ea ratione nititur explorare, quæ pia mens fidei vivacitate apprehendit. Fides piorum credit, non discutit. Sed iste Deum habens suspectum, credere non vult, nisi quod prius ratione discusserit.—*Epist.* 338.

NOTE TO PAGE 143.

In the eyes both of Anselm and Bernard, to deny the reality of Ideas is to cut off our only escape from the gross region of sense. Neither faith nor reason have then left them any basis of operation. We attain to truth only through the medium of Ideas, by virtue of our essential relationship to the Divine Source of Ideas—the Infinite Truth. That Supreme Truth which gives to existing things their reality is also the source of true thoughts in our minds. Thus our knowledge is an illumination dependent on the state of the heart towards God. On this principle all doubt must be criminal, and every heresy the offspring, not of a bewildered brain, but of a wicked heart.

The fundamental maxim of the mediæval religio-philosophy—Invisibilia non decipiunt, was fertile in delusions. It led men to reject, as untrustworthy, the testimony of sense and of experience. Thus, in the transubstantiation controversy of the ninth century, Realism and Superstition conquered together, It taught them to deduce all knowledge from certain mental abstractions, Platonic Ideas and Aristotelian Forms. Thus Bonaventura (who exhibits this tendency at its height) resolves all science into union with God. The successive attainment of various kinds of knowledge is, in his system, an approximation, stage above stage, to God—a scaling of the heights o Illumination, as we are more closely united with the Divine Word—the repertory of Ideas. Thus, again, the Scriptures were studied by the schoolmen less as a practical guide for the present life than as so much material whence they might deduce metaphysical axioms and propositions—discover more of those divine abstractions which they regarded as the seminal principles of all thought and all existence. They were constantly mistaking results which could only have been attained by revelation or tradition from without, for truth evolved from within the depths of the finite mind, by virtue of its immediate commerce with the Infinite. Anselm found no difficulty in assuming that the God of his ontological proof was identical with the God of the Bible.

NOTE TO PAGE 144.

Thus, speaking of the angelic state, he says,—Creatura cœli illa est, præsto habens per quod ista intueatur. Videt Verbum, et in Verbo facta per Verbum. Nec opus habet ex his quæ facta sunt, factoris notitiam mendicare.—*De Consid.* V. i., and comp. *Serm. in Cantica*, v. 4.

The three kinds of meditation, or stages of Christian proficiency, referred to in the text, Bernard calls *consideratio dispensativa, æstimativa*, and *speculativa*. The last is thus defined :—Speculativa est consideratio se in se colligens, et, quantum divinitus adjuvatur, rebus humanis eximens ad contemplandum Deum. He who reaches it is among the greatest in the Kingdom of Heaven. At omnium maximus, qui spreto ipso usu rerum et sensuum, quantum quidem humanæ fragilitati fas est, non ascensoriis gradibus, sed inopinatis excessibus, avolare interdum contemplando ad illa sublimia consuevit. Ad hoc ultimum genus illos pertinere reor excessus Pauli. Excessus non ascensus : nam raptum potius fuisse, quam ascendisse ipse se perhibet.—*De Consid.* v. ii. In one of the *Sermons on the Canticles*, Bernard discourses at more length on this kind of exaltation. Proinde et ego non absurde sponsæ exstasim vocaverim mortem, quæ tamen non vita, sed vitæ eripiat laqueis. . . . . Excedente quippe anima, etsi non vita certe vitæ sensu, necesse est etiam ut nec vitæ tentatis sentiatur. . . . . Utinam hac morte frequenter cadam. . . . Bona mors, quæ vitam non aufert, sed transfert in melius ; bona, qua non corpus cadit, sed anima sublevatur. Verum hæc hominum est. Sed moriatur anima mea morte etiam si dici potest, Angelorum, ut præsentium memoria excedens rerum se inferiorum corporearumque non modo cupiditatibus, *sed et similitudinibus* exuat. . . . . Talis, ut opinor, excessus, aut tantum, aut maxime contemplatio dicitur. Rerum etenim cupiditatibus vivendo non teneri, humanæ virtutis est ; corporum vero similitudinibus speculando non involvi, angelicæ puritatis est. . . . . Profecisti, separasti te ; sed nondum elongasti, nisi et irruentia undique phantasmata corporearum similitudinum transvolare mentis puritate prævaleas. Hucusque noli tibi promittere requiem.—*In Cantica, Serm.* lii. 4, 5.

NOTE TO PAGE 144.

Fateor et mihi adventasse Verbum, in insipientia dico, et pluries. Cumque sæpius intraverit ad me, non sensi aliquoties cum intravit. Adesse sensi, adfuisse recordor, interdum et præsentiæ potui introitum ejus, sentire nunquam, sed ne exitum quidem. . . . . Qua igitur introivit? An forte nec ntroivit quidem, quia non deforis venit ? Neque enim est unum aliquid ex iis que foris sunt. Porro nec deintra me venit quoniam bonum est, et scio quoniam non est in me bonum. Ascendi etiam superius meum : et ecce supra hoc Verbum eminens. Ad inferius quoque meum curiosus explorator descendi : et nihilominus infra inventum est. Si foras aspexi, extra omne exterius meum comperi illud esse : si vero intus, et ipsum interius erat. . . . . Ita igitur intrans ad me aliquoties Verbum sponsus, nullis unquam introitum suum

indiciis innotescere fecit, non voce, non specie, non incessu. Nullis denique
suis motibus compertum est mihi, nullis meis sensibus illapsum penetralibus
meis : tantum ex motu cordis, sicut præfatus sum, intellexi præsentiam ejus ;
et ex fuga vitiorum carnaliumque compressione affectuum, &c.—*In Cantica,
Serm.* lxxiv. 5, 6. The metaphors of Bernard are actual sounds, sights, and
fragrances with St. Theresa. From this sensuous extreme his practical
devotion is as far removed, on the one side, as from the cold abstraction of
Dionysius on the other. His contemplation is no staring at the Divine Essence
till we are blind—no oblivion or disdain of outward means. We see God, he
says, not as He is, but as He wills—*sicuti vult non sicuti est.* So when
describing that ascent of the soul to God, or descent of God into the soul, which
constitutes Union, he says,—In Spiritu fit ista conjunctio. . . . . Non ergo sic
affecta et sic dilecta (anima) contenta erit omnino vel illa, quæ multis per ea
quæ facta sunt ; vel, illa quæ paucis per visa et somnia facta est manifestatio
sponsi, nisi et speciali prærogativa intimis illum affectibus atque ipsis medullis
cordis cœlitus illapsum suscipiat, habeatque præsto quem desiderat non figura-
tum, sed infusum : non apparentem sed afficientem ; nec dubium quin eo
jucundiorem, quo intus, non foris. Verbum nempe est, non sonans, sed
penetrans ; non loquax, sed efficax ; non obstrepens auribus, sed affectibus
blandiens, &c.—*In Cantica, Serm.* xxxi. ; 6 and 1. Comp. also his remarks at
the close of the sermon, on the difference between faith and sight, p. 2868.

Bernard describes three kisses of the soul,—the kiss of the feet of God, of the
hand, and of the mouth. (*Serm. de diversis,* 87, and *In Cantica, Serm.* iv.)
This is his fanciful way of characterising, by the elaboration of a single figurative phrase of Scripture, the progress of the soul through conversion and grace
to perfection. Here, as in so many instances, his meaning is substantially
correct ; it is the expression which is objectionable. He is too much in earnest
for the artificial gradations and metaphysical refinements of later mysticism.
Compare him, in this respect, with John of the Cross. Bernard would have
rejected as unprofitable those descriptions of the successive absorption of the
several faculties in God ; those manifold kinds of prayer—prayers of quiet,
prayers of union, prayers of ecstasy, with their impalpable distinctions ; that
analysis, miraculously achieved, of miraculous ravishments, detailed at such
length in the tedious treatises of the Spanish mystics. The doctrine taught by
John of the Cross, that God compensates the faithful for the mortification of the
senses by sensuous gratifications of a supernatural kind, would have revolted the
more pure devotion of the simple-minded Abbot of Clairvaux.—See *La Montée
du Mont Carmel,* livre ii. chapp. 16, 17 ; pp. 457, &c.

It should be borne in mind that the highest kind of Consideratio is identical,
in Bernard's phraseology, with Contemplatio ; and the terms are thus often used
interchangeably. Generally, Consideratio is applied to inquiry, Contemplatio
to intuition. *De Consid.* lib. ii. cap. 2.

NOTE TO PAGE 146.

See *Vita,* ii. cap. 27, where his biographer gives Bernard's own modest
estimate of these wonders.

Wide, indeed, is the difference between the spiritual mysticism of Bernard
and the gross materialism and arrogant pretension which characterise the vision
and the prophecy to which Hildegard laid claim. The morbid ambition of
theurgic mysticism received a new impulse from the sanction afforded her by
Bernard and the contemporary popes. Bernard makes no doubt of the reality
of her gifts, and desires a place in her prayers. (*Epist.* 366.) He did not foresee
that the most extravagant and sensuous mysticism must soon of necessity displace the simpler and less dazzling. He would be afraid of taking his place

with Rationalist mockers, and a superstitious awe would readily persuade him that it was better to believe than to doubt. When emperors and popes corresponded on familiar terms with the seeress ; when haughty nobles and learned ecclesiastics sought counsel at her oracle concerning future events, and even for the decision of learned questions ; when all she said in answer was delivered as subject to and in the interest of the Church Catholic—was often the very echo of Bernard's own warnings and exhortations—who was he, that he should presume to limit the operations of the Spirit of God? Many of Hildegard's prophecies, denouncing the ecclesiastical abuses of the day, were decidedly reformatory in their tendency. In this respect she is the forerunner of the Abbot Joachim of Calabria, and of St. Brigitta, whose prophetic utterances startled the corrupt Church in the thirteenth and fourteenth centuries. In her supernatural gift of language, her attendant divine radiance, and her fantastic revelations, she, like her friend Elizabeth of Schonau (who had an angel to wait upon her, and saw the eleven thousand virgins), prepares the way for Catharine of Siena, Angela of Foligni, and St. Theresa.

CHAPTER II.

Licht und Farbe.

Wohne, du ewiglich Eines, dort bei dem ewiglich Einen!
Farbe, du wechselnde, komm' freundlich zum Menschen herab![1]
SCHILLER.

ON the next evening of meeting, Gower commenced as
follows his promised paper on Hugo and Richard of
St. Victor.

Hugo of St. Victor.

The celebrated School of St. Victor (so called from an
ancient chapel in the suburbs of Paris) was founded by William
of Champeaux at the commencement of the twelfth century.
This veteran dialectician assumed there the habit of the regular
canons of Augustine, and after an interval, began to lecture
once more to the students who flocked to his retirement. In
1114, king and pope combined to elevate the priory to an
abbacy. Bishops and nobles enriched it with their gifts. The
canons enjoyed the highest repute for sanctity and learning in
that golden age of the canonical institute. St. Victor colonized
Italy, England, Scotland, and Lower Saxony, with establish-
ments which regarded as their parent the mighty pile of building on the outskirts of Paris. Within a hundred years from its
foundation it numbered as its offspring thirty abbeys and more
than eighty priories.

Hugo of St. Victor was born in 1097, of a noble Saxon
family. His boyhood was passed at the convent of Hamers-

---

[1] *Light and Colour.*—Light, thou eternally one, dwell above by the great One Eternal; Colour, thou changeful, in love come to Humanity down!

leben.   There he gave promise of his future eminence.   His thirst after information of every kind was insatiable.   The youth might often have been seen walking alone in the convent garden, speaking and gesticulating, imagining himself advocate, preacher, or disputant.   Every evening he kept rigid account of his gains in knowledge during the day.   The floor of his room was covered with geometrical figures traced in charcoal. Many a winter's night, he says, he was waking between vigils in anxious study of a horoscope.   Many a rude experiment in musical science did he try with strings stretched across a board.   Even while a novice, he began to write.   Attracted by the reputation of the abbey of St. Victor, he enrolled his name among the regular canons there.   Not long after his arrival, the emissaries of an archdeacon, worsted in a suit with the chapter, murdered the prior, Thomas.   Hugo was elected to succeed him in the office of instructor.   He taught philo-sophy, rhetoric, and theology.   He seldom quitted the pre-cincts of the convent, and never aspired to farther preferment. He closed a peaceful and honoured life at the age of forty-four, leaving behind him those ponderous tomes of divinity to which Aquinas and Vincent of Beauvais acknowledge their obligations, and which gained for their author the name of a second Augustine.[2]

Hitherto mysticism, in the person of Bernard, has repudiated scholasticism.   In Hugo, and his successor Richard, the foes are reconciled.   Bonaventura in the thirteenth, and Gerson in the fifteenth century, are great names in the same province. Indeed, throughout the middle ages, almost everything that merits the title of mystical *theology* is characterized by some such endeavour to unite the contemplation of the mystic with the dialectics of the schoolman.   There was good in the

[2] Liebner's *Hugo of St. Victor*, p.   is given by Hugo in his *Didascalion*. 21.—This account of his early studies

attempt. Mysticism lost much of its vagueness, and scholasticism much of its frigidity.

Hugo was well fitted by temperament to mediate between the extreme tendencies of his time. Utterly destitute of that daring originality which placed Erigena at least two centuries in advance of his age, his very gentleness and caution would alone have rendered him more moderate in his views and more catholic in sympathy than the intense and vehement Bernard. Hugo, far from proscribing science and denouncing speculation, called in the aid of the logical gymnastics of his day to discipline the mind for the adventurous enterprise of the mystic. If he regarded with dislike the idle word-warfare of scholastic ingenuity, he was quite as little disposed to bid common sense a perpetual farewell among the cloudiest realms of mysticism. His style is clear, his spirit kindly, his judgment generally impartial. It is refreshing in those days of ecclesiastical domination to meet with at least a single mind to whom that Romanist ideal—an absolute uniformity in religious opinion— appeared both impossible and undesirable.[3]

A few words may present the characteristic outlines of his mysticism. It avails itself of the aid of speculation to acquire a scientific form—in due subjection, of course, to the authority of the Church. It will ground its claim on a surer tenure than mere religious emotion or visionary reverie. Hugo, with all his contemporaries, reverenced the Pseudo-Dionysius. His more devout and practical spirit laboured at a huge commentary on the *Heavenly Hierarchy*, like a good angel, condemned for some sin to servitude under a paynim giant. In the hands of his commentator, Dionysius becomes more scriptural and human—for the cloister, even edifying, but remains as uninteresting as ever.

Hugo makes a threefold division of our faculties. First, and lowest, *Cogitatio*. A stage higher stands *Meditatio :* by this

[3] Schmid, *Der Mysticismus des M. A.*, p. 303,

he means reflection, investigation. Third, and highest, ranges *Contemplatio :* in this state the mind possesses in light the truth which, in the preceding, it desired and groped after in twilight.[4]

He compares this spiritual process to the application of fire to green wood. It kindles with difficulty; clouds of smoke arise ; a flame is seen at intervals, flashing out here and there ; as the fire gains strength, it surrounds, it pierces the fuel ; presently it leaps and roars in triumph—the nature of the wood is being transformed into the nature of fire. Then, the struggle over, the crackling ceases, the smoke is gone, there is left a tranquil, friendly brightness, for the master-element has subdued all into itself. So, says Hugo, do sin and grace contend ; and the smoke of trouble and anguish hangs over the strife. But when grace grows stronger, and the soul's eye clearer, and truth pervades and swallows up the kindling, aspiring nature, then comes holy calm, and love is all in all. Save God in the heart, nothing of self is left.[5]

Looking through this and other metaphors as best we may, we discover that Contemplation has two provinces—a lower and a higher. The lower degree of contemplation, which ranks next above Meditation, is termed Speculation. It is distinct from Contemplation proper, in its strictest signification. The attribute of Meditation is Care. The brow is heavy with inquiring thought, for the darkness is mingled with the light. The attribute of Speculation is Admiration—Wonder. In it the soul ascends, as it were, a watch-tower (*specula*), and surveys everything earthly. On this stage stood the Preacher when he beheld the sorrow and the glory of the world, and pronounced all things human Vanity. To this elevation, whence he philosophizes concerning all finite things, man is raised by the faith,

---

[4] Comp. *De Sacramentis*, lib. v. p. x. c. 4 (tom. iii. p. 411. Garzon's edition of his works, Cologne, 1617.)

[5] See Liebner, p. 315.

the feeling, and the ascetic practice of religion. Speculative illumination is the reward of devotion. But at the loftiest elevation man beholds all things in God. Contemplation, in its narrower and highest sense, is immediate intuition of the Infinite. The attribute of this stage is Blessedness.

As a mystic, Hugo cannot be satisfied with that mediate and approximate apprehension of the Divine Nature which here on earth should amply satisfy all who listen to Scripture and to Reason. Augustine had told him of a certain spiritual sense, or eye of the soul. This he makes the organ of his mysticism. Admitting the incomprehensibility of the Supreme, yet chafing as he does at the limitations of our finite nature, Faith—which is here the natural resource of Reason—fails to content him. He leaps to the conclusion that there must be some immediate intuition of Deity by means of a separate faculty vouchsafed for the purpose.

You have sometimes seen from a hill-side a valley, over the undulating floor of which there has been laid out a heavy mantle of mist. The spires of the churches rise above it—you seem to catch the glistening of a roof or of a vane—here and there a higher house, a little eminence, or some tree-tops, are seen, islanded in the white vapour, but the lower and connecting objects, the linking lines of the roads, the plan and foundation of the whole, are completely hidden. Hugo felt that, with all our culture, yea, with Aristotle to boot, revealed truth was seen by us somewhat thus imperfectly. No doubt certain great facts and truths stand out clear and prominent, but there is a great deal at their basis, connecting them, attached to them, which is impervious to our ordinary faculties. We are, in fact, so lamentably far from knowing all about them. Is there not some power of vision to be attained which may pierce these clouds, lay bare to us these relationships, nay, even more, be to us like the faculty conferred by Asmodeus, and render the very roofs transparent, so that from topstone to foundation, within and without, we may gaze our fill? And if to realize this wholly be too much for sinful creatures, yet may not the wise and good approach such vision, and attain as the meed of their faith, even here, a superhuman elevation, and in a glance at least at the Heavenly Truth unveiled, escape the trammels of the finite?

Such probably was the spirit of the question which possessed, with a ceaseless importunity, the minds of men, ambitious alike to define with the schoolman and to gaze with the seer. Hugo answers that the eye of Contemplation—closed by sin, but opened more or less by grace—furnishes the power thus desiderated.[6] But at this, his highest point, he grasps a shadow instead of the substance. Something within the mind is mistaken for a manifestation from without. A mental creation is substituted for that Divine Existence which his rapture seems to reveal. He asserts, however, that this Eye beholds what the eye of sense and the eye of reason cannot see, what is both within us and above us—God. Within us, he cries, is both *what* we must flee and *whither* we must flee. The highest and the inmost are, so far, identical.[7] Thus do the pure in heart see God. In such moments the soul is transported beyond sense and reason, to a state similar to that enjoyed by angelic natures. The contemplative life is prefigured by the ark in the deluge. Without are waves, and the dove can find no rest. As the holy ship narrowed toward the summit, so doth this life of seclusion ascend from the manifold and changeful to the Divine Immutable Unity.

The simplification of the soul he inculcates is somewhat analogous to the Haplosis of the Neo-Platonists. All sensuous

[6] *De Sacramentis*, lib. i. p. i. cap. 12.—Quisquis sic ordinatus est, dignus est lumine solis: ut mente sursum erecta et desiderio in superna defixo lumen summæ veritatis contemplanti irradict : et jam non per speculum in ænigmate, *sed in seipsa ut est* veritatem agnoscat et sapiat.

[7] See Note, p. 170.

images are to be discarded ; we must concentrate ourselves upon the inmost source, the nude essence of our being. He is careful, accordingly, to guard against the delusions of the imagination.[8] He cautions his readers lest they mistake a mere visionary phantasm—some shape of imaginary glory, for a supernatural manifestation of the Divine Nature to the soul. His mysticism is intellectual, not sensuous. Too practical for a sentimental Quietism or any of its attendant effeminacies, and, at the same time, too orthodox to verge on pantheism, his mystical doctrine displays less than the usual proportion of extravagance, and the ardent eloquence of his 'Praise of Love' may find an echo in every Christian heart.

Richard of St. Victor.

Now, let us pass on to Richard of St. Victor. He was a native of Scotland, first the pupil and afterwards the successor of Hugo. Richard was a man whose fearless integrity and energetic character made themselves felt at St. Victor not less than the intellectual subtilty and flowing rhetoric which distinguished his prelections. He had far more of the practical reformer in him than the quiet Hugo. Loud and indignant are his rebukes of the empty disputation of the mere schoolman,— of the avarice and ambition of the prelate. His soul is grieved that there should be men who blush more for a false quantity than for a sin, and stand more in awe of Priscian than of Christ.[9] Alas ! he exclaims, how many come to the cloister to

[8] Tom. iii. p. 356.—In speaking of the days of creation and of the analogous seasons in the new creation within man, he says that as God first saw the light, that it was good, and then divided it from the darkness, so we must first try the spirit and examine our light with care, ere we part it from what we call darkness, since Satan can assume the garb of an angel of light.

For an elaborate account of his entire theology, the reader is referred to Liebner's *Hugo von St. Victor und die Theologischen Richtungen seiner Zeit ;* one of the best of the numerous monographs German scholarship has produced.

[9] *Richardi S. Victoris Opp.* (Lyons, 1534), *De Preparatione animi ad contemplationem,* fol. 39.

seek Christ, and find lying in that sepulchre only the linen clothes of your formalism! How many mask their cowardice under the name of love, and let every abuse run riot on the plea of peace! How many others call their hatred of individuals hatred of iniquity, and think to be righteous cheaply by mere outcry against other men's sins! Complaints like these are not without their application nearer home.[10]

His zeal did not confine itself to words. In the year 1162 he was made prior. Ervisius the abbot was a man of worldly spirit, though his reputation had been high when he entered on his office. He gradually relaxed all discipline, persecuted the God-fearing brethren, and favoured flatterers and spies; he was a very Dives in sumptuousness, and the fair name of St. Victor suffered no small peril at his hands. The usual evils of broken monastic rule were doubtless there, though little is specified—canons going in and out, whither they would, without inquiry, accounts in confusion, sacristy neglected, weeds literally and spiritually growing in holy places, wine-bibbing and scandal carried on at a lamentable rate, sleepy lethargy and noisy brawl, the more shameful because unpunished. Ervisius was good at excuses, and of course good for nothing else. If complaints were made to him, it was always that cellarer, that pittanciar, or that refectorarius—never his fault. These abuses must soon draw attention from without. Richard and the better sort are glad. The pope writes to the king about the sad accounts he hears. Bishops bestir themselves. Orders come from Rome forbidding the abbot to take any step without the consent of the majority of the chapter. Richard's position is delicate, between his vow of obedience to his superior and the good of the convent. But he plays his part like a man. An archbishop is sent to St. Victor to hold a commission of inquiry. All is curiosity and bustle, alarm and hope among the canons, inno-

---

[10] *Ibid.* cap. xli.

cent and guilty. At last, Ervisius, after giving them much trouble, is induced to resign. They choose an able successor, harmony and order gradually return, and Richard, having seen the abbey prosperous once more, dies in the following year.[11]

In the writings of Richard, as compared with those of Hugo, I find that what belongs to the schoolman has received a more elaborate and complex development, while what belongs to the mystic has also attained an ampler and more prolific growth. All the art of the scholastic is there—the endless ramification and subdivision of minute distinctions ; all the intellectual fortification of the time—the redoubts, ravelins, counterscarps, and bastions of dry, stern logic ; and among these, within their lines and at last above them all, is seen an almost oriental luxuriance of fancy and of rhetoric—palm and pomegranate, sycamore and cypress, solemn cedar shadows, the gloom in the abysses of the soul,—luscious fruit and fragrant flowers, the triumphs of its ecstasy, all blissful with the bloom and odours of the upper Paradise. He is a master alike in the serviceable science of self-scrutiny, and in the imaginary one of self-transcendence. His works afford a notable example of that fantastic use of Scripture prevalent throughout the Middle Age. His psychology, his metaphysics, his theology, are all extracted from the most unlikely quarters in the Bible by allegorical interpretation. Every logical abstraction is attached to some personage or object in the Old Testament history, as its authority and type. Rachel and Leah are Reason and Affection. Bilhah and Zilpah are Imagination and Sense. His divinity is embroidered on the garments of Aaron, engraven on the sides of the ark, hung on the pins and rings of the tabernacle. His definitions and his fancies build in the eaves of Solomon's temple, and make their 'pendent bed and procreant cradle' in the carved work of the holy place. To follow the thread of his religious philosophy,

[11] Engelhardt, *Richard von St. Victor*, p. 6.

you have to pursue his agile and discursive thoughts, as the
sparrow-hawk the sparrow, between the capitals, among the
cedar rafters, over the gilded roof, from court to court, column
to column, and sometimes after all the chase is vain, for they
have escaped into the bosom of a cloud.[12]

On a basis similar to that of Hugo, Richard erects six stages
of Contemplation. The two first grades fall within the province
of Imagination ; the two next belong to Reason ; the two highest to Intelligence. The objects of the first two are *Sensibilia ;*
of the second pair, *Intelligibilia* (truths concerning what is
invisible, but accessible to reason) ; of the third, *Intellectibilia*
(unseen truth above reason). These, again, have their subdivisions, into which we need not enter.[13] Within the depths of
thine own soul, he would say, thou wilt find a threefold heaven
—the imaginational, the rational, and the intellectual. The
third heaven is open only to the eye of Intelligence—that Eye
whose vision is clarified by divine grace and by a holy life.
This Eye enjoys the immediate discernment of unseen truth, as
the eye of the body beholds sensible objects. His use of the
word Intelligence is not always uniform. It would seem that
this divinely-illumined eye of the mind is to search first into the
deeps of our own nature (*inferiora invisibilia nostra*), and then

[12] See Note, p. 171.
[13] The six degrees of contemplation
are as follows (*De Contemp.* i.6, fol. 45):
1 In imaginatione secundum so-
lam imaginationem.
2 In imaginatione secundum rationem.
3 In ratione secundum imaginationem.
4 In ratione secundum rationem.
5 Supra rationem sed non præter
rationem.
6 Supra rationem videtur esse
præter rationem.
The office of Imagination to which
the first two belong is Thought (*Cogitatio*) ; the office of Reason, Investiga-

tion (*Meditatio*) ; that of Intelligence,
Contemplation (*Contemplatio*).—*Ibid.*
cap. 3. These three states are distinguished with much care, and his
definition of the last is as follows :—
Contemplatio est perspicax et liber
animi contuitus in res perspiciendas
undequaque diffusus.—*Ibid.* cap. 4.
He draws the distinction between intelligibilia and intellectibilia in cap. 7 ;
the former = invisibilia ratione tamen
comprehensibilia ; the latter = invisibilia et humanæ rationi incompre-
hensibilia. The four lower kinds are
principally occupied, he adds, with
created objects, the two last with what
is uncreated and divine.—Fol. 45.

upward into the heights of the divine (*superiora invisibilia divina*).[14]

For the highest degrees of Contemplation penitence avails more than science; sighs obtain what is impossible to reason. This exalted intuition begins on earth, and is consummated in heaven. Some, by divine assistance, reach it as the goal of long and arduous effort. Others await it, and are at times rapt away unawares into the heaven of heavens. Some good men have been ever unable to attain the highest stage; few are fully winged with all the six pinions of Contemplation. In the ecstasy he describes, there is supposed to be a dividing asunder of the soul and the spirit as by the sword of the Spirit of God. The body sleeps, and the soul and all the visible world is shut away. The spirit is joined to the Lord, and one with Him,— transcends itself and all the limitations of human thought. In such a moment it is conscious of no division, of no change; all contraries are absorbed, the part does not appear less than the whole, nor is the whole greater than a part; the universal is seen as particular, the particular as universal; we forget both all that is without and all that is within ourselves; all is one and one is all; and when the rapture is past the spirit returns from its trance with a dim and dizzy memory of unutterable glory.[15]

This account presents in some parts the very language in which Schelling and his disciples are accustomed to describe the privilege of Intellectual Intuition.

ATHERTON. I move thanks to Gower.

WILLOUGHBY. Which I second. It has been strange enough to see our painter turn bookworm, and oscillating, for the last fortnight or more, between the forest sunset on his easel and Atherton's old black-letter copy of *Richard of St. Victor.*

[14] See Note, p. 171.   [15] See Note, p, 172.

GOWER. The change was very pleasant. As grateful, I should think, as the actual alternation such men as Hugo and Richard must have enjoyed when they betook themselves, after the lassitude that followed an ecstasy, to a scholastic argumentation ; or again refreshed themselves, after the dryness of that, by an imaginative flight into the region of allegory, or by some contemplative reverie which carried them far enough beyond the confines of logic. The monastic fancy found this interchange symbolized in the upward and downward motion of the holy bell. Is it not in Longfellow's *Golden Legend* that a friar says—

> And the upward and downward motions show
> That we touch upon matters high and low ;
> And the constant change and transmutation
> Of action and of contemplation ;
> Downward, the Scripture brought from on high,
> Upward, exalted again to the sky ;
> Downward, the literal interpretation,
> Upward, the Vision and Mystery !

WILLOUGHBY. Much as a miracle-play must have been very refreshing after a public disputation, or as the most overwrought and most distinguished members of the legal profession are said to devour with most voracity every good novel they can catch.

ATHERTON. It is remarkable to see the mystical interpreters of that day committing the two opposite mistakes, now of regarding what is symbolical in Scripture as literal, and again of treating what is literal as symbolical.

GOWER. Somewhat like the early travellers, who mistook the hybrid figures of the hieroglyphic sculptures they saw for representations of living animals existing somewhere up the country, and then, at other times, fancied they found some profound significance in a simple tradition or an ordinary usage dictated by the climate.

WILLOUGHBY. Yet there lies a great truth in the counsel they give us to rise above all sensuous images in our contemplation of the Divine Nature.

ATHERTON. No doubt. God is (a) spirit. The Infinite Mind must not be represented to our thought through the medium of any material image, as though in that we had *all* the truth. We must not confound the medium with the object. But the object is in fact inaccessible without a medium. The Divine Nature is resolved into a mere blank diffusion when regarded as apart from a Divine Character. We are practically without a God in the presence of such an abstraction. To enable us to realize personality and character there must be a medium, a representation, some analogy drawn from relationships or objects with which we are acquainted.

The fault I find with these mystics is, that they encourage the imagination to run riot in provinces where it is not needed, and prohibit its exercise where it would render the greatest service. Orthodox as they were in their day, they yet attempt to gaze on the Divine Nature in its absoluteness and abstraction, apart from the manifestation of it to our intellect, our heart, and our imagination, which is made in the incarnate Christ Jesus. God has supplied them with this help to their apprehension of Him, but they hope by His help to dispense with it. They neglect the possible and practical in striving after a dazzling impossibility which allures their spiritual ambition. This is a natural consequence of that extravagance of spirituality which tells man that his highest aim is to escape from his human nature—not to work under the conditions of his finite being, but to violate and escape them as far as possible in quest of a superhuman elevation. We poor mortals, as Schiller says, must have *colour*. The attempt to evade this law always ends in substituting the mind's creation for the mind's Creator.

WILLOUGHBY. I cannot say that I clearly understand what this much-extolled introspection of theirs is supposed to reveal to them.

ATHERTON. Neither, very probably, did they. But though

an exact localization may be impossible, I think we can say *whereabout* they are in their opinion on this point. Their position is intermediate. They stand between the truth which assigns to an internal witness and an external revelation their just relative position, and that extreme of error which would deny the need or possibility of any external revelation whatever. They do not ignore either factor; they unduly increase one of them.

WILLOUGHBY. Good. Will you have the kindness first to give me the truth as you hold it? Then we shall have the *terminus a quo.*

ATHERTON. There is what has been variously termed an experimental or moral evidence for Christianity, which comes from within. If any one reverently searches the Scriptures, desiring sincerely to know and do the will of God as there revealed, he has the promise of Divine assistance. He will find, in the evil of his own heart, a reality answering to the statements of the Bible. He will find, in repentance and in faith, in growing love and hope, that very change taking place within which is described in the book without. His nature is being gradually brought into harmony with the truth there set forth. He has experienced the truth of the Saviour's words, 'If any man will do his will, he shall know of the doctrine whether it be of God.'

But in this experimental evidence there is nothing mystical. It does not at all supersede or infringe on the evidence of testimony,—the convincing argument from without, which may at first have made the man feel it his duty to study a book supported by a claim so strong. Neither does he cease to use his reason, when looking within, any more than when listening to witness from without. In self-observation, if in any exercise, reason must be vigilant. Neither is such inward evidence a miraculous experience peculiar to himself. It is common to multitudes. It is open to all who will take the same course he has done. He does not reach it by a faculty which transcends his human nature, and leaves in the distance every power which has been hitherto in such wholesome exercise. There is here no special revelation, distinct from and supplementary to the general. Such a privilege would render an appeal from himself to others impossible. It would entrench each Christian in his individuality apart from the rest. It would give to conscientious differences on minor points the authority of so many conflicting inspirations. It would issue in the ultimate disintegration of the Christian body.

The error of the mystics we are now considering consists in an exaggeration of the truth concerning experimental evidence. They seem to say that the Spirit will manifest to the devout mind verities within itself which are, as it were, the essence and original of the truths which the Church without has been accustomed to teach ; so that, supposing a man to have rightly used the external revelation, and at a certain point to suspend all reference to it, and to be completely secluded from all external influences, there would then be manifest to him, in God, the Ideas themselves which have been developed in time into a Bible and a historical Christianity. The soul, on this Platonist principle, enjoys a commerce once more with the world of Intelligence in the depth of the Divine Nature. She recovers her wings. The obliterations on the tablet of Reminiscence are supplied. . A theosophist like Paracelsus would declare that the whole universe is laid up potentially in the mind of man—the microcosm answering to the macrocosm. In a similar way these mystics would have us believe that there is in man a *microdogma* within, answering to the *macrodogma* of the Church without. Accordingly they deem it not difficult to discover a Christology in psychology, a Trinity in metaphysics. Hence, too, this erroneous assertion that if the heathen had only known themselves, they would have known God.

GOWER. If some of our modern advocates of the theory of Insight be right, they ought to have succeeded in both.

ATHERTON. That '*Know thyself*' was a precept which had its worth in the sense Socrates gave it. In the sense of Plotinus it was a delusion. Applied to morals,—regarded as equivalent to a call to obey conscience, it might render service. And yet varying and imperfect consciences—conflicting inner laws, could give men as an inference no immutable and perfect Lawgiver. Understood as equivalent to saying that the mind is in itself an all-sufficient and infallible repertory of spiritual truth, history in every page refutes it. The monstrosities of idolatry, the disputes of philosophical schools, the aspirations among the best of the sages of antiquity after a divine teaching of some sort—all these facts are fatal to the notion. It is one thing to be able in some degree to appreciate the excellence of revealed truth, and quite another to be competent to discover it for ourselves. Lactantius was right when he exclaimed, as he surveyed the sad and wasteful follies of heathendom, *O quam difficilis est ignorantibus veritas, et quam facilis scientibus !*

WILLOUGHBY. I must say I can scarcely conceive it possible to exclude from the mind every trace and result of what is external, and to gaze down into the depths of our simple self-consciousness as the mystic bids us do. It is like forming a moral estimate of a man exclusive of the slightest reference to his *character*.

GOWER. I think that as the result of such a process, we should find only what we bring. Assuredly this must continually have been the case with our friends Hugo and Richard. The method reminds me of a trick I have heard of as sometimes played on the proprietor of a supposed coal-mine in which no coal could be found, with a view to induce him to continue his profitless speculation. Geologists, learned theoretical men, protest that there can be no coal on that estate—there is none in that part of England. But the *practical* man puts some lumps slyly in his pocket, goes down with them, and brings them up in triumph, as fresh from the depths of the earth.

ATHERTON. Some German writers, even of the better sort have committed a similar mistake in their treatment of the life of Christ. First they set to work to construct the idea of Christ (out of the depths of their consciousness, I suppose), then they study and compare the gospels to find that idea realized. They think they have established the claim of Evangelists when they can show that they have found their idea developed in the biography they give us. As though the German mind could have had any idea of Christ at all within its profundities, but for the fishermen in the first instance.

GOWER. This said Eye of Intelligence appears to me a pure fiction. What am I to make of a faculty which is above, and independent of, memory, reason, feeling, imagination,—without cognizance of those external influences (which at least contribute to make us what we are), and without organs, instruments, or means of any kind for doing any sort of work whatever? Surely this complete and perpetual separation between intuition and everything else within and without us, is a most unphilosophical dichotomy of the mind of man.

ATHERTON. Equally so, whether it be regarded as natural to man or as a supernatural gift. Our intuitions, however rapid, must rest on the belief of some fact, the recognition of some relationship or sense of fitness, which rests again on a judgment, right or wrong.

WILLOUGHBY. And in such judgment the world without must have large share.

GOWER. For the existence of such a separate faculty as a spiritual gift we have only the word of Hugo and his brethren. The faith of Scripture, instead of being cut off from the other powers of the mind, is sustained by them, and strengthens as we exercise them.

ATHERTON. President Edwards, in his *Treatise on the Affec-*

tions, appears to me to approach the error of those mystics, in endeavouring to make it appear that regeneration imparts a new power, rather than a new disposition, to the mind. Such a doctrine cuts off the common ground between the individual Christian and other men. According to the Victorines it would seem to be the glory of Christianity that it enables man, at intervals at least, to denude himself of reason. To me its triumph appears to consist in this, that it makes him, for the first time, truly reasonable, who before acted unreasonably because of a perverted will.

NOTE TO PAGE 158.

The treatise by Hugo, entitled *De Vanitate Mundi,* is a dialogue between teacher and scholar, in which, after directing his pupil to survey the endless variety and vicissitude of life, after showing him the horrors of a shipwreck, the house of Dives, a marriage feast, the toils and disputes of the learned, the instructor bids him shelter himself from this sea of care in that ark of God, the religious life. He proceeds to describe that inner Eye, that *oculus cordis,* whose vision is so precious. 'Thou hast another eye,' he says (lib. i. p. 172), 'an eye within, far more piercing than the other thou speakest of,—one that beholds at once the past, the present, and the future ; which diffuses through all things the keen brightness of its vision ; which penetrates what is hidden, investigates what is impalpable ; which needs no foreign light wherewith to see, but gazes by a light of its own, peculiar to itself (luce aliena ad videndum non indigens, sed sua ac propria luce prospiciens).

Self-collection is opposed (p. 175) to distraction, or attachment to the manifold,—is declared to be *restauratio,* and at the same time *elevatio.* The scholar inquires, ' If the heart of man be an ark or ship, how can man be said to enter into his own heart, or to navigate the universe with his heart ? Lastly, if God, whom you call the harbour, be above, what can you mean by such an unheard-of thing as a voyage which carries the ship upwards, and bears away the mariner out of himself?' The teacher replies, ' When we purpose elevating the eye of the mind to things invisible, we must avail ourselves of certain analogies drawn from the objects of sense. Accordingly, when, speaking of things spiritual and unseen, we say that anything is highest, we do not mean that it is at the top of the sky, but that it is the inmost of all things. To ascend to God, therefore, is to enter into ourselves, and not only so, but in our inmost self to transcend ourselves. (Ascendere ergo ad Deum hoc est intrare ad semet ipsum, et non solum ad se intrare, sed ineffabili quodam modo in intimis etiam se ipsum transire, p. 176)

Hugo, like Richard, associates this illumination inseparably with the practices of devotion. The tree of Wisdom within is watered by Grace. It stands by Faith, and is rooted in God. As it flourishes, we die to the world, we empty ourselves, we sigh over even the necessary use of anything earthly. Devotion makes it bud, constancy of penitence causes it to grow. Such penitence (compunctio) he compares to digging in search of a treasure, or to find a spring. Sin has concealed this hoard—buried this water-source down beneath the many evils of the heart. The watching and the prayer of the contrite spirit clears away what is earthly, and restores the divine gift. The spirit, inflamed with heavenly desire, soars upward—becomes, as it ascends, less gross, as a column of smoke is least dense towards its summit, till we are all spirit; are lost to mortal ken, as the cloud melts into the air, and find a perfect peace within, in secret gazing on the face of the Lord. *De Arca morali,* lib. iii. cap. 7.

NOTE TO PAGE 162.

See the introductory chapters of the *Benjamin Minor,* or *De prep. anim. ad contemp.* fol. 34, &c.—Richard rates this kind of interpretation very highly, and looks for success therein to Divine Illumination. (*De eruditione interioris hominis,* cap. vi. fol. 25.) A passage or two from an appendix to his Treatise on Contemplation, may serve, once for all, as a specimen of his mystical interpretation. It is entitled *Nonnullæ allegoriæ tabernaculi fœderis.* ' By the tabernacle of the covenant understand the state of perfection. Where perfection of the soul is, there is the indwelling of God. The nearer we approach perfection, the more closely are we united with God. The tabernacle must have a court about it. Understand by this the discipline of the body ; by the tabernacle itself, the discipline of the mind. The one is useless without the other. The court is open to the sky, and so the discipline of the body is accessible to all. What was within the tabernacle could not be seen by those without. None knows what is in the inner man save the spirit of man which is in him. The inner man is divided into rational and intellectual ; the former represented by the outer, the latter by the inner part of the tabernacle. We call that rational perception by which we discern what is within ourselves. We here apply the term intellectual perception to that faculty by which we are elevated to the survey of what is divine. Man goes out of the tabernacle into the court in the exercise of works. He enters the first tabernacle when he returns to himself. He enters the second when he transcends himself. Self-transcendence is elevation into Deity. (Transcendendo sane seipsum elevatur in Deum.) In the former, man is occupied with the consideration of himself ; in the latter, with the contemplation of God.

' The ark of the covenant represents the grace of contemplation. The kinds of contemplation are six, each distinct from the rest. Two of them are exercised with regard to visible creatures, two are occupied with invisible, the two last with what is divine. The first four are represented in the ark, the two others are set forth in the figures of the cherubim. Mark the difference between the wood and the gold. There is the same difference between the objects of imagination and the objects of reason. By imagination we behold the forms of things visible, by ratiocination we investigate their causes. The three kinds of consideration which have reference to things, works, and morals, belong to the length, breadth, and height of the ark respectively. In the consideration of *form* and *matter,* our knowledge avails a full cubit. (It is equivalent to a cubit when complete.) But our knowledge of the *nature* of things is only partial. For this part, therefore, we reckon only half a cubit. Accordingly, the length of the ark is two cubits and a half.' . . . . And thus he proceeds concerning the crown, the rings, the staves, the mercy-seat, the cherubim, &c. —Fol. 63, &c.

NOTE TO PAGE 163.

The three heavens within the mind are described at length, (*De Contemp.* lib. iii. cap. 8.) In the first are contained the images of all things visible ; in the second lie the definitions and principles of things seen, the investigations made concerning things unseen ; in the third are contemplations of things divine, beheld as they truly are—a sun that knows no going down,—and there, and there alone, the kingdom of God within us in its glory.—Cap. x. fol 52.

The eye of Intelligence is thus defined (cap. ix.) :—Intelligentiæ siquidem oculus est sensus ille quo invisibilia videmus : non sicut oculo rationis quo occulta et absentia per investigationem quærimus et invenimus ; sicut sæpe causas per effectus, vel effectus per causas, et alia atque alia quocunque ratiocinandi modo comprehendimus. Sed sicut corporalia corporeo sensu videre solemus visibiliter potentialiter et corporaliter ; sic utique intellectualis ille sensus invisibilia capit invisibiliter quidem, sed potentialiter, sed essentialiter. (Fol. 52.) He then goes on to speak of the veil drawn over this organ by sin, and admits that even when illuminated from above, its gaze upon our inner self is not so piercing as to be able to discern the *essence* of the soul. The inner verities are said to be within, the upper, beyond the veil. ' It may be questioned, however, whether we are to see with this same eye of Intelligence the things beyond the veil, or whether we use one sense to behold the invisible things which are divine, and another to behold the invisible things of our own nature. But those who maintain that there is one sense for the intuition of things above and another for those below, must prove it as well as they can. I believe that in this way they introduce much confusion into the use of this word Intelligence,—now extending its signification to a speculation which is occupied with what is above, and now confining it to what is below, and sometimes including both senses. This twofold intuition of things above and things below, whether we call it, as it were, a double sense in one, or divide it, is yet the instrument of the same sense, or a twofold effect of the same instrument, and whichever we choose, there can be no objection to our saying that they both belong to the intellectual heaven.' There is certainly much of the confusion of which he complains in his own use of the word,—a confusion which is perhaps explained by supposing that he sometimes allows Intelligence to extend its office below its proper province, though no other faculty can rise above the limits assigned to it. Intelligence may sometimes survey from her altitude the more slow and laborious processes of reason, though she never descends to such toil.

He dwells constantly on the importance of self-knowledge, self-simplification, self-concentration, as essential to the ascent of the soul.—*De Contemp.* lib. iii. c. 3, c. 6 ; and on the difficulty of this attainment, lib. iv. c. 6.

Note to page 163.

De Contemp. lib. iv. cap. 6. *Ibid.* cap. 23, and comp. lib. v. cap. 1. Also iv. cap. 10. He calls it expressly a vision face to face :—Egressus autem quasi facie ad faciem intuetur, qui per mentis excessum extra semetipsum ductus summæ sapientiæ lumen sine aliquo involucro figurarum ve adumbratione ; denique non per speculum et in enigmate, sed in simplici (ut sic dicam) veritate contemplatur.—Fol. 56. See also lib. v. cœpp 4, 5, where he enters at large on the degrees and starting-points of self-transcendence. Comp. iv. c. 2, fol. 60.

De Contemp. i. cap. 10, describes the six wings, and declares that in a future state we shall possess them all. Speaking of ecstasy, he says :—' Cum enim per mentis excessum supra sive intra nosmetipsos in divinorum contemplationem rapimur exteriorum omnium statim immo non solum eorum quæ extra nos verum etiam eorum quæ in nobis sunt omnium obliviscimur.' When explaining the separation of soul and spirit, he exclaims,—' O alta quies, O sublimis requies, ubi omnis quod humanitus moveri solet motum omnem amittit ; ubi omnis qui tunc est motus divinitus fit et in Deum transit. Hic ille spiritus efflatus in manus patris commendatur, non (ut ille somniator Jacob) scala indiget ut ad tertium (ne dicam ad primum) cælum evolet. Quid quæso scala indigeat quem pater inter manus bajulat ut ad tertii cœli secreta rapiat intantum ut glorietur, et dicat, Dextera tua suscepit me. . . . . Spiritus ab infimis dividitur ut ad summa sublimetur.   Spiritus ab anima scinditur ut Domino uniatur.   Qui enim adhæret Domino unus spiritus est.—*De extermin. mali et promotione boni,* cap. xviii.   Again (*De Contemp.* lib. iv. c. 4), In hac gemina speculatione nihil imaginarium, nihil fantasticum debet occurrere.   Longe enim omnem corporeæ similitudinis proprietatem excedit quicquid spectaculi tibi hæc gemina novissimi operis specula proponit. . . . . Ubi pars non est minor suo toto, nec totum universalius suo individuo ; immo ubi pars a toto non minuitur, totum ex partibus non constituitur ; quia simplex est quod universaliter proponitur et universale quod quasi particulare profertur ; ubi totum singula, ubi omnia unum et unum omnia.   In his utique absque dubio succumbit humana ratio, et quid faciat ibi imaginatio ?   Absque dubio in ejusmodi spectaculo officere potest ; adjuvare omnino non potest.   Elsewhere he describes the state as one of rapturous spiritual intoxication.   Magnitudine jocunditatis et exultationis mens hominis a seipsa alienatur, quum intima illa internæ suavitatis abundantia potata, immo plene inebriata, quid sit, quid fuerit, penitus obliviscitur ; et in abalienationis excessum tripudii sui nimietate traducitur ; et in supermundanum quendam affectum sub quodam miræ felicitatis statu raptim transformatur.— *Ibid.* lib. v. c. 5, fol. 60.

BOOK THE FIFTH

—•—

MYSTICISM IN THE LATIN CHURCH

CHAPTER I.

I pray thee, peace ; I will be flesh and blood ;
For there was never yet philosopher,
That could endure the toothache patiently ;
However they have writ the style of gods,
And made a pish at chance and sufferance.

MUCH ADO ABOUT NOTHING.

It is more healthful and nutritive to dig the earth, and to eat of her fruits,
than to stare upon the greatest glories of the heavens, and live upon the beams
of the sun : so unsatisfying a thing is rapture and transportation to the soul ; it
often distracts the faculties, but seldom does advantage piety, and is full of
danger in the greatest of its lustre.—JEREMY TAYLOR.

THE approach of summer separated the members of the
Ashfield circle for a time. Atherton purposed spending
a few weeks in Germany, and Willoughby consented to accompany him. They were to visit once more Bonn, Heidelberg,
and Frankfort, then to make Strasburg their head quarters, and
thence to ramble about Alsace.

As soon as Atherton had left them, Mrs. Atherton and Kate
Merivale set out for the West of England, to visit their friends
Mr. and Mrs. Lowestoffe. Gower projected a sketching excur-
sion along the banks of the Wye. He knew the Lowestoffes,
and gladly bound himself by the promise they exacted, that he
would make Summerford House his home for a day or two now
and then, in the course of his wanderings. The beauty of the
grounds and neighbourhood would have rendered such visits
eminently delightful, even had the hospitable host and hostess
been less accomplished admirers of art, or had Gower found no
irresistible attraction in one of their guests.

The days at Summerford glided by in the enjoyment of

those innumerable minor *satisfactions* which, far more than
highly pleasurable excitements, make up the happiness of existence.   If you doubt it, consult Abraham Tucker on the matter.
To many persons, life at the Lowestoffes' would have been
intolerably dull.   There were few visitors.   The family seldom
emerged from their retirement to visit the neighbouring city.
Their amusements and their occupations, though varied, were
confined within limits which some would find lamentably narrow.
Lowestoffe himself was an early man and a punctual.   It cost
him something to smile a courteous forgiveness when even a
favourite guest transgressed any of the family regulations on
which his comfort so much depended.   His horses and dogs,
his grounds and his flowers, everything about him and all
dependent upon him, were methodically cared for, inspected,
or commanded by himself in person.   In one respect only was
there irregularity,—no servant, labourer, or workman could be
sure of any moment in which the master might not suddenly
appear to see that all went rightly.   Though scrupulously just,
and of a generous nature, Lowestoffe was only too subject to a
nervous dread of being defrauded by those he employed, and
used often to declare that men were ruined, not so much by
what they spent themselves, as by what they allowed others to
spend for them.   In his early days he had contented himself
with the mere necessaries of his position in life, to discharge the
debts which he inherited.   He would actually have gone into
business (to the horror of his aristocratic friends, but with the
applause of every impartial conscience), had there been no
other way whereby to emancipate his property and honour.   All
declared he would have made a fortune if he had.   A few years
of self-denial, and a few more of frugality and industrious vigi-
lance, realized the full accomplishment of his most cherished
desire.   His care and activity enabled him to deal very liberally
whatever his confidence was at last bestowed, and to expend

in discriminating charity a large annual sum. He was a con-
noisseur and a liberal patron of art, but no solicitation could
induce him to purchase an old master. He knew well how
skilfully imitations of antiquity are prepared, and had he bought
a reputed Titian or Correggio, he would have fidgeted himself
into a fever in a fortnight, by ruminating on the probabilities
of deception. He spent his money far more wisely on choice
pieces by living artists. When the morning was over, the
afternoon and evening found him a cheerful and fascinating
companion. His cares were thrown off, and he was restless
and anxious no longer about little things. Literature and art,
even mere frolic, play with a child, or a game of any kind, were
welcome. Gower whispered an antithesis one day, to the effect
that Lowestoffe gave one half the day to childish wisdom and
the other to wise childishness.

We have mentioned what was not to be found at Summerford. What the two sisters did find there was amply sufficient
for enjoyment. There was a long avenue winding up to the
house, so beset with ancient trees, that it seemed a passage
through the heart of a wood. The lawn on which it opened
was dotted with islands and rings of flower-bed,—perfect magic
circles of horticulture, one all blue, another red, another yellow.
There was the house itself, with its old-fashioned terraces, urns,
and balustrades, and behind it—oh, joy—a rookery! A conservatory shot out its transparent glittering wing on one side of
the edifice. At the foot of a slope of grass descending from the
flower-palace lay a pool, shut in by a mound and by fragments
of rock overgrown with flowers, and arched above by trees. On
the surface spread the level leaves of the water-lilies, with the
sparkling bubbles here and there upon their edges, and everywhere the shadowed water was alive with fish, that might be
seen darting, like little ruddy flames, in and out among the
arrowy sheaves of reeds. Then farther away there were old

irregular walks, richly furred with moss, wandering under trees
through which the sunbeams shot, now making some glossy
evergreen far in among the stems and underwood shine with a
startling brightness (so that the passer-by turned to see if there
were not running water there, and fancied Undine had been at
her tricks again),—now rendering translucent some plume of
fern, now kindling some rugged edge of fir, and again glistening
on some old tree-trunk, mailed with its circular plates of white
lichen. These wood pathways—often broken into natural steps
by the roots of the trees which ran across their course—led up
a steep hill. From the summit were seen, in front, opposite
heights, thickly covered with foliage, through which it was only
here and there that a jutting point of rock could show itself to
be reddened by the setting sun. Beneath, at a great depth, a
shallow brook idled on its pebbles, and you looked down on the
heads of those who crossed its rustic bridge. On the one hand,
here stretched away to the horizon a gentle sweep of hills,
crossed and re-crossed with hedgerows and speckled with trees
and sheep, and, on the other, lay the sea, in the haze of a sultry
day, seen like a grey tablet of marble veined with cloud-shadows.

All this without doors, and books, pictures, prints, drawing,
chess, chat, so choice and plentiful within, made Summerford
‘ a dainty place’—

> Attempred goodly well for health and for delight.

Meanwhile Atherton in Germany was reviving old acquaint-
anceships and forming new, studying the historic relics of old
Strasburg under the shadow of its lofty minster, and relieving
his research by rides and walks, now with student and now
with professor. Early in August he and Willoughby returned
to England, and repaired straightway to Summerford. There,
accordingly, the mystical circuit was complete once more. In
a day or two the discovery was made, through some mysterious
hints dropped by Willoughby, that Atherton had brought home

a treasure from the Rhine. Cross-examination elicited the fact that the said treasure was a manuscript. Something to do with mysticism? Partly so. Then we must hear it. Atherton consented without pretending reluctance. The document purported to be his translation of a narrative discovered among the Strasburg archives, written by one Adolf Arnstein, an armourer of that city,—a personage who appears to have lived in the fourteenth century, and kept some record of what he saw and heard.

So the manuscript was read at intervals, in short portions, sometimes to the little circle grouped on the grass under the trees, sometimes as they sat in the house, with open windows, to let in the evening song of the birds.

Atherton commenced his first reading as follows :—

THE CHRONICLE OF ADOLF ARNSTEIN OF STRASBURG.

This book was begun in the year after the birth of our Lord, one thousand three hundred and twenty. Whosoever readeth this book, let him pray for the soul of Adolf Arnstein, a poor sinful man, who wrote it. And to all who read the same, or hear it read, may God grant everlasting life. Amen.

1320. *September. St. Matthew's Day.*—Three days ago I was surprised by a visit from Hermann of Fritzlar,[1] who has travelled hither from Hesse to hear Master Eckart preach. How he reminded me of what seem old times to me now—ay, old times, though I am but twenty this day—of the days when my

---

[1] The *Heiligenleben* of Hermann von Fritslar has been recently edited by Franz Pfeiffer, in his *Ausgabe der Deutschen Mystiker* (Leipsig, 1845). Hermann says himself repeatedly that he had caused his book to be written (*schreiben lassen*) and there is every reason to believe that he was, like Rulman Merswin and Nicholas of Basle, his contemporaries, a devout layman, —one of a class among the laity characteristic of that age and neighbourhood, who, without entering into an order, spent the greater part of their time in the exercises of religion, and of their fortune on religious objects. Though he could not write, he could read, and his book is confessedly a compilation from many books and from the sermons and the sayings of learned and godly men. He says, Diz buch ist zu sammene gelesen ûzze vile anderen bucheren und ûzze vile predigâten und ûzze vil lêrêren.—*Vorrede.*

honoured father lived and I was a merry boy of fifteen, little thinking that I should so soon be left alone to play the man as I best might.

Hermann is the cause of my writing this. We were talking together yesterday in this room, while the workmen were hammering in the yard below, and the great forge-bellows were groaning away as usual. I told him how I envied his wonderful memory. He replied by reminding me that I could write and he could not. 'Ah,' said I, 'but your mind is full of things worth writing down. You scarcely hear or read a legend, a hymn, or a godly sermon, but it is presently your own, and after it has lain working in your brain for some time, you produce it again, and say or sing it after a way you have, so that it is quite delightful to hear.'

[The night before last I had taken him down into the workshop, and told the men to stop their clatter for awhile, and hear something to do them good—none of your Latin mumbling, but a godly history in their mother-tongue. And then did my friend tell them the Legend of Saint Dorothea, with such a simple tenderness that my rough fellows stood like statues till he had done. I saw a tear run down Hans' sooty face, making a white channel over his cheek. He would have it afterwards that some dust had blown into his eye.]

' My good friend,' said Hermann, ' I am a dozen years at least older than you ; let me counsel you not to set light by your gift, and let it lie unused. Had I that same scrivening art at my service, I should write me a book setting forth what I heard and observed while it was fresh in my mind. I know many good men who would hold such a book, written by a God-fearing man, as great treasure. They would keep it with care and hand it down to those who came after them, so that the writer thereof should be thought on when his hand was cold. I have it in my thoughts to dictate one day or other to some cunning scribe, some of the legends I so love. Haply they may not be the worse for their passage through the mind of a plain man with a loving heart, who has carried them about with him whithersoever he went, lived in them and grown one with them. But you can do much more if you list. I know, moreover, that you, Adolf, are not the man to turn away from your father's old friends because the great ones despise and daily vex them.'

This evening I do herewith begin to act on the resolution his words awakened. I am but a layman, and so is he, but for that matter I have hearkened to teachers who tell me that the layman may be nearer to heaven than the clerk, and that all such outer differences are of small account in the eye of God.

My father was an armourer and president of the guild. All looked up to him as the most fearless and far-seeing of our counsellors. He taught us how to watch and to resist the encroachments of the bishop and the nobles. We have to thank his wisdom mainly that our position has been not a little strengthened of late. Still, how much wrong have we oftentimes to suffer from the senate and their presidents! Strasburg prospers—marvellously, considering the dreadful pestilence seven years back ; but there is much to amend, Heaven knows ! My father fell on a journey to Spires, in an affray with Von Otterbach and his black band. He could use well the weapons he made, and wounded Von Otterbach well nigh to the death before he was overpowered by numbers. The Rhenish League was strong enough, and for once bold enough, to avenge him well. That castle of Otterbach, which every traveller and merchant trembled to pass, stands now ruinous and empty. I, alas ! was away the while, on my apprentice-travels. The old evil is but little abated, though our union has, I doubt not, prevented many of the worst mischiefs of the fist-law. Every rock along the Rhine is castled. They espy us approaching from far off, and

at every turn have we to wrangle, and now and then, if strong
enough, to fight, with these vultures about their robber-toll.
Right thankful am I that my father died a man's death, fighting—that I have not to imagine his fate as like that of some,
who, falling alive into their hands, have been horribly tortured,
and let down by a windlass, with dislocated limbs, into the
loathsome dog-hole of a keep, to writhe and die by inches in
putrid filth and darkness.   Yet our very perils give to our
calling an enterprise and an excitement it would otherwise lack.
The merchant has his chivalry as well as the knight.   Moreover, as rich old Gersdorf says, risk and profit run together—
though, as to money, I have as much already as I care for.   We
thrive, despite restrictions and extortions innumerable, legal and
illegal.   My brother Otto sends me word from Bohemia that he
prospers.   The Bohemian throats can never have enough of our
wines, and we are good customers for their metal.   Otto was
always a rover.   He talks of journeying to the East.   It seems
but yesterday that he and I were boys together, taking our
reading and writing lessons from that poor old Waldensian
whom my father sheltered in our house. How we all loved him! I
never saw my father so troubled at anything as at his death.   Our
house has been ever since a refuge for such persecuted wanderers.

The wrath of Popes, prelates, and inquisitors hath been especially kindled of late years against sundry communities, sects,
and residues of sects, which are known by the name of Beghards, Beguines, Lollards, Kathari, Fratricelli, Brethren of the
Free Spirit,[2] &c.   Councils, they tell me, have been held at
Cologne, Mayence, and Narbonne, to suppress the Beghards.

---

[2] Concerning these sects, see Ullmann, *Reformatoren vor der Reformation*, vol. ii. pp. 1-18.   The fullest
account is given of them in a masterly
Latin treatise by Mosheim, *De Beghardis et Beguinabus*.   He enters at length
into the discussion of their name and
origin ; details the various charges
brought against them, and gives the
bulls and acts issued for their suppression.   See especially the circular of
John Ochsenstein, Bishop of Strasburg,
cap. iv. § xi. p. 255.

Yet their numerous communities in the Netherlands and the Rhineland are a blessing to the poor folk, to whom the hierarchy are a curse. The clergy are jealous of them. They live single, they work with their hands, they nurse the sick, they lay out the dead, they lead a well-ordered and godly life in their Beguinasia, under the Magister or Magistra; but they are bound by no vows, fettered by no harassing minutiæ of austerity, and think the liberty of the Spirit better than monkish servitude. Some of them have fallen into the notions of those enthusiastic Franciscans who think the end of the world at hand, and that we live in, or near, the days of Antichrist. And no wonder, when the spiritual heads of Christendom are so unchristian. There are some sturdy beggars who wander about the country availing themselves of the name of Beghard to lead an idle life. These I excuse not. They say some of these Beghards claim the rank of apostles—that they have subterranean rooms, where both sexes meet to hear blasphemous preachers announce their equality with God. Yea, worse charges than these—even of grossest lewdness—do they bring. I know many of them, both here and at Cologne, but nothing of this sort have I seen, or credibly heard of. They are the enemies of clerical pomp and usurpation, and some, I fear, hold strange fantastical notions, coming I know not whence. But the churchmen themselves are at fault, and answerable for it all. They leave the artisans and labourers in besotted ignorance, and when they do get a solitary religious idea that comes home to them, ten to one but it presently confounds or overthrows what little sense they have. Many deeply religious minds among us, both of laity and clergy, are at heart as indignant at the crimes of the hierarchy as can be the wildest mob-leading fanatic who here and there appears for a moment, haranguing the populace, denouncing the de-nouncers, and bidding men fight sin with sin. We who sigh for reform, who must have more spiritual freedom, have our secret communications, our meetings now and then for counsel, our signs and counter-signs. Folks call the Rhineland the Parsons' Walk—so full is it of the clergy, so enjoyed and lorded over by them. Verily, it is at least as full of those hidden ones, who, in various wise which they call heresy, do worship God without man coming in between.

The tide of the time is with us.[3] Our once famous Godfrey of Strasburg is forgotten. Wolfram von Eschenbach is the universal model. His *Parzival and Titurel* live on the lips of the many rhymesters and minstrels who wander from town to town now, as once they did from court to court and castle to castle. It is the religiousness and the learning of Wolfram that finds favour for him and countless imitators. This is the good sign I mean. Our singers have turned preachers. They are practical, after their fashion. They are a Book of Proverbs, and give us maxims, riddles, doctrines, science, in their verses. If they sing of chivalry, it is to satirize chivalry—such knighthood as now we have. They are spreading and descending towards the people. Men may have their songs of chivalry in Spain, where, under the blessed St. Iago, good knights and true have a real crusade against those heathen hounds the Moors, whom God confound. But here each petty lord in his castle has nothing to do but quarrel with his neighbour and oppress all weaker than himself. What to such men, robbing, drinking, devouring their living with harlots, are Arthur and the Round Table, or Oliver and Roland? So the singers come to us. In good sooth, the old virtues of knighthood— its truth and honour, its chastity and courage—are found far more among the citizens than with the nobles. We relish the sage precepts and quaint abstruseness of Reimar of Zweter, though

---

[3] Authority for these statements concerning the literature of the period, will be found in Gervinus, *Geschichte* *der poetischen National-Literatur der Deutschen*, part vi. §§ 1, 2, 5.

he be somewhat of a pedant. Albertus Magnus is the hero
with him, instead of Charlemagne. His learning is a marvel,
and he draws all morality by allegory out of the Seven Sciences
in most wondrous wise. Frauenlob himself (alas! I heard
last year that he was dead) could not praise fair ladies more
fairly. He assails, in the boldest fashion, the Pope and Rome,
and their daughters Cologne and Mayence. The last time he
was over here from Bohemia, we laughed nigh to bursting at
his caricature of a tournament, and applauded till the rafters
rang again when he said that not birth, but virtue, made true
nobleness. Then our ballads and popular fables are full of
satire on the vices of ecclesiastics. All this tends to keep men
awake to the abuses of the day, and to deepen their desire for
reform. We shall need all the strength we can gather, political
and religious, if in the coming struggle the name of German is
not to be a shame. Our Holy Father promises to indemnify
himself for the humiliation he suffers at Avignon by heaping
insults upon Germany. If Louis of Bavaria conquers Frederick,
I should not wonder if we Strasburgers wake up some morning
and find ourselves excommunicate. All true hearts must be
stirring—we shall have cowards and sluggards enow on all
hands.

Last month the Emperor Louis was here with his army for
a few days. Our bishop Ochsenstein and the Zorn family
espouse the cause of his rival Frederick the Fair. Louis has
on his side, however, the best of us—the family of the Müllenheim, the chief burghers, and the people generally. Every
true German heart, every hater of foreign domination, must be
with him. Many a skirmish has there been in our streets
between the retainers of the two great houses of Zorn and
Müllenheim, and now their enmity is even more bitter than
heretofore. The senate received Louis with royal honours.
When Frederick was here five years ago, we would only enter-

tain him as a guest. The clergy and most of the nobles hailed him as Emperor. Now, when Louis came, it was their turn to stand aloof. There were few of them in the cathedral the other day, when he graciously confirmed our privileges. The bishop issued orders to put a stop to the performance of all church offices while Louis was here ; whereupon, either from prudence or consideration for our souls, he shortened his visit.[4]

1320. *September.   St. Maurice's Day.*—A long conversation with Hermann to-day.   He has heard Eckart repeatedly, and, as I looked for, is both startled and perplexed.   Of a truth it is small marvel that such preaching as his stirred up all Cologne, gathered crowds of wondering hearers, made him fast friends and deadly enemies, and roused the wrath of the heretic-hunting archbishop. Hermann brought me home some of the things this famous doctor said which most struck him.   I wrote them down from his lips, and place them here.

' He who is at all times alone is worthy of God.   He who is at all times at home, to him is God present.   He who standeth at all times in a present Now, in him doth God the Father bring forth his son without ceasing.[5]

' He who finds one thing otherwise than another—to whom God is dearer in one thing than another, that man is carnal, and still afar off and a child.   But he to whom God is alike in all things hath become a man.[6]

---

[4] *Johannes Tauler von Strasburg,* by Dr. Carl Schmidt, pp. 8-10 ; and La-guille's *Histoire d'Alsace,* liv. xxiv.

[5] Meister Eghart spricht : wer alle cit allein ist, der ist gottes wirdige ; vnt wer alliu cit do heimenen ist, dem ist got gegenwürtig ; vnt wer alliu cit stat in einem gegenwürtigen nu, in dem gebirt got der vatter sinen sune an vnderlas.—*Sprüche Deutscher Mysti-ker,* in Wackernagel's *Altdeutsches Lese-buch,* p. 889.

[6] Meister Eghart sprach : vnt wem in einem anders ist denne in dem andern, vnt dem got lieber ist in eime denne in dem andern, der mensche ist grobe, vnt noch verre vnt ein kint. Aber dem got gelich ist in allen, der ist ce man worden.—*Ibid.*

Both this saying and the foregoing are expressions for that total indiffer-ence and self-abandonment so strenu-ously inculcated by the mystics. He who lives weaned from the world,

'All that is in the Godhead is one. Thereof can we say nothing. It is above all names, above all nature. The essence of all creatures is eternally a divine life in Deity. God works. So doth not the Godhead. Therein are they distinguished,— in working and not working. The end of all things is the hidden darkness of the eternal Godhead, unknown and never to be known.[7]

'I declare, by good truth and truth everlasting, that in every man who hath utterly abandoned self, God must communicate Himself according to all His power, so completely that he retains nothing in His life, in His essence, in His Nature, and in His Godhead—He must communicate all to the bringing forth of fruit.[8]

'When the Will is so united that it becometh a One in oneness, then doth the Heavenly Father produce his only-begotten Son in Himself and in me. Wherefore in Himself and in me?

alone with God, without regrets, without anticipations, 'stands in a present Now,' and sees the divine love as clearly in his sorrows as in his joys,— does not find 'one thing other than another.' There is exaggeration in suppressing, as Eckart would do, the instinct of thanksgiving for special benefaction ; but in his strong language lies couched a great truth,—that only in utter self-surrender can man find abiding peace.

[7] Alles das in der gottheyt ist, das ist ein, vnd davon ist nicht zu sprechen. Got der würcket, die gotheyt nit, sy hat auch nicht zu würckende, in ir ist auch kein werck. Got vnt gotheyt hat underscheyd, an würcken vnd an nit würcken.

Was ist das letst end? Es ist die verborgen finsternusz der ewigen gotheit, vnd ist unbekant, vnd wirt nymmerme bekant. (See a paper on Eckart, by Dr. Carl Schmidt in the *Theol. Stud. u. Kritiken*, 1839, 3, p. 693.) Comp. the following :—Got

ist noch gut noch besser, noch allerbest, vnd ick thue also unrecht, wenn ick Got gut heisse, rechte ase ob ick oder er etwas wiz weiss und ick es schwarz heisse.—*Ibid.* p. 675. This last assertion was one of the counts of accusation in the bull of 1330.

[8] Martensen's *Meister Eckart* (Hamburg, 1842), p. 22.—The divine communication assumes with Eckart the form of philosophical necessity. The man emptied of Self is infallibly full of Deity, after the fashion of the old principle, 'Nature abhors a vacuum.' Yet even this doctrine is not wholly false. It is the misrepresentation of a Christian truth. Its correlative verity is this,—that the kingdom of grace, like the kingdom of nature, has its immutable laws. He who seeks shall find ; as we sow we reap, with unerring certainty. Gravitation is not more sure than the announcement, 'With that man will I dwell who is of a meek and contrite spirit.'

I am one with Him—He cannot exclude me. In the self-same operation doth the Holy Ghost receive his existence, and proceeds from me as from God. Wherefore? I am in God, and if the Holy Ghost deriveth not his being from me, He deriveth it not from God. I am in nowise excluded.[9]

'There is something in the soul which is above the soul, divine, simple, an absolute Nothing, rather unnamed than named, unknown than known. So long as thou lookest on thyself as a *Something*, so long thou knowest as little what this is as my mouth knows what colour is, or as my eye knows what taste is. Of this I am wont to speak in my sermons, and sometimes I have called it a Power, sometimes an uncreated Light, sometimes a divine Spark. It is absolute and free from all names and forms, as God is free and absolute in Himself. It is higher than knowledge, higher than love, higher than grace. For in all these there is still distinction. In this power doth blossom and flourish God, with all His Godhead, and the Spirit flourisheth in God. In this power doth the Father bring forth His only-begotten Son, as essentially as in Himself, and in this light ariseth the Holy Ghost. This Spark rejects all creatures, and will have only God, simply as he is in Himself. It rests satisfied neither with the Father, nor the Son, nor the Holy Ghost, nor with the three Persons, as far as each exists in its respective attributes. I will say what will sound

---

[9] Martensen, p. 23. Comp. *Stud. u. Krit. loc. cit.* Alles das denn got yn gegab seinem eingebornen sun, das hat er mir gegeben. . . . *Was got würcket, das ist ein,* darumb gebiret er mich seinen sun, on aller underscheyd.—These words exhibit the pantheistic principle on which this assumption is based. All spirit (whether in so-called creature or Creator) is substantially one and the same. It cannot be divided; it can have no distinctive operations. Our dividual personal consciousness is, as it were, a temporary accretion on the Universal Soul with which we are in contact. Escaping this consciousness, we merge in—that is, we become—the Universal Soul. We are brought into the Essence,—the calm, unknown oneness beyond all manifestation, above creation, providence, or grace. This is Eckart's escape from distinction,—lapse into the totality of spirit. This doctrine he teaches, not in opposition to the current Christian doctrine, but as a something above it,—at once its higher interpretation and its climax.

more marvellous yet.   This Light is satisfied only with the
super-essential essence.   It is bent on entering into the simple
Ground, the still Waste, wherein is no distinction, neither
Father, Son, nor Holy Ghost,—into the Unity where no man
dwelleth.   There is it satisfied in the light, there it is one ;
then is it in itself, as this Ground is a simple stillness in itself,
immoveable ; and yet by this Immobility are all things
moved.[10]

  ' God in himself was not God—in the creature only hath He
become God.   I ask to be rid of God—that is, that God, by
his grace, would bring me into the Essence—that Essence
which is above God and above distinction.   I would enter into
that eternal Unity which was mine before all time, when I was
what I would, and would what I was ;—into a state above all
addition or diminution ;—into the Immobility whereby all is
moved.[11]

  ' Folks say to me often—" Pray God for me."   Then I think

---

[10] These statements concerning the
' füncklin der vernunfft' are the substance of passages given by Martensen,
pp. 26, 27, and Schmidt (*Stud. u.
Krit. l. c.*) pp. 707, 709.—Ich sprich
es bey gutter warheit, und bey yem-
merwerender warheit, und bey ewiger
warheit, das disem liechte nit benüget
an dem einfaltigem stilstanden göt-
lichen wesen, von wannen disz wesen
harkommet, es will in den einfaltigen
grundt in die stillen wüste, das nye
underscheyd ingeluget, weder vatter
noch sun noch heiliger geist, in dem
einichen, da niemant daheim ist, da
benüget es im liechte, und da ist es
einicher, denn es sey in im selber, wann
diser grundt ist ein einfeltig stille
die in ir selber unbeweglich ist, und
von diser unbeweglichkeit werdent
beweget alle ding, &c.   Hermann von
Fritslar, in a remarkable passage,
enumerates the various and conflicting
names given to this organ of mysticism.
' Und das leben was daz licht der lûte.'

Daz meinet, daz di sêle einen funken in
ir hât, der ist in gote êwiclîchen gewest
leben und licht.   Und dirre funke ist
mit der sêle geschaffen in allen menschen und ist ein lûter licht in ime
selber und strafet allewege umme sunde
und hat ein stête heischen zu der tu-
gende und kriget allewege wider in
sînen ursprung. . . . Dar umme
heizen in etlîche meistere einen wechter
der sêle.   Also sprach Daniêl : 'der
wechter ûf dem turme der rufet gar
sêre.   Etlîche heizen disen funken einen
haven der sêle.   Etlîche heizen in di
worbele (axis, or centre) der sêle.   Etelîche heizen in ein gotechen in der sêle.
Etelîche heizen in ein antlize der sêle.
Etelîche heizen *intellectus*, daz ist ein
instênde kraft in der sêle.   Etlîche heizen *in sinderisis*.   Etlîche heizen in
daz wô der sêle.   Etlîche heizen in daz
nirgen der sêle.—*Heiligenleben*. *Di
dritte messe*, p. 32.

[11] Martensen, p. 27.   Schmidt, *loc.
cit.*

with myself, "Why go ye out? Why abide ye not in your own selves, and take hold on your own possession? Ye have all truth essentially within you?" [12]

'God and I are one in knowing. God's Essence is His knowing, and God's knowing makes me to know Him. Therefore is His knowing my knowing. The eye whereby I see God is the same eye whereby He seeth me. Mine eye and the eye of God are one eye, one vision, one knowledge, and one love.' [13]

'If any man hath understood this sermon, it is well for him. Had not a soul of you been here, I must have spoken the very same words. He who hath not understood it, let him not trouble his heart therewith, for as long as a man is not himself like unto this truth, so long will he never understand it, seeing that it is no truth of reflection, to be thought out, but is come directly out of the heart of God without medium.' [14]

Of all this I can understand scarcely anything. The perpetual incarnation of God in good Christians, the nameless Nothing, the self-unfolding and self-infolding of God (I know not what words to use) are things too high for my grosser apprehension. I shall let the sayings lie here; some one else who reads may comprehend them. I am content to be a child in such matters. I look with awe and admiration on men who have attained while yet in the flesh heights of wisdom which will be, perhaps to all eternity, beyond the reach of such as I am.

1320. *October. St. Francis' Day.*—Went with Hermann this morning to hear mass. Master Eckart preached again. Dr. Tauler in the church. How every one loves that man! As several of his brethren made their way to their places, I saw the people frown on some of them, and laugh and leer to each other as two or three of them passed. They had reason,

[12] The passage in Martensen, p. 20.   [14] *Ibid.* p. 29.
[13] Martensen, pp. 19, 29.

I know, to hate and to despise certain among them. But to Tauler all bowed, and many voices blessed him. He has a kind heart to feel for us, the commonalty. He and his sermons are one and the same. He means all he says, and we can understand much, at least, of what he means. There is a cold grandeur about Master Eckart. He seems above emotion: his very face, all intellect, says it is a weakness to feel. At him we wonder; with Master Tauler we weep. How reverently did Tauler listen, as a son to a father, to the words of the great Doctor. No doubt he understood every syllable. He is and shall be my sole confessor. I will question him, some day, concerning these lofty doctrines whereby it would seem that the poorest beggar may outpass in wisdom and in blessedness all the Popes of Christendom.

Master Eckart said to-day :—' Some people are for seeing God with their eyes, as they can see a cow, and would love God as they love a cow (which thou lovest for the milk and for the cheese, and for thine own profit). Thus do all those who love God for the sake of outward riches or of inward comfort; they do not love aright, but seek only themselves and their own advantage.[15]

' God is a pure good in Himself, and therefore will He dwell nowhere save in a pure soul. There He may pour Himself out; into that He can wholly flow. What is Purity? It is that man should have turned himself away from all creatures, and have set his heart so entirely on the pure good, that no creature is to him a comfort, that he has no desire for aught creaturely, save as far as he may apprehend therein the pure good which is God. And as little as the bright eye can endure aught foreign

[15] Etlich leut wöllent got mit den ougen ansehn, als sy ein ku ansent unnd wöllent gott liebhan, als sy ein ku liebhaben (die hastu lieb umb die milch, und umb den kätz, und umb dein eigen nutz). Also thund alle die leut die got liebhand, um uszwendigen reichtum, oder umb inwendigen trost, und die hand gott nit recht lieb, sunder sy suchent sich selbs und ir eigen nutz.—*Schmidt*, 712.

in it, so little can the pure soul bear anything in it, any stain, aught between it and God.   To it all creatures are pure to enjoy, for it enjoyeth all creatures in God, and God in all creatures.   Yea, so pure is that soul that she seeth through herself, she needeth not to seek God afar off, she finds him in herself, when, in her natural purity, she hath flowed out into the supernatural of the pure Godhead.   And thus is she in God and God in her, and what she doeth that she doeth in God and God doeth it in her.[16]

'Then shall a man be truly poor when he is as free from his creature will as he was before he was born.   And I say to you, by the eternal truth, that so long as ye desire to fulfil the will of God, and have any desire after eternity and God, so long are ye not truly poor.   He alone hath true spiritual poverty who wills nothing, knows nothing, desires nothing.[17]

'For us, to follow truly what God willeth, is to follow that whereto we are most inclined,—whereto we feel most frequent inward exhortation and strongest attraction.   The inner voice is the voice of God.'[18]

[16] Got ist ein luter guot an ime selben, vnt do von wil er nienen wonen denne in einer lutern sele : in die mag er sich ergiessen vnt genzeclichen in si fliessen. was ist luterkeit? das ist das sich der mensche gekeret habe von allen creaturen, vnt sin herce so gar uf gerichtet habe gen dem lutern guot, das ime kein creature trœstlichen si, vnt ir ouch nit begere denne als vil als si das luter guot, das got ist, darinne begriffen mag. vnt also wenig das liechte ouge icht' in ime erliden mag, also wenig mag diu luter sele icht an ir erliden keine vermasung vnt das si vermitlen mag. ir werdent alle creaturen luter ce niessen : wanne si niusset alle creaturen in got vnt got in allen creaturen. Denne si ist also luter, das si sich selben durschowet, denne endarf si got nit verre suchen : si vindet in ir selben, wanne s in ir natiurlichen luterkeit s[t] geflossen n das übernatiurliche der lutern gotheit. vnt also ist si in got, vnt got in ir ; vnt was si tuot, das tuot si in got, vnt tuot es got in ir.—*Wackernagel*, p. 891.

[17] Wann sol der mensch warlich arm sein, so soll er seynes geschaffnen willes also ledig sein, als er was do er noch nit was.   Und ich sag euch bey der ewigen warheit, *als lang ir willen hand zu erfüllend den willen gottes, vnd icht begerung hand der ewigkeit und gottes, also lang seind ir nitt recht arm*, wann das ist ein arm mensch der nicht wil, noch nicht bekennet, noch nicht begeret—*Schmidt*, p. 716.   Here again is the most extravagant expression possible of the doctrine of *sainte indifférence*, in comparison with which Madame Guyon is moderation itself.

[18] See *Schmidt*, p. 724.

After the service, Hermann left me to go and see a sick friend. I mingled with the crowd. There was a knot of people gathered before All-Saints, discussing what they had heard. A portly, capon-lined burgomaster declared he had first been hungry, then sleepy, and that was all he knew. He had verily, as a wag presently told him, obeyed the master, and lost consciousness of all external things. Whereat the jolly citizen was so tickled that he took the joker home to dine with him, promising mountains of pickled pork, a whole Black Forest of sauer kraut, and boundless beakers of hippocras.

An innocent novice from the country (looking fresh as a new-caught trout) began to say, 'Well, it doth seem to me that though Doctor Eckart received his Doctorate from Rome, at the hands of our Holy Father, though he hath studied and taught at Paris, though he hath been Provincial of our order in Saxony, and Vicar-General in Bohemia—where he played the cat with the mice, I can tell you—yet that some things he said were——'

'Hold your tongue for a jackass,' quoth a senior brother, who liked not, methinks, to hear a whisper against the orthodoxy of the order, by whomsoever or against whomsoever uttered.

'He is a blasphemer,' said a friar. 'Good people, did not you hear him say that what burned in hell was the Nothing?[19] Then nothing burns; *ergo*, there is no hell.'

'I don't think he believes in God at all,' cried one :—'Did he not say something about caring no more for God than for a stone?'

'Ay, but,' urged the friar, 'no hell, and so no purgatory—think of that. Why, he has swept the universe as clean of the devil as a housewife's platter at a christening.'

[19] He was charged with denying hell and purgatory, because he defined future punishment as deprivation,— 'Das Nicht in der helle brinnet.'—*Schmidt*, p. 722.

Some one in the crowd shouted out, 'That fellow cares not what becomes of God, but he can't give up his devil.' Whereon the friar grew very red in the face, as we all laughed, but could not bethink him of any answer, and went capped with the name of Brother Brimstone ever after.

'What was that he said,' asked a slip-shod, sottish-looking tailor, 'about doing what you like, and that is what God likes?'

'Friends,' cries next a rainbow-coloured, dandified puppy, a secretary of the bishop's, stroking the down of a would-be moustache, evidently as yet only in a state of Becoming (*Werden*)—'I would fain have moderately kicked him,——

'My friends' (smiling with a patronizing blandness at the tailor), 'you are right; the public morals are in danger. Evil men and seducers wax worse and worse. But the Holy Church will protect her children. We have heard pestilent heresy this day. To hear that man talk, you would fancy he thought there was as much divinity in his little finger as in the whole body of the Virgin Mother of God.'

Whereupon up starts a little man whom I knew for one of the brethren of the Free Spirit—takes his place on a stone that lay in the mud of the middle of the street, and begins— 'Good people, did you not hear the doctor say that those who cannot understand his doctrine are to hold by the common faith? Did not Saint Peter say of the Epistles of the blessed Saint Paul that there were some things therein hard to be understood, which the ignorant would wrest to their own destruction? I'll tell you the ignorance he means and the knowledge he means. Friend Crispin there, whom you carried home drunk in a barrow last night, and Master Secretary here, who transgresses in like wise and worse in a daintier style, and hath, by the way, as much perfumery about him as though the scent thereof, rising towards heaven, were so much incense for the taking away of his many sins—they are a couple of St. Paul's

ignoramuses. The knowledge St. Paul means is the thoughtful
love of doing the right thing for the love of Christ. But the
Pope himself may be one of these witless ones, if the love of
sin be stronger in him than the love of holiness. The preaching of all the twelve Apostles would be turned to mischief and
to licence by such as you, you feather-brained, civet-tanned
puppet of a man, you adulterous, quill-driving hypocrite.'

'Seize him,' shouts my Secretary, and darted forward; but
an apprentice put out his foot, and over he rolled into the mire,
grievously ruffling and besmutching all his gay feathers, while
the little man mingled with the laughing people, and made his
escape. I hope he is out of Strasburg, or he may be secluded
in a darkness and a solitude anything but divine. He was a
trifle free of tongue, assuredly; I suppose that makes a part of
the freedom of the Spirit with him. He had right, however,
beyond question.

The confusion created by this incident had scarcely ceased,
when I saw advancing towards us the stately form of Master
Eckart himself. He looked with a calm gravity about upon us,
as he paused in the midst—seemed to understand at once of
what sort our talk had been, and appeared about to speak.
There was a cry for silence—'Hear the Doctor! hear him!'
Whereon he spoke as follows :—

'There was once a learned man who longed and prayed full
eight years that God would show him some one to teach him
the way of truth. And on a time, as he was in a great longing, there came unto him a voice from heaven, and said, "Go to
the front of the church, there wilt thou find a man that shall
show thee the way to blessedness."

'So thither he went, and found there a poor man whose feet
were torn, and covered with dust and dirt, and all his apparel
scarce three hellers worth. He greeted him, saying, "God give
thee good morrow." Thereat made he answer, "I never had an

ill morrow."   Again said he,   "God prosper thee."   The other
answered. "Never had I aught but prosperity."

' "Heaven save thee," said the scholar, "how answerest thou
me so?"

' " I was never other than saved."

' " Explain to me this, for I understand not."

' " Willingly," quoth the poor man. "Thou wishest me good
morrow.   I never had an ill morrow, for, am I an hungered, I
praise God ; am I freezing, doth it hail, snow, rain, is it fair
weather or foul, I praise God ; and therefore had I never ill
morrow.   Thou didst say, God prosper thee.   I have been
never unprosperous, for I know how to live with God ; I know
that what he doth is best, and what God giveth or ordaineth
for me, be it pain or pleasure, that I take cheerfully from Him
as the best of all, and so I had never adversity.   Thou wishest
God to bless me.   I was never unblessed, for I desire to be only
in the will of God, and I have so given up my will to the will
of God, that what God willeth I will.'

' " But if God were to cast thee into hell," said the scholar,
" what wouldst thou do then?"

' " Cast me into hell?   His goodness holds him back therefrom.   Yet if he did, I should have two arms to embrace him
withal.   One arm is true Humility, and therewith am I one
with his holy humanity.   And with the right arm of Love,
that joineth his holy Godhead, I would embrace him, so He
must come with me into hell likewise.   And even so, I would
sooner be in hell, and have God, than in heaven, and not have
Him."

' Then understood this Master that true Abandonment, with
utter Abasement, was the nearest way to God.

' Moreover the Master asked : "From whence comest thou?"

' " From God."

' " Where hast thou found God?"

' " Where I abandoned all creatures. I am a king. My kingdom is my soul. All my powers, within and without, do homage to my soul. This kingdom is greater than any kingdom on the earth."

' " What hath brought thee to this perfection ?"

' " My silence, my heavenward thoughts, my union with God. For I could rest in nothing less than God. Now I have found God, and have everlasting rest and joy in Him." [20]

With that Master Eckart ceased, and went on his way again, leaving us in wonderment ; and I watched him, as far as I could see along the winding street, walking on under the overhanging gables, with his steady step and abstract air, and his silver locks fluttering out in the wind from under his doctor's hat. When I looked round, I found myself almost alone. He is a holy man, let what will be said about heresy.

I set down here a new hymn Hermann sang me—sweet, as he sang it—with a ringing repetition that chimes right pleasantly, and makes amends for some lack of meaning in the words. [21]

Oh be glad, thou Zion's daughter,
  Joyous news to thee are sent ;
Thou shalt sing a strain of sweetness,
  Sing it to thy heart's content.
Now the friend of God thou art,
Therefore shalt thou joy at heart,
Therefore know no sorrow-smart.
    Lo ! 'tis ju-ju-jubilation,
      Meditation ;
    Ju-ju-ju-ju-jubilation,
    Contemplation ;
    Ju-ju-ju-jubilation ;
    Ju-ju-ju-jubilation ;
    Speculation ;
    Ju-ju-ju-jubilation,
    Conciliation !

[20] The narrative here put into the mouth of Eckart is found in an appendix to Tauler's *Medulla animæ*. There is every reason to believe that it is Eckart's. Martensen gives it, p. 107.

[21] A literal translation of a curious old hymn in Wackernagel's collection, p. 896.

> Meditation, that is goodly,
>   When a man on God will muse ;
> Jubilation worketh wonder,
>   'Tis the harp the soul doth use.
> Speculation, that is sheen,
> Contemplation crowns, I ween,
> Concord leads, the dance's queen,
>   Lo ! ju-ju-ju-
>   Conciliation !
>   'Tis jubilation
>   At the sweets of contemplation !

Have been haunted by this ju-ju, in-doors and out, whatever I have been doing for the last three days, and I hear it in every stroke upon the anvil.

1320. *Second week in October.*—A ride over to Fegersheim about Sir Rudolf's new bascinet with the beaked ventaille. As I reached the castle the ladies were just coming out for hawking, with a brave company of knights and squires. They were fair to see, with their copes and kirtles blue and white, and those fanciful new-fashioned crowns on their heads, all glittering with gold and jewels. Sir Rudolf stayed for me awhile and then followed them.

On my way back, rested at noon at a little hostelry, where I sat before the door at a table, chatting with mine host. There ride up a priest and monk with attendants. Holy Mary, what dresses ! The monk with bells on his horse's bridle, his hood fastened with a great golden pin, wrought at the head into a true-love knot, his hair growing long so as to hide his tonsure, his shoes embroidered and cut lattice-wise.[22] There was the priest with broad gold girdle, gown of green and red, slashed after the newest mode, and a long sword and dagger, very truly militant. I marvelled at the variety and unction of the oaths they had at their service. The advantage of a theological training was very manifest therein.

---

[22] C. Schmidt (*Johannes Tauler von Strasburg*, p. 42) gives examples of the extravagant display in dress common among the clergy at that time.

Scarcely were these worthies, with bag and baggage, well on their way again when I espied, walking towards the inn, a giant of a man—some three inches higher than I am (a sight I have not often seen), miserably attired, dusty and travel-worn. When he came to where I was he threw down his staff and bundle, cast his huge limbs along the bench, gave a careless, surly glance at me, and, throwing back his shaggy head of black hair, seemed about to sleep. Having pity on his weariness I said, 'Art thirsty, friend? the sun hath power to-day.' Thereupon he partly raised himself, looked fixedly at me, and then drank off the tankard I pushed towards him, grunting out a something which methought was meant for thanks. Being now curious, I asked him straight, 'Where he came from?'

He. I never came from anywhere.

I. What are you?

He. I am not.

I. What will you?

He. I will not.

I. This is passing strange. Tell me your name.

He. Men call me the Nameless Wild.

I. Not far off the mark either; you talk wildly enough. Where do you come from? whither are you bound?

He. I dwell in absolute Freedom.

I. What is that?

He. When a man lives as he list, without distinction (Otherness, *Anderheit*), without before or after. The man who hath in his Eternal Nothing become nothing knows nought of distinctions.

I. But to violate distinction is to violate order, and to break that is to be a slave. That is not the freedom indeed, which the truth gives. He that committeth sin is the servant of sin. No man can be so utterly self-annihilated and lost in God,—

can be such a very nothing that there remains no remnant of the original difference between creature and Creator. My soul and body are one, are not separate ; but they are distinct. So is it with the soul united to God. Mark the difference, friend, I prithee, between separation and distinction (*Geschiedenheit und Unterschiedenheit*).

He. The teacher saith that the saintly man is God's son, and what Christ doth, that doth he.

I. He saith that such man followeth Christ in righteousness. But our personality must ever abide. Christ is son of God by nature, we by grace. Your pride blinds you. You are enlightened with a false light, coming whence I know not. You try and 'break through' to the Oneness, and you break through reason and reverence.

He replied by telling me that I was in thick darkness, and the boy coming with my horse, I left him.[23]

As I rode homeward I thought on the contrast I had seen. This man who came last is the natural consequent on the two who preceded him. So doth a hypocritical, ghostly tyranny produce lawlessness. I have seen the Priest and the Levite, and methinks one of the thieves,—where is our good Samaritan ? I know not which extreme is the worst. One is selfish abso-

---

[23] The substance of this dialogue will be found in the works of Heinrich Suso (ed. Melchior Diepenbrock, Regensburg, 1837), Book iii. chap. vii. pp. 310-14. Suso represents himself as holding such a conversation with ' ein vernunftiges Bilde, das war subtil an seinen Worten und war aber ungeübt an seinen Werken und war ausbrüchig in florirender Reichheit,' as he sat lost in meditation on a summer's day. Atherton has ventured to clothe this ideal of the enthusiast of those times in more than a couple of yards of flesh and blood, and supposed Arnstein to have picked up divinity enough in his sermon-hearing to be able to reason with him just as Suso does in his book.

The wandering devotees, who at this time abounded throughout the whole region between the Netherlands and Switzerland, approximated, some of them, to Eckart's portraiture of a religious teacher, others to Suso's ideal of the Nameless Wild. In some cases the enthusiasm of the same man may have approached now the nobler and now the baser type.

luteness, the other absolute selfishness.   Oh, for men among
us who shall battle with each in the strength of a truth above
them both !   Poor Alsace !

Here Atherton laid aside his manuscript, and conversation
commenced.

CHAPTER II.

For as though there were metempsychosis, and the soul of one man passed into another ; opinions do find, after certain revolutions, men and minds like those that first begat them.—SIR THOMAS BROWNE.

WILLOUGHBY. What struck me most as novel in the mysticism of this strange Master Eckart was the stress he laid on our own consciousness of being the sons of God. Neither the ecclesiastical nor the scholastic gradations and preparatives for mysticism, so important with his predecessors, seem of much moment with him in comparison with the attainment, *per saltum*, as it were, of this blessed certainty. Perhaps the secret of his reaction against the orthodoxy of his day lay here. He craves a firm resting-place for his soul. The Church cannot satisfy the want. He will supply it for himself, and, to do so, builds together into a sort of system certain current notions that suit his purpose, some new and others old, some in tolerable harmony with Christianity, others more hostile to it than he was altogether aware. These pantheistic metaphysics may have seemed to him his resource and justification—may have been the product of the brain labouring to assure the heart.

ATHERTON. A very plausible conjecture. Amalric of Bena, who had been famous as a teacher in Paris nearly a hundred years before Eckart went to study there, maintained that a personal conviction of our union to Christ was necessary to salvation. He was condemned for the doctrine, but it survived.

WILLOUGHBY. Thank you. That fact supports me. Might

not Eckart have desired to assert for our inward religious life a worthier and more independent place, as opposed to the despotic externalism of the time—to make our access to Christ more immediate, and less subject to the precarious mercies of the Church?

ATHERTON. A grand aim, if so : but to reach it he unfortunately absorbs the objective in the subjective element of religion —rebounds from servility to arrogance, and makes humanity a manifestation of the Divine Essence.

GOWER. In order to understand his position, the question to be first asked appears to me to be this. If Eckart goes to the Church, and says, ' How can I be assured that I am in a state of salvation ?' what answer will the Holy Mother give him? Can you tell me, Atherton ?

ATHERTON. She confounds justification and sanctification together, you will remember. So she will answer, ' My son, as a Christian of the ordinary sort, you cannot have any such certainty—indeed, you are much better without it. You may conjecture that you are reconciled to God by looking inward on your feelings, by assuring yourself that at least you are not living in any mortal sin. If, indeed, you were appointed to do some great things for my glory, you might find yourself among the happy few who are made certain of their state of grace by a special and *extra* revelation, to hearten them for their achievements.'

GOWER. Shameful ! The Church then admits the high, invigorating influence of such certainty, but denies it to those who, amid secular care and toil, require it most.

WILLOUGHBY. While discussing Eckart, we have lighted on a doctrine which must have produced more mysticism than almost any other you can name. On receiving such reply, how many ardent natures will strain after visions and miraculous manifestations, wrestling for some token of their safety !

GOWER. And how many will be the prey of morbid intro-spections, now catching the exultant thrill of confidence, and presently thrown headlong into some despairing abyss.

ATHERTON. As for the mass of the people, they will be enslaved for ever by such teaching, trying to assure themselves by plenty of sacraments, believing these the causes of grace, and hanging for their spiritual all on the dispensers thereof.

WILLOUGHBY. Then, to apply the result of your question, Gower, to Eckart,—as he has in him nothing servile, and nothing visionary, he resolves to grasp certainty with his own hand—wraps about him relics of the old Greek pallium, and retires to his extreme of majestic isolation.

GOWER. Pity that he could not find the scriptural *Via Media*—that common truth which, while it meets the deepest wants of the individual, yet links him in wholesome fellowship with others—that pure outer light which nurtures and directs the inner.

WILLOUGHBY. No easy way to find in days when Plato was installed high priest, and the whole biblical region a jungle of luxuriant allegoric conceits or thorny scholastic formulas.

GOWER. This daring Eckart reminds me of that heroic leader in Beaumont and Fletcher's *Bonduca.* I think I hear him cry with Caratach,

> Cease your fretful prayers,
> Your whinings, and your tame petitions ;
> The gods love courage armed with confidence,
> And prayers fit to pull them down : weak tears
> And troubled hearts, the dull twins of cold spirits,
> They sit and smile at. Hear how I salute 'em.

LOWESTOFFE. Did you not say yesterday, Atherton, that Eckart's system had received high praise from Hegel ?

ATHERTON. Oh yes, he calls it ' a genuine and profound philosophy.' Indeed the points of resemblance are very striking ;

and, setting aside for the moment some redeeming expressions and the more religious spirit of the man, Eckart's theosophy is a remarkable anticipation of modern German idealism. That abstract ground of Godhead Eckart talks about, answers exactly to Hegel's *Logische Idee.* The Trinity of process, the incarnation ever renewing itself in men, the resolution of redemption almost to a divine self-development, constitute strong features of family likeness between the Dominican and both Hegel and Fichte.[1]

GOWER. One may fancy that while Hegel was teaching at Heidelberg it must have fared with poor Eckart as with the dead huntsman in the Danish ballad, while a usurper was hunting with his hounds over his patrimony,—

> With my dogs so good,
> He hunteth the wild deer in the wood ;
> And with every deer he slays on the mould,
> He wakens me up in the grave so cold.

ATHERTON. Nay, if we come to fancying, let us call in Pythagoras at once, and say that the soul of Eckart transmigrated into Hegel.

GOWER. With all my heart. The Portuguese have a superstition according to which the soul of a man who has died, leaving some duty unfulfilled or promised work unfinished, is frequently known to enter into another person, and dislodging for a time the rightful soul-occupant, impel him unconsciously to complete what was lacking. On a dreamy summer day like this, we can imagine Hegel in like manner possessed by Eckart in order to systematize his half-developed ideas.

WILLOUGHBY. It is certainly very curious to mark the pathway of these pantheistic notions through successive ages. Seriously, I did not know till lately how venerably antique were the discoveries of absolute idealism.

[1] See Note, p. 212.

LOWESTOFFE. I confess that the being one in oneness, the nothing, the soul beyond the soul, the participation in the all-moving Immobility of which Eckart speaks, are to me utterly unintelligible.

GOWER. Do not trouble yourself.   No one will ever be able to get beyond the words themselves, any more than Bardolph could with the phrase which so tickled the ear of Justice Shallow.   'Accommodated ; that is, when a man is, as they say, accommodated : or, when a man is,—being,—whereby,— he may be thought to be accommodated ; which is an excellent thing.'

ATHERTON. Yet, to do Eckart justice, he has his qualifications and his distinctions in virtue of which he imagines himself still within the pale of orthodoxy, and he strongly repudiates the Antinomian consequences to which his doctrines were represented as tending.

GOWER. Ay, it is just in this way that the mischief is done. These distinctions many a follower of his could not or would not understand, and so his high philosophy produced in practice far oftener such men as the Nameless Wild than characters resembling the more pure and lofty ideal he drew himself in his discourse to the good people of Strasburg.   These philosophical edge-tools are full perilous.   Modern Germany is replete with examples of that fatal facility in the common mind for a practical application of philosophic paradox which our friend Adolf lamented at Fegersheim.   When a philosophy which weakens the embankments that keep licence out has once been popularized, the philosopher cannot stop the inundation by shouting from his study-window.   De Wette himself at last became aware of this, and regretted it in vain.   Such speculation resembles the magic sword of Sir Elidure—its mysterious virtue sometimes filled even its owner with a furor that hurried him to an indiscriminate slaughter, but wielded by any other hand its thirst could be satisfied only with the blood of every one around, and at last with the life of him who held it.

LOWESTOFFE. Still there is far more excuse for Eckart than for our nineteenth century pantheists. Even the desperation of some of those poor ignorant creatures, who exaggerated Eckart's paradoxes till they grew a plea for utter lawlessness, is not so unnatural, however lamentable. Who can wonder that some should have overwrought the doctrine of Christ *in* us and neglected that of Christ *for* us, when the *opus operatum* was in its glory, ghostly comfort bought and sold, and Christ our sacrifice pageanted about in the mass, as Milton says,—a fearful idol? Or that the untaught many, catching the first thought of spiritual freedom from some mystic, should have been intoxicated instantly. The laity, forbidden so long to be Christians on their own account, rise up here and there, crying, ' We will be not Christians merely, but so many Christs.' They have been denied what is due to man, they will dreadfully indemnify themselves by seizing what is due to God. Has not the letter been slaying them by inches all their days? The spirit shall give them life !

GOWER. Like the peasant in the apologue ;—religion has been so long doled out to them in a few pitiful drops of holy water, till in their impatience they must have a whole Ganges-flood poured into their grounds, obliterating, with a vengeance, ' all distinctions,' and drowning every logical and social landmark under the cold grey level—the blank neutral-tint of a stoical indifference which annihilates all order and all law.

ATHERTON. By a strange contradiction, Eckart employs Revelation at one moment only to escape it the next—and uses its beacon-lights to steer *from*, not to the haven. He pays homage to its authority, he consults its record, but presently leaves it far behind to lose himself in the unrevealed Godhead

—floats away on his 'sail-broad vans' of speculation through the vast vacuity in search of

——— a dark
Illimitable ocean, without bound,
Without dimension, where length, breadth, and height,
And time and place are lost.

When there, he finds his cloudy seat soon fail him ; he returns once more to the realities of revelation, only to forsake this lower ground again when he has renewed his strength. This oscillation betrays a fatal contradiction. To shut behind us the gate on this inferior world is not necessarily to open the everlasting doors of the upper one.

GOWER. I very much admire the absolute resignation of that devout mendicant described by Eckart. He is a Quietist of the very best sort—his life a 'Thy will be done.' He is a Fénélon in rags.

ATHERTON. After all, make what allowance we will,—giving Eckart all the benefit due from the fact that his life was pure, that he stood in no avowed antagonism to Christian doctrine or institute, that devout men like Tauler and Suso valued his teaching so highly,—still, he stands confessed a pantheist ; no charity can explain that away.

GOWER. I am afraid not. What else can we call him when he identifies himself and all Christian men with the Son, as we have heard, makes himself essential to God, will share with him in the evolution of the Holy Ghost, and, forbidding you to regard yourself as a something distinct from God, exhorts you (if you would be a justified person and child of God indeed) to merge the ground of your own nature in the divine, so that your knowledge of God and his of you are the same thing,— *i.e.*, you and He one and the same ? But can you conjecture, Atherton, by what process he arrived at such a pass ?

ATHERTON. Perhaps in this way :—John Scotus Erigena (with whose writings Eckart could scarcely have failed to make acquaintance at Paris) asserts the identity of Being and Willing, of the *Velle* and the *Esse* in God; also the identity of Being and Knowing. Applying this latter proposition to the relationship between God and man, he comes logically enough to this conclusion,—' Man, essentially considered, may be defined as God's knowledge of him; that is, man reduced to his ultimate —his ground, or simple subsistence—is a divine Thought. But, on the same principle, the thoughts of God are, of course, God. Hence Eckart's doctrine—the ground of your being lies in God. Reduce yourself to that simplicity, that root, and you are in God. There is no longer any distinction between your spirit and the divine,—you have escaped personality and finite limitation. Your particular, creature self, as a something separate and dependent on God, is gone. So also, obviously, your creaturely will. Henceforth, therefore, what seems an inclination of yours is in fact the divine good pleasure. You are free from law. You are above means. The very will to do the will of God is resolved into that will itself. This is the Apathy, the Negation, the Poverty, he commends.

With Eckart personally this self-reduction and deification is connected with a rigorous asceticism and exemplary moral excellence. Yet it is easy to see that it may be a merely intellectual process, consisting in a man's thinking that he is thinking himself away from his personality. He declares the appearance of the Son necessary to enable us to realize our sonship; and yet his language implies that this realization is the perpetual incarnation of that Son—does, as it were, constitute him. Christians are accordingly not less the sons of God by grace than is Christ by nature. Believe yourself divine, and the Son is brought forth in you. The Saviour and the saved are dissolved together in the blank absolute Substance.

WILLOUGHBY. So then, Eckart would say,—' To realize himself, God must have Christians ;' and Hegel,—'To realize him self, He must have philosophers.'

ATHERTON. Miserable inversion ! This result of Eckart's speculation was expressed with the most impious enormity by Angelus Silesius, in the seventeenth century. In virtue of the necessity God is under (according to this theory) of communicating himself, *bon gré, mal gré,* to whomsoever will refine himself down to his '*Nothing*,' he reduces the Almighty to dependence, and changes places with Him upon the eternal throne on the strength of his self-transcending humility !

NOTE TO PAGE 207.

Both Hegel and Eckart regard *Thought* as the point of union between the human nature and the divine. But the former would pronounce both God and man unrevealed, *i.e.,* unconscious of themselves, till Thought has been developed by some Method into a philosophic System. Mysticism brings Eckart nearer to Schelling on this matter than to the dry schoolman Hegel. The charge which Hegel brings against the philosophy of Schelling he might have applied, with a little alteration, to that of Eckart. Hegel says, 'When this knowledge which claims to be essential and ignores apprehension (is *begrifflose*), professes to have sunk the peculiarity of Self in the *Essence,* and so to give forth the utterance of a hallowed and unerring philosophy,* men quite overlook the fact that this so-called wisdom, instead of being yielded up to the influence of Divinity by its contempt of all proportion and definiteness, does really nothing but give full play to accident and to caprice. Such men imagine that by surrendering themselves to the unregulated ferment of the Substance (*Substanz*), by throwing a veil over consciousness, and abandoning the understanding, they become those favourites of Deity to whom he gives wisdom in sleep ; verily, nothing was ever produced by such a process better than mere dreams.'—*Vorrede zur Phænomenologie,* p. 6.

These are true and weighty words : unfortunately Hegel's remedy proves worse than the disease.

We seem to hear Eckart speak when Fichte exclaims, 'Raise thyself to the height of religion, and all veils are removed ; the world and its dead principle passes away from thee, and the very Godhead enters thee anew in its first and original form, as Life, as thine own life which thou shalt and oughtest to live.'—*Anweisung zum sel. Leben,* p. 470.

And again, ' Religion consists in the inward consciousness that God actually lives and acts in us, and fulfils his work.'—*Ibid.* p. 473.

But Eckart would not have affirmed with Fichte (a few pages farther on) that, were Christ to return to the world, he would be indifferent to the recognition or the denial of his work as a Saviour, provided a man were only united to God *somehow !*

---

* Eckart does not make use of his lapse   is simply his religious *ultimatum.*
into the Essence to philosophise withal ; it

CHAPTER III.

With that about I tourned my hedde,
And sawe anone the fifth rout
That to this lady gan lout,
And doune on knees, anone, to fall,
And to her tho besoughten all,
To hiden hir good workes eke,
And said, they yeve not a leke
For no fame, ne soch renoun,
For they for contemplacioun,
And Goddes love had it wrought,
Ne of fame would they nought.

CHAUCER: THE HOUSE OF FAME.

ON the next occasion when our little Summerford circle was ready to hear some more of Arnstein's Chronicle, they were informed by Atherton that four years of the manuscript were missing,—that such intervals were only too frequent,—in fact, the document was little more than a collection of fragments.

'The next entry I find,' said he, 'is in 1324, and the good armourer, in much excitement, begins with an exclamation.

1324. *July. St. Kylian's Day.*—What a day this has been! Strasburg, and all the states which adhere to Louis, are placed under the bann. The bells were ringing merrily at early morning ; now, the Interdict is proclaimed, and every tongue of them is silent. As the news flew round, every workman quitted his work. The busy stalls set out on either side of the streets were left empty. The tools and the wares lay unlooked at and untouched. The bishop and the clergy of his party, and most of the Dominicans, keep out of sight. My men are furious. I have been all day from house to house, and group to group, telling the people to keep a good heart. We shall have a sad time of it, I see. It is so hard for the poor creatures to shake off a fear in which they have been cradled.

The clergy and the monks will pour out of Strasburg, as out of a Sodom, in shoals. A mere handful will stay behind,— not nearly enough to christen those who will be born and to shrive those who will die in this populous city. They may name their price : the greedy of gain may make their fortunes. The miserable poor will die, numbers of them, in horror, unable to purchase absolution. And then, out of the few priests who do remain, scarcely any will have the courage to disobey the pope, and, despite the Interdict, say mass.

'Tis an anxious time for either party. Louis has most of the states on his side, and the common voice, in all the towns of the Rhineland—(in the princely Cologne most of all), is, I hear, loud in his favour. The Minorites will be with him, and all of that sort among the friars, who have little favour to lose with his Holiness. But France is with the Pope against him ; Duke Leopold is a doughty adversary ; John of Bohemia restless and fickle, and no doubt the Pope will set on the Polacks and pagan Lithuanians to waste most horribly all the north and eastern frontiers. Since the victory of Mühldorf, Frederick has lain in prison. That battle is the grievance. The enemies of the Emperor are more full of rancour than ever. Yet, with all the mischief it may bring in the present, what lover of the Father-land can sorrow therefor ? Gallant little Schweppermann, with his lame foot and grey hair, and his glorious two eggs, long may he live to do other such deeds !¹ Louis holds a high spirit

---

¹ Louis was indebted for this important victory to the skill of Schweppermann. After the battle the sole supply of the imperial table was found to consist of a basket of eggs, which the emperor distributed among his officers, saying, ' To each of you one egg—to our gallant Schweppermann two.'— *Menzel.*

at present, and goes about under the bann with a brave heart. But it is only the outset as yet. I much fear me he may lack the staunchness to go through as he has begun. There is store of thunder behind at Avignon. Methinks he hankers, like a child, mainly after the lance and sword and crown of Charlemagne, to dress him out perfectly withal King of the Romans, and seeth not the full bearing of the very war he wages.

We shall not be idle. It is already proposed to send off troops to the aid of Louis. I have half a mind to go myself; but home can ill spare me now, and I render the Emperor more service by such little influence as I have in Strasburg. To-morrow, to consult about the leagues to be formed with neighbouring towns and with the Swiss burghers, to uphold the good cause together.

* * * * * *

1326. *March. St. Gregory's Day.*—Duke Leopold died here yesterday, at the Ochsenstein Palace.[2] After ravaging the suburbs of Spires, he came hither in a raging fever to breathe his last. The bishop told him he must pardon the Landgrave of Lower Alsace from the bottom of his heart. They say he struggled long and wrathfully against the condition, till, finding the bishop firm in refusing absolution on other terms, he gave way. But, just as he was about to receive the host, a fit of vomiting came on, wherein he presently expired, without the sacrament after all.

Frederick has been now at liberty some months. Louis visited him in his prison. To think of their having been together all their boyhood, and loving each other so, to meet thus! Frederick the Handsome, haggard with a three years' imprisonment—his beard down to his waist; and Louis, successful and miserable. They say Frederick cut off his beard at

[2] See Laguille, *Histoire d'Alsace*, liv. xxiii. p. 271.

first, and sent it, by way of memorial, to John of Bohemia, and
that when he went back to his castle he found his young wife
had wept herself blind during his captivity.   He swore on the
holy wafer to renounce his claim to the empire.   The Pope
released him from his oath soon after, but he keeps his word
like knight, not like priest, and holds to it yet.   It is whispered that they have agreed to share the throne.   But that can
never be brought to pass.

Heard to-day, by a merchant, of Hermann.[3]   He is travelling
through Spain.   I miss him much.   Before he left Strasburg
he was full of Eckart's doctrine, out of all measure admiring the
wonderful man, and hoarding every word that dropped from his
lips.   Eckart is now sick at Cologne, among his sorrowing
disciples.   Grieved to hear that the leeches say he hath not
long to live.

A long conversation with Henry of Nördlingen.[4]   He has
journeyed hither, cast down and needy, to ask counsel of Tauler.
Verily he needs counsel, but hath not strength of mind to take
it when given.   Tauler says Henry has many friends among
the excellent of the earth; all love him, and he is full of love,
but sure a pitiful sight to see.   His heart is with us.   He
mourns over the trouble of the time.   He weeps for the poor
folk, living and dying without the sacraments.   But the Interdict crushes his soul.   Now he has all but gathered heart to do
as Tauler doth—preach and labour on, unmoved by all this
uproar, but anon his courage is gone, and he falls back into
his fear again as soon as he is left alone.   He sits and pores over
those letters of spiritual consolation which Margaret Ebner has
written to him.   He says sometimes she alone retains him on

---

[3] Many passages in his *Heiligen-leben* are altogether in the spirit of Eckart, and have their origin, beyond question, in his sayings, or in those of his disciples.—See pp. 114, 225, 150, 187 (*Pfeiffer*), and also the extracts in Wackernagel, *Altd. Leseb.* p. 853.

[4] See Schmidt's Tauler, Appendix, p. 172, &c., where such information as can be obtained concerning Henry of Nördlingen is given.

the earth.　Verily I fear me that, priest as he is, some hopeless earthly love mingles with his friendship for that saintly woman. He has had to flee from his home for refusing to perform ser-vice.　Strasburg, in that case, can be no abiding place for him. I see nothing before him but a wretched wandering, perhaps for years.　I cannot get him to discern the malice of Pope John, rather than the wrath of heaven, in the curse that withers us. I gave him a full account of what the Pope's court at Avignon truly is, as I gathered from a trusty eye-witness, late come from thence, whom I questioned long the other day.[5]　I told him that gold was the one true god there—our German wealth, wrung out from us, and squandered on French courtiers, players, buffoons, and courtezans—Christ sold daily for it—the palace full of cardinals and prelates, grey-haired debauchees and filthy mockers, to a man—accounting chastity a scandal, and the soul's immortality and coming judgment an old wife's fable ;—yea, simony, adultery, murder, incest, so frequent and unashamed, that the Frenchmen themselves do say the Pope's coming hath corrupted them.　I asked him if these were the hands to take up God's instruments of wrath to bruise with them his creatures ? But all in vain.　There is an awfulness in the very name of Pope which blinds reason and strikes manhood down, in him, as in thousands more.

*　　*　　*　　*　　*　　*

A.D. 1332.　*Fourth week after Easter.*—But now awaked from the first sleep I have had for the last three days and nights.　I set down in a word or two what hath happened, then out to action again.　Last Wednesday, at the great festival, the nobles, knights, and senators, with a brave show of fair ladies,

---

[5] Compare Petrarch's account in his letters, cited by Gieseler : ' Mitto stupra, raptus, incestus, adulteria, qui jam pontificalis lasciviæ ludi sunt : mitto raptarum viros, ne mutire audeant, non tantum avitis laribus, sed finibus patriis exturbatos, quæque contumeliarum gravissima est, et violatas conjuges et externo semine gravidas rursus accipere, et post partum reddere ad alternam satietatem abutentium coactos.'

banqueted at the grand house in the Brandgasse.[6]   Within, far
into the night, minstrelsy and dancing; without, the street
blocked up with a crowd of serving men and grooms with
horses, torch-bearers, and lookers-on of all sorts—when, suddenly, the music stopped—they heard shouts and the clash of
swords and shrill screams.   There had been a quarrel between
a Zorn and a Müllenheim—they drew—Von Hunefeld was
killed on the spot, another of the Zorns avenged him by cutting
down Wasselenheim ; the conflict became general, in hall, in
the antechambers, down the great staircase, out on the steps, the
retainers took part on either side, and the fray ended in the
flight of the Zorns, who left six slain in the house and in the
street.   Two were killed on the side of the Müllenheims.   All
who fell were of high rank, and several of either faction are
severely wounded.   They draw off to their quarters, each breath-
ing vengeance, preparing for another conflict at daybreak.   All
the rest of the night the Landvogt and Gotzo von Grosstein
were riding to and fro to pacify them—to no purpose.   Each
party declared they would send for the knights and gentry of
their side from the country round about.   I was with Burckard
Zwinger when we heard this.   'Now,' said I, 'or all is lost.
Off, and harangue the people.   I will get the best of the
burghers together.'   We parted.   All the city was as ˙r.   As
I made my way from house to house, I sent the people I met
off to the market place to hear Zwinger.   I could hear their
shouts, summons enough now, without any other.   When I
got back to the Roland's pillar, I found that his plain, home-
thrust speech had wrought the multitude to what we would, and
no more.   Snatches of it flew from mouth to mouth, like sparks
of fire,—he had struck well while the iron was hot.   'To the
Stadtmeister !' was the cry.   'The keys!   The seal !   The
standard !   We will have our standard.   Let the citizens defend

[6] Laguille gives an account of this revolution, *Hist. d'Alsace*, p. 276.

their own !'   Most of the burghers were of one mind with
Zwinger, and we went in a body (the crowd shouting behind us,
a roaring sea of heads, and the bell on the townhouse ringing
as never before) to demand the keys of young Sieck. He yielded
all with trembling.   By daybreak we had dispersed; the
several corporations repaired armed to their quarters; the gates
were shut; the bridges guarded; the walls manned.   All was
in our hands.   So far safe.   The nobles, knights, and gentry
of the neighbourhood came up in the morning in straggling
groups, approaching the city from various quarters, with as
many of their men as could be hastily gathered, but drew off
again when they saw our posture of defence.   It was truly no
time for them.   This promptitude has saved Strasburg from
being a field of battle in every street for counts and men at
arms, who despise and hate the citizens—whose victory, on
whatever side, would have been assured pillage and rapine,
and, in the end, the loss of our privilege to deal solely for ourselves in our own affairs.   Well done, good Zwinger, thou prince
of bakers, with thy true warm heart, and cool head, and ready
tongue !   To our praise be it said, no deed of violence was
done; there was no blood-thirstiness, no spoiling, but a steady
purpose in the vast crowd that, hap what would, no strangers
should come in to brawl and rob in Strasburg.

While the gates have been closed and the Town Hall guarded,
we have been deliberating on a new senate. ' Four new Stadt-
meisters elected.   Zwinger made Amtmeister.   The magistracy
taken out of the exclusive hands of the great families and open
to the citizens generally, gentlemen, burghers, and artizans, side
by side.   The workmen no longer to be slaves to the caprice of
the gentry.   The nobles are disarmed for a time, to help them
settle their quarrel more quickly.   I go the rounds with the
horse patrol every night.   The gates are never to be opened
except when the great bell has rung to give permission.   We

sit in the Town Hall with our swords.   I took my place there this morning, armed to the teeth, and verily my Margarita seemed proud enough when she sent me forth, with a kiss, to my new dignity, clad in good steel instead of senatorial finery. We have every prospect of peace and prosperousness.   The nobles see our strength, and must relinquish with as good a grace as they may a power they have usurped.   The main part of the old laws will abide as before.   All is perfectly quiet. There has been no mere vengeance or needless rigour.   I hear nothing worse than banishment will be inflicted upon any—that only on a few.   The bishop's claws will be kept shorter.

*   *   *   *   *   *

1338.   *August.   St. Bartholomew's Day.*—Now is the rent between clerk and layman, pope and emperor, wider even than heretofore.   Last month was held the electorial diet at Rhense. The electors, by far the greater part, with Louis ; and their bold doings now apparent.   Yesterday was issued, at Frankfort, a manifesto of the Emperor's, wherein Benedict, he and all his curses, are set at nought, and the mailed glove manfully hurled in his teeth.   Thereby he declares, that whomsoever the electors choose they will have acknowledged rightful emperor, whether the pope bless or bann, and all who gainsay this are traitors ;—that the emperor is not, and will not be, in anywise dependent on the pope.   All good subjects are called on to disregard the Interdict, and such towns or states as obey the same are to forfeit their charters.[7]

It was indeed high time to speak out.   Louis, losing heart, tried negotiation, and made unworthy concessions to the pope, whereon he (impatient, they say, to get back to Italy) would have come to an agreement, but the French cardinals took care to cross and undo all.   The emperor even applied to Philip personally—asking the King of France, forsooth, to suffer him

[7] Schmidt's Tauler, p. 12.

to be king of the Romans—then, finding that vain, is leagued with the English king, and war declared against France. This sounds bravely. Shame on the electors if they hold not to their promise now.

As to our Strasburg, we stand by the emperor, as of old, despite our bishop Berthold, who, with sword instead of crook, has done battle with the partizans of Louis for now some years, gathering help from all parts among the nobles and the gentry, burning villages, besieging and being besieged, spoiling and being spoiled ; moreover, between whiles, thinking to win himself the name of a zealous pastor by issuing decrees against long hair growing on clerks' heads, and enforcing fiercely all the late bulls against the followers of Eckart, the Beghards, and others.[8] Last year he tasted six weeks' imprisonment, having quarrelled with the heads of the chapter. Rudolph von Hohenstein and others of the opposite party, surrounded one night the house of the Provost of Haselach, where he lay, and carried him off in his shirt to the Castle of Vendenti ; and smartly did they make him pay before he came out. We have full authority to declare war against him, if he refuses now to submit to Louis, as I think not likely, seeing how matters go at present. He had the conscience to expect that we magistrates would meddle in his dispute and take his part. Even the senators, who adhere mainly to the Zorn family, were against him, and methinks after all he has done to harass and injure us, we did in a sort return good for evil in being merely lookers-on.

Tauler is away on a visit to Basle, where the state of parties is precisely similar to our own, the citizens there, as in Friburg, joining our league for Louis and for Germany ; and the bishop against them, tooth and nail.[9] My eldest boy (God bless him, he is fifteen this day, and a lad for a father to be proud of) hath accompanied the Doctor thither, having charge of sundry mat-

---

[8] Laguille, liv. xxiv. p. 280.   [9] Schmidt, p. 22.

ters of business for me there.   Had word from him last week.
They have somehow procured a year's remission of the Interdict
for Basle.   He says Suso came to see Tauler, and that they had
long talk together for two days.   Henry of Nördlingen is there
likewise, and now that the pope hath kennelled his barking curse
for a twelvemonth, preaches, to the thronging of the churches,
wherever he goes.

A.D. 1339. *January.*—The new year opens gloomily. Without loss of time, fresh-forged anathemas are come, and coming,
against the outspoken emperor and this troublesome Germany.
Some of the preachers, and the bare-footed friars especially,
have yet remained to say mass and perform the offices ; now,
even these are leaving the city.   Some cloisters have stood for
now two or three years quite empty.   Many churches are deserted altogether, and the doors nailed up.   The magistracy
have issued orders to compel the performance of service.   The
clerks are fairly on the anvil ; the civil hammer batters them
on the one side, and the ecclesiastical upon the other with
alternate strokes.

Bitter wind and sleet this morning.   Saw three Dominicans
creeping back into the town, who had left it a month ago, refusing to say mass.   Poor wretches, how starved and woe-begone
they looked, after miserable wanderings about the country in the
snow, winter showing them scant courtesy, and sure I am the
boors less ; and now coming back to a deserted convent and to
a city where men's faces are towards them as a flint.   Straight,
as I saw them, there came into my mind that goodly exhortation
of Dr. Tauler's, that we should show mercy, as doth God, unto
all, enemies and friends alike, for he that loveth not his brother
whom he hath seen, how can he love God, whom he hath not
seen ?[10]   Ran after them, called them in, thawed them, fed

---

[10] Tauler's *Sermon on the Twenty-
second Sunday after Trinity* contains
an exhortation to Christian love, remarkable for beauty and discrimination.   Tauler's *Predigten*, vol. ii. p.
591 (Berlin, 1841).

them, comforted them with kind words and good ale by the
great fire,—then argued with them. They thought it a cruel
thing that they must starve because pope and emperor are at
feud. 'And is it not,' urged I, 'a crueller that thousands of
innocent poor folk should live without sacrament, never hear a
mass, perhaps die unshriven, for the very same reason? Is not
God's law higher than the pope's,—do to others as ye would
they should do unto you? Could you look for other treatment
at the hands of our magistrates, and expect to be countenanced
and sustained by them in administering the malediction of their
enemies? Thought it most courteous, however, to ply them
more pressingly with food than with arguments.

While they were there, in comes my little Otto, opens his
eyes wide with wonder to see them, and presently breaks out
with the words, now on the tongue of every Strasburger, a
rhyming version of the decree :—

> They shall still their masses sing,
> Or out of the city we'll make them spring.[11]

Told him he should not sing that just then, and, when he was
out of the room, bade them mark by that straw which way the
wind blew.

I record here a vision vouchsafed to that eminent saint the
abbess Christina Ebner, of Engelthal, near Nurnberg. She beheld the Romish Church in the likeness of a great minster, fair
to see, but with doors closed by reason of the bann. Priestly
voices, solemn and sweet, were heard to chant within; and,
without, stood a multitude waiting and hearkening, but no
man dared enter. Then came there to the nun one in the habit
of a preacher, and told her that he would give her words to
speak to comfort the poor folk withal that stood outside,—and
that man was the Lord Christ.

[11] Schmidt, p. 14 :—
> ' do soltent sü ouch fürbas singen
> oder aber us der statt springen.'

And verily, in some sort, so hath God done, having pity upon us, for through all Rhineland hath he moved godly men, both clerks and laity, to draw nearer the one to the other, forming together what we call the association of the *Friends of God*, for the better tending of the inward life in these troublous times, for wrestling with the Almighty on behalf of his suffering Christendom, and for the succour of the poor people, by preaching and counsel and sacrament, that are now as sheep without a shepherd, and perishing for lack of spiritual bread.[12] Tauler is of the foremost among them, and with his brethren, Egenolph of Ehenheim and Dietrich of Colmar, labours without ceasing, having now the wider field and heavier toil, as so few are left in Strasburg who will perform any church service for love or money. Ah ! well might the Abbess Christina say of him that the Spirit of God dwelt within him as a sweet harping. He has travelled much of late, and wherever he goes spreads blessing and consolation ; the people flock to hear him ; the hands of the Friends of God are strengthened ; and a savour of heavenly love and wisdom is left behind. His good name hath journeyed, they say, even beyond the Alps, and into the Low Countries. Neither are there wanting many like-minded, though none equal to him. He found at Cologne Henry of Löwen, Henry, and Franke, and John of Sterngasse,[13] brother Dominicans all of them, preaching constantly, with much of his own fervour, if with a doctrine more like that of Eckart. In Switzerland there is Suso, and I hear much of one Ruysbroek, in the Netherlands, a man younger than Tauler, and a notable master in the divine art of contemplation.

Among the Friends of God are numbers both of men and women of every rank, abbots and farmers, knights and nuns,

[12] Schmidt's Tauler, *Anhang über die Gottesfreunde.*

[13] Passages from two of these mystics, Heinrich von Löwen and Johannes von Sterngasse, are given among the *Sprüche Deutscher Mystiker,* in Wackernagel, p. 890.

monks and artizans. There is Conrad, Abbot of Kaisersheim :
there are the nuns of Unterlinden and Klingenthal, at Colmar
and Basle, as well as the holy sisters of Engelthal ; the knights
of Rheinfeld, Pfaffenheim, and Landsberg ; our rich merchant
here, Rulman Merswin, and one, unworthy of so good a name,
that holds this pen. Our law is that universal love commanded
by Christ, and not to be gainsaid by his vicar. Some have
joined themselves to us for awhile, and gone out from us
because they were not of us ; for we teach no easy road to
heaven for the pleasing of the flesh. Many call us sectaries,
Beghards, brethren of the Free Spirit, or of the New Spirit,
and what not. They might call us by worse names, but we are
none of these. The prophecies of some among us, concerning
judgments to be looked for at the hands of God, and the faithful warnings of others, have made many angry. Yet are not
such things needed, when, as Dr. Tauler saith, the princes and
prelates are, too many of them, worse than Jews and infidels,
and mere horses for the devil's riding.[14] So far from wishing
evil, we mourn as no others over the present woe, and the
Friends of God are, saith Dr. Tauler again, pillars of Christendom, and holders off for awhile of the gathered cloud of wrath.
Beyond all question, if all would be active as they are active
in works of love to their fellows, the face of the times would
brighten presently, and the world come into sunshine.

It was but yesterday that in his sermon Tauler repeated the
saying of one—an eminent Friend of God—' I cannot pass my
neighbour by without wishing for him in my heart more of the
blessedness of heaven than for myself ;'—' and that,' said the
good Doctor, ' I call true love.' Sure I am that such men
stand between the living and the dead.[15]

---

[14] See Tauler's *Predigten*, vol. ii. p.
584 ; and also, concerning the charge
of sectarianism, p. 595 ; and the services of the Friends of God, vol. i.
pred. xxvi. p. 194 ; pred. xi. p. 85.
[15] *Ibid.*, vol. ii. pred. lxvi. p. 594.

1339. *March.*—Much encouraged on hearing Dr. Tauler's sermon on 'Whose is the image and superscription?'[16] It was the last part that gladdened me more especially, when he was enforcing watchfulness and self-examination, and yet showed that the command might be obeyed by men such as I am, in the midst of a worldly calling. Many, said he, complain that they are so busied with outward things as to have no time to look inward. But let such, for every six steps they have to take outward in their daily duty, take one step inward, and observe their hearts, and their business will be to them no stumbling-block. Many are cloistered in body while thought and desire wander to and fro over the earth. But many others do, even amid the noise and stir of the market-place and the shop, keep such watch over their hearts, and set such ward on their senses, that they go unharmed, and their inner peace abides unbroken. Such men are much more truly to be called monks than those who, within a convent wall, have thought and senses so distraught that they can scarce say a single Paternoster with true devotion.

He said that God impressed his image and superscription on our souls when he created us in his image. All true Christians should constantly retire into themselves, and examine throughout their souls wherein this image of the Holy Trinity lieth, and clear away therefrom such images and thoughts as are not of God's impressing,—all that is merely earthly in love and care, all that hath not God purely for its object. It must be in separateness from the world, withdrawn from all trust and

---

[16] The sermon referred to is that on the *Twenty-third Sunday after Trinity,* vol. ii. p. 598.

While he is careful to warn his hearers against the presumption of attempting at once to contemplate Deity apart from its manifestation in the humanity of Christ, he yet seems to admit that when the soul has been thoroughly exercised in the imitation of Christ,—has become conformed, as far as man can be, to his spirit and his sufferings, then there commences a period of repose and joy in which there is an extraordinary intuition of Deity, which approximates to that perfect vision promised hereafter, when we shall see, not 'through a glass darkly,' but face to face. —Vol. ii. p. 609.

satisfaction in what is creaturely, that we present God the image he hath engraven, clear and free from rust. This image and superscription lies in the inmost inmost of the soul, whither God only cometh, and neither men nor angels, and where he delights to dwell. He will share it with no other. He hath said, ' My delight is in the sons of men.' Thus is the inmost of our soul united to the inmost of the very Godhead, where the eternal Father doth ever speak and bring forth his eternal essential Word, his only-begotten Son, equal in honour, power, and worthiness, as saith the Apostle—' He is the brightness of his glory and the express image of his person.' By him hath the Father made all things. As all things have their beginning and source from the Godhead, by the birth of the eternal Word out of the Father, so do all creatures in their essence subsist by the same birth of the Son out of the Father, and therefore shall they all return in the same way to their source, to wit, through the Son to the Father. From this eternal birth of the Son ariseth the love of God the Father to his divine Son, and that of the Son to his divine Father, which love is the Holy Ghost—an eternal and divine Bond, uniting the Father and the Son in everlasting Love. These three are essentially one—one single pure essential unity, as even the heathen philosophers bear witness. Therefore, saith Aristotle, ' There is but one Lord who ordaineth all things.'

He, therefore, that would be truly united to God must dedicate the penny of his soul, with all its faculties, to God alone, and join it unto Him. For if the highest and most glorious Unity, which is God himself, is to be united to the soul, it must be through oneness (*Einigkeit*). Now when the soul hath utterly forsaken itself and all creatures, and made itself free from all manifoldness, then the sole Unity, which is God, answers truly to the oneness of the soul, for then is there nothing in the soul beside God. Therefore between such a soul and God (if a man be so prepared that his soul hangs on nothing but God himself) there is so great a oneness that they become one, as the Apostle saith, 'He that is joined to the Lord is one spirit.'

But there are some who will fly before they have wings, and pluck the apples before they are ripe, and, at the very outset of the Divine life, be so puffed up that it contents them not to enter in at the door and contemplate Christ's humanity, but they will apprehend his highness and incomprehensible Deity only. So did once a priest, and fell grievously, and bitterly mourned his folly, and had to say, 'Ah, most Merciful! had I followed truly the pattern of thy holy humanity, it had not been thus with me!' Beware of such perilous presumption— your safe course is to perfect yourselves first in following the lowly life of Christ, and in earnest study of the shameful cross.

Methinks this is true counsel, and better, for our sort at least, than Master Eckart's exhortation to break through into the essence, and to exchange God made manifest for the absolute and inscrutable Godhead.

1339. *March* 20.—Finished to-day a complete suit of armour for young Franz Müllenheim. The aristocratic families bear the change of government more good-humouredly than I looked for. Their influence is still great, and they can afford to make a virtue of necessity. Most of them now, too, are on the right side.

A great improvement—locking our doors at night.[17] This is the first time I have thought to record it, though the custom has been introduced these nine years. Before, there was not a lock to a house-door in Strasburg, and if you wanted to shut it, on ever so great a need, you had to work with spade and shovel to remove a whole mountain of dirt collected about the threshold. Several new roads, too, made of late by the merchant-league of the Rhineland.

[17] Meiners, *Hist. Vergleichung der Sitten, &c., des Mittelalters,* vol. ii. p. 117.

CHAPTER IV.

If you would be pleased to make acquaintance with a solid theology of the good old sort in the German tongue, get John Tauler's sermons ; for neither in Latin nor in our own language have I ever seen a theology more sound or more in harmony with the Gospel.—LUTHER (*to Spalatin*).

> Die Sehnsucht und der Traüme Weben
> Sie sind der weichen Seele süss,
> Doch edler ist ein starkes Streben
> Und macht den schönen Traum gewiss.[1]
>
> UHLAND.

ON another evening, after Kate had played a plaintive air on the piano as an overture ; when Atherton had praised it as expressive of the upward fluttering struggle of the Psyche of Mysticism, and Gower had quoted Jean Paul's fancy, where he says that sweet sounds are the blue waves that hide the sea-monsters which lurk in the deeps of life—Adolf's journal was continued, as follows :—

1339. *December. St. Barbara's Day.*—Three days ago, at the close of his sermon, Doctor Tauler said he would preach to-day on the highest perfection attainable in this life. Went to hear him. The cloister-chapel crowded long before the time. He began by telling us that he had much to say, and so would not to-day preach from the gospel according to his wont, and moreover would not put much Latin into his sermon, but would make good all he taught with Holy Writ. Then he went on to preach on the necessity of dying utterly to the world and to our own will, and to yield ourselves up, 'dying-wise,' into

---

[1] To long and weave a woof of dreams is sweet unto the feeble soul, but nobler is stout-hearted striving, and makes the dream reality.

the hands of God. He gave further four-and-twenty marks, whereby we may discern who are the true, righteous, illuminated, contemplative men of God.[2]

Observed close under the pulpit a stranger (by his dress, from the Oberland) who did diligently write down, from time to time, what the Doctor said—a man of notable presence, in the prime of life, with large piercing eyes under shaggy brows, eagle nose, thoughtful head—altogether so royal a man as I never before saw. He mingled with the crowd after sermon, and I could not learn who he was. Several others, as curious, and no wiser than myself. This mysterious personage may perhaps be one of the Friends of God, who are numerous in the Oberland. Methought he wished to escape notice. Perhaps he is a Waldensian, and dreads the evil eye of the inquisitor.

1340. *January. Eve of St. Agnes.*—Strange; nothing has been seen of the Doctor for this whole month. His penitents are calling continually at the convent, craving admittance to their confessor, but he will see no one. He is not ill, they say, and takes his part in the convent services with the rest, but never stirs beyond the walls. None of his many friends can tell us what is the matter.

1340. *July. St. Alexius' Day.*—All things much as aforetime, that is, ill enough. Business slack generally, but our hammers going. The worst is this loss of Tauler, our comfort in our trouble. Many reports, no certainty. Some say he has committed some crime, and sits now in the convent prison. This I everywhere contradict. Others will have it that he is gone mad. Many of his former friends are now turned against him, and his enemies make them merry. Went again to the convent to get what news I could. Enquired of the porter why the

---

[2] This sermon is given entire in the second chapter of the *Lebenshistorie des ehrwürdigen Doctors Johann Tauler*, prefixed to his sermons. The succeeding incidents are all related by the same authority. The cellarer only and the family affairs of Adolf, appear to be invented by Atherton.

Doctor had shut himself up. He replied, 'Indeed, sir, and I cannot know.' Methought a wonderful close answer for a porter. Went into the locutory. In the passage the cook ran by me, having just received twenty-five cuffs on the head for leaving the vessels and linen dirty on Saturday night. Much laughter thereat. Several monks in the locutory, among them brother Bernard, the cellarer, an acquaintance of mine—a bustling, shrewd little man, provider of the monastic prog[3] to general satisfaction, talking often of pittances and profound in beeves,—a brave blade, and seen swaggering now and then on holidays with sword at his side, affecting, more than beseems, secular gallantry. Said, when I asked him concerning Tauler, 'Oh, poor fellow, the devil's clawing him a bit, that's all.' Another said, 'We always knew it would be this way.' A third, 'I said so from the first—spiritual pride, Lucifer's sin, Lucifer's sin !' Looked at the rascal's paunch—thought he ran little danger of such sin from any over-mortifying of the flesh. His flesh ought to have mortified *him*, the brazen-face. Spake up for Tauler as I could, but saw that he was the jest of his brethren—having doubtless to bear cruelty and mocking along with some melancholy inward fight of afflictions—and came away home with a heavy heart. Could not get speech with the abbot, who was busy looking to the monks' beds, that they were not too soft.

1342. *New Year's Day.*—Public notice given, that in three days Tauler will preach once more. The news makes great talk. My heart sings jubilate thereat. I look back on two weary years that he has now been hidden from those who so need him. I have confessed to no one the while—somehow, could not to any other—yet I fear me such neglect is a sin. Those like-minded with Tauler have been busy among us in their work of love, but the master-spirit is sorely missed, notwithstanding.

3 Atherton defends this word by the usage of Thomas Fuller.

One Ludolph of Saxony, who was a Dominican, and has come over hither from Cologne lately, to be prior of the new Carthusian convent, has been a great blessing unto us. He speaks out boldly against abuses, and persuades men tenderly to follow Christ carrying the cross.

Bishop Berthold quieter of late; finds it prudent to keep on better terms at present with the emperor.

Little Hans a month old to-day. A household of now five children. Henry of great service to me. Think sometimes of leaving the business with him almost altogether, if only to have him near. Margarita not again ill since the first times of the interdict. A great mercy! Getting richer yet, and tremble sometimes lest it should ensnare my soul, therefore, I disencumber myself at intervals of considerable sums for sick and poor folk. Must bear in mind Tauler's counsel to use and enjoy everything intending God therein. Find my affections go forth much—I hope not too much—towards this last babe. He thrives well; verily, no child could be more unlike the blessed St. Nicholas, of whom I have heard a friar say that, when hanging on his mother's breast, he fasted Wednesdays and Fridays, and could not be brought to suck more than once a day. But if I stay to number up my blessings, I shall have a list longer than the curse-roll of the Pope. God give me an unworldly, thankful, watchful spirit!

1342. *January* 6.—Alas! that I should have to write what now I must! I forced a way into the crowded church—every part filled with people, wedged in below so that they could not move, clustered like bees where they had climbed above into every available place, and a dense mass in the porch besides. The Doctor came, looking woefully ill, changed as I scarce ever saw a man, to live. He mounted the lectorium, held his cap before his eyes, and said:

'O merciful and eternal God, if it be thy will, give me so to

speak that thy divine name may be praised and honoured, and
these men bettered thereby.'

With that he began to weep. We waited, breathless. Still
he wept, and could speak no word, his sobs audible in the
stillness, and the tears making their way through his fingers as
he hid his face in his hands. This continued till the people
grew restless. Longer yet, with more manifest discontent. At
last a voice cried out from among the people (I think it was that
roughspoken Carvel, the butcher), 'Now then, Sir, how long are
we to stop here? It is getting late, if you don't mean to preach,
let us go home.'

I saw that Tauler was struggling to collect himself by prayer,
but his emotion became only the more uncontrollable, and at
last he said, with a broken voice,—

'Dear brethren, I am sorry from my heart to have kept you
so long, but at this time I cannot possibly speak to you. Pray
God for me that he would help me, and I may do better at
another time.'

So we went away, and the report thereof was presently all
over Strasburg. The snowball had plenty of hands to roll it,
and lost nothing by the way. The people, numbers of them,
seemed to me with a wicked glee to delight in showing how the
learned Doctor had made a fool of himself. Those who had
counted him mad before reckoned themselves now little short
of prophets. Many such whom I met in the streets looked and
spoke with such a hateful triumph of the matter as well nigh
put me beside myself. Not so long ago, no one could satisfy
them but Tauler; not the name of the most popular of saints
oftener on their lips; the very ground he trod on was blessed;
a kindly word from his lips food for days—and now the hands
stretched out almost in adoration, throw mire on the fallen idol,
and not a 'prentice lad behind his stall but hugs himself in his
superior sanity. Had he been a hunter after popularity, what

a judgment !   Verily that man has the folly of a thousand fools who lives for the applause of the multitude.   But I know how Tauler's heart bled for them.

Friar Bernard came over this evening.   He says the superiors are wroth beyond measure with Tauler for the scandal he has brought upon the order, and will forbid him to preach more.   Entertained my jovial gauger of monks' bellies with the best cheer I had—he has a good heart after all, and is unfeignedly sorry for Tauler's disgrace.   Says he thinks the Doctor has fasted and done penance beyond his strength, that the sudden coming out from his cell to preach to such numbers was too much for his weakness,—that he will get over it and be himself again, and much more,—to the hope whereof he pledged me in another glass, and left me not a little comforted.

1342. *January. St. Vincent's Day.*—Saw Bernard again, who gives me the good news that Dr. Tauler obtained permission from the prior to deliver a Latin address in the school, and did acquit himself to such admiration, that he is to be allowed to preach in public when he will.

1342. *January* 23.—Tauler preached to-day in the chapel of the nunnery of St. Agatha, on 'Behold the bridegroom cometh; go ye out to meet him.'   A wondrous discourse—a torrent that seems to make me dizzy yet.   As he was describing, more like an angel than a man, the joy of the bride at the approach of the bridegroom, a man cried out, 'It is true !' and fell senseless on the floor.   As they were about him to bring him to himself, a woman among them shrieked, 'Oh, stop, sir, stop ! or he will die in our arms !'   Whereat he said calmly, and with his face lighted up as though he saw the heavens opened, 'Ah, dear children, and if the bridegroom will call home the bride, shall we not willingly suffer him ?   But nevertheless I will make an end.'   Then after sermon he read mass again, and, as I came out, I saw the people gathered about several persons in the court who lay on the ground, as though dead, such had been the power of his words.

1342. *February. St. Blasius' Day.*—Now Tauler is continually preaching, not only in the church of his convent, but in those of various monasteries and nunneries, in the Beguinasia, and in the cells wherein little companies of pious women have gathered themselves together to hide from the dangers of the world. He never cited so much Latin as some, now less than heretofore. More alive than ever, it would seem, to our wants, he addresses himself mightily to heart and conscience, which he can bind up or smite at will. His love and care, for the laity most of all, is a marvel ; he lives for us, and yet appears to hold himself no greater than the least. Before, there was none like him, now we feel that in heavenliness of nature he has gone beyond his former self. So earnestly does he exhort to active love to man, as well as to perfect resignation to God, that already a new spirit seems to pervade many, and they begin to care for others, as he tells us the first Christians did. He tells them mere prayers, and mass, and alms, and penance, will help them nothing unless the Holy Spirit breathes life into them. He says the priests are not of necessity better men because they oftener taste the Lord's body, that outward things such as those profit nothing alone, and that those who love their fellows most are the truest instructors, and teach more wisely than all the schools.

1344. *March.*—Tauler hath of late, besides preaching constantly as ever, begun to send forth from time to time sundry small books, full of consolation and godly counsel for these days. Copies of them are fast multiplied, and people gather to hear them read at each other's houses. This is a new thing, and works powerfully,

The greatest stir has been made by two letters issued by Tauler, Ludolph the Carthusian, and others, and sent out, not

only through Strasburg, but all the region round about.[4]   The
bishop is very angry thereat ; though, before, he had come
several times to hear Tauler, and had professed no small admiration of him.   One of these letters is to comfort the people,
and exhorts all priests to administer the sacraments to all who
shall desire, the bann notwithstanding.   ' For,' it saith, ' ye are
bound to visit and console the sick, remembering the bitter pain
and death of Christ, who hath made satisfaction, not for your
sins only, but also for those of the whole world, who doth represent us all before God, so that if one falleth innocently under
the bann, no Pope can shut him out of heaven.   Ye should,
therefore, give absolution to such as wish therefor—giving heed
rather to the bidding of Christ and his Apostles than to the
bann, which is issued only out of malice and avarice.'

Thus truly have these good men done, and many with them,
so that numbers have died in peace, fearing the bann not a
whit, whereas before, many thousands, unshriven, gave up the
ghost in the horrors of despair.

The other letter is addressed to the learned and great ones
among the clergy.   It saith that there are two swords—a
spiritual, which is God's word, and the temporal, the secular
power :—that these two are to be kept distinct ; both are from
God, and ought not to be contrary the one to the other.   The
spiritual power should fulfil its proper duty and uphold the
temporal, while that again should protect the good and be a
terror to evil-doers.   If temporal princes sin, such as are spiritual
should exhort them, in love and humility, to amend their ways.
It is against the law of Christ that the shepherds, when one of
these falls beneath their displeasure, should for that reason presume to damn a whole country, with all its cities, towns, and

---

[4] These letters are preserved in substance in Specklin's *Collectanea,* and
are inserted, from that source, in the
introduction by Görres to Diepenbrock's edition of Suso's works ; pp.
xxxv. &c.

villages, where dwell the poor innocent folk who are no partakers in the sin.   It cannot be proved from Scripture that all
those who will not kiss the Pope's foot, or receive a certain
article of faith, or who hold by an emperor duly elected and
well fulfilling his office, and do him service as set over them by
God, do therein sin against the Church and are heretics.   God
will not demand of vassals an account of the sins of their
lords, and neither should subjects, bound to obey the emperor
as the highest temporal power, be given over to damnation as
though answerable for the faults of their rulers.   Therefore all
who hold the true Christian faith, and sin only against the
person of the Pope, are no heretics.   Those, rather, are real
heretics who obstinately refuse to repent and forsake their sins;
for let a man have been what he may, if he will so do, he
cannot be cast out of the Church.   Through Christ, the truly
penitent thief, murderer, traitor, adulterer, all may have forgiveness.   Such as God beholdeth under an unrighteous bann,
he will turn for them the curse into a blessing.   Christ himself
did not resist the temporal power, but said, My kingdom is not
of this world.   Our souls belong unto God, our body and goods
to Cæsar.   If the emperor sins, he must give account to God
therefor—not to a poor mortal man.

CHAPTER V.

The meanes, therefore, which unto us is lent
Him to behold, is on his workes to looke,
Which he hath made in beautie excellent,
And in the same, as in a brasen booke,
To read enregistred in every nooke
His goodnesse, which his beautie doth declare ;
For all that's good is beautifull and faire.

Thence gathering plumes of perfect speculation,
To impe the wings of thy high-flying mynd,
Mount up aloft through heavenly contemplation,
From this darke world, whose damps the soule do blynd,
And, like the native brood of eagles kynd,
On that bright Sunne of Glorie fixe thine eyes,
Cleared from grosse mists of fraile infirmities.

SPENSER : HYMNE OF HEAVENLY BEAUTIE.

WILLOUGHBY. I did not think Atherton had so much artifice in him. He broke off his last reading from Arnstein's Chronicle with a mystery unexplained, quite in the most approved *feuilleton* style.

GOWER. You have excited the curiosity of the ladies most painfully, I assure you. I believe I am empowered to say that they cannot listen to any more of the armourer's journal until you have accounted for Tauler's singular disappearance.

KATE. One word for us and two for yourself, Mr. Gower.

ATHERTON. Ungrateful public ! You all know I haven't a particle of invention in my nature. It is just because I am not a novelist that I have not been able to explain everything. Arnstein is, like me, a matter-of-fact personage, and could not be in two places at once.

However, to relieve you, I am ready to acknowledge that I am in possession of information about these incidents quite independent of the irregular entries in his record. There is no secret; it is all matter of sober history. The facts are these—

One day there came a stranger to Tauler, desiring to confess to him. It was the remarkable man who had so attracted the attention of Adolf in the church. He was called Nicholas of Basle, and was well known in the Oberland as an eminent 'Friend of God.' He was one of those men so characteristic of that period—a layman exercising a wider spiritual influence than many a bishop. He was perhaps a Waldensian, holding the opinions of that sect, with a considerable infusion of visionary mysticism. The Waldenses, and the Friends of God, were drawn nearer to each other by opposition, and the disorders of the time, as well as by the more liberal opinions they held in common, and it is not always easy to distinguish them.

After confession, the layman requested, much to the Doctor's surprise, that he would preach a sermon on the highest spiritual attainment a man may reach in time. Tauler yielded at length to his importunity, and fulfilled his promise. Nicholas brought his notes of the sermon to Tauler, and in the course of their conversation, disclosed the object of his visit. He had travelled those thirty miles, he said, not merely to listen to the doctor, of whom he had heard so much, but, by God's help, to give him some counsel that should do him good. He told him plainly that the sermon, though excellent in its way, could teach him nothing—the Great Teacher could impart to him more knowledge in an hour than Tauler and all his brethren, preaching till the day of doom. Tauler was first astonished, then indignant, to hear a mere layman address him in such language. Nicholas appealed to that very anger as a proof that the self-confidence of the Pharisee was not yet cleansed away, that the preacher trusted with unbecoming pride in his mastership and great learning.

You must remember the vast distance which at that day

separated the clerk from the layman, to give to the candour and humility of Tauler its due value. The truth flashed across his mind. Deeply affected, he embraced the layman, saying, 'Thou hast been the first to tell me of my fault. Stay with me here. Henceforth I will live after thy counsel ; thou shalt be my spiritual father, and I thy sinful son.'

Nicholas acceded to his request, and gave him, to begin with, a kind of spiritual A B C,—a list of moral rules, commencing in succession with the letters of the alphabet, which he was to commit to memory and to practise, together with sundry bodily austerities, for five weeks, in honour of the five wounds of Christ. But the discipline which followed was yet more severe. Tauler was directed to abstain from hearing confession, from study and from preaching, and to shut himself up in his cell, that, in solitary contemplation of the sufferings and death of Christ, he might attain true humility and complete renewal. The anticipated consequences ensued. His friends and penitents forsook him ; he became the by-word of the cloister ; his painful penances brought on a lingering sickness. Borne down by mental and bodily sufferings together, he applied to his friend for relief. The layman told him that he was going on well—it would be better with him ere long—he might remit his severer self-inflictions, and should recruit the body by a more generous diet.

Nicholas was now called away by important business, he said, and Tauler was left to himself. His parting advice to his spiritual scholar was, that if he came to want, he should pawn his books, but sell them on no account, for the day would come when he would need them once more.

Tauler continued in this trying seclusion for nearly two years, contemned by the world without as one beside himself, oppressed within by distress of mind and feebleness of body. It had been forbidden him to desire, even when thus brought low, any special communication from God that might gladden him with rapture or consolation. Such a request would spring from self and pride. He was there to learn an utter self-abandonment—to submit himself without will or choice to the good pleasure of God—to be tried with this or any other affliction, if need were, till the judgment day.

Now it came to pass, when he had become so ill that he could not attend mass or take his place in the choir as he had been wont, that, as he lay on his sickbed, he meditated once more on the sufferings and love of our Lord and Saviour, and thought on his own life, what a poor thing it had been, and how ungrateful. With that he fell into a marvellous great sorrow, says the history, for all his lost time and all his sins, and spake, with heart and mouth, these words :—

'O merciful God, have mercy upon me, a poor sinner ; have mercy in thine infinite compassion, for I am not worthy to live on the face of the earth.'

Then as he sat up waking in his sickness and sorrow, he heard a voice saying, 'Stand fast in thy peace, trust God, remember that he was once on the earth in human nature, healing sick bodies and sick souls.' When he heard these words he fell back fainting, and knew no more. On coming to himself, he found that both his inward and outward powers had received new life. Much that had before been strange now seemed clear. He sent for his friend, who heard with joy what he had to tell.

'Now,' said Nicholas, 'thou hast been for the first time moved by the Highest, and art a partaker of the grace of God, and knowest that though the letter killeth, the Spirit giveth life. Now wilt thou understand the Scripture as never before —perceive its harmony and preciousness, and be well able to show thy fellow Christians the way to eternal life. Now one of thy sermons will bring more fruit than a hundred aforetime,

coming, as it will, from a simple, humbled, loving heart; and
much as the people have set thee at nought, they will now far
more love and prize thee.　But a man with treasure must
guard against the thieves.　See to it that thou hold fast thy
humility, by which thou wilt best keep thy riches.　Now thou
needest my teaching no longer, having found the right Master,
whose instrument I am, and who sent me hither.　Now, in all
godly love, thou shalt teach me in turn.'

Tauler had pledged his books for thirty gulden.　The layman
went immediately and redeemed them at his own cost, and by
his advice Tauler caused it to be announced that in three days
he would preach once more.　You have already heard how our
good friend Adolf records the unhappy result of this first attempt.　Tauler went with his trouble to Nicholas, who comforted him by the assurance that such farther trial was but a
sign of the careful love which carried on the work within.
There must have been some remnant of self-seeking which was
still to be purged away.　He advised him to wait awhile, and
then apply for permission to deliver a Latin address to the
brethren in the school.　This he at last received, and a better
sermon they never heard.　So the next preacher, at the close of
his discourse, made the following announcement to the congre-
gation : 'I am requested to give notice that Doctor Tauler will
preach here to-morrow.　If he succeeds no better than before,
the blame must rest with himself.　But this I can say, that he
has read us in the school a prelection such as we have not heard
for many a day; how he will acquit himself now, I know not,
God knoweth.'

Then followed the overpowering discourse, of whose effects
you have heard ; and from this time forward commenced a new
æra in Tauler's public life.　For full eight years he laboured
unremittingly, with an earnestness and a practical effect far sur-
passing his former efforts, and in such esteem with all classes

that his fellow-citizens would seem to have thought no step should be taken in spiritual matters, scarcely in temporal, without first seeking counsel of Tauler.

LOWESTOFFE. A most singular story. But how have all these minute circumstances come down to us?

ATHERTON. When Tauler was on his death-bed he sent for Nicholas, and gave him a manuscript, in which he had written down their conversations, with some account of his own life and God's dealings towards him, His unworthy servant, requesting him to make thereof a little book. The layman promised to do so. ' But see to it,' continued the Doctor, ' that you can conceal our names. You can easily write 'The Man and the Doctor'—for the life and words and works which God hath wrought through me, an unworthy, sinful man, are not mine, but belong unto Almighty God for ever. So let it be, for the edifying of our fellow men; but take the writing with thee into thy country, and let no man see it while I live.' This narrative has been preserved, and there is no difficulty in discerning in the Doctor and the man, Tauler and Nicholas of Basle.[1]

You will now let me resume my reading, I suppose.

Chronicle of Adolf Arnstein, continued.

1344. *Eve of St. Dionysius.*—I here set down passages from sermons I have at sundry times heard Doctor Tauler preach. I have made it my wont to go straight home as soon as the service has been ended, and write what I could best remember. The goodly sayings which follow are copied from those imperfect

---

[1] The substance of the foregoing narrative concerning Tauler and the laymen will be found in the *Lebenshistorie des ehrwürdigen Doctors Joh. Tauler.* See also C. Schmidt's account of Nicholas in his monograph on Tauler (p. 28), and a characteristic letter by Nicholas concerning visions of coming judgment given in the Appendix.

records, and placed here for my edification and that of my children and others after me.

From a sermon on Christ's teaching the multitude out of the ship.—The soul of the believing man, wherein Christ is, doth find its representation in that ship.   Speaking of the perpetual peace such souls may have, despite what storm and commotion soever, he added (not a little to my comfort) : ' But some of you have not felt all this ; be not ye dismayed.   There are poor fishers as well as rich ; yea, more poor than rich.   Hold this as unchangeably sure, that the trials and struggle of no man are of small account.   If a man be but in right earnest, longeth to be a true lover of God, and perseveres therein, and loves those he knows or deems to be such,—doth heartily address himself to live fairly after Job's pattern, and intend God unfeignedly in his doing or not doing, such a man will assuredly enter into God's peace, though he should tarry for it till his dying day.   Even those true friends and lovers of God who enjoy so glorious a peace have disquiet and trouble of their own in that they cannot be towards their faithful God all they would, and in that even what God giveth is less large than their desires.'

' In the highest stage of divine comfort is that peace which is said to pass all understanding.   When that noblest part of the soul to which no name can be given is completely turned to God and set on Him, it takes with it all those faculties in man to which we can give names.   This conversion involves both that in God which is Nameless and that in the consciousness of man which can be named.   These are they whom St. Dionysius calls godly-minded men.   As Paul saith, ' That ye may be rooted and grounded in love ; and understand with all saints what is the breadth, and length, and height, and depth.'   For the height and depth which are revealed in such men can be apprehended by no human sense or reason ; they reach beyond all sense out into a deep abyss.   This great good, light, and comfort, is inwardly revealed only to those who are outwardly sanctified and inwardly illuminated, and who know how to dwell inwardly within themselves.   To such, heaven and earth and all creatures are as an absolute Nothing, for they themselves are a heaven of God, inasmuch as God dwelleth and rests in them.'

'God draweth these men in such wise into Himself, that they become altogether pleasing unto Him, and all that is in them becomes, in a super-essential way, so pervaded and trans-formed, that God himself doeth and worketh all their works. Wherefore, clearly, such persons are called with right—Godlike (*Gottformige*).   For if we could see such minds as they truly are, they would appear to us like God, being so, however, not by nature, but by grace.   For God lives, forms, ordaineth, and doeth in them all his works, and doth use Himself in them.'

' It fares with such men as with Peter, when, at the miracu-lous draught of fishes, he exclaimed, ' Depart from me, for I am a sinful man, O Lord !'   See ! he can find no words, no way of utterance, for that within.   So is it, I say, with such men— they find themselves empty of fit words and works.   And that is the first mode.   The other is that they fall utterly into their own groundless Nothing (*in ihr grundloses Nichts*), and become so small and utterly nothing in God as quite to forget all gifts they have received before, and do, as it were, pour themselves back again absolutely into God (whose they properly are) as though such bestowments had never been theirs.   Yea, they are withal as barely nothing as though they had never been.   So sinks the created Nothing in the Uncreated, incomprehensibly, unspeakably.   Herein is true what is said in the Psalter, ' Deep calleth unto deep.'   For the uncreated Deep calls the created, and these two deeps become entirely one.   Then hath the created spirit lost itself in the spirit of God, yea, is drowned in

the bottomless sea of Godhead.   But how well it is with such
a man passeth all understanding to comprehend.   Such a man
becomes, thirdly, essential, virtuous, godly ; in his walk, loving
and kindly, condescending and friendly towards all men, so that
no man can detect in him any fault or transgression, any vice or
crime.   Moreover, he is believing and trustful towards all men,
hath mercy and sympathy for every man without distinction;
is not austere and stern, but friendly, gentle, and good, and it is
not possible that such men should ever be separated from God.
Unto such perfectness may all we be graciously helped of God
our Saviour, unto whom be praise for ever.   Amen.' [2]

'The ground or centre of the soul is so high and glorious a
thing, that it cannot properly be named, even as no adequate
name can be found for the Infinite and Almighty God.   In this
ground lies the image of the Holy Trinity.   Its kindred and
likeness with God is such as no tongue can utter.   Could a
man perceive and realize how God dwelleth in this ground, such
knowledge would be straightway the blessedness of salvation.
The apostle saith, 'be renewed in the spirit of your mind
(*Gemüthes*).'   When the mind is rightly directed, it tendeth
towards this ground whose image is far beyond its powers.   In
this mind we are to be renewed, by a perpetual bringing of ourselves into this ground, truly loving and intending God immediately.   This is not impossible for the mind itself, though our
inferior powers are unequal to such unceasing union with God.
This renewal must take place also in the spirit.   For God is a
spirit, and our created spirit must be united to and lost in the
uncreated, even as it existed in God before its creation.   Every
moment in which the soul so re-enters into God, a complete
restoration takes place.   If it be done a thousand times in a
day, there is, each time, a true regeneration : as the Psalmist
saith,—'This day have I begotten thee.'   This is when the

---

[2] See Note, p. 254.

inmost of the spirit is sunk and dissolved in the inmost of the Divine Nature, and thus new-made and transformed. God pours Himself out thus into our spirit, as the sun rays forth its natural light into the air, and fills it with sunshine, so that no eye can tell the difference between the sunshine and the air. If the union of the sun and air cannot be distinguished, how far less this divine union of the created and the uncreated Spirit! Our spirit is received and utterly swallowed up in the abyss which is its source. Then the spirit transcends itself and all its powers, and mounts higher and higher towards the Divine Dark, even as an eagle towards the sun.'

'Yet let no man in his littleness and nothingness think of himself to approach that surpassing darkness,—rather let him draw nigh to the darkness of his ignorance of God, let him simply yield himself to God, ask nothing, desire nothing, love and mean only God, yea, and such an unknown God. Let him lovingly cast all his thoughts and cares, and his sins too, as it were, on that unknown Will. Beyond this unknown will of God he must desire and purpose nothing, neither way, nor rest, nor work, neither this nor that, but wholly subject and offer himself up to this unknown will. Moreover, if a man, while busy in this lofty inward work, were called by some duty in the Providence of God to cease therefrom and cook a broth for some sick person, or any other such service, he should do so willingly and with great joy. This I say that if it happened to me that I had to forsake such work and go out to preach or aught else, I should go cheerfully, believing not only that God would be with me, but that He would vouchsafe me it may be even greater grace and blessing in that external work undertaken out of true love in the service of my neighbour than I should perhaps receive in my season of loftiest contemplation.'

'The truly enlightened man—alas! that they should be so few—scarce two or three among a thousand—sinks himself the deeper in his Ground the more he recognises his honour and his blessedness, and of all his gifts ascribes not even the least unto himself. Our righteousness and holiness, as the prophet saith, is but filthiness.   Therefore must we build, not on our righteousness, but on the righteousness of God, and trust, not in our own words, works, or ways, but alone in God.   May this God give us all power and grace to lose ourselves wholly in Him, that we may be renewed in truth, and found to His praise and glory.   Amen.'[3]

Speaking of the publican in the temple, he put up a prayer that God would give him such an insight as that man had into his own Nothing and unworthiness ;—'That,' said he, 'is the highest and most profitable path a man can tread. For that way brings God continually and immediately into man. Where God appears in His mercy, there is He manifest also with all His nature—with Himself.'[4]

I understand the Doctor as teaching three states or conditions wherein man may stand ; that of nature, by the unaided light of reason, which in its inmost tends Godward, did not the flesh hinder ; that of grace ; and a higher stage yet, above grace, where means and medium are as it were superseded, and God works immediately within the transformed soul. For what God doeth that He is. Yet that in this higher state, as in the second, man hath no merit ; he is nothing and God all. In the course of this same sermon he described humility as indispensable to such perfectness, since the loftiest trees send their roots down deepest. He said that we should not distress ourselves if we had not detailed to our confessor all the short-coming and sin of our hearts, but confess to God and ask His mercy. No ecclesiastical absolution can help us unless we are contrite for our sin before God. We are not to keep away from the Lord's body because we feel so deeply our unworthiness to partake of

[3] See first Note, p. 256.   [4] *Serm. on Eleventh Sun. after Trinity,* ii. p. 436.

the sacrament, seeing that they who are whole need not a physician, but they that are sick.[5]

'There are some who can talk much and eloquently of the incarnation and bitter sufferings of Christ, who do with tears apostrophise him from head to foot as they present him to their imagination. Yet is there often in this more of sense and self-pleasing than of true love to God. They look more to the means than to the end. For my part, I would rather there were less of such excitement and transport, less of mere sweet emotion, so that a man were diligent and right manful in working and in virtue, for in such exercise do we learn best to know ourselves. These raptures are not the highest order of devotion, though would that many a dull heart had more of such sensibility! There are, as St. Bernard hath said, three kinds of love, the sweet, the wise, and the strong. The first is as a gilded image of wood, the second as a gilded image of silver, the third an image of pure gold. One to whom God hath vouchsafed such sweetness should receive it with lowliness and thankfulness, discerning therein his weakness and imperfection, in that God has to allure and entice him as a little child. He should not rest at this point, but press on, through images, above all image and figure; through the outward exercise of the senses to the inward ground of his soul, where properly the kingdom of God is. There are many altogether at home amid sensuous imagery, and having great joy therein, whose inner ground is as fast shut to them as a mountain of iron through which there is no way.'

'Dionysius writeth how God doth far and superessentially surpass all images, modes, forms, or names that can be applied to Him. The true fulness of divine enlightenment is known herein that it is an essential illumination, not taking place by

[5] *Serm. on Eleventh Sun. after Trin.* ii. pp. 442, 443. Also, *Predigten,* vol. iii. p. 19, and *Schmidt,* p. 125.

means of images or in the powers of the soul, but rather in the ground itself of the soul, when a man is utterly sunk in his own Nothing.   This I say against the 'free spirits,' who persuade themselves that by means of certain appearances and glances of revelation they have discerned the truth, and please themselves with their own exaltation, knowledge, and wisdom ; going about in a false emptiness (*Ledigkeit*) of their own ; and speaking to others as though they were not yet advanced beyond the use of forms and images ; bringing, with their frivolous presumption, no small dishonour upon God.   But know ye, Christians beloved, that no truly pious and God-fearing man gives himself out as having risen above all things, for things in themselves utterly insignificant and mean are yet, in the truth, right and good ; and though any one may be in reality elevated above such lesser matters, yet doth he love and honour them not less than heretofore ; for the truly pious account themselves less than all things, and boast not that they have surpassed or are lifted above them.'[6]

' O, dear child, in the midst of all these enmities and dangers, sink thou into thy ground and thy Nothingness, and let the tower with all its bells fall on thee, yea, let all the devils in hell storm out upon thee, let heaven and earth with all their creatures assail thee, all shall but marvellously serve thee—sink thou only into thy Nothingness, and the better part is thine !'[7]

' Yet some will ask what remains after a man hath thus lost himself in God?   I answer, nothing but a fathomless annihilation of himself, an absolute ignoring of all reference to himself personally, of all aims of his own in will and heart, in way, in purpose, or in use.   For in this self-loss man sinks so deep into the ground that if he could, out of pure love and lowliness, sink himself deeper yet, and become absolutely nothing, he

---

[6] *Third Serm. on Thirteenth Sun. after Trin.*, ii. pp. 474-478.

[7] *First Serm. on Thirteenth Sun. after Trin.*, ii. p. 459.

would do so right gladly. For such a self-annihilation hath
been brought to pass within him that he thinketh himself unworthy to be a man, unfit to enter God's house and temple, and
to look upon a crucifix painted on the wall ; yea, such a man
deemeth himself not so good by far as the very worst. Nevertheless, as far as regards the sufferings and death of the Lord
—the birth and incarnation of the Son of God—His holy and
perfect life that He lived on earth among sinful men, all this
such a man did never before so heartily and strongly love as
now he doth ; yea, now his care is how he may order his life
right Christianly, and fashion it anew, and out of fervent love
toward his Lord and Saviour, exercise himself without ceasing
in all good work and virtue.'[8]

' There are those who thoughtlessly maim and torture their
miserable flesh, and yet leave untouched the inclinations which
are the root of evil in their hearts. Ah, my friend, what hath
thy poor body done to thee, that thou shouldst so torment it?
Oh folly ! mortify and slay thy sins, not thine own flesh and
blood.'[9]

WILLOUGHBY. My dear Atherton, this is grand doctrine.
May I never be farther from the kingdom of heaven than such
a mystic. Surely Luther's praise is just. Compare such theology as this with the common creed and practice of that day.
The faults are nearly all those of the time—the excellence
his own.

ATHERTON. It is wonderful to see how little harm his Platonism can do to a man so profoundly reverent, so fervent in
his love to Christ. How often he seems to tread the verge of
Eckart's pantheistic abyss, but never falls into it! His heart is
true ; he walks uprightly, and so, surely. That conception of
sin as selfishness—that doctrine of self-abandonment, death in

---

[8] See second Note, p. 256.   [9] *Twenty-first Sun. after Trin.*, ii. p. 584,

ourselves and life in God—these are convictions with him so
deep and blessed—so far beyond all Greek philosophy—so fatal
to the intellectual arrogance of pantheism, that they bear him
safe through every peril.

GOWER. His sermons cannot fail to do one good—read with
the heart and imagination. But if you coldly criticise, and can
make no allowance for the allegories and metaphors and vehement language of the mystic, you may shut the book at once.

ATHERTON. And shut out blessing from your soul. It is
not difficult to see, however, where Tauler's danger lies. There
is an excess of negation in his divinity. He will ignore, deny,
annihilate almost everything you can name,—bid you be know-
ledgeless, desireless, motionless,—will enjoin submission to the
unknown God (when it is our triumph in Christ that we submit
to the Revealed and Known)—and, in short, leaves scarcely
anything positive save the mysterious lapse of the soul's
Ground, or Spark, into the Perfect, the Essential One. He
seems sometimes to make our very personality a sin, as though
the limitations of our finite being were an element in our guilt.
The separation of a particular faculty or higher power of the
soul which unites with God, while the inferior powers are either
absorbed or occupied in the lower sphere, this is the great
metaphysical mistake which lies at the root of so many forms
of mysticism. With Tauler the work of grace consists too much
of extremes—it dehumanizes in order to deify.

WILLOUGHBY. But that, remember, is no fault of Tauler's
especially. He does but follow here the ascetic, superhuman
aspiration of a Church which, trying to raise some above
humanity, sinks myriads below it.

ATHERTON. Granted. That error does not lessen my love
and admiration for the man.

GOWER. Your extracts show, too, that the Nothingness
towards which he calls men to strive is no indolent Quietism,

nor, as with Eckart, a kind of metaphysical postulate, but in fact a profound spiritual self-abasement and the daily working out of a self-sacrificing Christ-like character.

ATHERTON. Blessed are his contradictions and inconsistencies! Logic cannot always reconcile Tauler with himself—our hearts do.[10]

WILLOUGHBY. Never surely was a theory so negative combined with an action more fervently intense—a positiveness more benign.

GOWER. In his life we understand him,—that is at once the explanation and vindication of what his mysticism means.

ATHERTON. Few, however, of his fellow-mystics rose, so far as Tauler, above the peculiar dangers of mysticism. Even the good layman, Nicholas of Basle, was a man of vision, and assumed a kind of prophecy. Tauler and the *Theologia Germanica* stand almost alone in rejecting the sensuous element of mysticism—its apparitions, its voices, its celestial phantasmagoria. With many of his friends mysticism became secluded, effeminate, visionary, because uncorrected, as in his case, by benevolent action, by devoted conflict against priestly wrong.

KATE. Tauler, then, was a Protestant in spirit—a genuine forerunner of the Reformation?

ATHERTON. Unquestionably.

MRS. ATHERTON. But what could the common people make of this high ideal he sets before them? Could they be brought heartily to care about that kind of ultra-human perfectness? Beautiful it must have been to hear this eloquent man describe the divine passion of the soul, how—

Love took up the harp of life and smote on all the chords with might,
Smote the chord of Self, that, trembling, passed in music out of sight,

—but bewildering, rather?

[10] See Note, p. 257.

ATHERTON. I am afraid so. Yet there was much they evidently did understand and relish.

GOWER. In fact the Reformers were wanted, with their Bible, with their simpler, homelier teaching—so much less ascetic, so much more human—and with their written word, interpreted more soundly; coming, not to extinguish that inner light, but to enclose, as in a glass, the precious flame, otherwise fitfully blown about by the gusts of circumstance and feeling.

WILLOUGHBY. But none the less let us praise the man who lived so nobly by the light he had—who made human works as nothing, that God might be all—who took the heavenly kingdom from the hands of the priest, and proclaimed it in the heart of every spiritual worshipper.

GOWER. Though Tauler adopts at times the language of Eckart, no one can fail to discern a very different spirit. How much more profound his apprehension of sin—his sense of need; how much more prominent Christ, rescuing and purifying the stricken soul. Tauler lays man in the dust, and keeps him there. Eckart suffers him to expand from Nothing to Infinity. Summarily, I would put the difference thus:—With Eckart the language of Christianity becomes the metaphorical expression for pantheism; with Tauler, phraseology approaching pantheism is the metaphorical expression of a most truly Christian conviction. If the former sins even more in the spirit than in the letter, in the case of the latter the sins of the letter are redeemed by the excellence of the spirit.

NOTE TO PAGE 246.

The passages in the text are from the second *Sermon on Fifth Sunday after Trinity, Predigten,* ii. pp. 353, &c. The spiritual conflict and desolation which had shaken Tauler's nature to its depths bears fruit in this profound humility. Self-abasement is the cardinal doctrine of all his sermons; his lowliness of spirit the safeguard of his theology from all dangerous error. The troubles through which he and Suso were made to pass, gave them an antidote to the poison of the current ecclesiastical doctrine. Consciences so stirred were not to be cast into a sleep by the mesmeric passes of a priestly hand.   He only who had hurt could heal ; they fled from man to God—from means to the End, and so, like the patriarch, their eye saw God, and they repented and abhorred themselves as in dust and ashes,   Never after that could they believe in salvation by works, and so they became aliens from the spirit of that Church whose pale retained them to the last.   *what Church ?*

Tauler and his brethren will 'escape *distinction ;*'—not that which is between creature and Creator, or between good and evil—that rather which the Pharisee makes when he says, 'I am holier than thou.'   It is their very anxiety to escape all assumption of merit which partly vitiates the letter of their theology, and makes them speak as though grace substituted God for man within the renewed nature.   They will escape the dry and fruitless distinctions of the schoolman. They will escape the distinction which selfish comfort-worshippers make so broad between ease and hardship.   Sorrow and joy, pain and pleasure, are trustfully accepted as alike coming from the hand of love.

Even when Tauler speaks of self-surrender to an '*unknown* Will,' we must not press his words too far.   It is very evident that he who reaches this coveted abandonment is not supposed to have forgotten that gracious character under which God has made Himself known—of which Christ is the manifestation. In casting his care on an unknown Will, Tauler acts on the conviction that he is cared for,—this fact he knows ; but precisely what that care may deem best for him he does not know.   He surrenders, in true self-distrust, his personal notion of what may be the Divine good pleasure in any particular case.   Few lessons were more needed than this in Tauler's day, when superstition found signs and wonders everywhere, and fanaticism so recklessly identified human wrath and Divine righteousness.

Tauler's 'state above grace,' and 'transformed condition of the soul, in which God worketh all its works,' are perhaps little more than injudicious expressions for that more spontaneous and habitual piety characteristic of the established Christian life,—that religion which consists so much more in a pervading spirit of devotion than in professed and special religious acts.   He certainly inculcates no proud and self-complacent rejection and depreciation of any means.   Rather would the man who learnt Tauler's doctrine well find all persons, objects, and circumstances, made more or less 'means of grace' to him.   In a landscape or a fever, an enemy or an accident, his soul would find discipline and blessing, and not in mass and penance and paternoster merely ;—for is not God in all things near us, and willing to make everything minister to our spiritual growth ? Such teaching was truly reformatory, antagonistic as it was to that excessive value almost everywhere attached in those days to works and sacraments.

So again with Tauler's exhortation to rise above symbol, image, or figure. He carries it too far, indeed.   Such asceticism of the soul is too severe a strain for ordinary humanity.   It is unknown to His teaching, who spake as never man spake.   Yet there lay in it a most wholesome protest against religious sentimentalism, visionary extravagance, hysterical inoperative emotions,—against the fanciful prettinesses of superstitious ritual and routine.

Tauler's 'Nothing,' or 'Ground' of the soul, may be metaphysically a fiction—religiously it indicates the sole seat of inward peace.   Only as we put no trust in things earthly,—only as amidst our most strenuous action the heart saith ever, 'Thy will be done,'—only as we strive to reduce our feverish hopes and fears about temporal enjoyment as nearly as we can to Nothing,—are we calm and brave, whatever may befal.   This loving repose of Faith is Eternal Life, as sin is so much present death;—it is a life lived, in harmony with the everlasting, above the restlessness of time ;—it is (in Eckart's phrase, though not in Eckart's sense) a union with the Allmoving Immobility—the divine serenity of Love Omnipotent, guiding and upholding all without an effort.

NOTE TO PAGE 248.

The above is from the *Sermon on the Nineteenth Sunday after Trinity*, ii.
p. 546. He says in this discourse that the soul has various names, according to
the different operations and attributes belonging to it. It is called Anima, or
soul ; Spirit ; and Disposition (*gemüth*), a marvellous and very lovely thing
—for the memory, the understanding, and the will of man are all collected
therein. The Disposition hath an *objectum* above the other powers, and as
it follows or forsakes that aim so is it well or ill with the rest of man's
nature. Fourthly, the soul is called mens or mensch (*man*), and that is the
ground which is nameless, and wherein dwells hidden the true image of the
Holy Trinity. (Compare *Third Serm. on Third Sunday after Trin.*, ii. p. 305,
and *Serm. on Eleventh Sunday after Trin.*, ii. p. 435.) By the synteresis, or
synderesis, Tauler appears to mean the native tendency of the soul towards
God. With Tauler and the mystics generally this tendency is an original
capacity for knowing God immediately. The term is not peculiar to the
mystics, but it bears in their writings a signification which non-mystical
theologians refuse to admit. The distinction usually made between συντήρησις
and συνείδησις is simply this: the former expresses that constitution of our nature
whereby we assent at once to the axioms of morality, while the latter denotes
that judgment which man passes on himself in conformity with such constitution
of his moral nature. The second is related to the first somewhat as recollection
is to memory.

On this divine centre or substratum of the soul rests the fundamental doctrine
of these mystics. So Hermann of Fritslar says, speaking of—di kraft in der sêle
di her heizit *sinderisis*. In dirre kraft mac inkein krêatûre wirken noch inkein
krêatûrlich bilde, sunder got der wirket dar in âne mittel und âne underlâz.
Heiligenleben, p. 187. Thus, he says elsewhere, that the masters speak of two
faces of the soul, the one turned toward this world, the other immediately to
God. In the latter God doth flow and shine eternally, whether man knoweth it
or not. It is, therefore, according to man's nature as possessed of this divine
ground, to seek God, his original ; it must be so for ever, and even in hell the
suffering there has its source in the hopeless contradiction of this indestructible
tendency.

NOTE TO PAGE 251.

This passage is from the *Third Serm. on Thirteenth Sun. after Trin.*, ii. p. 480.
The same remarkable combination of inward aspiration and outward love and
service is urged with much force and beauty in the *Sermon on Fifth Sunday after
Trinity*, and in that on the *Sixteenth Sunday after Trinity*, ii. p. 512.

Tauler speaks of this Ground of the soul as that which is inseparable from the
Divine nature, and wherein man hath by Grace what God is by nature. *Predigten*, ii. p. 199. He quotes Proclus as saying that, while man is busied with
images, which are beneath us, and clings to such, he cannot possibly return into
his Ground or Essence. ' If thou wilt know by experience that such a Ground
truly is, thou must forsake all the manifold and gaze thereon with thine intellectual eye alone. But wouldst thou come nearer yet, turn thine intellectual
eyesight therefrom—for even the intellect is beneath thee—and become one with
the One—that is, unite thyself with Unity.' This unity Proclus calls the ' calm,
silent, slumbering, and incomprehensible divine Darkness.' ' To think, beloved
in the Lord, that a heathen should understand so much and go so far, and we be
so behind, may well make us blush for shame. To this our Lord Jesus Christ
testifies when he says the kingdom of God is within you. That is, this kingdom
is born in the inmost Ground of all, apart from all that the powers of the mind
can accomplish. . . . . In this Ground the eternal heavenly Father doth bring

forth his only-begotten Son, a hundred thousand times quicker than an instant, according to our apprehension, —ever anew in the light of Eternity, in the glory and unutterable brightness of his own Self. He who would experience this must turn himself inward far away from all working of his outward and inward powers and imaginations—from all that ever cometh from without, and then sink and dissolve himself in the Ground. Then cometh the power of the Father, and calls the man into Himself through his only-begotten Son ; and so the Son is born out of the Father and returneth unto the Father, and such a man is born in the Son of the Father, and floweth back with the Son into the Father again, and becomes one with them' (p. 203, and Schmidt, p. 127). Yet, with all this, Tauler sincerely repudiates any pantheistic confusion of the Divine and human, and is always careful to state that this highest attainment—the vanishing point of Humanity, is the work of Grace. Some of his expressions in describing this union are almost as strong as those of Eckart (*Third Serm. on Third Sun. after Trin.* ii. p. 310), but his general tone far more lowly, practical, and true.

Note to page 253.

We best ascertain the true meaning of Tauler's mystical phraseology, and discover the point at which he was desirous that mysticism should arrest its flight, by listening to the rebukes he administers to the unrighteous, pantheistic, or fantastical mystics of the day. A sermon of his on Psalm xci. 5 (*Pred.* vol. i. p. 228) is of great importance in this respect.

Speaking of such as embrace a religious life, without any true vocation, he points out how, as they follow only their own inclinations, they naturally desire rest, but are satisfied with a merely natural inaction instead of that spiritual calm which is the gift of God. Consequently, while the devout mind (as Gregory saith) cannot tolerate self-seeking, or be content with any such mere negation, these men profess to have attained the elevation of true peace while they have done nothing more than abstain from all imagination and action. Any man, remarks Tauler, very sensibly, may do this, without any especial grace from God. Such persons live in indolence, become self-complacent and full of pride. True love ever longs to love more ; the more of God it hath the more it covets. God is never to be found in the pretended quiet of such men, which any Turk or heathen could find in the same way, as easily as they. They are persuaded by the devil that devout exercises and works of charity will only disturb their inward quiet, and do, in fact, disobey and resist God in their self-satisfied delusion.

He next exposes the error of those who undergo great austerities to be thought holy,—suffering for their own glory rather than that of God ; and who think their penance and their works give them an extraordinary claim on the Most High. He shows how often they fall into temptation by their wayward and passionate desire after special spiritual manifestations, and by their clamorous importunity for particular bestowments on which their unmortified self-will has been obstinately set. Divine love, he says, offers itself up without reserve to God —seeks His glory alone, and can be satisfied with nothing short of God Himself. Natural love seeks itself in all things, and falls ere long, as Adam did, into mortal sin—into licence, pride, and covetousness.

Then he proceeds to describe an error, ' yet more dangerous than this,' as follows :—' Those who compose this class call themselves God-seeing (*Gott schauende*) men. You may know them by the natural rest they profess to experience, for they imagine themselves free from sin and immediately united to God. They fancy themselves free from any obligation to obey either divine or human laws, and that they need no longer be diligent in good works. They believe the quiet to which they have devoted themselves so lofty and glorious a

thing that they cannot, without sin, suffer themselves to be hindered or disturbed
therein. Therefore will they be subject to no man—will work not at all, either
inwardly or outwardly, but lie like an idle tool awaiting its master's hand. They
think, if they were to work, God's operation within them would be hindered ; so
they sit inactive, and exercise themselves in no good work or virtue. In short,
they are resolved to be so absolutely empty and idle that they will not so much
as praise and thank God—will not desire or pray for anything—will not know
or learn anything. All such things they hold to be mischievous—persuade themselves that they possess already all that can be requested, and that they have
the true spiritual poverty because, as they flatter themselves, they live without
any will of their own, and have abandoned all choice. As to the laws and ordinances of the Church, they believe that they have not only fulfilled them, but
have advanced far beyond that state for which such institutions were designed.
Neither God nor man (they say) can give or take from them aught, because they
suffered all that was to be suffered till they passed beyond the stage of trial
and virtue, and finally attained this absolute Quiet wherein they now abide.
For they declare expressly that the great difficulty is not so much to attain
to virtue as to overcome or surpass it, and to arrive at the said Quiet and
absolute emptiness of all virtue. Accordingly they will be completely free and
submit to no man,—not to pope or bishops, or to the priests and teachers set
over them ; and if they sometimes profess to obey, they do not in reality yield
any obedience either in spirit or in practice. And just as they say they will be
free from all laws and ordinances of the Holy Church, so they affirm, without a
blush, that as long as a man is diligently striving to attain unto the Christian virtues he is not yet properly perfect, and knows not yet what spiritual poverty and
spiritual freedom or emptiness really are. Moreover, they believe that they are
exalted above the merits of all men and angels ; that they can neither add to
their virtues nor be guilty of any fault or sin, because (as they fancy) they live
without will, have brought their spirit into Quiet and Emptiness, are in themselves nothing, and veritably united unto God. They believe, likewise, madly
enough, that they may fulfil all the desires of their nature without any sin, because, forsooth, they have arrived at perfect innocence, and for them there is no
law. In short, that the Quiet and freedom of their spirit may not be hindered,
they do whatsoever they list. They care not a whit for fasts, festivals, or ordinances, but what they do is done on account of others, they themselves having
to conscience about any such matters.'

A fourth class brought under review are less arrogant than these enthusiasts,
and will admit that they may progress in grace. They are 'God-suffering
(*Gottesleidende*) men'—in fact, mystics of the intransitive theopathetic species
par excellence. Their relation toward God is to be one of complete passivity,
and all their doings (of whatever character) are His work. Tauler acknowledges
duly the humility and patient endurance of these men. Their fault lies, he says,
in their belief that every inward inclination they feel is the movement of the Holy
Ghost, and this even when such inclinations are sinful, 'whereas the Holy Spirit
worketh in no man that which is useless or contrary to the life of Christ and
Holy Scriptures.' In their constancy as well as in their doctrine they nearly
resemble the early Quakers. They would sooner die, says Tauler, than swerve a
hair's breadth from their opinion or their purpose.

Tauler's reprobation of these forms of mysticism—which his own expressions,
too literally understood, might appear sometimes to approach—shows clearly
that he was himself practically free from such extremes. His concluding remarks
enforce very justly the necessity of good works as an evidence to our fellow-men
of our sincerity. He dwells on the indispensableness of religious ordinance,
worship, and thanksgiving, as at once the expression and the nourishment

of devout affection. He precludes at the same time, in the strongest language, all merit in the creature before God. 'I say that if it were possible for our spiritual nature to be deprived of all its modes of operation, and to be as absolutely inactive as it was when it lay yet uncreated in the abyss of the Divine Nature,—if it were possible for the rational creature to be still as it was when in God prior to creation,—neither the one nor the other could even thus merit anything, yea, not now any more than then; it would have no more holiness or blessedness in itself than a block or a stone' (p. 243). He points to the example of Christ as the best refutation of this false doctrine of Quiet, saying, ' He continued without ceasing to love and desire, to bless and praise his Heavenly Father, and though his soul was joined to and blessed in the Divine Essence, yet he never arrived at the Emptiness of which these men talk.'

CHAPTER VI.

Keep all thy native good, and naturalize
All foreign of that name ; but scorn their ill.
Embrace their activeness, not vanities ;
Who follows all things forfeiteth his will.

HERBERT.

THE day after the conversation recorded in the last chapter, Atherton was called to a distance from Summerford on legal business. Before leaving, he had some further talk with Willoughby on several topics suggested by what had passed on the previous day. The lawyers did not release him so promptly as he had expected, and as he had taken a copy of Tauler's sermons with him, and had time at his disposal, he wrote more than once to his friend in the course of the next week. This chapter will consist of extracts from the letters thus written, and will form a fitting supplement to matters dealt with in several preceding conversations.

*　　*　　*　　*　　*　　*

I scarcely need remind you that there are great practical advantages to be derived from a course of mental travel among forms of Christian belief in many respects foreign to our own. Nothing so surely arrests our spiritual growth as a self-complacent. insular disdain of other men's faith. To displace this pride by brotherly-kindness—to seek out lovingly the points whereon we agree with others, and not censoriously those wherein we differ, is to live in a clearer light, as well as a larger love. Then again, the powers of observation and of discrimination called into exercise by such journeyings among brethren of another speech will greatly benefit us. The very endeavour to distinguish between the good in others which we should naturalize and assimilate for ourselves, and the error which could be profitable neither for them nor for us, is most wholesome. Such studies lead us to take account of what we already have and believe ; so that we come to know ourselves better by the comparison both in what we possess and in what we lack. Every section of the Church of Christ desires to include in its survey the whole fabric of revealed truth. What party will admit to an antagonist that its study of the divine edifice has been confined to a single aspect ? And yet the fact is beyond all candid questioning that each group of worshippers, with whatever honesty of intention they may have started to go round about the building, and view it fairly from every side, have, notwithstanding, their favourite point of contemplation—one spot where they are most frequently to be found, intent on that side of truth to which, from temperament or circumstance, they are most attached. There is both good and evil in this inevitable partiality ; but the good will be most happily realized, and the evil most successfully avoided, if we have liberality enough now and then to take each other's places. It is possible, in this way, both to qualify and to enrich our own impressions from the observations of those who have given themselves, with all the intensity of passion, to some aspect of truth, which, while it may be the opposite, is yet the complement of the view preferred by ourselves. How often, as the result of an acquaintance made with some such diverse (and yet kindred) species of devotion, are we led to ask ourselves— ' Is there not a fuller meaning than I had supposed in this passage, or that other, of Holy Writ ? Have I not, because certain passages have been abused, allowed myself unconsciously to slight or to defraud them of their due significance ?' And, in this way, both those parts of Scripture we have most deeply studied, and those which we have but touched with our plummet, may disclose their blessing to us, and fill higher the measure of our joy.

Nor is this all. We gather both instruction and comfort from the spiritual history of others who have passed through the same darkness, doubt, or sorrow, which we ourselves have either encountered, or may be on our way to meet. How glad was Christian when he heard the voice of a fellow-pilgrim in the Valley of the Shadow of Death! And when suns are bright, and the waters calm, and the desired wind blows steadily, he is the wise mariner who employs his leisure in studying the records of others who have made voyage already in those latitudes; who learns from their expedients, their mishaps, or their deliverances, how best to weather the storms, or to escape the quicksands that await him. Of all who have sailed the seas of life, no men have experienced a range of vicissitude more wide than has fallen to the lot of some among the mystics. Theirs have been the dazzling heights; the lowest depths also have been theirs. Their solitary vessels have been swept into the frozen North, where the ice of a great despair has closed about them like the ribs of death, and through a long soul's winter they have lain hidden in cold and darkness, as some belated swallow in the cleft of a rock. It has been theirs, too, to encounter the perilous fervours of that zone where never cooling cloud appears to veil insufferable radiance, and to glow beneath those glories with an ardour so intense that some men, in their pity, have essayed to heal it as a fever, and others, in their wrath, to chain it as a frenzy. Now afflicted, tossed with tempest, and not comforted, ere long there hath been built for them at once a palace and a place of rest; their foundations have been laid with sapphires, their windows have been made of agates, and their gates of carbuncles, and all their borders of pleasant stones.

A place of rest! Yes, in that one word REST lies all the longing of the mystic. Every creature in heaven above, and in the earth beneath, saith Master Eckart, all things in the height and all things in the depth, have one yearning, one ceaseless, unfathomable desire, one voice of aspiration: it is for rest; and again, for rest; and ever, till the end of time, for rest! The mystics have constituted themselves the interpreters of these sighs and groans of the travailing creation; they are the hierophants to gather, and express, and offer them to heaven; they are the teachers to weary, weeping men of the way whereby they may attain, even on this side the grave, a serenity like that of heaven. What the halcyon of fable is among the birds, that are the mystics among their kind. They essay to build them a marvellous nest, which not only floats upon the waves of life, but has the property of charming those waves to a glassy stillness, so that in mid-winter, and the very heart of storms, their souls enjoy, for a season, what the ancients called 'the halcyon days,'—that wondrous week of calm ordained for the favoured bird when the year is roughest. 'Tis pity, murmurs old Montaigne, that more information hath not come down to us concerning the construction of these nests. Tradition has it, that the halcyon first of all fashions the said nest by interlacing the bones of some fish. When it is put together she takes it, like a boat ready for launching, and lays it on the beach: the waves come up: they lift it: they let it fall: they toss it gently among the rocks and pebbles; what is faultily made their play breaks, or makes to gape, so that the bird discovers the weak places, and what parts must be more duly finished; what is well knit together already, their strokes only season and confirm. Now when we read the lives of the mystics—each of whom has a method, more or less his own, of weaving such a nest, in other words, his *Theory and Practice of Quietude*—we see the structure on trial. Experience, with

its buffeting, tests each man's method for the attainment of
Rest. If we watch carefully, we shall see that some things in
the doctrine of many of them break away under trial, while
others are rendered only more compact and buoyant thereby.
The examination of the appliances and the processes adopted
by these searchers after the Divine Stillness, ought to be very
helpful to ourselves. As far as we have their history before
us, we can try them by their fruits. We ask, in the case of one
man, by what divine art was it that his ark was so skilfully
framed as to out-ride those deluges of trouble as though they
had been the waters of some windless mere? We ask, in the
case of another, by what fault came it in the structure of his
sailing nest, that the waters entered, and he sank, or seemed to
sink, finding not the rest of soul he sought, but the vexation of
soul he fled? We ask, in the several most signal examples of
the class, how far did their mysticism help them to realize true
manhood—make them strong to bear and strong to do? How
far did it tend, or did it not tend, towards the complete development and consecration of their nature?

To derive from such inquiries their full benefit, two qualifications are indispensable:—the judgment must be clear, the
sympathies must be warm. The inquirer must retain self-pos-
session enough not to be too readily fascinated, or too soon
offended, by certain strange and startling forms of expression;
he must not suppose, that because, for a long time, the mystics
have been unduly depreciated, it is wisdom now to cover them
with thoughtless and indiscriminate praise. He must not suppose that the mystics are an exception to the ordinary limitations
of mortals—that the glorious intensity of some among them
was realized without any diminution of breadth, and that their
view embraced, with equal fondness and with equal insight,
every quarter in the heaven of truth. And, on the other hand,
let him beware how he seeks to understand these men without

fellow-feeling and without love.   The weak and volatile nature
is smitten, on a first interview with the mystics, with a rage for
mysticism—is for turning mystic straightway, and is out of
patience, for six weeks, with every other form of Christianity.
The cold and proud nature scorns their ardour as a phantasy,
and (to its own grievous injury) casts out the warmth they
bring.   The loving nature and the wise says not, ' I will be
blind to their errors,' but, ' I will always look at those errors in
the light of their excellences.'

'The critic of Tauler no man has a right to become, who has
not first ascertained that he is a better man than Tauler.'[1]
What are we to understand by these words ?   If such an assertion be true at all, it cannot be true for Tauler only.   Would
Mr. Kingsley say that no man has a right to become the critic
of Augustine, of Luther, of Calvin, of Wesley, of George Fox,
who has not first ascertained himself a better man ?   Ought
every biographer, who is not a mere blind eulogist, to start with
the presumption that he is a better man than he of whom he
writes ?   Ought the historian, who forms his critical estimate
of the qualities possessed or lacking—of the service rendered
in this direction or in that, by the worthies of the Church,
to suppose himself superior to each in turn ?   As in art he
who estimates the worth of a poem is not required to write
better poetry, so in morals, he who estimates the worth of a
character is not required to display superior virtue.   Or is it
the *opinions*, rather than the character of Tauler, which only a
better man than Tauler may criticise ?   Any one who, on being
made acquainted with certain opinions, differs from them, is
supposed to have criticised them.   In as far as Mr. Kingsley
may not agree with some of the well-known opinions of Augustine, Luther, or Fox, so far has he ventured to be their critic ;
yet he does not suppose himself a better man.   Why should

[1] Preface to Tauler's *Life and Sermons* by Susanna Winkworth.

Tauler alone be thus fenced about with a statement that virtually
prohibits criticism ? Such advocacy harms a client's cause.
People are apt to suspect that their scrutiny is feared, when
such pains are taken to keep them at a distance. So confident
am I that the dross in Tauler is as nothing beside the
gold, that I would invite, rather than deter, the most candid
and sober exercise of the critical judgment with regard to
him. Perhaps Mr. Kingsley may be, in reality, much of the
same mind ; if so, he should not write as though he thought
quite otherwise.

I cannot suppose that Mr. Kingsley would seriously maintain that the mystic ought, from the very nature of his claims,
to be exempt from that scrutiny to which history continually
subjects the fathers, the schoolmen, and the reformers. Yet
there are those who would have us hearken to every voice professing to speak from the ' everlasting deeps' with a reverence
little more discriminating than that which the Mussulman
renders to idiocy and madness. Curiously ignorant concerning
the very objects of their praise, these admirers would seem to
suppose that every mystic repudiates the exercise of understanding, is indifferent to the use of language, and invariably
dissolves religious opinion in religious sentiment. These
eulogists of mysticism imagine that they have found in the virtues of a Tauler, a platform whence to play off with advantage
a volley of commonplaces against ' literalisms,' ' formulas,'
' creeds,' ' shams,' and the like. It is high time to rescue the
mystics from a foolish adoration, which the best among them
would be the most eager to repudiate. So far from forbidding
men to try the spirits, the most celebrated among the mystics
lead the way in such examination. It is the mystics themselves
who warn us so seriously that mysticism comprises an evil
tendency as well as a good, and has had its utterances from
the nether realms as well as from the upper. The great

mystics of the fourteenth century would have been indignant with any man who had confounded, in a blind admiration, their mysticism with the self-deifying antinomianism that prevailed among the ' Brethren of the Free Spirit.'   In many of Tauler's sermons, in the *Theologia Germanica*, in the writings of Suso and of Ruysbroek, care is taken to mark, with all the accuracy possible to language, the distinction between the False Light and the True.   There is not a confession of faith in the world which surpasses in clearness and precision the propositions in Fenelon's *Maxims of the Saints*, whereby it is proposed to separate the genuine Quietism from the spurious.   The mystic Gerson criticises the mystic Ruysbroek.   Nicholas of Strasburg criticises Hildegard and Joachim ;   Behmen criticises Stiefel and Meth ;   Henry More criticises the followers of George Fox.   So far are such mystics from that indifference to the true or the false in doctrine, which constitutes, with some, their highest claim to our admiration.   It is absurd to praise men for a folly : it is still more absurd to praise them for a folly of which they are guiltless.

But here I can suppose some one ready to interrupt me with some such question as this :—Is it not almost inevitable, when the significance of the word mysticism is so broad and ill-defined, that those who speak of it should misunderstand or be misunderstood ?   What two persons can you meet with who will define the term in precisely the same way ?   The word is in itself a not less general and extensive one than *revolution*, for instance.   No one speaks of revolution in the abstract as good or evil.   Every one calls this or that revolution glorious or disastrous, as they conceive it to have overthrown a good government or a bad.   But the best among such movements are not without their evil, nor are the worst perhaps absolutely destitute of good.   Does not mysticism, in like manner, sometimes rise up against a monstrous tyranny, and sometimes

violate a befitting order? Has there been no excess in its
triumphs? Has there been no excuse for its offences? See,
then, what opposites are coupled under this single word! Is
it not mainly for this reason that you hear one man condemning
and another extolling mysticism? He who applauds is thinking of such mystics as Bernard, or Tauler, or Fenelon; he who
denounces is thinking of the Carlstadts, the Münzers, or the
Southcotes. He who applauds is thinking of men who vanquished formalism; he who denounces is thinking of men who
trampled on reason or morality. Has not each his right? Are
not your differences mere disputes about nomenclature, and can
you ever come to understanding while you employ so ambiguous
a term?

So it seems to me that Common Sense might speak, and very
forcibly, too. It is indeed to be regretted that we have not two
words—one to express what may be termed the true, and
another for the false, mysticism. But regret is useless. Rather
let us endeavour to show how we may employ, least disad-
vantageously, a term so controverted and unfortunate.

On one single question the whole matter turns :—Are we or
are we not to call St. John a mystic? If we say ' Yes,' then
of course all those are mystics whose teaching is largely impregnated with the aspect of Christianity presented in the writings
of that Apostle. Then he is a mystic who loves to dwell on
the union of Christians with Christ; on His abode in us, and
our abiding in Him; on the identity of our knowledge of God
with our likeness to Him; of truth with love; of light with
life; on the witness which he who believes hath within himself.
Then he is a mystic who regards the Eternal Word as the
source of whatever light and truth has anywhere been found
among men, and who conceives of the Church of Christ as the
progressive realization of the Redeemer's prayer—' I in them
and thou in me, that they may be made perfect in one.'

Now, I think that, in the strict use of language, the word mystic should be applied, not to St. John, but to those who more or less exaggerate his doctrine concerning spiritual influence and life in God. The Scripture is the standard whereby alone the spirits are to be tried, in all candour and charity. To those who repudiate this authority I do not write. But if any one, understanding by 'mystics' simply those who give full force to the language of St. John, shall praise them, however highly, I am perfectly at one with him in his admiration—my only difference is about the use of the mere word.

So much then is settled. It will be obvious, however, that the *historian* of mysticism will scarcely find it possible always to confine his use of the word to the exaggeration just specified. For he must take up, one after the other, all those personages who have at any time been reckoned by general consent among the mystics. But an age which has relapsed into coldness will inevitably stigmatize as a mystic any man whose devout ardour rises a few degrees above its own frigidity. It is as certain as anything can be that, if a German had appeared among the Lutherans of the seventeenth century, teaching in his own way just as St. John taught, without one particle of exaggeration, he would have been denounced as a mystic from a hundred pulpits. Hence it has come to pass that some men, who have figured largely as mystics in the history of the Church, have in them but a comparatively small measure of that subjective excess which we would call mysticism, in the strict sense. Tauler is one of these.

But it may be said,—You talk of testing these men by Scripture; yet you can only mean, by *your interpretation* of Scripture. How are you sure that your interpretation is better than theirs? Such an objection lies equally against every appeal to Scripture. For we all appeal to what we suppose to be the meaning of the sacred writers, ascertained according to the best exercise of our judgment. The science of hermeneutics has established certain general principles of interpretation which are acknowledged by scholars of every creed. But if any one now-a-days resolves the New Testament into allegory, and supposes, for example, that by the five husbands of the woman of Samaria we are to understand the five Senses, I cannot of course try my cause with him before a Court where he makes the verdict what he pleases. I can only leave him with his riddles, and request him to carry my compliments to the Sphinx.

There is, then, a twofold test by which Tauler and other mystics are to be judged, if their teaching is to profit rather than to confuse and mislead us. We may compare the purport of his discourses with the general tenor and bearing of the New Testament, as far as we can apprehend it as a whole. Are some unquestionable truths but rarely touched, and others pushed to their utmost limits? If we think we see a certain disproportionateness—that there is a joyousness, and freedom, and warm humanity about the portraiture of Christian life in St. John, which we lack in his very sincere disciple, the ascetic and the mystic,—we trifle with truth if we do not say so. The other test is the *historical.* Was a certain mystic on the side of the truth and onwardness of his time, or against it? Did he rise above its worst errors, or did he aggravate them? And here Tauler stands with a glory round his head. Whatever exaggeration there may have been of the inward as against the outward, it was scarcely more than was inevitable in the case of a man who had to maintain the inmost verities of Christian life amidst almost universal formality and death.

What then, it may be asked, is that exaggeration of which you speak? For hitherto your account of mysticism proper is only negative—it is a something which St. John does *not* teach.

I will give a few examples. If a man should imagine that

his inward light superseded outward testimony, so that the words of Christ and his inspired disciples became superfluous to him ; if he regarded indifference to the facts and recorded truths of the New Testament as a sign of eminent spirituality, such a man would, I think, abuse the teaching of St. John concerning the unction from the Holy One. The same Apostle who declares that he who hateth his brother abideth in darkness, refuses to bid God speed to him who brings not the doctrine of Christ, and inseparably associates the ' anointing' which his children had received, with their abiding in the truth they had heard from his lips. (1 John ii. 24.) If, again, any man were to pretend that a special revelation exempted him from the ordinary obligations of morality—that his union with God was such as to render sinless in him what would have been sin in others, he would be condemned, and not supported, by conscience and Scripture. Neither could that mystic appeal to St. John who should teach, instead of the discipline and consecration of our faculties, such an abandonment of their use, in favour of supernatural gifts, as should be a premium on his indolence, and a discouragement to all faithful endeavour to ascertain the sense of Holy Writ. Nor, again, does any mystic who disdains hope as a meanness abide by the teaching of St. John. For the Apostle regards the hope of heaven as eminently conducive to our fitness for it, and says—' He that hath this hope purifieth himself.' The mystical ascetic who refuses to pray for particular or temporal bestowments is wrong in his practice, however elevated in his motive. For St. John can write,—' I pray (εὔχομαι) above all things that thou mayest prosper and be in health, even as thy soul prospereth.' (3 John 2.) Nowhere does that Apostle prescribe absolute indifference, or absolute passivity. Lastly, John is not so afraid of anthropomorphism as to discourage or refine away the symbol and the figure. It is evident that he regards the father-hoods and the brotherhoods of this earthly life, not as fleshly ideas which profane things spiritual, but as adumbrations, most fit (however inadequate) to set forth the divine relationship to us,—yea, farther, as facts which would never have had place in time, had not something like their archetype from the first existed in that Eternal Mind who has made man in his own image.

I remember hearing of an old lady, a member of the Society of Friends, who interrupted a conversation in which the name of Jerusalem had been mentioned, by the exclamation, ' Jerusalem—umph—Jerusalem—it has not yet been revealed to me that there is such a place !' Now I do not say that our friend the Quakeress might not have been an excellent Christian ; but I do venture to think her far gone in mysticism. Her remark puts the idea of mysticism, in its barest and most extreme form, as a tendency which issues in refusing to acknowledge the external world as a source of religious knowledge in any way, and will have every man's Christianity evolved *de novo* from the depths of his own consciousness, as though no apostle had ever preached, or evangelist written, or any Christian existed beside himself. It is not, therefore, the holding the doctrine of an inward light that makes a mystic, but the holding it in such a way as to ignore or to diminish the proper province of the outer.

*　　*　　*　　*　　*　　*

I should certainly like to see some one settle for us definitively the questions which lie at the root of mysticism, such as these, for example :—Is there an immediate influence exerted by the Spirit of God on the spirit of man ? And if so, under what conditions ? What are those limits which, once passed, land us in mysticism ? But the task, I fear, is beyond all hope of satisfactory execution. Every term used would have to be defined, and the words of the definition defined again, and every definition and subdefinition would be open to some doubt or some objection. Marco Polo tells us that the people of Kin-sai throw into the fire, at funerals, pieces of painted paper, representing servants, horses, and furniture ; believing that the deceased will enjoy the use of realities corresponding to these in the other world. But, alas, for our poor definition-cutter, with his logical scissors ! Where shall he find a faith like that of the Kin-sai people, to believe that there actually exist, in the realm of spirit and the world of ideas, realities answering to the terms he fashions? No ; these questions admit but of approximate solution. The varieties of spiritual experience defy all but a few broad and simple rules. Hath not One told us that the influence in which we believe is as the wind, which bloweth as it listeth, and we cannot tell whence it cometh and whither it goeth?

For my own part, I firmly believe that there is an immediate influence exerted by the Divine Spirit. But is this immediate influence above sense and consciousness, or not? Yes, answers many a mystic. But, if it be above consciousness, how can any man be conscious of it? And what then becomes of the doctrine—so vital with a large class of mystics—of perceptible guidance, of inward impulses and monitions? Speaking with due caution on a matter so mysterious, I should say that, while the indwelling and guidance of the Spirit is most real, such influence is not ordinarily perceptible. It would be presumption to deny that in certain cases of especial need (as in some times of persecution, sore distress, or desolation) manifestations of a special (though not miraculous) nature may have been vouchsafed.

With regard to the witness of the Spirit, I think that the language of St. John warrants us in believing that the divine life within us is its own evidence. Certain states of physical or mental distemper being excepted, in so far as our life in Christ is vigorously and watchfully maintained, in so far will

the witness of the Spirit with our spirit give us direct conviction of our sonship. How frequently, throughout his first
Epistle, does the Apostle repeat that favourite word, οἴδαμεν,
' *we know !*'

Again, as to the presence of Christ in the soul. Says the
Lutheran Church; 'We condemn those who say that the gifts
of God only, and not God himself, dwell in the believer.' I
have no wish to echo any such condemnation, but I believe that
the Lutheran affirmation is the doctrine of Scripture. Both
Christ himself and the Spirit of Christ are said to dwell within
the children of God. We may perhaps regard the indwelling
of Christ as the abiding source or principle of the new life, and
the indwelling of the Spirit as that progressive operation which
forms in us the likeness to Christ. The former is vitality itself;
the latter has its degrees, as we grow in holiness.

Once more, as to passivity. If we really believe in spiritual
guidance, we shall agree with those mystics who bid us abstain
from any self-willed guiding of ourselves. When a good man
has laid self totally aside that he may follow only the leading of
the Spirit, is it not essential to any practical belief in Divine
direction that he should consider what then appears to him as
right or wrong to be really such, in his case, according to the
mind of the Spirit? Yet to say thus much is not to admit that
the influences of the Spirit are ordinarily perceptible. The
motion of a leaf may indicate the direction of a current of air;
it does not render the air visible. The mystic who has gathered
up his soul in a still expectancy, perceives at last a certain
dominant thought among his thoughts. He is determined, in
one direction or another. But what he has perceived is still
one of his own thoughts in motion, not the hand of the Divine
Mover. Here, however, some mystics would say, 'You beg
the question. What we perceive *is* a something quite separate
from ourselves—in fact, the impelling Spirit.' In this case the

matter is beyond discussion. I can only say, my consciousness is different. I shall be to him a rationalist, as he to me a
mystic ; but let us not dispute.

Obviously, the great difficulty is to be quite sure that we
have so annihilated every passion, preference or foregone conclusion as to make it certain that only powers from heaven can
be working on the waters of the soul. That ripple, which
has just stirred the stillness ! Was it a breath of earthly air ?
Was it the leaping of a desire from within us ? Or was it
indeed the first touch, as it were, of some angelic hand, commissioned to trouble the pool with healing from on high ? If
such questions are hard to answer, when judging ourselves,
how much more so when judging each other !

When we desire to determine difficult duty by aid of the
illumination promised, self must be abandoned. But what self?
Assuredly, selfishness and self-will. Not the exercise of those
powers of observation and judgment which God has given us
for this very purpose. A divine light is promised, not to supersede, but to illuminate our understanding. Greatly would that
man err who should declare those things only to be his duty to
which he had been specially 'drawn,' or 'moved,' as the Friends
would term it. What can be conceived more snug and comfortable, in one sense, and more despicable, in another, than the
easy, selfish life which such a man might lead, under pretence
of eminent spirituality ? Refusing to read and meditate on the
recorded example of Christ's life—for that is a mere externalism
—he awaits inertly the development of an inward Christ. As
he takes care not to expose himself to inducements to unpleasant
duty — to any outward teachings calculated to awaken his conscience and elevate his standard of obligation—that conscience
remains sluggish, that standard low. He is honest, respectable,
sober, we will say. His inward voice does not as yet urge him
to anything beyond this. Others, it is true, exhaust themselves

in endeavours to benefit the souls and bodies of men. They
are right (he says), for so their inward Christ teaches them.
He is right (he says), for so does *not* his inward Christ teach
him.　It is to be hoped that a type of mysticism so ignoble as
this can furnish but few specimens.　Yet such is the logical
issue of some of the extravagant language we occasionally
hear concerning the bondage of the letter and the freedom of
the spirit.　When the letter means what God chooses, and the
spirit what *we* choose, Self is sure to exclaim, 'The letter
killeth.'　If the light that is in thee be darkness, how great is
that darkness !

Such, then, in imperfect outline, is what I hold to be true on
this question concerning the reality and extent of the Spirit's
influence.　As there are two worlds—the seen and the unseen
—so have there been ever two revelations—an inward and an
outward—reciprocally calling forth and supplementing each
other.　To undervalue the outward manifestation of God, in
nature, in providence, in revelation, because it *is* outward—
because it is vain without the inward manifestation of God in
the conscience and by the Spirit, is the great error of mysticism.
Hence it has often disdained means because they are not—what
they were never meant to be—the end.　An ultra-refinement of
spirituality has rejected, as carnal and unclean, what God has
commended to men as wholesome and helpful.　It is not wise
to refuse to employ our feet because they are not wings.

*　　*　　*　　*　　*　　*

But it is not mysticism to believe in a world of higher realities, which are, and ever will be, beyond sight and sense ; for
heaven itself will not abrogate manifestation, but substitute a
more adequate manifestation for a less.　What thoughtful
Christian man supposes that in any heaven of heavens, any
number of millenniums hence, the Wisdom, Power, or Goodness
of God will become manifest to him, as so many visible entities,

with form, and hue, and motion? It is not mysticism to believe that the uncreated underlies all created good. Augustine
will not be suspected of pantheism ; and it is Augustine who
says—'From a good man, or a good angel, take away angel,
take away man—and you find God.' We may be realists (as
opposed to the nominalist) without being mystics. For the
surmise of Plato, that the world of Appearance subsisted in and
by a higher world of Divine Thoughts is confirmed (while it is
transcended) by Christianity, when it tells us of that Divine
Subsistence, that Eternal Word, by whom and in whom, all
things consist, and without whom was not anything made that
is made. And herein lies that real, though often exaggerated,
affinity between Platonism and Christianity, which a long succession of mystics have laboured so lovingly to trace out and to
develop. In the second and third centuries, in the fourteenth,
and in the seventeenth ; in the Christian school at Alexandria,
in the pulpits of the Rhineland, at Bemerton, and at Cambridge,
Plato has been the 'Attic Moses' of the Clements and the
Taulers, the Norrises and the Mores.

But when mysticism, in the person of Plotinus, declares all
thought essentially one, and refuses to Ideas any existence external to our own minds, it has become pantheistic. So, also,
when the Oriental mystic tells us that our consciousness of not
being infinite is a delusion (*maya*) to be escaped by relapsing
ecstatically into the universal Life. Still more dangerous does
such mysticism become when it goes a step farther and says—
That sense of sin which troubles you is a delusion also ; it is
the infirmity of your condition in this phantom world to suppose
that right is different from wrong. Shake off that dream of
personality, and you will see that good and evil are identical in
the Absolute.

In considering the German mysticism of the fourteenth century it is natural to inquire, first of all, how far it manifests

any advance beyond that of preceding periods.   An examination of its leading principles will show that its appearance marks an epoch of no mean moment in the history of philosophy.   These monks of the Rhineland were the first to break away from a long-cherished mode of thought, and to substitute a new and profounder view of the relations subsisting between God and the universe.   Their memorable step of progress is briefly indicated by saying that they substituted the idea of the *immanence* of God in the world for the idea of the *emanation* of the world from God.   These two ideas have given rise to two different forms of pantheism ; but they are neither of them necessarily pantheistic.   To view rightly the relationship of God to the universe it is requisite to regard Him as both above it and within it.   So Revelation taught the ancient Hebrews to view their great ‘ I am.’   On the one hand, He had His dwelling in the heavens, and humbled Himself to behold the affairs of men ; on the other, He was represented as having beset man behind and before, as giving life to all creatures by the sending forth of His breath, as giving to man understanding by His inspiration, and as dwelling, in an especial sense, with the humble and the contrite.   But philosophy, and mysticism, frequently its purest aspiration, have not always been able to embrace fully and together these two conceptions of transcendence and of immanence.   We find, accordingly, that from the days of Dionysius Areopagita down to the fourteenth century, the emanation theory, in one form or another, is dominant. The daring originality of John Scotus could not escape from its control.   It is elaborately depicted in Dante’s *Paradiso*.   The doctrine of immanence found first utterance with the Dominican Eckart ; not in timid hints, but intrepid, reckless, sounding blasphemous. What was false in Eckart’s teaching died out after awhile ; what was true, animated his brother mystics, transmigrated eventually into the mind of Luther, and did not die.

To render more intelligible the position of the German mystics it will be necessary to enter into some farther explanation of the two theories in question. The theory of emanation supposes the universe to descend in successive, widening circles of being, from the Supreme—from some such 'trinal, individual' Light of lights, as Dante seemed to see in his Vision. In the highest, narrowest, and most rapid orbits, sing and shine the refulgent rows of Cherubim and Seraphim and Thrones. Next these, in wider sweep, the Dominations, Virtues, Powers. Below these, Princedoms, Archangels, Angels, gaze adoring upwards. Of these hierarchies the lowest occupy the largest circle. Beneath their lowest begins our highest sphere—the empyrean, enfolding within its lesser and still lesser spheres, till we reach the centre—'that dim spot which men call earth.' Through the hierarchies of heaven, and the corresponding hierarchies of the church, the grace of God is transmitted, stage by stage, each order in its turn receiving from that above, imparting to that below. This descent of divine influence from the highest point to the lowest is designed to effect a similar ascent of the soul from the lowest to the highest. Of such a theory John Scotus Erigena is the most philosophical exponent. With him the restitution of all things consists in their resolution into their ideal sources (*causæ primordiales*). Man and nature are redeemed in proportion as they pass from the actual up to the ideal ; for in his system, the actual is not so much the realization of the ideal as a *fall* from it. So, in the spirit of this theory, the mounting soul, when it anticipates in imagination the redemption of the travailing universe, will extract from music the very essence of its sweetness, and refine that again (far above all delight of sense) into the primal idea of an Eternal Harmony. So likewise, all form and colour—the grace of flowers, the majesty of mountains, the might of seas, the red of evening or of morning clouds, the lustre of precious stones and gold in the gleaming heart of mines—all will be concentrated and subtilized into an abstract principle of Beauty, and a hueless original of Light. All the affinities of things, and instincts of creatures, and human speech and mirth, and household endearment, he will sublimate into abstract Wisdom, Joy, or Love, and sink these abstractions again into some crystal sea of the third heaven, that they may have existence only in their fount and source—the superessential One.

Very different is the doctrine of Immanence, as it appears in the *Theologia Germanica*, in Eckart, in Jacob Behmen, and afterwards in some forms of modern speculation. The emanation theory supposes a radiation from above ; the theory of immanence, a self-development, or manifestation of God from within. A geometrician would declare the pyramid the symbol of the one, the sphere the symbol of the other. The former conception places a long scale of degrees between the heavenly and the earthly : the latter tends to abolish all gradation, and all distinction. The former is successive ; the latter, immediate, simultaneous. A chemist might call the former the sublimate, the latter the diluent, of the Actual. The theory of immanence declares God everywhere present with all His power—will realize heaven or hell in the present moment—denies that God is nearer on the other side the grave than this—equalizes all external states—breaks down all steps, all partitions—will have man at once escape from all that is not God, and so know and find only God everywhere. What are all those contrasts that make warp and woof in the web of time ; what are riches and poverty, health and sickness ; all the harms and horrors of life, and all its joy and peace,—what past and future, sacred and secular, far and near? Are they not the mere raiment wherewith our narrow human thought clothes the Ever-present, Ever-living One? Phantoms, and utter nothing—all of them ! The one sole reality is even this—that God through Christ does assume flesh in every Christian man ; abolishes inwardly his creature self, and absorbs it into the eternal stillness of His own 'all-moving Immobility.' So, though the storms of life may beat, or its suns may shine upon his lower nature, his true (or uncreated) self is hidden in God, and sits already in the heavenly places. Thus, while the Greek Dionysius bids a man retire into himself, because there he will find the foot of that ladder of hierarchies which stretches up to heaven ; the Germans bid man retire into himself because, in the depths of his being, God speaks immediately to him, and will enter and fill his nature if he makes Him room.

In spite of some startling expressions (not perhaps unnatural on the first possession of men by so vast a truth), the advance of the German mysticism on that of Dionysius or Erigena is conspicuous. The Greek regards man as in need only of a certain illumination. The Celt saves him by a transformation from the physical into the metaphysical. But the Teuton, holding fast the great contrasts of life and death, sin and grace, declares an entire revolution of will—a totally new principle of life essential. It is true that the German mystics dwell so much on the bringing forth of the Son in all Christians *now*, that they seem to relegate to a distant and merely preliminary position the historical incarnation of the Son of God. But this great fact is always implied, though less frequently expressed. And we must remember how far the Church of Rome had really banished the Saviour from human sympathies, by absorbing to the extent she did, his humanity in his divinity. Christ was by her brought really near to men only in the magical transformation of the Sacrament, and was no true Mediator. The want of human sympathy in their ideal of Him, forced them to have recourse to the maternal love of the Virgin, and the intercession of the saints. Unspeakable was the gain, then, when the Saviour was brought from that awful distance to

The humanity of Christ is not sufficiently real to most ofus.

become the guest of the soul, and vitally to animate, here on earth, the members of his mystical body. Even Eckart, be it remembered, does not say, with the Hegelian, that every man is divine already, and the divinity of Christ not different in kind from our own. He attributes a real divineness only to a certain class of men—those who by grace are transformed from the created to the uncreated nature. It is not easy to determine the true place of Christ in his pantheistic system; but this much appears certain, that Christ and not man—grace, and not nature, is the source of that incomprehensible deification with which he invests the truly perfect and poor in spirit.

On the moral character of Eckart, even the malice of persecution has not left a stain. Yet that *unknown* God to which he desires to escape when he says 'I want to be rid of God,' is a being without morality. He is *above* goodness, and so those who have become identical with Him 'are indifferent to doing or not doing,' says Eckart. I can no more call him good, he exclaims, than I can call the sun black. In his system, separate personality is a sin—a sort of robbery of God: it resembles those spots on the moon, which the angel describes to Adam as 'unpurged vapours, not yet into her substance turned.' I am not less than God, he will say, there is no distinction: if I were not, He would not be. 'I hesitate to receive anything from God—for to be indebted to Him would imply inferiority, and make a distinction between Him and me; whereas, the righteous man is, without distinction, in substance and in nature, what God is.' Here we see the doctrine of the immanence of God swallowing up the conception of his transcendence. A pantheism, apparently apathetic and arrogant as that of the Stoics, is the result. Yet, when we remember that Eckart was the friend of Tauler and Suso, we cannot but suppose that there may have lain some meaning in such language less monstrous than that which the words themselves imply.

Eckart would probably apply such expressions, not to his actual self;—for that he supposes non-existent, and reduced to its true nothing—but to the divine nature which, as he thought, then superseded within him the annihilated personality. Tauler (and with him Ruysbroek and Suso) holds in due combination the correlative ideas of transcendence and of immanence.

*   *   *   *   *   *

Such, then, is one of the most important characteristics of German mysticism in the fourteenth century. I have next to ascertain in which of the leading orders of mystics Tauler should be assigned a place.

'Divination,' saith Bacon, 'is of two kinds—primitive, and by influxion.' The former is founded on the belief that the soul, when by abstinence and observances it has been purified and concentrated, has 'a certain extent and latitude of pre-notion.' The latter is grounded on the persuasion that the foreknowledge of God and of spirits may be infused into the soul when rendered duly passive and mirror-like. Of these two kinds of divining the former is characterized by repose and quiet, the latter by a fervency and elevation such as the ancients styled *furor*. Now our mystical divines have this in common with the diviners, that they chiefly aim to withdraw the soul within itself. They may be divided most appropriately after a like manner. A cursory inspection will satisfy any one that theopathetic mysticism branches into two distinct, and often contrasted, species. There is the serene and contemplative mysticism; and over against it, the tempestuous and the active. The former is comparatively self-contained and intransitive; the latter, emphatically transitive. Its subject conceives himself mastered by a divine seizure. Emotions well-nigh past the strain of humanity, make the chest to heave, the frame to tremble; cast the man down, convulsed, upon the earth. Or visions that will not pass away, burn into his soul their glories and their terrors.   Or words that will not be kept down, force an articulation, with quaking and with spasms, from organs no longer under his control.   The contemplative mystic has most commonly loved best that side of Christian truth which is nearest to Platonism ; the enthusiastic or practical mystic, that which connects it with Judaism.   The former hopes to realize within himself the highest ascents of faith and hope—nay, haply, to surpass them, even while here below.   The latter comes forth from his solitude, with warning, apocalyptic voice, to shake a sleeping Church.   He has a word from the Lord that burns as a fire in his bones till it be spoken.   He lifts up his voice, and cries, exhorting, commanding, or foretelling, with the authority of inspiration.

The Phrygian mountaineer, Montanus, furnishes the earliest example, and a very striking one, of this enthusiastic or pro-phetic kind of mysticism.   He and his followers had been cradled in the fiercest and most frantic superstitions of heathen-dom.   Terrible was Cybele, the mountain mother, throned among the misty fastnesses of Ida. Maddest uproar echoed through the glens on her great days of festival.   There is beat-ing of drum and timbrel, clashing of cymbals, shrill crying of pipes ; incessant the mournful sound of barbarous horns ; loud, above all, the groans and shrieks and yells from frenzied votaries whom the goddess has possessed.   They toss their heads ; they leap ; they whirl ; they wallow convulsed upon the rocks, cutting themselves with knives ; they brandish, they hurl their weapons ; their worship is a foaming, raving, rushing to-and-fro, till the driving deity flings them down exhausted, senseless. Among these demoniacs—*sanguine fleti, Terrificas capitum quatientes numine cristas*, as Lucretius has described them— these Corybantes, or head-tossers, Christianity made its way, exorcising a legion of evil spirits.   But the enthusiastic tem-perament was not expelled.   These wild men, become Christians, carried much of the old fervour into the new faith. Violent excitement, ecstatic transport, oracular utterance, were to them the dazzling signs of the divine victory—of the forcible dislodgment of the power of Darkness by the power of Light. So Montanus readily believes, and finds numbers to believe, that he is the subject of a divine possession. Against the bloodthirsty mob in the villages and towns—against a Marcus Aurelius, ordaining massacre from the high places of the Cæsars —had not God armed his own with gifts beyond the common measure—with rapture—with vision—with prophecy? Yes! the promised Paraclete was indeed among them, and it was not they, but He, who spake. So thought the Montanists, as they announced new precepts to the Church; as they foretold the gathering judgment of Antichrist and the dawning triumph of the saints; as they hastened forth, defiant and sublime, to provoke from their persecutors the martyr's crown. Let us not overlook the real heroism of these men, while touching on their errors. But their conception of the Church of Christ, so analogous, in many respects, to that of the early Quakers— was it the right one? According to Montanus, the Church was to be maintained in the world by a succession of miraculous interventions. From time to time, fresh outpourings of the Spirit would inspire fresh companies of prophets to ordain ritual, to confute heresy, to organize and modify the Church according to the changing necessities of each period. He denied that the Scripture was an adequate source, whence to draw the refutation of error and the new supplies of truth demanded by the exigencies of the future. As Romanism sets up an infallible Pope to decide concerning truth, and in fact to supplement revelation, as the organ of the Divine Spirit ever living in the Church; so these mystics have their inspired teachers and prophets, raised up from time to time, for the same purpose. But the contemplative mystics, and indeed Christians generally, borne out, as we think, by Scripture and by history, deny any such necessity, and declare this doctrine of supplementary inspiration alien from the spirit of Christianity. While Montanus and his prophetesses, Maximilla and Priscilla, were thus speaking, in the name of the Lord, to the country-folk of Phrygia or to the citizens of Pepuza, Clement at Alexandria was teaching, on the contrary, that we *have* the organ requisite for finding in the Scriptures all the truth we need—that they are a well of depth sufficient, nay inexhaustible ; and that the devout exercise of reason in their interpretation and application is at once the discipline and prerogative of the manhood proper to the Christian dispensation. We are no longer Jews, he would say, no longer children. The presence of the Spirit with us is a part of the *ordinary* law of the economy under which we live. It is designed that the supernatural shall gradually vindicate itself as the natural, in proportion as our nature is restored to its allegiance to God. It is *not* necessary that we should be inspired in the same way as the sacred writers were, before their writings can be adequately serviceable to us.

Such was the opposition in the second century, and such has it been in the main ever since, between these two kinds of mystical tendency. The Montanist type of mysticism, as we see it in a Hildegard, among the Quakers, among the Protestant peasantry of the Cevennes, and among some of the ' Friends of God,' usually takes its rise with the uneducated, is popular, sometimes revolutionary. Animated by its spirit, Carlstadt filled Wittenberg with scandal and confusion ; and the Anabaptist mob reddened the sky with the burning libraries of Osnaburg and Munster. The Alexandrian mysticism, so far from despising scholarship and philosophy, as so much carnal wisdom, desires to appropriate for Christianity every science and every art. It is the mysticism of theologians, of philosophers, and scholars. It exists as an important element in the theology of Clement, of Origen, and of Augustine. It assumes still greater prominence in a Hugo or a Richard of St. Victor. It obtained its fullest proportions in these German mystics of the fourteenth century. It refined and elevated the scholarship of Reuchlin, Ficinus, and Mirandola. It is at once profound and expansive in our English Platonists.

Yet let it not be supposed that the extravagance of the enthusiastic mysticism has not its uses, or that the serenity of the contemplative is always alike admirable. Both have, in their turn, done goodly service. Each has had a work given it to do in which its rival would have failed. The eccentric impetuosity of Montanism, ancient and modern, has done good, directly and indirectly, by breaking through traditional routine —by protesting against the abuses of human authority—by stirring many a sleeping question, and daring many an untried path of action. On the other hand, the contemplative mysticism has been at times too timid, too fond of an elegant or devout, but still unworthy, ease. The Nicodemuses of the sixteenth century, the Briçonnets and the Gerard Roussels, were nearly all of them Platonists. They were men whose mysticism raised them above the wretched externalism of Rome, and at the same time furnished them with an ingenious excuse for abiding safely in her communion. 'What,' they would say, 'are the various forms of the letter, to the unity of the Spirit? Can we not use the signs of Romanism in the spirit of Protestantism— since, to the spiritual and the wise, this outward usage or that, is of small matter?' The enthusiastic mysticism tends to multiply, and the contemplative to diminish, positive precept and ordinance. The former will sometimes revolt against one kind of prescription only to devise a new one of its own. So the followers of Fox exchanged surplice and 'steeple-house' for a singularity of hat, coat, and pronouns. The contemplative mystic loves to inform his common life with the mysterious and the divine. Certain especial sanctities he has, but nothing unsanctified; and he covers his table with an altar-cloth, and curtains his bed with a chasuble, and drinks out of a chalice every day of his life. A Montanus commends celibacy; an Origen sees typified in marriage the espousals of the Church. The zeal of the enthusiastic mysticism is ever on the watch for signs—expects a kingdom coming with observation—is almost always Millenarian. The contemplatist regards the kingdom of heaven as internal, and sees in the history of souls a continual day of judgment. The one courts the vision and hungers after marvel: the other strives to ascend, above all form and language, from the valley of phantasmata to the silent heights of 'imageless contemplation.' The one loves violent contrasts, and parts off abruptly the religious world and the irreligious, the natural and the supernatural. The other loves to harmonize these opposites, as far as may be—would win rather than rebuke the world—would blend, in the daily life of faith, the human with the divine working: and delights to trace everywhere types, analogies, and hidden unity, rather than diversity and strife. The Old Testament has been always the favourite of the prophetic mysticism: the contemplative has drunk most deeply into the spirit of the New.

* * * * * *

Mysticism, as exhibited in Tauler's sermons, is much more likely to win appreciation at the hands of English readers than mysticism in the *Theologia Germanica*. The principles which were there laid down as bare abstractions are here warmed by sunshine and clothed with verdure. To the theory of mysticism we find added many a suggestive hint concerning its practice. There were general statements in the *Theologia Germanica* so dim, so vast, so ultra-human, that many readers would be at a loss to understand how they could possibly become a practice or a joy in any soul alive. In the sermons, a brother mystic supplies the requisite qualification, and shows that the old Teutonic knight had, after all, a meaning not so utterly remote from all the ways and wants of flesh and blood.

Brought out to view by Tauler's fervour, his invisible ink becomes a legible character. The exhortations of the pulpit thus interpret the soliloquy of the cell; and when the preacher illuminates mysticism with the many-coloured lights of meta-phor and passion—when he interrogates, counsels, entreats, rebukes, we seem to return from the confines of the nameless, voiceless Void to a region within the rule of the sun, and to beings a little lower than the angels. It will reassure many readers to discover from these sermons that the mystics whom Tauler represents are by no means so infatuated as to disdain those external aids which God has provided, or which holy men of old have handed down—that they do not call history a husk, social worship a vain oblation, or decent order bondage to the letter—that when they speak of transcending time and place, they pretend to no new commandment, and do but repeat a truth old as all true religion—that they are on their guard, beyond most men, against that spiritual pride which some think inseparable from the mystical aspiration—that so far from encouraging the morbid introspection attributed to them, it is their first object to cure men of that malady—that instead of formulating their own experience as a test and regimen for others, they tell men to sit down in the lowest place till God calls them to come up higher—and finally, that they are men who have mourned for the sins, and comforted the sorrows of their fellows, with a depth and compass of lowly love such as should have disarmed every unfriendly judgment, had their errors been as numerous as their excellence is extraordinary.

Any one who has attentively read Tauler's discourses as now accessible may consider himself familiar with the substance of Tauler's preaching. From whatever part of Scripture history, prophecy, song, or precept, his text be taken, the sermons, we may be sure, will contain similar exhortations to self-abandonment, the same warnings against a barren externalism, the same directions to prepare the way for the inward Advent of the Lord in the Ground of the Soul. The allegorical interpretation, universal in those days, rendered easy such an ever-varied presentation of a single theme. Did the multitude go out into the wilderness to the preaching of John? We are to go forth into the wilderness of the spiritual life. Did Joseph and Mary seek their son in vain among their friends and acquaintance, and find him in his Father's house? We also must retire to the inmost sanctuary of the soul, and be found no more in the company of those hindering associates, our own Thoughts, Will, and Understanding. Did Christ say to Mary Magdalen, 'I have not yet ascended to my Father?' He meant, ' I have not yet been spiritually raised within thy soul;' for he himself had never left the Father.

From the sermon on the fifteenth Sunday after Trinity I select a passage which contains in two sentences the kernel of Tauler's doctrine—the principle which, under a thousand varieties of illustration and application, makes the matter of all his sermons. 'When, through all manner of exercises the outward man has been converted into the inward, reasonable man, and thus the two, that is to say, the powers of the senses and the powers of the reason, are gathered up into the very centre of the man's being—the unseen depths of his spirit wherein lies the image of God,—and thus he flings himself into the divine abyss, in which he dwelt eternally before he was created; then when God finds the man thus simply and nakedly turned towards Him, the Godhead bends down and descends into the depths of the pure, waiting soul, and transforms the created soul, drawing it up into the uncreated essence, so that the spirit becomes one with Him. Could such a man behold himself, he would see himself so noble that he would fancy himself God, and see himself a thousand times nobler than he is in himself, and would perceive all the thoughts and purposes, words and works, and have all the knowledge of all men that ever were.'

An explanation of this extract will be a summary of Tauler's theology. First of all, it is obvious that he regards human nature as tripartite—it is a temple in three compartments : there is the outer court of the senses ; there is the inner court of the intellectual nature, where the powers of the soul, busy with the images of things, are ever active, where Reason, Memory, Will, move to and fro, as a kind of mediating priests; there is, lastly, and inmost, a Holy of Holies—the Ground of the Soul, as the mystics term it.

'Yes !' exclaims some critic, 'this *Ground*, of which we hear so much, which the mystics so labour to describe, what is it, after all?' Let Tauler answer. He here calls it 'the very centre of man's being'—'the unseen depths of his spirit, wherein lies the image of God.' I believe that he means to indicate by these and other names that element in our nature by virtue whereof we are moral agents, wherein lies that idea of a right and a wrong which finds expression (though not always adequate) in the verdicts of conscience—that *Synderesis* (to use an Aristotelian word) of which the *Syneidesis* is the particular action and voice—that part of our finite nature which borders on the infinite—that gate through which God enters to dwell with man. Nor is the belief in such a principle by any means peculiar to the mystics ; men at the farthest remove, by temperament and education, from mysticism, are yet generally found ready to admit that we can only approach a solution of our great difficulties concerning predestination and free will, by supposing that there is a depth in our nature where the divine and human are one. This is Tauler's spark and potential divinity of man—that face of man's soul wherein God shineth always, whether the man be aware thereof or not. This, to speak Platonically, is the ideal part of man—that part of him whereby, as a creature, he participates in the Word by whose thought and will all creatures exist. It is the unlost and inalienable nobleness of man—that from which, as Pascal says, his misery as well as his glory proceeds—that which, according to Tauler, must exist even in hell, and be converted into the sorrow there. The Christian Platonist expresses his conception of the consummated redemption of man by saying that he is restored to his original idea—becomes what he was designed to be before sin marred him—puts off the actual sinful self, and puts on the truer primal self which exists only in God. In this sense Eckart says, ' I shall be sorry if I am not younger to-morrow than I am to-day—that is, a step nearer to the source whence I came'—away from this Eckart to the Divine Idea of man.

Such, then, in this Ground. Next, how is the lapse, or transit into it, effected? Tauler reminds us that many men live as though God were not in this way nearer to them than they are to themselves. They possess inevitably this image—this immediate receptivity of God, but they never think of their prerogative, never seek Him in whom they live and move. Such men live in the outside of themselves—in the sensuous or intellectual nature ; but never lift the curtain behind which are the rays of the Shekinah. It will profit me nothing, says Tauler, to be a king, if I know it not. So the soul must break away from outward things, from passion and self, and in abandonment and nothingness seek God immediately. When God is truly found, then indeed the simplified, self-annihilated soul, is passive. But the way thereto, what action it demands, what strong crying and tears, what trampling out of subtle, seemly, darling sins !

First of all, the senses must be mastered by, and absorbed in, the powers of the soul. Then must these very powers them-selves—all reasonings, willings, hopings, fearings, be absorbed in a simple sense of the Divine presence—a sense so still, so blissful, as to annihilate before and after, obliterate self, and sink the soul in a Love, whose height and depth, and length and breadth, passing knowledge, shall fill it with all the fulness of God.

'What!' it may be said, 'and is this death—not of sin merely, but of nature—the demand of your mysticism? Is all peace hollow which is not an utter passivity—without knowledge, without will, without desire—a total blank?'

Not altogether so, the mystic will reply. These powers of the soul must cease to act, in as far as they belong to self; but they are not destroyed: their absorption in the higher part of our nature is in one sense a death; in another, their truest life. They die; but they live anew, animated by a principle of life that comes directly from the Father of lights, and from the Light who is the life of men. That in them which is fit to live, survives. Still are they of use in this lower world, and still to be employed in manifold service; but, shall I say it? they are no longer quite the same powers. They are, as it were, the glorified spirits of those powers. They are risen ones. They are in this world, but not of it. Their life has passed into the life which, by slaying, has preserved and exalted them. So have I heard of a nightingale, challenged by a musician with his lute; and when all nature's skill was vain to rival the swift and doubling and redoubling mazes and harmonies of mortal science, the bird, heart-broken, dropt dead on the victorious lute;—and yet, not truly dead, for the spirit of music which throbbed in that melodious throat had now passed into the lute; and ever afterward breathed into its tones a wild sweetness such as never Thessalian valley heard before—the consummate blending of the woodland witchery with the finished height of art.

'You see,' our mystic continues—and let us hear him, for he has somewhat more to say, and to the purpose, as it seems— 'you see that we are no enemies to the symbol and the figure in their proper place, any more than we are to the arguments of reason. But there are three considerations which I and my brethren would entreat you to entertain. First of all, that logical distinctions, and all forms of imagery, must of necessity be transcended when we contemplate directly that Being who is above time and space, before and after,—the universal Presence, —the dweller in the everlasting Now. In the highest states of the soul, when she is concentrated on that part of her which links her with the infinite, when she clings most immediately to the Father of spirits, all the slow technicalities, and the processes and the imaginations of the lower powers, must inevitably be forgotten. Have you never known times when, quite apart from any particular religious means, your soul has been filled, past utterance, with a sense of the divine presence,—when emotion has overflowed all reasoning and all words, and a certain serene amazement—a silent gaze of wonder—has taken the place of all conclusions and conceptions? Some interruption came, or some reflex act dissolved the spell of glory and re-called you to yourself, but could not rob you of your blessing. There remained a divine tranquillity, in the strength whereof your heaviest trouble had grown lighter than the grasshopper, and your hardest duty seemed as a cloud before the winds of the morning. In that hour, your soul could find no language ; but looking back upon it, you think if that unutterable longing and unutterable rest could have found speech, it would have been in words such as these—"Whom have I in heaven but Thee? and there is none upon earth that I desire beside Thee."

‘ Then again, we would have you consider that the mere con-clusions of the intellect, the handiwork of imagination, the effervescence of sentiment, yea, sensible delight in certain religious exercises—all these things, though religion's hand-maidens, are not religion herself. Sometimes they are delusive ; always are they dangerous, if they, rather than God, become in any way our dependence. If the heart—the central fount of life's issues—be not God's, what avail the admitted propositions, and touching pictures, and wafts of sweetness—the mere furniture, adornment, and incense, of the outer courts of thy nature? Christ in thy soul, and not the truth about Him in thy brain, is thy life's life; and his agony of love must pierce thee somewhat deeper than the pathos of a tragedy. There are those who live complacently on the facilities and enjoyments they have in certain practices of devotion, when all the while it is rather they themselves, as thus devout, and not their Lord, whom they love. Some such are not yet Christians at all. Others, who are, have yet to learn that those emotions they set such store by, belong, most of them, to the earliest and lowest stages of the Christian life. The lotus-flowers are not the Nile. There are those who violently excite the imagination and the feeling by long gazing on the crucifix—by picturing the torments of martyrs—by performing repeated acts of Contrition,—by trying to wish to appropriate to themselves, for Christ's sake, all the sufferings of all mankind—by praying for a love above that of all seraphim, and do often, in wrestling after such extraordinary gifts, and harrowing their souls with such sensuous horrors, work out a mere passion of the lower nature, followed by melancholy collapse, and found pitiably wanting in the hour of trial.[2] In these states does it oftenest happen that the phantoms of imagination are mistaken for celestial manifestations; and forms which belong to middle air, for shiny ones from the third heaven. I have been told that astronomers have sometimes seen in the field of their glass, floating globes of light—as it seemed, new planets swimming within their ken; and these were but flying specks of dust, hovering in the air; but magni-

[2] Nicole, in his *Traité de la Prière*, describes and criticises this style of devotion. It must always be borne in mind that the warnings of Tauler with regard to the image and the symbol are addressed, not to us sober Protestant folk, but especially to the devotees of the cloister. Those who have some acquaintance with the fantastic excesses he combats, will not think his language too strong.

fied and made luminous by the lenses through which they
looked, and by the reflection of the light.   The eye of the mind
may be visited by similar illusions.   I counsel all, therefore,
that they ask only for grace sufficient against present evil, and
covet not great things, but be content with such measures of
assurance and sensible delight as God shall think safe for them ;
and that, above all, they look not at His gifts in themselves,
but out of themselves, to Him, the Giver.

  ' The third consideration I have to urge, in justification of
precepts which appear to you unnatural, is this :—there are
certain trials and desolations of soul, to which the best are ex-
posed, wherein all subordinate acts are impossible ; and then
happy is he who has never exalted such helps above their due
place.   I scarcely know how to make myself understood to any
save those who have been at some time on the edge, at least,
of those unfathomable abysses.   Good men of prosperous and
active life may scarcely know them.   Few who have lived much
in retirement, with temperament meditative, and perhaps melancholy, have altogether escaped.   There are times when, it may
be that some great sorrow has torn the mind away from its
familiar supports, and laid level those defences which in prosperity seemed so stable—when the most rooted convictions of
the reason seem rottenness, and the blossom of our heavenward
imaginations goes up before that blast as dust—when our works
and joys and hopes, with all their multitude and pomp and
glory, seem to go down together into the pit, and the soul is
left as a garden that hath no water, and as a wandering bird
cast out of the nest—when, instead of our pleasant pictures, we
have about us only doleful creatures among ruins—when a
spirit of judgment and a spirit of burning seem to visit the city
of the heart, and in that day of trouble and of treading down
and of perplexity, the noise of viols, and the mirth of the tabret,
and the joy of the harp, are silent as the grave.   Now, I say,

blessed is the man who, when cast into this utter wretchedness, far away from all creatures and from all comfort, can yet be willing, amidst all his tears and anguish, there to remain as long as God shall please—who seeks help from no creature—who utters his complaint to the ear of God alone—who still, with ever-strengthening trust, is ready to endure till self shall have been purged out by the fires of that fathomless annihilation—who, crying out of the depths, while the Spirit maketh intercession within him with groanings that cannot be uttered, shall presently be delivered when the right time hath come, and rejoice in that glorious liberty of the children of God, wherein they are nothing and He is all !'

Now, somewhat thus, I think, would that class of mystics whom Tauler represents, reply to the very natural objections urged by many in our times. Nor does such reply, so far, seem to me either unsatisfactory in itself, or in any way contrary to Scripture. It is with the aim, and under the qualifications, I have endeavoured to set forth, that these mystics would refuge the soul in a height above reasonings, outward means and methods, in a serenity and an abstraction wherein the subtlest distinctions and most delicate imaginations would seem too gross and sensuous—where (as in Endymion's ecstasy)

> 'Essences
> Once spiritual, are like muddy lees,
> Meant but to fertilize our earthly root,
> And make our branches lift a golden fruit
> Into the bloom of heaven.'

On the latter part of the extract given just now I have not yet commented. It suggests a question of no small moment. What, it will be asked, is the relation sustained by the Saviour of mankind to this mystical process—this drawing up of the created soul into the uncreated essence ? Is not a blank abstraction—an essential nothing, substituted for the Son of man ? How does the abstract Essence in which Tauler would sink the

soul, differ from the abstract Essence or super-essential Unity
in which a Plotinus would lose himself, or from that Divine
substance in which the pantheistic Sufis sought to dissolve
their personality? In this region (confessedly above distinction),
the mystic cannot, by his own admission, distinguish one
abstraction from the other. There is a story of a lover who,
Leander-like, swam nightly across a strait to visit the lady
of his heart. A light which she exhibited on the shore was
the beacon of the adventurous swimmer. But two brothers
(cruel as those who murdered Isabella's lover in the wood)
removed the light one dark and stormy night, and placed it in
a boat anchored not near shore, but in mid-waters, where the
strait was broadest. Their victim struggled as long as mortal
strength might endure, towards the treacherous light—farther
and farther out—into the ocean which engulphed him. Have
not the mystics, in like manner, shifted the beacon and substituted an expanse—an abyss, as the object of man's effort, instead of that love and sympathy which await him in the heart
of the Son of man?

Can it be possible that the best thing to do with a revelation
of God, now we have one, is to throw it behind our backs?
Now that the light the wisest heathen longed for has come, are
we to rid ourselves of it, with all speed, and fly, like Eckart,
from the known to the old, *unknown* God? To do this, is to
account as foolishness the wisdom of God manifest in the flesh.
Is it not all—as the enemies of Quietism used to say—a device
of the Devil? Does it not look as though the Arch-enemy,
unable to undo the work of redemption, had succeeded, by a
master-stroke of policy, in persuading men to a false spirituality,
which should consist in obliterating the facts of that redemption
from their own minds as completely as though it had never
been wrought?

Now it is much better, I think, to put objections like these

in all their strength, and to give them fair hearing.   They will
occur to many persons in the reading of these sermons.   They
will awaken a distrust and a perplexity which are not to be
talked down by high words, or by telling men that if they do
not sufficiently admire these mystics, so much the worse for
them.   One of the objections thus urged is logically unanswer-
able.   If Eckart and Plotinus both succeed in reducing their
minds to a total emptiness of all memory, knowledge, and
desire, in order to contemplate a super-essential Void, equally
blank, the Christian and the heathen pantheist are indistin-
guishable.   Vacuum A, would be a vacuum no longer if it
contained anything to distinguish it from vacuum B ; and to
escape, in the most absolute sense, all distinction, is Eckart's
highest ambition.   But it is to be remembered, first of all, that
Tauler does not go so far as Eckart in his impatience of everything intelligible, conceivable, or utterable.   And next, that,
happily, neither Eckart, Tauler, nor any man, can really reduce
himself to that total nescience and apathy demanded by the
theory which makes personality a sin, knowledge an infirmity,
imagination a folly.   Humanity is still too strong for any such
de-humanizing ideal.   The Absolute of Tauler is not, like the
Absolute of Plotinus, an abstraction above morality.   His link
between finite and infinite—his image of God, is moral, not
metaphysical merely.   It is his knowledge, first of all, of God
in Christ which enables him to contemplate the Infinite, not as
boundless being, but as unfathomable love.   So he stands firm
on the grand Christian foundation, and the Son is his way to
the Father.   Following Dionysius, that arch-mystagogue, he
does indeed invite the trembling soul into the shadows of a
Divine darkness, wherein no specific attribute or act is perceptible to the baffled sight.   But across that profound obscure
and utter silence, there floats, perceptible, some incense from
the censer, of the Elder Brother—the eternal High Priest.   It

is a darkness, but such an one as we have when we close our eyes after spectacles of glory—a darkness luminous and living with the hovering residue of splendours visible no longer. It is a silence, but such an one as we have after sweet music—a silence still stirred by inward echoes, and repetitions, and floating fragments of melodies that have ceased to fall upon the ear. It seems a chilling purity, a hueless veil—but such a veil as the snowfall lays upon an Alpine church-yard, hiding all colour but not all form, and showing us still where the crosses are. By their fruits we know these mystics. No men animated by a love so Christ-like as was theirs, could have put an abstraction in the place of Christ.

With regard to the work of Christ, Tauler acknowledges (more readily than George Fox) that the divine element or inward light in man must remain a mere surmise or longing, apart from the historic manifestation of God in the flesh. It is Jesus of Nazareth who at once interprets to the soul, while He satisfies, its own restless heavenward desire. It is His grace alone which makes a mere capacity of God, a possession—a mere potentiality, actual. The view of Christ which Tauler loves to present most frequently is that expressed by those passages of Scripture which speak of Him as the first-born among many brethren, and which remind us that both He that sanctifieth and they that are sanctified are all of one. He would say that the Saviour now lives upon the earth, in the person of all true believers; and that, in a subordinate sense, the Word is being continually made flesh, as Christ is formed in the hearts of Christians. With one voice Eckart and Tauler, Ruysbroek and Suso, exclaim—'Arise, O man ! realize the end of thy being : make room for God within thy soul, that he may bring forth his Son within thee.'

The Saviour's obedience unto death is regarded by Tauler, rather in its exemplary, than in its propitiatory aspect. Very

important, as characteristic of his theology, is the distinction
he makes between our union to the humanity of Christ, and
our union to his divinity. As man, He is the ideal of humanity
—the exemplar of self-surrender. All that He received from
the Father was yielded up to Him in that absolute devotedness
which all His brethren imitate. We are united to His humanity
in proportion as we follow the obedience and self-sacrifice of His
earthly life. But above this moral conformity to His example,
Tauler sets another and a higher union to His divinity. And
this union with the Godhead of the Son is not a superior
degree of moral likeness to Him, it is rather an approximation
to another mode of existence. It is an inward transit from our
actual to our ideal self—not to the *moral* ideal (for that is
already realized in proportion as we are united to His humanity),
but to our Platonic archetypal ideal. This higher process of
union to the Word, or return to our ideal place in Him, consists in escaping from all that distinguishes us as creatures on
this earth—in denuding ourselves of reasonings, imaginations,
passions,—humanities, in fact, and reducing ourselves to that
metaphysical essence or germ of our being, which lay from
eternity—not a creature, but the *thought* of a creature, in the
Divine Word.

Now it appears to me that this self-spiritualizing process
which seeks by a refined asceticism to transcend humanity
and creatureliness, is altogether a mistake. An ideal sufficiently high, and ever beyond us, is already given in the moral
perfection of Christ Jesus. This desire to escape from all the
modes and means of our human existence came not from Paul,
but from Plato. It revives the impatience of that noble but
one-sided, Greek ideal, which despised the body and daily
life, abhorred matter as a prison-house, instead of using it as
a scaffolding, and longed so intensely to become pure, passion-
less intellect. I know no self-transcendence, and I desire none,

higher than the self-sacrifice of the good Shepherd, who laid
down his life for the sheep. You will probably be reminded
here of another great Platonist. Origen, also, makes a distinction between those who know Christ, according to the flesh, as
he terms it, *i.e.*, in his sufferings, death, and resurrection, and
that higher class of the perfect, or *Gnostici*, who, on the basis
of that fundamental knowledge, rise from the historical Christ
to the spiritual essence of the Word. Origen, however, supposed that this communion with the Logos, or eternal Reason,
might become the channel of a higher knowledge, illumining
the *Gnosticus* with a divine philosophy. With Tauler, on the
contrary, the intellectual ambition is less prominent; and he
who has ascended into the uncreated essence cannot bring
down from thence any wisdom for this lower world. Thus, in
our extract, he says that if the soul united to the word could
perceive itself, it would seem altogether like God, and would
appear possessed of all knowledge that ever was. Such is the
ideal; but the first reflex act would dissolve that trance of
absolute, immediate oneness, and restore the mystic to the
humbling consciousness of a separate, actual self; and here
lies the great difference between Tauler and Eckart. Tauler,
Suso, and Ruysbroek say, that in these moments of exaltation
the soul (above distinctions) is not conscious of its distinction
as a separate, creature entity. Eckart says, not that the soul
has, for a moment, forgotten all that is personal, and that parts
it off from God, but that the distinction does not exist at all,—
not that *we* do not know ourselves as separate, but that *God*
does not. To draw the line between theism and pantheism,
is not always easy; but I think it must lie somewhere
hereabout.

With regard to the doctrines of holy indifference and disinterested love, the German mystics are by no means so extreme
as the French. Their views of the divine character were more

profound and comprehensive ; their heaven and hell were less external and realistic.   A mysticism like theirs could not concentrate itself, as Quietism did, on the degrees and qualities of one particular affection.   Their God was one who, by a benign necessity of nature, must communicate Himself in blessing, one whose love lay at the root of His being.   ' If men would only believe,' cries Tauler, in one of his sermons, ' how passionately God longs to save, and bring forth His Son in them !' They care little for being themselves accused of making matter eternal, and creatures necessary to God, if they can free Him from the imputation of selfishness or caprice.   And so they have no scruples as to whether it be not selfish and criminal to pray for our own salvation.   In the sense of Tauler—a true and deep one—no man can say, ' Thy will be done,' and ' Thy kingdom come,' without praying for his own salvation.   When Tauler seems to demand a self-abnegation which consents to perdition itself, he is to be understood in one of two ways : either he would say that salvation should be desired for the sake of God, above our own, and that we should patiently submit, when He sees fit to try us by withdrawing our hope of it ; or that the presence and the absence of God make heaven and hell—that no conceivable enjoyment ought to be a heaven to us without Him, no conceivable suffering a hell with Him.   But how different is all this from teaching, with some of the Quietists, that, since (as they say) God is equally glorified in our perdition and in our salvation, we should have no preference (if our love be truly disinterested) for the one mode of glorifying Him above the other.   That any human being ever attained such a sublime indifference I shall not believe, until it is attested by a love for man as much above ordinary Christian benevolence, as this love for God professes to be above ordinary Christian devotion ; for what is true of the principle of love, is true of its degrees—' He that loveth not his brother

whom he hath seen, how shall he love God whom he hath
not seen?'

The strongly ascetic language of Tauler and his brethren,
their almost Manichean contempt of the world, must be read
by the light of their times, so full of misery and corruption;
and by the light, also, of those fearful furnaces of trial through
which they had personally passed. What soul, into which the
iron has entered, will say, while the pain is still fresh, that the
words of Tauler, or of Thomas à Kempis, are intemperate?
It is probable that Tauler would have been less impatient to
abolish his very personality, in order to give place to God, had
he been able, like Luther, to regard salvation, in greater
measure, as consisting in a work done *for*, as well as wrought
in him. But his justification is a progressive, approximate
process. It is not a something he accepts, but a something he
has to work out; and seeing, as, with his true humility, he was
sure to do, how unsatisfactory was his likeness to God, how
great the distance still, the only resource open to him is to
ignore or annihilate that sorry and disappointing personality
altogether, that God, instead of it, may perform his actions,
and be, in fact, the substitute for his soul. Both Tauler and
Luther believe in substitution. The substitution of Tauler is
internal—God takes his place within himself. The substitution of Luther is external—when he believed on Christ, the
Saviour associated him with Himself, and so brought him into
sonship. So inevitable is the idea of *some* substitution, where
the sense of sin is deep. Luther believes as profoundly as
Tauler in a present, inward, living Saviour, as opposed to a
remote historic personage, intellectually acknowledged. In
the theology of both the old dualism is broken down, and God
is brought near to man, yea, within him. But the Son to whom
Tauler is united, is the uncreated essence, the super-essential
Word, from the beginning with the Father. The Son to whom

Luther is united is emphatically the Godman, as truly human, in all sympathy and nearness, as when He walked the Galilean hills. The humanity of Christ is chiefly historic with Tauler, and for any practical purpose can scarcely be said to have survived His exaltation; but with Luther that humanity is so vital and so perpetual that he will even transfer to it the attributes of Deity. So far from desiring to pass upward from the man Christ Jesus to the Logos, as from a lower to a higher, Luther calls 'that sinking himself so deep in flesh and blood,' the most glorious manifestation of Godhead. He does not, with the Platonists, see degradation in the limitations of our nature; that nature has been honoured unspeakably, and is glorified, not annihilated, by the Incarnate One. According to Luther, the undivine consists in sin, and sin alone; not in our human means and modes, and processes of thought. Thus with him the divine and human are intimately associated, not merely in the religious life, as it is termed, but in our temporal hopes and fears, in every part of our complicated, struggling, mysterious humanity. The theology of Luther is more free, joyous, and human, partly because the serene and superhuman ideal of Tauler did not appear to him either possible or desirable, partly because sanctification was, with him, a change of state consequent on a change of relation—the grateful service of one who, by believing, has entered into rest; and partly, also, because he does not lose sight of the humanity of Christ, in His divinity, to the extent which Tauler does. Both Luther and Tauler say—the mere history alone will not profit: Christ must be born in you. Luther adds—Christ begins to be born in you as soon as you heartily believe upon Him. Tauler adds—Christ is born in you as soon as you have become nothing.

It would be very unfair to make it a matter of blame to Tauler that he did not see with Luther's eyes, and do Luther's work. Luther in one century, and Tauler in another, had their

tasks appointed, and quitted themselves like men.   It was for
Tauler to loosen the yoke of asceticism : it was for Luther to
break it in pieces.   But it would be just as culpable to disguise
the real differences between Tauler and Luther, and to conceal
the truth, from a desire to make Tauler appear a more complete reformer than he really was.   Our High Churchmen, in
their insular self-complacency, love to depreciate Luther and
the Continental reformers.   Idolaters of the past as they are,
we do not think that they will be better pleased with that
noblest product of the Middle Age—the German mysticism of
the fourteenth century, now placed within their reach.   These
sermons of Tauler assert so audaciously against sacerdotalism,
the true priesthood of every Christian man.   There is so
little in them of the ' Church about us,' so much of the ' Christ
within us.'

*   *   *   *   *   *

It would have moved the scorn of some of the mystics, and
the sorrow of others, could they have been made aware of the
strange uses to which some persons were to turn them in this
nineteenth century. The Emersonian philosophy, for example,
is grieved that one series of writings should arrogate inspiration
to themselves alone.   It is obvious that a ready credence given
to professed inspiration in other quarters, and later times, must
tend to lower the exclusive prestige of the Scriptures.   Thus
the mystics may be played off against the Apostles, and all
that is granted to mysticism may be considered as so much
taken from the Bible.   A certain door has been marked with a
cross.   Emerson, like the sly Abigail of the Forty Thieves,
proceeds to mark, in like manner, all the doors in the street.
Very gratifying truly, and comic in the highest degree, to
witness the perplexity of mankind, going up and down, seeking
some indication of the hoped-for guidance from above !   I
do not believe that the inspired writers were (to use Philo's

comparison) as passive as a lyre under the hand of a musician. But some, who are much shocked at this doctrine in their case, would have us be awe-stricken, rather than offended, by similar pretension on the part of certain mystics. *Then*, they tell us to tread delicately—to remember how little the laws of our own nature are known to us—to abstain from hasty judgment. In this way, it is supposed that Bibliolatry may be in some measure checked, and one of the greatest religious evils of the time be happily lessened. Criticise, if you will, John's history, or Paul's letters, but let due reverence restrain you from applying the tests of a superficial common sense to the utterances of the Montanuses, the Munzers, the Engelbrechts, the Hildegards, the Theresas. But what saith History as to mysticism? Very plainly she tells us that the mystics have been a power in the world, and a power for good, in proportion as their teaching has been in accordance with the Bible ;—that the instances wherein they have failed have been precisely those in which they have attempted (whether wittingly, or not) to substitute another and a private revelation for it. They have come as a blessing to their age, just in proportion as they have called the attention of men to some of the deepest lessons of that book—to lessons too commonly overlooked. The very men who might seem, to superficial observers, to bear witness *against* the Bible, do in reality utter the most emphatic testimony *for* it. A fact of this nature lends additional importance to the history of mysticism at the present time.

Again, there are some who may suppose there is a real resemblance between the exhortations of Tauler, and the counsel given men by such philosophers as Fichte or Herr Teufelsdröckh. Do not both urge men to abandon introspections—to abstain from all self-seeking—to arise and live in the transcendental world, by abandoning hope and fear, and by losing our finite in an Infinite Will? Some similarity of sound there may occasionally be, but the antipathy of principle between the two kinds of teaching is profound and radical.

I will suppose that there comes to our Teufelsdröckh some troubled spirit, full of the burden of 'this unintelligible world,' questioning,—as to an oracle. The response is ready. 'What do you come whining to me about your miserable soul for? The soul-saving business is going down fast enough now-a-days, I can tell you. So you want to be happy, do you? Pining after your Lubberland, as usual,—your Millennium of mere Ease and plentiful supply. Poor wretch! let me tell you this,—the very fact of that hunger of yours proves that you will never have it supplied. Your appetite, my friend, is too enormous. In this wild Universe of ours, storming-in, vague-menacing, it is enough if you shall find, not happiness, but existence and footing to stand on,—and that only by girding yourself for continual effort and endurance. I was wretched enough once —down in the "Everlasting Nay," thinking this a Devil's-world, because, in the universal scramble of myriads for a handful, I had not clutched the happiness I set my heart on. Now, here I am in the "Everlasting Yea," serene as you see me. How? Simply by giving up wanting to be happy, and setting to work, and resigning myself to the Eternities, Abysses, or whatsoever other name shall be given to the fontal Vortices of the inner realms. . . . . Miracles! Fiddlestick! Are not you a miracle to your horse? What can they prove? . . . . Inspiration!— Try and get a little for yourself, my poor friend. Work, man: go work, and let that sorry soul of thine have a little peace.'

'Peace,' repeats our 'poor friend,' as he goes discomfited away. 'Peace! the very thing this soul of mine will not let me have, as it seems. I know I am selfish. I dare say this desire of happiness is very mean and low, and all that; but I would fain reach something higher. Yet the first step thereto he does not show me. To leap into those depths of stoical

apathy which that great man has reached, is simply impossible
to poor me. His experience is not mine. He tells a bedridden
man to climb the mountains, and he will straightway be well.
Let him show me the way to a little strength, and in time I
may.   I will not hunger any more after mere " lubberly enjoyment," if he will offer my affections something more attractive.
But Infinite Will, and Law, and Abysses, and Eternities, are
not attractive—nay, I am not sure that they are intelligible to
me or any mortal.'

  Now the doctrine of Tauler is nowhere more in contrast with
that just uttered than in its tenderness of Christian sympathy
and adaptation, as compared with the dreary and repellent pride
of the philosopher.   Instead of overwhelming the applicant by
absurdly demanding, as the first step, a sublimity of self-sacrifice
which only the finished adept may attain, Tauler is not too
proud to begin at the beginning.   Disinterested love is, with
him, a mountain to which he points in the distance, bright with
heavenly glory.   Disinterested love, with Teufelsdröckh, is an
avalanche hurled down right in the path of the beginner.
Tauler does not see, in the unhappiness of the man, so much
mere craven fear, or thwarted selfishness. He sees God's image
in him ; he believes that that hunger of his soul, which he
vainly tries to satisfy with things earthly, is a divine craving, a
proof that he was born to satisfy it with things heavenly.   He
does not talk grandiloquently about Duty, and the glory of
moral Freedom.   He tells him that the same Saviour who died
upon the cross is pleading and knocking at his heart, and doth
passionately long to bless him.   He sends him away to think
over this fact, till it shall become more real to him than house
and home, or sun and stars.   He does not think that he can
improve on 'the low morality' of the gospel by disdaining to
appeal to hope and fear in order to snatch men from their sins.
If so to plead be to speak after the flesh, after the flesh he will

speak, to save a brother. There will be time enough, he thinks, if God sees fit to lead the man to the heights of absolute self-loss ; and God will take His own way to do it. All Tauler has to do is to declare to him the truth concerning a Saviour, not to prescribe out of his own experience a law beyond that which is written. In this way, instead of striking him into despair, or bidding him bury care in work, he comforts and strengthens him. He does not despise him for keeping the law simply out of love to Him who gave it. He does not think it unmanly, but true manhood rather, when he sees him living, a suppliant, dependent on a life higher than his own—on a Person, whose present character and power were attested of old by history and miracle, as well as now by the ' witness of the Spirit.'

I think the candid reader of Tauler's sermons, and of *Sartor Resartus*, will admit that a difference in substance such as I have pointed out, does exist between them. If so, those who follow the philosophy of Teufelsdröckh cannot claim Tauler—have no right to admire him, and ought to condemn in *him* that which they condemn in the Christianity of the present day.

CHAPTER VII.

Alas poor country ;
Almost afraid to know itself !   It cannot
Be called our mother, but our grave.   Where nothing,
But who knows nothing, is once seen to smile ;
Where sighs, and groans, and shrieks that rend the air,
Are made, not mark'd ; where violent sorrow seems
A modern ecstasy ; the dead man's knell
Is there scarce asked, for who ; and good men's lives
Expire before the flowers in their caps,
Dying or ere they sicken.

MACBETH.

THE day after Atherton's return, Willoughby and Gower
met about noon, at Lowestoffe's lodge gate, the one returning from a piscatory expedition of six hours, with fish, the
other from a pictorial ramble of four days, with sketches.
Willoughby had to tell of the escapades of tricksy trout, and
of the hopes and fears which were suspended on his line.   But
not a word, of course, had he to say of the other thoughts
which busied him the while,—how his romance was in his
head, as he carried those credentials of idleness, the fishing-
tackle, and how, while he was angling for fish, he was devising
the fashion in which Blanche should throw the fly for Florian.
Gower had seen such glades and uplands—such wondrous
effects of light and shadow—he, too, had had his adventures,
and could show his trophies.

Dinner was succeeded by that comparatively somnolent period
which preceded the early tea so dear to Lowestoffe.   Atherton
found that a book of Schubert's, which had interested him in
the morning, was, in the afternoon, only a conducting-rod to

lure down the subtile influence of sleep.   Lowestoffe, lulled by the buzzing flies, dropped off into an arm-chair doze, without apology or disguise.   He had been early up, and had been riding about all day on a new chestnut mare.   Violently had he objurgated that wretch of a groom for giving her too many beans, thereby rendering her in danger of flying at the heels ; and what was worse, the monster had put on a gag snaffle with the martingale, and narrowly escaped getting her into mischief. But the flying storm had long since swept away.   Before tea, Lowestoffe was in his good-humoured, irrational humour ; after tea he would be in his good-humoured rational one.   As for Gower and Kate, they had quietly withdrawn together to see a water-lily that had just blown, and were not heard of till tea-time.

After tea, when certain sleepy people had again become responsible creatures, conversation began.

GOWER. Don't you think Atherton has a very manuscriptural air to-night ?

KATE. There is a certain aspect of repletion about him.

MRS. ATHERTON. We must bleed him, or the consequences may be serious.   What's this ? (*Pulls a paper out of his pocket.*)

KATE. And this ! (*Pulls out another.*)

WILLOUGHBY. He seems better now.

ATHERTON (*abstractedly*).   I was thinking of the difference between Gower's studies and mine for the last few days.   I have been reading a dark, miserable chapter in the history of man.   He has been the chronicler of pleasant passages in the history of rocks and trees,—his great epochs, a smile of sunshine or sudden chill of shadow,—the worst disasters, a dull neutral-tint kind of day, or a heavy rain,—his most impractic. able subjects, beauties too bright or evanescent to be caught. It is sad to think how every subject of our study deepens in sorrow as it rises in dignity.

WILLOUGHBY. And yet it is only by the manful struggles of

past generations through calamity and against wrong, that we have bequeathed to us the leisure, the liberty, and the knowledge essential to the highest enjoyment of nature. Atherton, in fact, studies the chequered and intricate causes which issue in the taste of Gower as one of their effects. I should think it must be no small gain for an artist to be placed beyond the mediæval idea which set the *Inferno* in the centre of the earth, and imagined, far below the roots of the mountains and the channels of the sea, eternal flames as the kernel of the world.

GOWER. I have sometimes endeavoured, while lying on the grass, to realise in my own way the conception of the world by the light-hearted Greeks as an animal, or as a robe or peplus. I have imagined the clouds the floating breath of the great creature, rising against the crystal sphere of the sky, under which it lies as in an enchanter's glass ;—the seas, some delicate surfaces of the huge organism, that run wrinkled into a quick shiver at the cold touch of wind ;—the forests, a fell of hair which is ruffled by the chafing hand of the tempest. Then, when I look at the earth in the other aspect, as a variegated woven robe, I see it threaded silverly with branching rivers spangled with eyes of lakes ; where the sleek meadows lie, it is rich with piled velvet, and where the woods are, tufted with emerald feathers. But now I want to hear something more about our Strasburg people.

ATHERTON. Bad news. There is a great hiatus in Arnstein's journal, which history fills up with pestilence and bloodshed. I have drawn up a few notes of this interval which must serve you as an outline. (*Reads.*)

In the year 1348 that terrible contagion, known as the Black Death, which journeyed from the East to devastate the whole of Europe, appeared at Strasburg.[1] Everywhere famine, floods,

[1] See Hecker's *Black Death* (trans. by Dr. Babington, 1853).—Hecker

the inversion of the seasons, strange appearances in the sky, had been its precursors. In the Mediterranean Sea, as afterwards in the Baltic, ships were descried drifting masterless, filled only by plague-stricken corpses. Every man dreaded, not merely the touch and the breath of his neighbour, but his very eye, so subtile and so swift seemed the infection. In many parts of France it was computed that only two out of every twenty inhabitants were left alive. In Strasburg sixteen thousand perished ; in Avignon sixty thousand. In Paris, at one time, four or five hundred were dying in a day. In that city, in the midst of a demoralization and a selfish horror like that Thucydides has painted, the Sisters of Mercy were seen tending the sufferers who crowded the Hôtel Dieu ; and, as death thinned their martyr-ranks, numbers more were ready to fill the same office of perilous compassion. Pausanias says that in Athens alone out of all Greece there was raised an altar to mercy. But it was an altar almost without a ministry. Heathendom, at its best, might glory in the shrine ; Christianity, at its worst, could furnish the priesthood.

In Strasburg Tauler laboured fearlessly, with Thomas and Ludolph, among the panic-stricken people—doubly cursed by the Interdict and by the plague. Great fires of vine-wood, wormwood, and laurel were kept burning in the squares and market-places to purify the air, lighting up the carved work of the deserted town-hall, and flickering aslant the overhanging gables of the narrow crooked streets and the empty tradesmen's stalls. The village was ravaged as fatally as the town. The herds grew wild in the fields of the dead peasants, or died strangely themselves—victims, apparently, to the universal blight of life. The charlatans of the day drove for awhile a golden traffic with quintessences and distillations, filthy and

gives the documents relating to the trial of the Neustadt Jews in an ap-

pendix, from the *Chronicle* of Jacob of Königshoven. See also pp. 103-127.

fantastic medicines, fumigation of shirts and kerchiefs, charms and invocations, only at last to perish in their turn, Even the monks had lost their love for gold, since every gift was deadly. In vain did trembling men carry their hoards to the monastery or the church. Every gate was barred, and the wealthy might be seen tossing their bags of bezants over the convent walls. In the outskirts of towns and cities, huge pits were opened, whose mouths were daily filled with hideous heaps of dead. The pope found it necessary to consecrate the river Rhone, and hundreds of corpses were cast out at Avignon, from the quays and pleasant gardens by the water-side, to be swept by the rapid stream under the silent bridges, past the forgotten ships and forsaken fields and mourning towns, livid and wasting, out into the sea.

In a frenzy of terror and revenge the people fell upon the miserable Jews. They were accused of poisoning the wells, and every heart was steeled against them. Fear seemed to render all classes more ferocious, and the man who might sicken and die to-morrow found a wretched compensation in inflicting death to-day on the imagined authors of his danger. Toledo was supposed to be the centre of an atrocious scheme by which the Jews were to depopulate Christendom. At Chillon several Jews, some after torture and some in terror of it, confessed that they had received poison for that purpose. It was a black and red powder, made partly from a basilisk, and sent in the mummy of an egg. The deposition of the Jews arrested at Neustadt was sent by the castellan of Chillon to Strasburg. Bishops, nobles, and chief citizens held a diet at Binnefeld in Alsace, to concert measures of persecution. The deputies of Strasburg, to their honour be it spoken, declared that nothing had been proved against the Jews. Their bishop was the most pitiless advocate of massacre. The result was a league of priests, lords, and people, to slay or banish every Jew. In some places the senators and burgomasters were disposed to mercy or to justice. The pope and the emperor raised their voices, alike in vain, in behalf of the victims. Some Christians, who had sought from pity or from avarice to save them, perished in the same flames. The noble of whom they bought protection was stigmatised as a Jew master, execrated by the populace, at the mercy of his enemies. No power could stem the torrent. The people had tasted blood ; the priest had no mercy for the murderers of the Lord ; the baron had debts easily discharged by the death of his creditor. At Strasburg a monster scaffold was erected in the Jewish burial ground, and two thousand were burnt alive. At Basle all the Jews were burnt together in a wooden edifice erected for the purpose. At Spires they set their quarter in flames, and perished by their own hands. A guard kept out the populace while men commissioned by the senate hunted for treasure among the smoking ruins. The corrupting bodies of those slain in the streets were put up in empty wine casks, and trundled into the Rhine. When the rage for slaughter had subsided, hands, red with Hebrew blood, were piously employed in building belfries and repairing churches with Jewish tombstones and the materials of Jewish houses.

The gloomy spirit of the time found fit expression in the fanaticism of the Flagellants.[2] Similar troops of devotees had

---

[2] These fanatics were everywhere foremost among the instigators of the cruelties perpetrated on the Jews. Women, and even children, joined their ranks in great numbers, wearing the hats with red crosses, carrying flags, and scourging themselves with the rest. The particulars given are taken from the account in Jacob von Königshoven's *Elsassische u. Strassburgische Chronik*, inserted entire in Wackernagel,—(p.931). The chronicler says:—'Zuo Strôsburg kam mêdenne tûsent manne in ire geselleschaft, und siu teiltent sich zuo Strôsburg : eine parte der geischelaere gieng das lant abe, die ander parte das lant ûf. und kam sô vîl volkes in ire bruoderschaft, das es verdrôs den bôbest uud den keiser und die phafheit. und der keiser verschreip dem bôbeste das er etwas hie zuo gedaechte : anders die geischeler verkêrtent alle die welt.' The Flagellants claimed power to confess and give absolution. The thirty-four days' scourging among them was to make a man as innocent as a babe— the virtue of the lash was above all sacraments. Thus the people took religion into their own hands, blindly

in the preceding century carried throughout Italy the mania of
the scourge ; but never before had the frenzy of penance been
so violent or so contagious. It was in the summer of 1349
that they appeared in Strasburg. All the bells rang out as two
hundred of them, following two and two many costly banners
and tapers, entered the city, singing strange hymns. The
citizens vied with each other in opening to them their doors
and seating them at their tables. More than a thousand joined
their ranks. Whoever entered their number was bound to
continue among them thirty-four days, must have fourpence of
his own for each day, might enter no house unasked, might
speak with no woman. The lash of the master awaited every
infraction of their rule. The movement partook of the popular,
anti-hierarchical spirit of the day. The priest or friar could
hold no rank, as such, among the Flagellants. The mastership
was inaccessible to him, and he was precluded from the secret
council. The scourging took place twice a day. Every
morning and evening they repaired in procession to the place
of flagellation outside the city. There they stripped themselves, retaining only a pair of linen drawers. They lay down
in a large circle, indicating by their posture the particular sin
of which each penitent was principally guilty. The perjured
lay on his side, and held up three fingers ; the adulterer on his
face. The master then passed round, applying his lash to each
in succession, chanting the rhyme—

> Stand up in virtue of holy pain,
> And guard thee well from guilt again.

One after the other, they rose and followed him, singing and
scourging themselves with whips in which were great knots and
nails. The ceremony closed with the reading of a letter, said

and savagely,—no other way was then
possible. It was a spasmodic movement of the mass of life beneath,
when the social disorder that accompanied the pestilence had loosened the
grasp of the power temporal and
spiritual which held them down so
long.

to have been brought by an angel from heaven, enjoining their practice, after which they returned home in order as they came. The people crowded from far and near to witness the piteous expiation, and to watch with prayers and tears the flowing blood which was to mingle with that of Christ. The pretended letter was reverenced as another gospel, and the Flagellant was already believed before the priest. The clergy grew anxious as they saw the enthusiasm spreading on every side. But the unnatural furor could not last; its own extravagance prepared its downfall. An attempt made by some Flagellants in Strasburg to bring a dead child to life was fatal to their credit. The Emperor, the Pope, and the prelates took measures against them simultaneously, in Germany, in France, in Sicily, and in the East. The pilgrimage of the scourge was to have lasted four-and-thirty years. Six months sufficed to disgust men with the folly, to see their angelic letter laughed to scorn, their processions denounced, their order scattered.

Meanwhile the enemies of Tauler were not idle. Louis of Bavaria was dead. The new Emperor Charles IV. was of the papal party, and called the Parsons' Kaiser, but a man of vigour and enlightenment; so weary Germany, broken by so many calamities, was generally inclined to acknowledge his claim. About the year 1348 he visited Strasburg, and the clergy brought Tauler and his two friends before him. They were to answer for their hard words against priests and princes. Charles listened attentively to the statement of their principles, and to their spirited defence of what they had said and done. At last he said (conceive the dismay of the prelates!) that, after all, 'he was very much of their mind.' But the ecclesiastics did not rest till they had procured a condemnatory sentence. The accused were commanded to publish a recantation, and to promise to refrain for the future from such contumacious language concerning the Church and the Interdict, on pain of excommunication. It is said that, in spite of this decision, they did but speak and write the more in the same spirit. This, however, is not certain. It is known that Tauler shortly after-wards left his native city, and fixed his residence in Cologne, where he mostly spent the remainder of his life, actively engaged as a preacher in endeavouring to promote a deeper spirituality, and in combating the enthusiasm of the pantheistic Beghards who abounded in that city.[3]

Chronicle of Adolf Arnstein, continued.

STRASBURG. 1354. *January.*—In the comparative leisure of the winter time, I set down in order (from such fragmentary notes as I then made) records of a journey undertaken last year to Flanders.

When I left Strasburg, to sail down the Rhine, our city had enjoyed at last nearly two years' prosperity. We could scarcely believe the respite real. First of all, after so many troubles and dissensions, the Black Death had laid us waste. Then came the Flagellants, turning all things upside down—the irresistible infection of their fury—the thirst for blood they stirred up everywhere—the slaughter of the miserable Jews. Then we had the Emperor among us, demanding unrighteous imposts. Our old spirit rose. For two years and a half our chains and guard-ships barred the passage of the Rhine.[4] We would endure any extremity rather than submit, and our firm-ness won the day. Now, for the last three years,—the pestilence and its horrors over; blockaded business free again;—our little world has been gambolling like children let loose from school. Never such rapid and fruitful buying and selling, such marrying and giving in marriage, such feasting, pageantry, and merriment, among high and low alike.[5] All the

---

[3] See Schmidt's *Tauler*, p. 58.

[4] Laguille's *Histoire d'Alsace*, liv. xxv. p. 290.   [5] Hecker, p. 81

year is May for the morris-dancers. No one remembers now
the scourge or the torch.

The clergy might have learnt a lesson from the outbreak of
the Flagellants. It should have shown them how hateful their
vices and their pride had made them to the people. But the
universal levity now pardons clerical crime and folly as it does
every other. The odious exaggeration of the Flagellants has
given men a pretext for licence, and ruined the hopes of reform.
The cause of emperor against pope exists no longer. In the
hour of conflict and of sorrow, men hailed the help and listened
to the teaching of the Friends of God. Tauler himself, were he
among us, would find it another Strasburg.

Landed at Cologne, I hastened to the cloister of St. Gertrude
to find Dr. Tauler. With what delight did I see him once
more! I thought him looking much older, and, indeed, he
said he thought the same of me. The time has been long but
a stepmother to merry faces and ruddy cheeks. He told me
that he had met with great kindness in this city, which he had
always loved. His friends were numerous; his preaching, he
hoped not without fruit, and he had succeeded in reforming
much that had been amiss.[6] I had many messages for him
from his old friends in Strasburg, and he had so many questions
to ask, he knew not where to begin.

He inquired particularly after Rulman Merswin. This rich
merchant had withdrawn from the world (with the consent of
his wife) and devoted himself altogether to the contemplative
life, a short time previous to the coming of the Black Death.
His austerities had been almost fatal. Tauler's last counsel to
him was to lessen their severity. I saw him before I left, and
he desired me to tell Tauler that the Layman had visited him
more than once, and was now his spiritual guide. I informed
the Doctor, moreover, that during the last year Merswin had

[6] Schmidt's *Tauler*, p. 59.

been privately busied in writing a book, to be called *The Nine Rocks*, of which he did me the honour of reading to me a part.[7] The Doctor asking what I thought, I said it seemed to be the work of a powerful and sombre imagination, excited by the sufferings he had inflicted on himself, yet containing many solemn and most just rebukes of the vices prevalent. Tauler said that such excessive mortification in all classes, and especially among the clergy, often weakened, instead of exalting the intellect. He feared that the good Rulman would always lean too much on visions, voices, ecstasies, and the like, and never rise to the higher calm of unsensuous, imageless contemplation.

The second time I visited Tauler, I found him reading—he told me for the fourth time—a book called *The Spiritual Nuptials*, by John Ruysbroek.[8] The Doctor praised it highly, and as I questioned him about it, offered to lend it me to read. I had heard of Ruysbroek as a master in spiritual mysteries, often holding intercourse by letter with the Friends of God in Cologne, Alsace, and even in the Oberland. I took the book home to my inn, and shut myself up to read it. Many parts of it I copied out. Not a few things in it I found hard to be understood, and consulting with the Doctor about them, he told me he purposed setting out in a few days to visit the author. Should I like to accompany him? I said 'Yes, with all my heart.' So we left Cologne to travel to the convent of Grünthal, in the heart of the forest of Soigne, not far from Louvain, whither the holy man, now sixty years of age, had of late retired.[9]

From Cologne we journeyed direct to Aix-la-Chapelle. There we saw the chair in which the emperors sit when they are

---

[7] See Note, p. 336.

[8] Ruysbroek sent a copy of his book, *De ornatu spiritualium nuptiarum*, to the Friends of God in the Oberland. He had many friends in Cologne, and it is very likely that the work may have reached Tauler there, either through them or from the author, who must have heard of him.

[9] See *Johannes Ruysbroek*, by Engelhardt, p. 168.

crowned. Its sides are of ivory, and the bottom is made of a piece of wood from Noah's Ark. Tasted the water in the famous hot springs there. It is saltish ; the physicians say of singular virtue, whether taken inwardly or outwardly. Saw near the town a water which is lukewarm, by reason of one of the hot springs which passes under it. There are bred in it fine fish, they say, which must be put in cold water two months before they are eaten.

From Aix-la-Chapelle we went to Maestricht, and thence through Tirlemont, to Louvain. This last is a wealthy city, with a fine town-hall. The Flemings seem very fond of bells, which are always chiming, and the great multitude of storks was a strange thing to me ; they make their nests on the tops of the chimneys. The country round is very fertile, and the great guilds exceeding prosperous. The small handicrafts have more power there than with us at Strasburg. At Ypres, I hear, they lately mustered five thousand strong in the market-place, and headed by their deacons, engaged and routed the knights and men-at-arms who wished to hold the town against the men of Ghent.[10] They are very brave and determined, and keep better together, as it seems to me, than our folk. I found no small excitement in the city, on account of the war then carrying on between the men of Ghent and their allies, on the one side, and the Earl of Flanders on the other. It began with the old rivalry between Ghent and Bruges—some dispute about a canal from the Lys. The real struggle is between lords and commons. What Bishop Berthold and his party have been to us, that is the Count de Male to these Flemings. The popular side has lost a brave leader in John Lyon. He revived the White Hoods, and stirred up all Flanders against the earl. But two at least of the new captains, John Boule and Peter du Bois, bid fair to fill his place. When I was at Louvain, the

---

[10] Froissart, book ii. chap. 40.

troops of the earl were besieged in Oudenarde by upwards of a hundred thousand men, gathered out of all the principal towns, well provisioned and appointed. The besiegers were very strong in cross-bow men, and had with them some great guns, which did no small damage. Many hot assaults were made, both by land and water, and on both sides many brave men slain (Heaven rest their souls!) for the Flemings were no whit behind the knights in foolhardiness. When I left Brabant, report said that a peace was, or soon would be concluded, to be ratified, according to their wont there, by enormous dinners. Certain it is that neither Oudenarde nor Dendermonde were carried after all.[11]

They still talked at Louvain about that flower of chivalry Edward III. of England, who was there for a season some few years back.[12] His princely entertainments to lords and ladies left the country full of golden traditions about him. The islanders won all hearts by their unparalleled magnificence and generosity. They say the English king called James von Artaveld—brewer of metheglin as he was—his cousin, and was passing wroth when he heard of his murder. Yet methinks he cares but little after all for the Flemish weavers, save as they may help him and his knights against France. Nevertheless, the weaker France, the better for Germany. I think I understand why our emperor Charles so flatters the pope. If his Holiness could confide in Germany he would fain break with France. Be this as it may, not a word now is heard about the claims of the empire. The Ghibelline cause finds no leader. The spirit of the Hohenstaufen lives only in the rhymes of the minstrel. No doubt times are changed. There may be policy in the submission, but I love it not. The Doctor interpreted to me the other day the emperor's Latin motto, which set me thinking. It means—the best use you can make of your own

---

[11] Froissart, chapp. 41, 42.   [12] *Ibid.*, book i. chap. 34.

wits is to turn to good account the follies of other people.[13] So cardinals and envoys riding to and fro, plotting and treaty-making, will manage Christendom now, not strong arms and sword-strokes. Whether, in the end, this change will lead to better or to worse, it baffles my poor brain to decide.

We set out from Louvain for Grünthal, quite a troop of us. There was a noble widow-lady, with her attendants, who was going to crave ghostly counsel from the prior. She had lost her husband by the plague, three years since, and appeared still overwhelmed with grief, speaking to no one, and never suffering her face to be seen. Her women, when not near her, were merry enough with the followers of a young Frenchman of family who carried letters to Ruysbroek from his uncle, an abbot in Paris. We had with us besides two Minorite friars from Guelders. The head dresses of the women were fit for giantesses, rising up like a great horn, with long ribbons fluttering from the top. One of them had a little dagger in her girdle, and managed a spirited horse to admiration. The Frenchman, with whom I had much talk, was an arrant fop, yet a shrewd fellow withal. He jingled like a jester with his many silver bells, his hair was tied behind in a tail, the points of his shoes turned up, his parti-coloured doublet cut short round (a new fashion, adopted for greater swiftness in flying from an enemy), and his beard, long and bushy, trimmed with a sort of studied negligence. He gave me a melancholy account of the state of France, divided within, overrun by the English invaders, nobles plundering and burning—here to-day and there to-morrow, without pity, law, or loyalty ; knights destroying, not helping the weak : troops of robbers surprising castles and even taking towns ; and the wretched peasantry fain often to hide themselves and their cattle for weeks and months in great caves hollowed out underneath the ground.

[13] Optimum aliena insania frui.

One of the friars told me a story current about Prior Ruys-broek, how, one day, he was absent longer than usual in the forest, whither he was accustomed to retire for meditation, and as some of the brethren went to seek him they saw a tree at a distance which appeared surrounded by fiery glory. The holy man was sitting at its foot, lost in contemplation! The Saviour and our Blessed Lady herself are said to have appeared to him more than once.[14]

We reached Grünthal—a great building of exceeding plain-ness—soon after nightfall. Found there visitors from Brussels, so that, between us, nearly all the guest chambers were filled. The good Ruysbroek has been there but a year, yet if he is always to be thus sought unto, methinks he is as far from his longed-for seclusion as ever.[15]

We remained three weeks at Grünthal, for whenever the Doctor would be going, the good Prior so besought him to tarry longer that he could not in courtesy say him nay. Often Ruys-broek and Tauler would spend all the summer morning in the forest, now walking, now sitting under the trees, talking of the concerns of the soul, or of the fears and hopes awakened by these doubtful times. I was permitted repeatedly to accompany them, and afterwards wrote down some of the more remarkable things I heard said. These two saintly men, prepared to love each other as brothers in a common experience, seemed at once to grow together into a friendship as strong as though many years had been employed in the building thereof. Neither of them vain, neither jealous, each was for humbling himself beneath the other, and seemed desirous rather to hear and learn than to talk about himself.

Speaking about the Son of God and the soul of man, Ruys-

---

[14] Engelhardt, p. 326.

[15] It is certain that Ruysbroek was visited during the many years of his residence in Grünthal, much after the manner described, and also that Tau-ler was among the visitors, though the exact time of his journey is not known.

broek said—' I believe that the Son is the Image of the Father, that in the Son have dwelt from all eternity, foreknown and contemplated by the Father, the prototypes of all mankind. We existed in the Son before we were born—He is the creative ground of all creatures—the eternal cause and principle of their life. The highest essence of our being rests therefore in God, —exists in his image in the Son. After our creation in time, our souls are endowed with these properties, which are in effect one ; the first, the Imageless Nudity, (*die bildlose Nacktheit*) —by means of this we receive and are united to the Father ; the second, the Higher Reason of the Soul (*die höhere Vernunft der Seele*), the mirror of brightness, by which we receive the Son ; the third, the Spark of the Soul (*Funken der Seele*) by which we receive the love of God the Holy Ghost. These three faculties are in us all the ground of our spiritual life, but in sinners they are obscured and buried under their transgressions.[16]

' The office of the Son in time was to die for us, fulfil the

---

[16] See Engelhardt, pp. 189, 288.— According to Ruysbroek, the Trinitarian process lies at the basis of the kingdoms both of Nature and of Grace. There is a flowing forth and manifestation in the creative Word, —a return and union of love by the Holy Ghost. This process goes on continually in the providential government of the universe, and in the spiritual life of believers. The upholding of the world, and the maintenance of the work of grace in the heart, are both in different ways a perpetual bringing forth of the Son, by whom all things consist, and who is formed in every devout soul. Ruysbroek is careful to state (as a *caveat* against pantheism) that such process is no necessary development of the divine nature,—it is the good pleasure of the Supreme. (See *Vier Schriften von J. Ruysbroek, in niederdeutscher Sprache*,* by A. v. Arnswaldt ; Hanover, 1848.) ' Wi hebben alle boven onse ghescapenheit een ewich leuen in gode als in onse leuende sake die ons ghemaect ende ghescapen heest van niete, maer wi en sijn niet god noch wi en hebben ons seluen niet ghemaeckt. *Wi en sijn ooc niet wt gode ghevloten van naturen*, maer want ons god ewelijc ghevoelt heest ende bekent in hem seluen, so heest hi ons ghemaeckt, niet van naturen noch van node, *maer van vriheit sijns willen*,'—p. 291. (*Spiegel der Seligkeit*, xvii.)

The bosom of the Father, he says, is our proper ground and origin (der schois des vaders is onse eygen gront ind onse oirsprunck) ; we have all, therefore, the capacity for receiving God, and His grace enables us to recognise and realise this latent possibility (offenbairt ind brengit vort die verboirgenheit godes in wijsen),—p. 144.

* (1) Die Zierde der Geistlichen Hochzeit ; (2) Von dem funkelnden Steine ; (3) Von Vier Versuchungen ; (4) Der Spiegel der Seligkeit.

law, and give us a divine pattern of humility, love, and patience He is the fountain whence flows to us all needed blessing, and with him works the Holy Spirit. What the Son did he did for all—is Light-bringer for all mankind, for the Catholic Church especially, but also for every devoutly-disposed mind. Grace is common, and whoever desires it has it. Without it no natural powers or merits can save us. The will is free by nature, it becomes by grace more free; yea, a king, lord of every lower power, crowned with Love, clad in the might of the Holy Ghost. There is a natural will towards good (*Synderesis*) implanted in us all, but damped by sin. We can will to follow this better impulse, and of ourselves desire the help of divine grace, without which we can never overcome sin and rise above ourselves. Everything depends on will. A man must will right strongly. Will to have humility and love, and they are thine. If any man is without the spirit of God, it is his own fault, for not seeking that without which he cannot please Him.[17]

'True penitence is of the heart; bodily suffering is not essential. No one is to think he is shut out from Christ because he cannot bear the torturing penance some endure. We must never be satisfied with any performance, any virtue—only in the abyss, the Nothingness of Humility, do we rise beyond all heavens. True desire after God is not kept back by the sense of defect. The longing soul knows only this, that it is

[17] Engelhardt, pp. 183, 186. Ruysbroek speaks as follows of that fundamental tendency godward of which he supposes prevenient grace (vurloiffende gracie) to lay hold :—'Ouch hait der mynsche eyn naturlich gront neygen zo gode overmitz den voncken der sielen ind die overste reden die altzijt begert dat goide ind hasset dat quaide. Mit desen punten voirt got alle mynschen na dat sijs behoeven ind ecklichen na sinre noit,' &c.— *Geistl. Hochzeit*, cap. 3.

Ruysbroek lays great stress on the exercise of the will. 'Ye are as holy as ye truly will to be holy,' said he one day to two ecclesiastics, inquiring concerning growth in grace. It is not difficult to reconcile such active effort with the passivity of mysticism. The mystics all say, 'We strive towards virtue by a strenuous use of the *gifts* which God communicates, but when God communicates *Himself*, then we can be only passive—we repose, we enjoy, but all operation ceases.'

bent on God. Swallowed up in aspiration, it can take heed of nothing more."[18] (A very weighty saying this, methinks, and helpful.)

Speaking of the inner life, and the union of the soul with God, Ruysbroek said—

'God dwells in the highest part of the soul. He who ascends this height has all things under his feet. We are united to God when, in the practice of the virtues, we deny and forsake ourselves, loving and following God above all creatures. We cannot compel God by our love to love us, but He cannot sanctify us unless we freely contribute our effort. There is a reciprocal desire on our part and that of God. The free inspiration of God is the spring of all our spiritual life. Thence flows into us knowledge—an inner revelation which preserves our spirit open, and, lifting us above all images and all disturbance, brings us to an inward silence. Here the divine inspiration is a secret whispering in the inner ear. God dwells in the heart pure and free from every image. Then first, when we withdraw into the *simplicitas* of our heart, do we behold the immeasurable glory of God, and our intellect is as clear from all considerations of distinction and figurative apprehensions, as though we had never seen or heard of such things. Then the riches of God are open to us. Our spirit becomes desireless, as though there were nothing on earth or in heaven of which we stood in need. Then we are alone with God, God and we—nothing else. Then we rise above all multiplicity and distinction into the simple nakedness of our essence, and in it become conscious of the infinite wisdom of the Divine Essence, whose inexhaustible depths are as a vast waste, into which no corporeal and no spiritual image can intrude. Our created is absorbed in our uncreated life, and we are as it were transformed into God. Lost in the abyss of our eternal blessedness, we perceive no

[18] Engelhardt, pp. 195, 199.

distinction between ourselves and God. As soon as we begin to reflect and to consider what that is we feel, we become aware of such distinction, and fall back to the level of reason.'[19]

Here Tauler asked whether such language was not liable to abuse by the heretics who confound man and God? He referred to a passage in the *Spiritual Nuptials*, in which Ruysbroek said that we became identical, in this union, with the glory by which we are illumined.[20]

Ruysbroek answered, that he had designed to qualify duly all such expressions. 'But you know, Doctor,' continued he, 'I have not your learning, and cannot at all times say so accurately as I would what I mean. Out of the mouths of babes and sucklings!—I would say that in such a state all our powers are in repose, not that they are annihilated. If so, we should lose our existence as creatures. We are one with God, but yet always creature existences distinct from God. I do humbly believe, let my enemies say what they may, that I wrote no word of that book save at the impulse of the Holy Ghost, and with a peculiar and most blessed presence to my soul of the Holy Trinity. But what shall I call this blessedness? It includes peace, inward silence, affectionate hanging on the source of our joy, sleep in God, contemplation of the heaven of darkness, far above reason.'[21]

The conversation then turned on the heresies of the time, the

[19] Engelhardt, pp. 201, 213. In the season of spiritual exaltation, the powers of the soul are, as it were, absorbed in absolute essential enjoyment (staen ledich in een weselic gebrucken). But they are not annihilated, for then we should lose our creatureliness.—Mer si en werden niet te niete, want soe verloeren wy onse gescapenheit. Ende alsoe lange als wy mit geneichden geeste ende mit apen ogen sonder merken ledich staen,

alsoe lange moegen wy schouwen ende gebruken. Mer in den seluen ogenblijc dat wy proeven ende merken willen wat dat is dat wy geuoelen, so vallen wy in reden, ende dan vynden wy onderscheit ende anderheit tusschen ons ende gade, ende dan vynden wy gade buten ons in onbegripelicheiden. — *Von dem funkelnden Steine*, x.

[20] See first Note, p. 338.

[21] See second Note, p. 338.

corruptions of the Church and of the State, and other practical matters more within my compass. Ruysbroek said that the great sin and error of these heretics lay in their aspiring to union with God by a summary and arrogant method of their own. They persuaded themselves that, merely by ceasing to think and distinguish, they could withdraw themselves into the essence of their nature, and so, without the help of grace or the practice of virtue, attain by bare nature the rest and blessedness of absolute simplicity and superiority to all modes and images.

'Verily,' quoth Tauler, 'though they give themselves out for the wisest and the holiest, it is only themselves, not God, they enjoy. Yet mischievous as they are, often as I have preached against them, I never have taken, nor shall I take, any part in their persecution.'[22]

'I have had plentiful opportunity,' continued Ruysbroek, 'for observing these men. I would divide them into four classes.[23]

---

[22] Engelhardt, p. 225. Schmidt's *Tauler*, p. 61.—The same doctrine which furnished a sanctuary for the devotion of purer natures supplied also an excuse for the licence of the base. Wilful perversion, or mere ignorance, or some one of the manifold combinations of these two factors, would work the mystical exhortation into some such result as that denounced by Ruysbroek. We may imagine some bewildered man as speaking thus within himself :—'So we are to covet ignorance, to surmount distinctions, to shun what is clear or vivid as mediate and comparatively carnal, to transcend means and bid farewell to the wisdom of the schools. Wise and devout men forsake all their learning, forget their pious toil and penance, to lose themselves in that ground in which we are united to God,—to sink into vague abstract confusion. But may I not do at first what they do at last? Why take in only to take out? I am empty already.

Thank heaven! I haven't a distinct idea in my head.'

It is so that the popular mind is sure to travesty the ultra-refinements of philosophy.

[23] Engelhardt, pp. 224-228.—Eckart, like Hegel, would seem to have left behind him a right-hand and a left-hand party,—admirers like Suso and Tauler, who dropped his extreme points and held by such saving clauses as they found ; and headstrong spirits, ripe for anarchy, like these New-Lights or High-Fliers, the representatives of mysticism run to seed. Ruysbroek's classification of them is somewhat artificial ; fanaticism does not distribute itself theologically. In the treatise entitled *Spiegel der Seligkeit*, § 16, he describes them generally as follows :—'Ander quade duulische menschen vint men, die segghen dat si selue Cristus sijn of dat si god sijn, ende dat haer hant hemel ende erde ghemaect heest, ende dat an haer hant hanghet hemel

First of all there are those whose doctrine sins especially against
the Holy Ghost.   They say the essential Godhead works not,
but the Holy Ghost doth : that they belong to that Divine
Essence, and will rest in like manner ;—that they are, therefore, above the Spirit of God.   They hold that, after time, all
things will be God, one absolute Quiescence, without distinction and without change.   So they will neither know nor act,
neither think nor thank, but be free from all desire, all obligation.   This they call Poverty of Spirit.   I say it is a devilish
poverty, and such souls must be poor as hell in divine love and
knowledge.

'The second class say, with like blasphemy, 'We are divine
by nature.   There is one God, and we are identical with Him.
We with Him have created all things ; if we had not chosen,
we had not been born.   It was our own choice to exist as we
do.   God can do nothing without us, and we give Him therefore no preference, pay Him no homage.   Honour to Him is
honour to us.   What we are we would be, what we would be
we are ; with God we have created ourselves and all things ;
heaven and earth hang on our will.'   This insane spiritual
pride is flatly contrary to all catholic doctrine.

'The third class sin not less against the Son.   They say, we
are as much incarnate as Christ was, and, in the same sense,
divine sons of God.   Had He lived long enough, He would

ende erde ende alle dinc, ende dat si
verheuen sijn boven alle die sacra-
menten der heiligher kerken, ende dat
si der niet en behoeuen noch si en
willen der ooc niet.' He represents
their claim to identity with God as
leading to a total moral indifference
(§ 17) :—'Ende sulke wanen god sijn,
ende si en achten gheen dinc goet noch
quaet, in dien dat si hem ontboelden
connen ende in bloter ledicheit haer
eighen wesen vinden ende besitten mog-
hen.' Their idea of the consummation
of all things savours of the Parisian
heresy—the offspring of John Scotus,
popularised by David of Dinant and
his followers.   The final restitution is
to consist in the resolution of all
creatures into the Divine Substance :—
'So spreken si voort dat in den lesten
daghe des ordels enghele ende duuele,
goede ende quade, dese sullen alle
werden *een eenvoudighe substancie der
godheit* . . . . ende na dan, spreken si
voort, en sal god bekennen noch minnen hem seluen noch ghene creature'—
(§ 16).

have attained to the same contemplative quiet we enjoy. Retired into our inmost selves, we find ourselves the same Wisdom of God which Christ is. When He is honoured, we are honoured, for we are identical with Him.

'The fourth class declare that neither God nor themselves, heaven nor hell, action nor rest, good nor evil, have any real existence. They deny God and the work of Christ, Scripture, sacraments,—everything. God is nothing; they are nothing; the universe is nothing.

'Some hold doctrines such as these in secret, and conform outwardly, for fear. Others make them the pretext for every kind of vice and insolent insubordination. Of a truth we should cross ourselves when we but speak of them, as in the neighbourhood of spirits from the pit.'

'And what hope,' said Tauler, 'of better things, while the Church is crowded with hirelings, and, with lust and bravery, everywhere leads on the world in sin?'

'What hope, indeed!' mournfully responded Ruysbroek. 'The grace of the sacraments is shamefully bought and sold. Rich transgressors may live as they list. The wealthy usurer is buried before the altar, the bells ring, the priest declares him blessed. I declare that if he died in unrighteousness, not all the priests in Christendom, not all his hoards lavished to feed the poor, could save him from perdition. See, too, the monks, mendicants and all, what riches! what sumptuous fare! what licence, in violation of every vow! what odious distinctions! Some have four or five garments, another scarcely one. Some revel with the prior, the guardian, and the lector in the refectory, at a place of their own. Others must be content with herring and cabbage, washed down with sour beer. Little by little the habit is changed, black becomes brown, grey is exchanged for blue, the white must be of the finest stuff, the shape of the newest cut.'

'This,' said Tauler, 'is what I so much admire in your little community here. You have practically abolished those mischievous distinctions, the cause of so much bitterness in our religious houses. Every one has his place, but no one is degraded. You yourself will perform the meanest offices, as the other morning, when Arnstein found you sweeping the lectorium. Yours is the true canonical life—the life of a family. Every one is ready to do kind offices for his brethren, and your own example teaches daily forgetfulness of self.'

Ruysbroek looked uneasy under these praises, and they spoke again of the prevalent evils in the Church.[24]

'How many nuns have I seen,' said Ruysbroek, 'daintily attired, with silver bells to their girdles, whose prison was the cloister and their paradise the world! A retinue of forty reiters is a moderate attendance for a prelate out on a visitation. I have known some priests who engaged themselves as business agents to laymen; others who have entered the service of ladies of rank, and walked behind them as footmen into church. A criminal has but to pay money down, and he may serve the devil for another year. A trim reckoning, and satisfaction for all parties! The bishop gets the gold, the devil gets the soul, and the miserable fool the moment's pleasure of his lust.'[25]

When, one day, they were conversing on future rewards and punishments, I remember hearing Ruysbroek say—'I trust I am

[24] Engelhardt, pp. 326-336.—Good Ruysbroek was fully entitled to the encomium placed in the mouth of Tauler. He himself, like Bernard, would frequently perform the meanest offices of the cloister. The happy spirit of brotherhood which prevailed among the canons of Grünthal made a deep impression on that laborious practical reformer, Gerard Groot, when, in 1378, he visited the aged prior. What he then saw was not without its influence in the formation of that community with which his name is associated—the Brethren of the Common Life.— See Ullmann, *Reformatoren vor der Reformation*, vol. ii.

[25] Engelhardt, p. 330.—Ruysbroek inveighs with much detail against the vanities of female dress—as to those hair-pads, sticking up like great horns, they are just so many 'devil's nests.'

ready for all God sends me, life or death, or even hell-pains themselves.' An attainment of virtue inconceivable to me.[26]

At Grünthal I saw much of a lay brother named John Affliginiensis, the cook of the community.[27] He accompanied Ruysbroek thither. Though wholly unlettered, he serves daily as a goodly ensample of the active and contemplative life united. It is his calling to see to the dinners of the brethren ; he is scarce less helpful to their devotions. That he is a good plain cook I can bear witness, and to the edifying character of the discourses he sometimes delivers to the canons, all testify. He scarcely sleeps at all, goes meanly clad, and eats the veriest refuse of the convent fare. He is one of the meekest and most humble of men —has had his sore fights of temptation, fierce inward purgations, and also his favoured hours and secret revelations. Ruysbroek loves him like a brother. The esteem in which he is held, and the liberty of speech allowed him, is characteristic of the simple and brotherly spirit which dwells among these worthy canons. Grünthal is not, like so many religious houses, a petty image of the pettiest follies of the world. There they do seem to have withdrawn in spirit from the strife and pomp of secular life.

---

[26] Ruysbroek expressed himself in these words to Gerard Groot (Engelhardt, p. 168). In his touching description of the 'desolation' endured by the soul on its way upward toward the 'super-essential contemplation,' he makes the sufferer say,—'O Lord, since I am thine (want ich din eygen bin), I would as soon be in hell as in heaven, if such should be thy good pleasure ; only do thy glorious will with me, O Lord !'—*Geistl. Hochzeit,* § 30. Ruysbroek, like Fénélon, abandons himself thus only on the supposition that even in hell he should still retain the divine favour ;—so impossible after all is the absolute disinterestedness toward which Quietism aspires. The Flemish mystic distinguishes between the servants of God,

the friends, and the sons. Those worshippers who stand in the relation of friends have still something of their own (besitten oer inwendichkeit mit eygenscap) in their love to God. The sons ascend, 'dying-wise,' to an absolute emptiness. The friends still set value on divine bestowments and experiences ; the sons are utterly dead to self, in bare modeless love (in bloeter ; wiseloeser mynnen). Yet, very inconsistently, he represents the sons as more assured of eternal life than the friends. (*Von dem funkelnden Steine,* § 8.)

[27] A veritable personage. He died in 1377, and left behind him a book recording the conflicts he underwent and the revelations vouchsafed him. (Engelhardt, p. 326.)

Gladly would I spend my last years among the beeches and the oaks that shut in their holy peace. But while I may I must be doing ; had my call been to the contemplative life I should have been moulded in another fashion.

On our journey back from Louvain I had rare entertainment. We had scarcely passed out beyond the gates, when Tauler rode forward, in deep discourse with an ecclesiastic of the party. A hasty glance at our fellow-travellers, as we mustered at the door of the hostelry, had not led me to look for any company likely to eke out a day's travel with aught that was pleasant or of profit. But I was mistaken. I espied ere long, a neat, merry-looking little man, in a minstrel's habit, with a gittern slung at his back. To him I joined himself, and he, pleased evidently with the notice I took of him, sang me songs and told me stories all the way. He said his name was Muscatblut, and I was not sorry to be able to gratify him by answering that his fame had already reached my ears.[28] He had store of songs, with short and long lines curiously interwoven in a way of his own, a very difficult measure to write, as he assured me—the very triumph of his heart. These love-lays he interspersed with riddles and rhyming proverbs, with quaint allegories, satires on clerks and monks, and stories about husbands and wives, making all within hearing roll in their saddles with laughter. He had likewise certain coarse songs, half amatory, half devotional, tagged with bits of slang and bits of Latin, about the wooing of our Lady. I told him, to his surprise, to stop ; it was flat blasphemy. He said the voluptuous passages of his lay were after Frauenlob's best manner, and as to the sacred personages, by St. Bartholomew ! many a holy clerk had praised that part most of all, calling it a deep allegory, most edifying to the advanced believer.

---

[28] The lyrics of Muscatblut are characterised by Gervinus (ii. p. 225), and the same authority gives some account, from the *Limburg Chronicle*, of the famous friar, leper, and poet mentioned by Arnstein.

At Cologne I parted from the Doctor with many embraces. On my way back to Strasburg I took boat up the Mayne to Frankfurt, whither business called me. We passed a little woody island in the midst of the river, which was pointed out to me as the residence of the leprous barefooted friar, whose songs and airs are so popular throughout the Rhineland. I looked with reverence at the melancholy spot. There he dwells alone, shut out from mankind, yet delighting and touching every heart. His songs are sweet as the old knightly lays of love, full of courtly grace and tenderness, and yet they are songs for the people from one truly of themselves. The burgher has his minstrelsy now, as well as the noble. This at least is a good sign.

NOTE TO PAGE 321.

From this time forward, Rulman Merswin gave himself up to the spiritual guidance of Nicholas the layman—taking him to be to him 'in God's stead.' He took no step without his direction, and wrote at his command his book entitled *Von den vier ioren sins anevohenden lebendes*—a record of what may be called his spiritual apprenticeship. Nicholas took a copy of it back with him to the Oberland. Schmidt has brought together what is known of Merswin, in the Appendix to his life of Tauler, pp. 177, &c.

The *Book of the Nine Rocks* was commenced in 1352. It has been published in Diepenbrock's edition of the works of Suso, to whom it was, till recently, attributed. The claim of Merswin to its authorship is established beyond question—(Schmidt, 180). The work opens by relating how, early one morning in Advent, a man (the author) was warned of God to prepare himself, by inward retirement, for that which He should show him. He was made to behold a vision full of strange and alarming appearances. He cried out, 'Ah, my heart's Love! what meanest thou with these mysterious symbols?' He struggled hard against the phantoms of his trance, but the marvellous forms only multiplied the more. He was constrained by a divine voice to gaze, and commanded, in spite of his humble remonstrances, to write in a book what he saw—the image of the corruptions of Christendom, for the warning of the guilty and the edification of the faithful. The dialogues are given at length between him and God—'the Man' and 'the Answer.' For eleven weeks, in sickness and spiritual distress, he wavered. He was but a poor, ignorant layman; how should he presume to exhort the Church? 'The Voice of the Answer' is heard saying, 'Came not thy reluctance from humility, I would consign thee to the pit. I see I must compel thee. In the name of the Holy Trinity, I command thee to begin to write this day.'

The souls of men proceeding from God, but few of them returning to their Original, are shown him under the similitude of multitudes of fish, brought down by the descent of great waters from the summit of a mountain. Men in the valley are catching them in nets. Scarce half of them reach the sea below. There the remnant swim in all directions, and at length endeavour to leap back, up to the source whence they came. Numbers are taken in the nets ; only a few reach even the base of the mountain. Some who ascend higher fall back upon the rocks and die. A very few, springing from rock to rock, reach exhausted, the fountain at the top, and there forget their pains.

The twenty following chapters are occupied with a dialogue, in which the divine Voice enumerates the characteristic sins of all classes of mankind, from the pope to the begging friar—from the emperor to the serf.

Then commences the vision of the Nine Rocks. A mountain, enormous in breadth and height, fills all the scene. As the eye travels up the ascent, it beholds nine steep rocks, each loftier than that which preceded it,—the highest lost in the heavens. From the lowest the whole surface of the earth is visible. A net is spread over all the region beneath, but it does not reach the mountain. The multitudes seen beneath it are men in mortal sin. The men standing on the first and lowest rock are religious persons, but such as are lukewarm, defective in aspiration and in zeal. They dwell dangerously near the net—(cap. xxiii.). Some, from the first rock, are seen making their way up the precipice, and reaching the second, where they become of dazzling brightness. Those on the second rock have heartily forsaken the world ; they will suffer less in purgatory, enjoy more in heaven, than those beneath ; but they, too, are far from their Origin yet, and in danger of spiritual pride, self-seeking, and of growing faint and remiss in their painful progress—(cap. xxiv.). Those on the third rock, fewer in number, suffering far more severely in time, are nearer to God, will suffer little in purgatory, and are of yet more glorious aspect than their predecessors—(cap. xxv.). Such is the process to the summit. All the nine rocks must be surmounted, would we return to our Divine Source. But few attain the last, which is indeed the Gate of the Origin—the consummate blessedness, in which the believer, fearless of hell and purgatory, has annihilated self, and hath no wish or will save that of God. One of these true worshippers brings more blessing to Christendom than thousands of such as live after their own will, and know not that they are nothing.

Finally, 'the man' is permitted a moment's glance into the Divine 'Origin.' The rapture of that moment he attempted in vain to describe ;—no reflection, no image, could give the least hint of it.

Both Rulman and 'the Friend of God in the Oberland' believed themselves repeatedly warned of God in visions, that they should build a house for him in Strasburg. The merchant purchased a ruined cloister on a little island in the river Ill, without the city walls. He restored the church, and erected a stone belfry. Nicholas advised him to bestow it on the Johannites, in preference to any other Order,—for there had been no little rivalry among the monks as to who was to enjoy the gift. The conditions of the deed for which he stipulated with the Master of the Order are indicative of the new and more elevated position which mysticism had taught the laity to claim. The government of the house was to rest entirely with a lay triumvirate ; the two survivors always to choose a third. The first three governors were Rulman himself, Heinzmann Wetzel, knight, and John Merswin, burg-graf. The admission of brethren rested with these heads of the house, and they were free to receive any one, clerk or layman, knight or serving man, whether belonging to the order of St. John or not, requiring only that he should bring with him the moderate sum requisite to render his residence no burden on the convent. (Schmidt, p. 189.)

NOTE TO PAGE 329.

The passage to which Tauler is made to refer is contained in the third book of the Spiritual Nuptials, chap. 5:—'Ind alle die minschen die bouen ir geschaffenheit verhauen sin in eyn schauwende leuen, die synt eyn mit deser gotlicher clairheit, ind sij sint die clairheit selver. Ind sy sien ind gevoilen ind vynden sich selver ouermitz dit gotliche licht, dat sy sin der selue eynveldige gront na wijse irre ungeschaffenheit, da de clairheit sonder mias vs schynt in gotlicher wijsen ind na sympelheit des wesens eynueldich binnen blijfft ewelich sonder wise. Ind hervm soilen die innyge schauwende minschen vsgayn na wijse des schauwens bouen reden ind bouen vnderscheit ind bouen ir geschaffen wesen mit ewigen instarren ouermitz dat ingeboiren licht, soe werden sy getransformeirt ind eyn mit desem seluen licht da sy mede sien ind dat sy sien. Ind also vervolgen die schauwende minschen ir ewich bilde da si zo gemacht sin ind beschauwen got ind alle dinck sonder vnderscheit in eyme eynveldigen sien in gotlicher clairheit. In dat is dat edelste ind dat vrberlichste schauwen da men zo komen mach in desem leuen.'—*Vier Schriften*, p. 144.

[And all men who are exalted above their creatureliness into a contemplative life are *one with this divine glory,*—*yea, are that glory.* And they see, and feel, and find in themselves, by means of this divine light, that they are the same simple Ground as to their uncreated nature (*i.e.*, in respect of their ideal pre-existence in the Son), since the glory shineth forth without measure, after the divine manner, and abideth within them simply and without mode (particular manifestation or medium), according to the simplicity of the essence. Wherefore interior contemplative men should go forth in the way of contemplation above reason and distinction, beyond their created substance, and gaze perpetually by the aid of their inborn light, and so they become transformed, and *one with the same light, by means of which they see, and which they see.* Thus do contemplative men arrive at that eternal image after which they were created, and contemplate God and all things without distinction in a simple beholding, in divine glory. And this is the loftiest and most profitable contemplation whereto men may attain in this life.]

This passage, and others like it, gave rise to the charge of pantheism brought by Gerson against Ruysbroek in the following century. The prior of Grünthal found a defender in Schönhoven, who pointed with justice to numerous expressions in the writings of the accused, altogether incompatible with the heresy alleged. Quite inconsistent with any confusion of the divine and human is Ruysbroek's fine description of the insatiable hunger of the soul—growing by that it feeds on,—the consciousness that all possessed is but a drop to the illimitable undeemed Perfection yet beyond. ('Wi leren in waerheit sijns aenschijns dat al dat wi gesmaken tegen dat ons ontblijft dat en is niet een draep tegen al die zee, dit verstormt onsen geest in hetten ende in ongeduer van mynnen.'—*Von dem funkelnden Steine*, x. p. 194.) So again he says, 'Want wy enmogen te mael niet got werden ende onse gescapenheit verliesen, dat is onmoegelic'—p. 190 ; and similarly that we become one with God in love, not in nature, ('ouerformet ende een mit hem in sijnre minnen, niet in sijnre naturen.') —*Spiegel der Seligkeit*, xxiv.

NOTE TO PAGE 329.

Ruysbroek expressed to Gerard Groot, in these very words, his belief in the special guidance of the Holy Spirit vouchsafed for the composition of his books on these 'deep things' of the kingdom. (Engelhardt, p. 168.)

The doctrine of Ruysbroek is substantially the same with that of his friend and brother-mystic, Tauler. Whether speaking the high German of the upper

Rhine or the low German of the Netherlands, mysticism gives utterance to the same complaint and the same aspiration. Ruysbroek is individually less speculative than Eckart, less practical than Tauler. The Flemish mystic is a more submissive son of the Church than the stout-hearted Dominican of Strasburg, and lays proportionally more stress on what is outward and institutional. He is fond of handling his topics analytically. His numerous divisions and subdivisions remind us of the scholastic Richard of St. Victor, but Ruysbroek, less methodical by nature, and less disciplined, more frequently loses sight of his own distinctions. The subject itself, indeed, where it possesses the writer, repudiates every artificial treatment. While he specifies with minuteness the stages of the mystical ascent, Ruysbroek does not contend that the experience of every adept in the contemplative life must follow the precise order he lays down. (*Geistl. Hochzeit*, ii. § 30, p. 71.) He loves to ally the distinctions he enumerates in the world of nature, in the operations of grace, in the heavenly state, and in the Divine Being, by a relationship of correspondence. Thus the seven planets and the seven gifts of the Holy Spirit answer to each other. The Empyrean in the external world corresponds to Pure Being in the divine nature, to the Spark of the soul in man, and to the Contemplative stage of his spiritual experience. This scheme of analogies, incidental in Ruysbroek and the earlier mystics, makes up almost the whole system of mystics like Behmen and Swedenborg. His elaborate comparison of the operations of grace to a fountain with three streams (one of which refreshes the memory, another clarifies the understanding, while a third invigorates the will), resembles strikingly the fanciful method of Madame Guyon in her *Torrents*, and of St. Theresa in her *Degrees of Prayer*. (*Geistl. Hochzeit*, xvii. § 36, p. 80.) The mysticism of Ruysbroek is less sensuous than that of the poetical Suso. Beyond question the higher elevation of the contemplative life must have been a welcome refuge to many devout minds wearied with vain ritual, penance, and routine. As acknowledged contemplatists, they could escape without scandal from contact with the grosser machinery of their religion. Accordingly, to claim superiority to means and modes was by no means always the arrogant pretension it may seem to us. Tauler's 'state above grace' was the ark of an unconscious Protestantism. Where the means were made the end, wisdom forsook them, and rejoiced to find that the name of mystic could shelter spirituality from the dangers of the suspected heretic. Ruysbroek, however, felt the want of such a protection for freer thought, much less than did Tauler and some of his more active followers.

CHAPTER VIII.

Unde planctus et lamentum?
Quid mentem non erigis?
Quid revolvis monumentum?
Tecum est quem diligis;
Jesum quæris, et inventum
Habes, nec intelligis.

Unde gemis, unde ploras?
Verum habes gaudium.
In te latet quod ignoras
Doloris solatium.
Intus habes, quæris foras
Languoris remedium.[1]

HYMN OF THE FIFTEENTH CENTURY.

Vivo sin vivir mi,
Y tan alta vida espero
Que muero porque no muero.[2]

ST. THERESA.

ON the next evening Atherton resumed his reading as
follows:—

Chronicle of Adolph Arnstein, continued.

1354. *March. St. Brigitta's Day.*—A fortnight ago this
day, there came to me, to buy as goodly a battle-axe as could
be made, young Sir Ulric—the same who, at the tourney the

[1] Why smite thy breast and lament?
why not lift up thy soul? why meditate
for ever on the sign? He thou lovest
is within thee. Thou seekest Jesus—
thou hast him; he is found. and thou
perceivest it not. Why these groans,
this weeping? The true joy is thine;
hidden within thee, though thou knowest it not, lies the solace of thine anguish; thou hast within, thou seekest
without, the cure for thy languishing
soul.

[2] I live, but with no life of mine, and
long towards a life so high—I die because I do not die.

other day, graced his new-won spurs by such gallant feats of
arms.   We fell into talk about the great floods which have
everywhere wrought of late such loss of life, and cattle, and
husbandry.   He said he had but the day before saved the life
of a monk who, with his companion, had been carried beyond
his depth by the force of the water, as they were wading across
the fields.

' The one most in danger,' said Ulric, ' had a big book in his
bosom.   As he flounders about, out tumbles the book ; he lets
go his staff, and makes after it ; and souse he goes, over head
and ears in a twinkling.   The other stands stock still, and
bawls out to me for help.   I, just sworn to succour the distressed and be true to the Church, spur Roland, plunge in, and
lift out the draggled, streaming father by the hood, half throt-
tled and half drowned, but clutching the book in his frozen
fingers as though it were a standard or a fair lady's token.   I
lay him before me across my horse ; his fellow catches hold of
my stirrup, and we land on the rising ground.   When my
monk had somewhat come to himself, he pours as many blessings on my head as there were drops running from his habit ;
not, he said, for saving his poor life merely, but that the book
was safe.   He had just finished writing it—there was not
another copy in the world—the devil had an especial spite
against it—no doubt the fiend had raised the waters to destroy
the seed which fed men's souls as well as the grain which
nourished their bodies ; but the faithful God had sent me, like
his angel, just in time for rescue.   I saw them in safety, and
he promised to remember me in his orisons.   His name, I
think he said, was Seusse or Suso.'[3]

<hr>

[3] The *Life of Suso,* published in
Diepenbrock's edition of his works, was
written by his spiritual daughter, Elsbet
Stäglin, according to the account she
received at various intervals from his
own lips.   He sprang from a good
family,—his name, originally Heinrich
vom Berg.   The name of Suso he
adopted from his mother, a woman
remarkable for her devotion.   The

So Suso is in Strasburg, thought I,—the man I have long wished to see. I lost no time in inquiring after him at the Dominican convent. There I found, with no small satisfaction, that he was none the worse for his mishap ; saw him several times, and persuaded him, at last, to honour for a few days my unworthy roof. He has been with us for a week, but must pursue his journey to-morrow. On my part, I could tell him news about Ruysbroek, and Tauler, and some of his old friends at Cologne. On his, he has won the love of all the household by his gentle, affectionate nature, blessed us by his prayers, and edified every heart by his godly conversation. My good wife would love him, if for nothing else, because he so loves the little ones. They love him because he always goes with them to feed the old falcon, and to throw out crumbs for the sparrows, because he joins them in petting Argus, and talks so sweetly about the Virgin and Child, and the lilies and violets and roses, and the angels with gold-bright wings that live in heaven. Those three tall fellows, my boys, fonder of sword-play, wrestling, and camping the bar, than of churchmen or church-going, will listen to him by the hour, while he tells of his visions, his journeys, his dangers, and his deliverances. Rulman Merswin also came over and spent two evenings with us. He talked much with Suso about Master Eckart. Suso was full of reminiscences and anecdotes about him. In his youthful days he had been his disciple at Cologne.

' At one time,' said Suso, ' I was for ten years in the deepest spiritual gloom. I could not realize the mysteries of the faith. A decree seemed to have gone forth against me, and I thought I was lost. My cries, my tears, my penance,—all were vain. I bethought me at last of consulting my old teacher, left my

secret name of Amandus, concealed till after his death, was supposed to have been conferred by the Everlasting Wisdom himself on his beloved servant. The incident of the rescue of him-self and his book from the floods, by the timely intervention of a knight passing that way, is related in the twenty-ninth chapter of the *Life*, p. 68.

cell, sailed down the Rhine, and at Cologne the Lord gave to the words of the master such power that the prison-doors were opened, and I stepped out into the sunshine once more. Neither did his counsel cease with life. I saw him in a vision, not long after his death. He told me that his place was in the ineffable glory, and that his soul was divinely transformed in God. I asked him, likewise, several questions about heavenly things, which he graciously answered, strengthening me not a little in the arduous course of the inner life of self-annihilation. I have marvelled often that any, having tasted of the noble wine of his doctrine, should desire any of my poor vintage.'[4]

In talking with the brethren at the convent, while Suso was their guest, I heard many things related concerning him altogether new to me. I was aware that he had been greatly sought after as a preacher in German throughout the Rhineland, and stood high in the esteem of holy men as a wise and tender-hearted guide of souls. That he was an especial friend of the Friends of God wherever he found them, I knew. When at Cologne I heard Tauler praise a book of his which he had in his possession, called the *Horologe of Wisdom*.[5] Something of the fame of his austerities, conflicts, and revelations, had come to my ears, but the half had not been told me.

It seems that his life, from his eighteenth to his fortieth year, was one long self-torture. The Everlasting Wisdom (who is a tree of life to them that lay hold upon her, more precious than rubies, and with whom are durable riches and righteousness) manifested herself to him. This was his call to the spiritual

---

[4] Heinrich Suso's *Leben und Schriften*, von M. Diepenbrock (1837), pp. 15, 51, 86. Diepenbrock's book is an edition of the biography by Stäglin, and of the *Book of the Everlasting Wisdom*, &c., from the oldest manuscripts and editions, and rendered into modern German.

[5] *Leben*, cap. 48,—where it is also said that, on one occasion, as 'the servant was preaching at Cologne, one of his auditors beheld his face luminous with a supernatural effulgence.' It is known that Tauler possessed a copy of the *Horologium Sapientiæ*.

See also Schmidt's *Tauler*, p. 169. Comp. *Leben*, cap. xxxi. p. 72, and cap. xlix.

life. He seemed to behold her—a maiden, bright as the
sun,—her crown, eternity;—her raiment, blessedness;—her
words, sweetness; unknown, and yet well known; near, and yet
afar off; smiling on him, and saying, 'My son, give me thine
heart!' From that time forth he dedicated his life to her
service. He called himself the servant of the Eternal Wisdom,
armed his soul as her knight, wooed her as his heart's queen,
bore without a murmur the lover's pangs of coyness, doubt,
and distance, with all the hidden martyrdom of spiritual
passion.[6]

But the rose of his love, as he is wont to term it, had fearful
thorns. I heard with a shudder of what he underwent that he
might crush to death his naturally active, buoyant, impulsive
temperament. Day and night he wore a close-fitting shirt in
which were a hundred and fifty sharp nails, the points turned
inward on the flesh. In this he lay writhing, like a mangled
worm; and lest in his sleep he should find some easier posture,
or relieve with his hands in any way the smart and sting that,
like a nest of vipers, gnawed him everywhere, he had leather
gloves made, covered with sharp blades, so that every touch
might make a wound. Time after time were the old scars
opened into new gashes. His body appeared like that of one
who has escaped, half dead, from the furious clutches of a bear.
This lasted sixteen years, till a vision bade him cease.

Never satisfied with suffering, he devised a new kind of
discipline. He fashioned a wooden cross, with thirty nails whose
points stood out beyond the wood, and this he wore between
his shoulders underneath his garments, till his back was one
loathly sore. To the thirty nails he added afterwards seven
more, in honour of the sorrows of the Mother of God. When
he would administer the discipline, he struck a blow on this
cross with his fist, driving the points into his wounded flesh.

[6] *Leben*, cap. iv.

He made himself, moreover, a scourge, one of the iron tags of which was bent like a fisher's hook, and with this he lashed himself till it broke in his hand. For many years he lay at nights in a miserable hole he called his cell, with an old door for his bed, and in the depth of winter thought it sin to approach the stove for warmth. His convent lay on a little island where the Rhine flows out of the Lake of Constance. He could see the sparkling water on every side. His wounds filled him with feverish thirst; yet he would often pass the whole day without suffering a drop to moisten his lips. His recompence was the vision in which, at one time, the Holy Child brought him a vessel of spring-water; and, at another, Our Blessed Lady gave him to drink from her own heart. Such, they tell me, was his life till his fortieth year, when it was signified to him that he should remit these terrible exercises. He is now, I believe, little more than fifty years old—the mere wreck of a man to look at; but with such life and energy of spirit that, now he hath begun to live more like other people, he may have a good thirty years before him still.[7]

I questioned him about his book called the *Horologe of Wisdom*, or *Book of the Eternal Wisdom*, for it hath gone abroad under both names. He said it was finished in the year 1340, since which time he hath written sundry other pieces. He declared to me that he wrote that treatise only in his most favoured moments, himself ignorant and passive, but under the immediate impulse and illumination of the Divine Wisdom. He afterwards carefully examined all he had written, to be sure that there was nothing in his pages other than the holy Fathers had taught, and the Church received.[8] Methought, if he was

[7] *Leben*, cap. xvii.-xx. Suso died in 1385 at Ulm; he was born about the commencement of the century.

[8] Suso sent a Latin version of the book of the Everlasting Wisdom, under the title *Horologium Sapientiæ*, to Hugo von Vaucemain, Master of the Order, for his approval. The date of the work is fixed between 1333 and 1341. The prologue contains the ac-

sure of his inspiration, he might have spared himself this pain,
unless the Holy Spirit could in some sort gainsay his own words.

He is strongly moved by music,—but what must have been
his rapture to hear the hymns of the heavenly host ! He has
seen himself surrounded by the choir of seraphim and cherubim.
He has heard a voice of thrilling sweetness lead the response,
' Arise and shine, Jerusalem,' and has wept in his cell with joy
to hear from angels' lips, at early dawn, the soaring words,
' Mary, the morning star, is risen to-day.' Many a time has
he seen a heavenly company sent down to comfort him. They
have taken him by the hand, and he has joined in spirit in their
dance,—that celestial dance, which is a blissful undulation to
and fro in the depths of the divine glory. One day, when thus
surrounded in vision, he asked a shining prince of heaven to
show him the mode in which God had His secret dwelling in
his soul. Then answered the angel, ' Take a gladsome look
into thine inmost, and see how God in thy loving soul playeth
His play of love.' Straightway (said Suso to me) I looked,
and behold the body about my heart was clear as crystal, and
I saw the Eternal Wisdom calmly sitting in my heart in lovely
wise: and, close by that form of beauty, my soul, leaning on
God, embraced by His arm, pressed to His heart, full of
heavenly longing, transported, intoxicated with love !⁹

We were talking one evening of May-day eve, and asking
Suso wherein their custom of celebrating that festival differed
from our own. He said that in Suabia the youths went out,
much in our fashion, singing songs before the houses of the
maidens they loved, and craving from them garlands in honour
of the May. He told us how he, in like manner, besought Our

count of the '*inspiratio superna*'
under which the work was written.—
(*Diepenb. Vorbericht*, p. 6.) It was
translated ere long into French, Dutch,
and English, and appears to have been

in the fourteenth century almost what
the *Imitatio Christi* became in the
fifteenth.—*Ibid.* p. 15.

⁹ *Leben,* cap. vi.

Lady with prayers and tears that he might have a garland from
her Son, the Eternal Wisdom.   It was his wont, he said, to set
up a spiritual May-pole—the holy cross, that May-bough of the
soul, blossoming with grace and beauty.   ' Before this,' he continued, ' I performed six venias,[10] and sung the hymn, ' Hail,
holy cross !' thereafter praising God somewhat thus :—

' Hail ! heavenly May of the Eternal Wisdom, whose fruit is
everlasting joy.   First, to honour thee, I bring thee, to-day, for
every red rose a heart's love ; then, for every little violet a lowly
inclination ; next, for every tender lily, a pure embrace ; for
every bright flower ever born or to be born of May, on heath or
grassplot, wood or field, tree or meadow, my heart doth bring
thee a spiritual kiss ; for every happy song of birds that ever
sang in the kindly May, my soul would give thee praises inexhaustible ; for every grace that ever graced the May, my heart
would raise thee a spiritual song, and pray thee, O thou blest
soul's May ! to help me so to glorify thee in my little time below,
that I may taste thy living fruit for evermore above !'[11]

The beginning of a new stage of trial was made known to
him by the appearance, in a vision, of an angel, bringing him
the attire and the shoes of a knight.   With these he was to gird
himself for new and yet more terrible conflicts.   Concerning his
own austerities he never speaks, nor does he show to any one
the letters of the name of Jesus, which he is said to have cut
with a style upon his bosom.   But of the sufferings which came
upon him from without, he talks freely.   At one time, when in
Flanders, he was brought before the chapter on a charge of
heresy ; but his enemies gained not their wicked end.[12]   He was
in greatest danger of his life shortly before the coming of the
plague, when the fearful rumour was abroad about the poisoning
of the wells.   He himself told me the story, as follows :—

[10] Reverences or prostrations.   [12] *Leben*, cap. xxii. p. 5 ; and xxv.
[11] *Leben*, capp. x. and xiv.

' I was once despatched on a journey in the service of the convent, and they gave me as my companion a half-witted lay-brother.   We had not been many days on the road, when, one morning, having early left our quarters for the night, we arrived, after a long, hungry walk through the rain, at a village on the banks of the Rhine.   It happened to be the fair-time. The street was full of booths and stalls, horses and cattle, country-folk, players, pedlers, and idle roystering soldiers.   My fellow-traveller, Peter, catches sight of a sign, and turns in straightway to warm himself at the fire, telling me I can go on, do what I have to do, and I shall find him there.   As I learnt after, he sits himself down to table with a ruffianly set of drovers and traders that had come to the fair, who first of all make him half-drunk, and then seize him, and swear he has stolen a cheese. At this moment there come in four or five troopers, hardened fellows, ripe for any outrage, who fall on him also, crying, 'The scroundrel monk is a poisoner.'   The clamour soon gathers a crowd.

' When Peter sees matters at this pass, he piteously cries out to them to loose him, and stand still and listen : he will confess everything.   With that they let go their hold, and he, standing trembling in the midst of them, begins : ' Look at me, sirs,— you see I am a fool ; they call me silly, and nobody cares for what I say : but my companion, he is a wise man, so our Order has given him the poison-bag, and he is to poison all the springs between here and Alsace.   He is gone now to throw some into the spring here, to kill every one that is come to the fair.   That is why I stayed here, and would not go with him.   You may be sure that what I say is true, for you will see him when he comes with a great wallet full of bags of poison and gold pieces, which he and the Order have received from the Jews for this murderous business.'

' At these words they all shouted, ' After the murderer ! Stop

him! Stop him!' One seized a spear, another an axe, others
the first tool or weapon they could lay hands on, and all hurried
furiously from house to house, and street to street, breaking
open doors, ransacking closets, stabbing the beds, and thrusting
in the straw with their swords, till the whole fair was in an
uproar. Some friends of mine, who heard my name mentioned,
assured them of my innocence of such an abominable crime, but
to no purpose. At last, when they could nowhere find me,
they carried Peter off to the bailiff, who shut him up in the
prison.

' When I came back to the inn, knowing nothing of all this,
the host told me what had befallen Peter, and how this evil
rumour had stirred up the whole fair against me. I hastened
off to the bailiff to beg Peter's release. He refused. I spent
nearly the whole day in trying to prevail with him, and in
going about in vain to get bail. At last, about vesper time,
with a heavy sum of gulden I opened the heart of the bailiff and
the doors of the jail.

' Then my greatest troubles began. As I passed through the
village, hoping to escape unknown, I was recognised by some of
the mob, and in a moment they were swarming about me.
' Down with the poisoner!' they cried. ' His gold shall not
serve him with us as it did with the bailiff.' I ran a little way,
but they closed me in again, some saying, ' Drown him in the
Rhine;' others answering, ' No, burn him! he'll poison the
whole river if you throw him in.' Then I saw (methinks I see
him now) a gigantic peasant in a russet jerkin, forcing his way
through the crowd, with a pike in his hand. Seizing me by the
throat with one hand, and flourishing the pike in the other, he
shouted, ' Hear me, all of you. Let me spit him with my long
pike, like a poisonous toad, and then plant it in this stout
hedge here, and let the caitiff howl and twist in the air till his
soul goes home to the devil. Then every one that goes by will

see his withered carcass, rotting and wasting, and sink him deeper down in hell with curses. Come on,—it serves him right.'

' My brain swam round. I closed my eyes. I expected the next instant to feel the iron. By some merciful interposition, the wretch was not suffered to execute his purpose. I thought I saw some of the better sort looking on with horror-stricken faces, but they dared not interfere. The women shrieked and wrung their hands. I made my way from one to another of those who seemed least pitiless, beseeching them to save me. Heaven must have heard my cries, though man did not. They stood round watching me, disputing with horrid oaths among themselves what they should do. At length—as I had sunk on my knees under the hedge, praying for deliverance—I saw a priest, more like an angel than a man, mightily thrusting them from side to side, and when he reached me, laying his hand on my arm, he looked round on the ring of savage faces, and threatened them with the hottest curses of the Church if they harmed a hair upon the head of her servant ; outvoiced their angry cries with loud rebukes of their cowardice, cruelty, and sacrilege, and led me out safely through them all. He brought me to his house, made fast the doors, refreshed and sheltered me for the night, and by the earliest dawn I was away and safe upon my journey, while that abode of the wicked was sunk in its drunken sleep. I keep the anniversary of that dreadful day, and never shall I cease to praise the goodness which answered my prayer in the hour of need, and delivered me as a bird from the snare of the fowler.[13]

' On one other occasion only,' continued Suso, 'did I taste so nearly the bitterness of death.'

---

[13] This incident is related at length in the twenty-seventh chapter of the *Life;* and the adventure with the robber, which follows, in the succeeding. The account given in the text follows closely in all essential particulars the narrative in the biography.

We begged him to tell us the adventure, and so he did, somewhat thus—

' I was once on my way home from Flanders, travelling up the Rhine A great feebleness and sickness had been upon me for some days, so that I could not walk fast, and my companion, young and active, had gone on about two miles ahead. I entered an old forest whose trees overhung the steep river bank. It was evening, and it seemed to grow dark in a moment as I entered the chilling shadow of a wood, in which many a defenceless passenger had been robbed and slain. I had gone on deeper and deeper into the growing gloom, the wind among the pines sounding like a hungry sea. The fall of my own footsteps seemed like the tread of one coming after me. I stood still and hearkened. It was no one ; when suddenly I saw, not far off among the trees, two persons, a man and a woman, talking together and watching me. I trembled in every limb, but I made the sign of the cross, and passed on. Soon I heard quick footsteps behind me. I turned—it was the woman. She was young and fair to look on. She asked my name, and when she learnt it, said she knew and reverenced me greatly, told me how that robber with whom I saw her had forced her to become his wife, and prayed me there and then to hear her confession.

' When I had shriven her, think how my fear was heightened to see her go back and talk long and earnestly with the robber, whose brow grew dark, as he left her without a word, and advanced gloomily towards where I stood. It was a narrow pathway ; on the one side the forest, on the other the precipice, sheer down to the rapid river. Alas, thought I, as my heart sank within me, now I am lost. I have not strength to flee : no one will hear a cry for help : he will slay me, and hide the body in the wood. All was still. I listened in vain for the sound of a boat, a voice, or even the bark of a dog. I only heard the feet of the outlaw and the violent beating of my own heart. But, lo ! when he approached me, he bowed his knee, and began to confess. Blessed Mary, what a black catalogue ! While he spake I heard, motionless, every word of the horrible recital, and yet I was all the time listening for rescue, watching his face, and minutely noting every little thing about his person. I remember the very graining of the wood of his lance which he laid aside on the grass when he knelt to me—the long knife in his belt—his frayed black doublet—his rough red hair, growing close down to his shaggy eyebrows—two great teeth that stood out like tusks—and his hands clasped, covered with warts, and just the colour of the roots of the tree by which I stood. Even during those fearful moments, I can call to mind distinctly how I marked a little shining insect that was struggling among the blades of grass, climbing over a knot of wood, and that got upon a fir-cone and fell off upon its back.

'After revealing to me crimes that made my blood run cold, he went on to say, ' I was once in this forest, just about this hour of the day, on the look-out for booty as I was this evening, when I met a priest, to whom I confessed myself. He was standing just where you are now, and when my shrift was ended, I drew out this knife, stabbed him to the heart, and rolled his body down there into the Rhine.' When I heard this, the cold sweat burst out upon my face ; I staggered back giddy, almost senseless, against the tree. Seeing this, the woman ran up, and caught me in her arms, saying, ' Good sir, fear nothing, he will not kill you.' Whereat the murderer said, ' I have heard much good of you, and that shall save your life to-day. Pray for me, good father, that, through you, a miserable sinner may find mercy in his last hour.' At this I breathed again, and promised to do as he would have me. Then we walked on some way together, till they parted from me, and I reached the skirts of the wood, where sat my companion waiting.

I could just stagger up to him, and then fell down at his side, shivering like a man with the ague.   After some time I arose, and we went on our way.   But I failed not, with strong inward groaning, to plead with the Lord for the poor outlaw, that he might find grace and escape damnation..   And, in sooth, I had so strong an assurance vouchsafed to me of God, that I could not doubt of his final salvation.'

With stories such as these of what befel himself, and many others, whom he knew in Suabia and the Oberland, or met with on his journeys, the holy man whiled away our windy March nights by the ingle.   Very edifying it was to hear him and Rulman Merswin talk together about the higher experiences of the inward life.

Concerning the stages thereof, Suso said that the first consisted in turning away from the world and the lusts of the flesh to God: the second, in patient endurance of all that is contrary to flesh and blood, whether inflicted of God or man: the third, in imitating the sufferings of Christ, and forming ourselves after his sweet doctrine, gracious walk, and pure life.   After this, the soul must withdraw itself into a profound stillness, as if the man were dead, willing and purposing nought but the glory of Christ and our heavenly Father, and with a right lowly demeanour toward friend and foe.   Then the spirit, thus advanced in holy exercise, arriveth at freedom from the outward senses, before so importunate ; and its higher powers lose themselves in a supernatural sensibility.   Here the spirit parts with its natural properties, presses within the circle which represents the eternal Godhead, and reaches spiritual perfection.   It is made free by the Son in the Son.

'This I call,' he said, 'the transit of the soul,—it passes beyond time and space, and is, with an amorous inward intuition, dissolved in God.   This entrance of the soul banishes all forms, images, and multiplicity ; it is ignorant of itself and of all things; it hovers, reduced to its essence, in the abyss of the Trinity. At this elevation there is no effort, no struggle; the beginning and the end are one.[14] Here the Divine Nature doth, as it were, embrace, and inwardly kiss through and through, the soul; that they may be for ever one.[15] He who is thus received into the Eternal Nothing is in the Everlasting Now, and hath neither before nor after. Rightly hath St. Dionysius said that God is Non-being—that is, above all our notions of being. We have to employ images and similitudes, as I must do in seeking to set forth these truths, but know that all such figures are as far below the reality as a blackamoor is unlike the sun.[17] In this absorption whereof I speak, the soul is still a creature, but, at the time, hath no thought whether it be creature or no.'[18]

Suso repeated several times this saying—'A man of true self-abandonment must be *un*built from the creature, *in*-built with Christ, and *over*-built into the Godhead.'[19]

We bid adieu with much regret to this excellent man, and his visit will abide long in our memory. We drew from him a half promise that he would come to see us yet again.

May, 1354.—Oh, most happy May ! My brother Otto hath returned, after trading to and fro so long in foreign parts. He is well and wealthy, and will venture forth no more. What store of marvellous tales hath he about the East ! What hairs'-

---

[14] *Leben*, cap. lvii. Suso speaks to this effect in a dialogue with his spiritual daughter. She describes in another place (p. 74) how she drew Suso on to talk on these high themes, and then wrote down what follows.

[15] *Ibid.*, cap. xxxiv. p. 80; and comp. *Buch. d. E. Weisheit*, cap. vii. p. 199.

[16] *Buchlein von d. E. Weisheit*, Buch. iii. cap. ii.; and *Leben*, cap. lvi. p. 168, and p. 302.

[17] *Leben*, p. 171.

[18] Extravagant as are his expressions concerning the absorption in God, Suso has still numerous passages designed to preclude pantheism; declaring that the distinction between the Creator and the creature is nowise infringed by the essential union he extols. The dialogue with the 'nameless Wild,' already alluded to, is an example.— Comp. *Leben*, cap. lvi. pp. 166, 167, and *Buch. d. E. W.*, Buch. iii. cap. vi.

[19] *Leben*, cap. liii. p. 148. See Note, p. 357.

breadth escapes to relate, and what precious and curious things to show ! Verily, were I to write down here all he hath to tell of, I might be writing all my days.

Only one thing will I note, while I think of it. He visited Mount Athos, now fourteen years ago : he described to me the beauty of the mountain, with its rich olives and lovely gardens, and the whole neighourhood studded with white convents and hermitages of holy men. Some of the monasteries were on rocks so steep that he had to be drawn up by a rope in a basket to enter them. The shrines were wondrous rich with gold and silver and precious stones. But nowhere, he said, was he more martyred by fleas. When he was there, a new doctrine or practice which had sprung up among the monks (taught, it is said, by a certain Abbot Simeon), was making no small stir. There was to be a synod held about it at that time in Constantinople. It seems that some of the monks (called, if I mistake not, Hesychasts) held that if a man shut himself up in a corner of his cell, with his chin upon his breast, turning his thoughts inward, gazing towards his navel, and centering all the strength of his mind on the region of the heart ; and, not discouraged by at first perceiving only darkness, held out at this strange inlooking for several days and nights, he would at length behold a divine glory, and see himself luminous with the very light which was manifested on Mount Tabor. They call these devotees Navel-contemplators. A sorry business ! All the monks, for lack of aught else to do, were by the ears about it,—either trying the same or reviling it.[20]

Methought if our heretics have their extravagances and utmost reaches of mystical folly here, there are some worse still among those lazy Greeks.

*   *   *   *   *   *

[20] Schröckh's *Kirchengeschichte*, vol. xxxiv. pp. 431-450.

KATE. And is that the end of Arnstein's journal?

ATHERTON. No more has come down to posterity.

MRS. ATHERTON. That last piece of news from Mount Athos seems quite familiar to me. I have just been reading Curzon's *Monasteries of the Levant*, and thanks to him, I can imagine the scenery of the mountain and its neighourhood : the Byzantine convents, with their many little windows rounded at the top, the whole structure full of arches and domes,—the little farms interspersed, with their white square towers and cottages of stone at the foot,—the forests of gigantic plane trees, with an underwood of aromatic evergreens,—flowers like those in the conservatory everywhere growing wild,—waterfalls at the head of every valley, dashing down over marble rocks,—and the bells, heard tinkling every now and then, to call the monks to prayer.

WILLOUGHBY. The crass stupidity of those Omphalopsychi shows how little mere natural beauty can contribute to refine and cultivate,—at any rate when the pupils are ascetics. The contemporary mysticism of the East looks mean enough beside the speculation, the poetry, and the action of the German mystics of the fourteenth century. It is but the motionless abstraction of the Indian Yogi over again.

ATHERTON. Yet you will be unjust to the Greek Church (which has little enough to boast of) if you reckon this gross materialist Quietism as the only specimen of mysticism she has to show during this period. There was a certain Cabasilas, Archbishop of Thessalonica,[21] a contemporary of our German friends, an active man in the political and religious movements of the time, whose writings exhibit very fairly the better

---

[21] See *Die Mystik des Nikolaus Cabasilas vom Leben in Christo*, von Dr. W. Gass (1849).—In this work, Dr. Gass publishes, for the first time, the Greek text of the seven books, *De Vita in Christo*, with an able introduction. The authority for this summary of the theological tendency of Cabasilas will be found, pp. 210-224.

characteristics of Byzantine mysticism. His earnest practical
devotion rests on the basis of the traditional sacerdotalism, but
he stands between the extremes of the objective and the subjective mysticism, though naturally somewhat nearer to the
former. He presents, however, nothing original to detain us ;—
so let us away to supper.

Note to page 354.

The following passage, placed in the mouth of the Everlasting Wisdom
may serve as a further specimen of the sensuous and florid cast of Suso's
language :—
'I am the throne of joy, I am the crown of bliss. Mine eyes are so bright,
my mouth so tender, my cheeks so rosy-red. and all my form so winning fair,
that were a man to abide in a glowing furnace till the Last Day, it would be a
little price for a moment's vision of my beauty. Behold ! I am so beauteously
adorned with a robe of glory, so delicately arrayed in all the blooming colours
of the living flowers—red roses, white lilies, lovely violets, and flowers of every
name, that the fair blossoms of all Mays, and the tender flowerets of all sunny
fields, and the sweet sprays of all bright meadows, are but as a rugged thistle
beside my loveliness.' (Then he breaks into verse):—

> 'I play in the Godhead the play of joy,
>   And gladden the angel host on high
> With a sweetness such that a thousand years
>   Like a vanishing hour of time run by.

' . . . . Happy he who shall share the sweet play, and tread at my side the joy-
dance of heaven for ever in gladsome security. One word from my sweet
mouth surpasses all the songs of angels, the sound of all harps, and all sweet
playing on stringed instruments. . . . . Lo ! I am a good so absolute that he
who hath in time but one single drop thereof finds all the joy and pleasure of
this world a bitterness,—all wealth and honour worthless. Those dear ones who
love me are embraced by my sweet love, and swim and melt in the sole Unity
with a love which knows no form, no figure, no spoken words, and are borne and
dissolved into the Good from whence they sprang,' &c.—*Leben*, cap. vii. p. 199.
    The following is a sample of Suso's old Suabian German, from the extracts
given by Wackernagel, p. 885 :—
    '*Entwürt der ewigen weisheit.* Zuo uallende lon lit an sunderlicher froed. die
diu sel gewinnet von sunderlichen vnd erwirdigen werken mit dien si hie gesiget
hat. Alz die hohen lerer, die starken martyrer. Vnd die reinen iung frowen.
Aber wesentliche lon. lit an schöwlicher ver einung der sele mit der blossen gotheit.
Wan e geruowet si niemer, e si gefueret wirt über alle ir Krefte vnd mugentheit.
vnd gewiset wirt in der personen naturlich wesentheit. Vnd in dez wesens
einvaltig blosheit. Vnd in dem gegenwurf vindet si denn genuegde vnd ewige
selikeit. Vnd ie abgescheidener lidiger usgang. ie frier uf gang. Vnd ie frier
uf gang. ie neher in gang. in die wilden wuesti. vnd in daz tief ab gründe der
wise losen gotheit in die siu versenket ver swemmet vnd ver einet werdent. daz
siu nit anderz mugen wellen denn daz got wil. vnd daz ist daz selb wesen daz do
got ist. daz ist daz siu selig sint. von genaden, als er selig ist von nature.
[*Answer of the Everlasting Wisdom.—Adventitious* reward consists in a par-

ticular joy which souls receive for particular worthy deeds wherein they have here been conquerors,—such, for example, are the lofty teachers, the stout martyrs, and the pure virgins. But *essential* reward consists in contemplative union of the soul with the bare Godhead : for she resteth not until she be carried above all her own powers and possibility, and led into the natural essentiality of the Persons, and into the simple absoluteness of the Essence. And in the reaction she finds satisfaction and everlasting bliss. And the more separate and void the passage out (of self), the more free the passage up ; and the freer the passage up, the nearer the passage into the wild waste and deep abyss of the unsearchable Godhead, in which the souls are sunk and dissolved and united, so that they can will nothing but what God wills, and become of one nature with God,—that is to say, are blessed by grace as He is blessed by nature.]

CHAPTER IX.

Di Meistere sprechen von zwein antlitzen der sêle. Daz eine antlitze ist gekart in dise werlt. Daz ander antlitze ist gekart di richte in got. In diseme antlitze lûchtet und brennet got êwiclîchen, der mensche wizzes oder enwizzes nicht.[1]—
HERMANN VON FRITZLAR.

KATE. I should like to know what became of our mysterious 'Layman,' Nicholas of Basle.

ATHERTON. He lived on many years, the hidden ubiquitous master-spirit of the Friends of God; expending his wealth in restless rapid travels to and fro, and in aiding the adherents of the good cause; suddenly appearing, now in the north and now in the south, to encourage and exhort, to seek out new disciples and to confirm the old; and again vanishing as suddenly, concealing his abode even from his spiritual children, while sending them frequent tracts and letters by his trusty messenger Ruprecht; growing ever more sad and earnest under repeated visions of judgment overhanging Christendom; studying the Scriptures (which had opened his eyes to so much of Romanist error) somewhat after the old Covenanter fashion, with an indiscriminate application of Old Testament history, and a firm belief that his revelations were such as prophets and apostles enjoyed,—till, at last, at the close of the century, he was overtaken at Vienna by the foe he had so often baffled, and the

[1] The Masters speak of two faces the soul hath. The one face is turned towards this world The other face is turned direct toward God. In this latter face shineth and gloweth God eternally, whether man is ware or unaware thereof.

Inquisition yet more ennobled a noble life by the fiery gift of martyrdom.[2]

GOWER. I can well imagine what a basilisk eye the Inquisition must have kept on these lay-priests—these indefatigable writers and preachers to the people in the forbidden vernacular —these Friends of God, Beghards, and Waldenses ; and on those audacious Ishmaels, the Brethren of the Free Spirit, most of all. I fancy I see it, lurking always on the edge of any light, watching and watching, as they say the Indian lizard does, crouched in the shadow just outside the circle of light a lamp makes upon the ceiling, to snatch up with its arrowy tongue the moths which fly toward the fascinating brightness.

WILLOUGHBY. And do not let us forget that even those pantheistic Brethren of the Free Spirit, with all their coarseness and violence of exaggeration, held at least some little truth, and might plead a large excuse. If some of them broke blindly through all restraint, they made at any rate a breach in priest-craft better used by better men.—

GOWER.—Just as the track where buffaloes have made their huge crashing way through the forest, has often guided the hunter of the backwoods.

ATHERTON. We must not think that the efforts of such a man as Nicholas were fruitless, whatever the apparent success of his persecutors.—

GOWER.—Though history has paid him too little attention, and though the Inquisition paid him too much. How I love to find examples of that consoling truth that no well-meant effort for God and man can ever really die—that the relics of vanished, vanquished endeavours are gathered up and conserved, and by the spiritual chemistry of Providence transformed into a new

[2] Schmidt's *Tauler*, pp. 205, &c.— Mosheim gives the passage in Nieder relating the apprehension and death of Nicholas :—'Acutissimus enim erat (says this authority) et idcirco manus Inquisitorum diu evaserat.'—*Mosheim de Beghardis et Beguinabus*, cap. iv. § 42, p. 454.

life in a new age, so that the dead rise, and mortality puts on immortality. The lessons such men scattered, though they might seem to perish, perpetuated a hidden life till Luther's time ;—like the dead leaves about the winter tree, they preserved the roots from the teeth of the frost, and covered a vitality within, which was soon to blossom on every bough in the sunshine of the Reformation.

ATHERTON. Our fourteenth century, so full of mysticism both in East and West, has some other mystical products to show, principally of the visionary, theurgic species. There is St. Brigitta, a widow of rank, leaving her Swedish pine forests to visit Palestine, and after honouring with a pilgrimage every shrine and relic in southern Europe, fixing her residence at Rome, to the great pecuniary advantage of the faithful there. She writes a discourse on the Blessed Virgin at the dictation of an angel, who visited her punctually for the purpose : indites bombastic invocations to the eyes, ears, hair, chin, &c., of the Saviour ; and *ditto* to *ditto* of the Virgin ; and, what was not quite so bad, gives to the world a series of revelations and prophecies, in which the vices of popes and prelates are lashed unsparingly, and threatened with speedy judgment.[3]

WILLOUGHBY. It would be interesting to trace this series of

[3] See *Revelationes Selectæ S. Brigittæ* (Heuser, 1851).—This is a selection for the edification of good Catholics, and contains accordingly the most Mario-latrous and least important of her writings. Rudelbach gives some speci-mens of her spirited rebuke of papal iniquity in his *Savonarola*, pp. 300, &c. In her prophetic capacity she does not hesitate to call the pope a murderer of souls, and to declare him and his greedy prelates forerunners of Anti-christ. She says,—'If a man comes to them with four wounds, he goes away with five.' Like Savonarola, she placed her sole hope of reform in a general council.

A common mode of self-mortifica-tion with her found an imitator in Madame Guyon :—the Swede dropped the wax of lighted tapers on her bare flesh, and carried gentian in her mouth —*Vita*, p. 6. The Frenchwoman burned herself with hot sealing-wax in the same manner, and chewed a quid of coloquintida.

The *Revelationes de Vitâ et Passione Jesu Christi et gloriosæ Virginis*, con-tain a puerile and profane account of the birth, childhood, and death of our Lord, in the style of the apocryphal *Gospel of the Infancy*, professedly conveyed in conversations with the authoress by the Mother and her Son.

reformatory prophets, male and female. From the twelfth to
the close of the fifteenth century there is a succession of them,
called forth by the hideousness of ecclesiastical corruption—
Hildegard, Joachim, Brigitta, Savonarola.

GOWER. Do not forget Dante.

ATHERTON. You hear them all executing variations, plaintive
or indignant, menacing or despairing, on the old and never
antiquated theme—

> Curia Romana non petit ovem sine lanâ,
> Dantes exaudit, non dantibus ostia claudit.

GOWER. And, to silence these complaints, the Church found
inquisitors and censors of service, but most of all—her pattern
children—those enthusiasts whose painful labours were employed to quiet the croaking, much as the lord in old feudal
times would often exercise his right of compelling a vassal to
spend a night or two in beating the waters of the ponds, to
stop the frog-chorus there, and procure his master an easy
sleep. Obedient enthusiasm toils all night that cardinals may
snore.

ATHERTON. Angela de Foligni, who made herself miserable
—I must say something the converse of flourished—about the
beginning of the fourteenth century, was a fine model pupil of
this sort, a genuine daughter of St. Francis. Her mother, her
husband, her children dead, she is alone and sorrowful. She
betakes herself to violent devotion—falls ill—suffers incessant
anguish from a complication of disorders—has rapturous
consolations and terrific temptations—is dashed in a moment
from a seat of glory above the empyrean to a depth so low that
the floor of hell might be its zenith. She tells us how, on her

---

The Virgin tells her, in reference to
her Son,—'quomodo neque aliqua
immunditia ascendit super eum;' and
that his hair was never in a tangle—
(nec perplexitas in capillise jus appa-
ruit).

way to Assisi, the Saviour addressed her, called her his love, his
sweet, his joy; and manifested himself within her soul as he
had never done to evangelist or apostle.   On one occasion, her
face shone with a divine glory, her eyes were as flaming lamps;
on another, a star proceeded from her side, broke into a thousand
beautiful colours, and glided upwards into the sky.[4]

WILLOUGHBY. A notable example of mystical pyrotechny.

ATHERTON. Her etherialised olfactories were gratified by
odours of indescribable fragrance; and to her exalted taste, the
consecrated wafer became almost insupportably delicious.
Visions and ecstasies by scores are narrated from her lips in the
wretched Latin of Arnold the Minorite.   All is naught!   The
flattest and most insipid reading in the world—from first to last

---

[4] '*Angela de Foligni.*' See *Beatæ
Angelæ de Fulginio Visionum et In-
structionum Liber;* (recens.]. H.
Lammertz; Cologne, 1851.)—The account of the wonderful star is given by
Arnold in his *Prologue,* p. 12.   At one
time it is promised by the Lord that
the 'whole Trinity shall enter into her,'
(capit. xx.); at another, she is transported into the midst of the Trinity.
—(Capit. xxxii.) In chapter after
chapter of monotonous inflation, she
wearies and disappoints the curious
reader by declaring her 'abysses of
delectation and illumination' altogether
unutterable,—such as language pro-
fanes rather than expresses—'inen-
arrabiles,' 'indicibiles,' &c. So the
miraculous taste of the host to her
favoured palate was not like bread or
flesh, but a 'sapor sapidissimus,'—like
nothing that can be named.—Capit. xl.
The following act of saintship we
give in the original, lest in English it
should act on delicate readers as an
emetic.   She speaks of herself and a
sister ascetic :—' Lavimus pedes femi-
narum ibi existentium pauperum, et
manus hominum, et maxime cujus-
dam leprosi, qui habebat manus valde
fœtidas et marcidas et præpeditas et

corruptas; *et bibimus de illâ loturâ.*
Tantam autem dulcedinem sensimus
in illo potu, quod per totam viam
venimus in magnâ suavitate, et vide-
batur mihi per omnia quod ego gus-
tassem mirabilem dulcedinem, quantum
ad suavitatem quam ibi inveni.   Et
quia quædam squamula illarum plaga-
rum erat interposita in gutture meo,
conata sum ad diglutiendum eam, sicut
si communicassem, donec deglutivi
eam.   Unde tantam suavitatem inveni
in hoc, quod eam non possum expri-
mere.'—Capit. l. p. 176.
In her ' Instructions,' she lays it
down as a rule that none can ever be
deceived in the visions and manifestations vouchsafed them who are truly
poor in spirit,—who have rendered
themselves as 'dead and putrid' into
the hands of God.   (Capp. liv. lv.)
She says that when God manifests
Himself to the soul, 'it sees Him,
without bodily form, indeed, but more
distinctly than one man can see another man, for the eyes of the soul
behold a spiritual plenitude, not a corporeal, whereof I can say nothing,
since both words and imagination fail
here.'   (Capit. lii. p. 192.) Angela
died in 1309.

a repetition of the old stock phrase, 'feelings more readily imagined than described.' She concludes every account by saying, 'No words can describe what I enjoyed;' and each rapture is declared to surpass in bliss all the preceding.

LOWESTOFFE. Enough! enough!

ATHERTON. Catharine of Siena——

WILLOUGHBY. No more, pray.

ATHERTON. Only this one. Catharine of Siena closes the century. She is a specimen somewhat less wretched, of this delirious mysticism. Her visions began when she was six years old, and a solemn betrothal to our Lord was celebrated, with ring and vow, not very long after. She travelled through the cities and hamlets of Italy, teaching, warning, expostulating, and proclaiming to assembled crowds the wonders she had seen in heaven and hell during that trance in which all had thought her dead. She journeyed from Florence to Avignon, and back to Florence again, to reconcile the Pope and Italy; she thrust herself between the spears of Guelph and Ghibelline—a whole Mediæval Peace-Society in her woman's heart—and when she sank at last, saw all her labour swept away, as the stormy waters of the Great Schism closed over her head.[5]

GOWER. What a condemning comment on the pretended tender mercies of the Church are those narratives which Rome delights to parade of the sufferings, mental and bodily, which her devotees were instructed to inflict upon themselves! I am reminded of the thirsting mule, which has, in some countries, to strike with its hoof among the spines of the cactus, and drink, with lamed foot and bleeding lips, the few drops of milk which ooze from the broken thorns. Affectionate suffering natures came to Rome for comfort; but her scanty kindness is only to be drawn with anguish from the cruel sharpness of asceticism.

---

[5] '*Catharine of Siena.*' Görres gives a short account of her in his In-troduction to Diepenbrock's edition of *Suso,* p. 96.

The worldly, the audacious, escape easily; but these pliant excitable temperaments, so anxiously in earnest, may be made useful. The more dangerous, frightful, or unnatural their performances, the more profit for their keepers. Men and women are trained by torturing processes to deny their nature, and then they are exhibited to bring grist to the mill—like birds and beasts forced to postures and services against the laws of their being—like those who must perform perilous feats on ropes or with lions, nightly hazarding their lives to fill the pockets of a manager. The self-devotion of which Rome boasts so much is a self-devotion she has always thus made the most of for herself. Calculating men, who have thought only of the interest of the priesthood, have known well how best to stimulate and to display the spasmodic movements of a brainsick disinterestedness. I have not the shadow of a doubt that, once and again, some priest might have been seen, with cold grey eye, endeavouring to do a stroke of diplomacy by means of the enthusiastic Catharine, making the fancied ambassadress of heaven in reality the tool of a schemer. Such unquestionable virtues as these visionaries may some of them have possessed, cannot be fairly set down to the credit of the Church, which has used them all for mercenary or ambitious purposes, and infected them everywhere with a morbid character. Some of these mystics, floating down the great ecclesiastical current of the Middle Age, appear to me like the trees carried away by the inundation of some mighty tropical river. They drift along the stream, passive, lifeless, broken; yet they are covered with gay verdure, the aquatic plants hang and twine about the sodden timber and the draggled leaves, the trunk is a sailing garden of flowers. But the adornment is not that of nature—it is the decoration of another and a strange element; the roots are in the air; the boughs, which should be full of birds, are in the flood, covered by its alien products, swimming side by side with the alligator.

So has this priestcraft swept its victims from their natural place and independent growth, to clothe them in their helplessness, with a false spiritual adornment, neither scriptural nor human, but ecclesiastical—the native product of that overwhelming superstition which has subverted and enslaved their nature. The Church of Rome takes care that while simple souls think they are cultivating Christian graces, they shall be forging their own chains; that their attempts to honour God shall always dishonour, because they disenfranchise themselves. To be humble, to be obedient, to be charitable, under such direction, is to be contentedly ignorant, pitiably abject, and notoriously swindled.

ATHERTON. Strong language, Lionel,—yet not unjust to the spirit of the Romanist system. The charity which pities the oppressed is bound to denounce the oppressor.

WILLOUGHBY. *Rem acu tetigisti.* If you call priestcraft by smooth names, your spurious charity to the tyrant is uncharitableness to the slave. It is sickening to hear the unctuous talk with which now-a-days ultra-liberalism will sometimes stretch out a hand to spiritual tyranny.

ATHERTON. Not surprising. It is just like the sentimental sympathy got up for some notorious criminal, which forgets the outrage to society and the sufferings of the innocent, in concern for the interesting offender.

And now let us bid adieu to that fourteenth century which has occupied us so long. I shall only afflict you with one more paper,—to-morrow, Lowestoffe, if we don't go to Hawksfell. Some notes I have drawn up on the contemporary Persian mysticism.

WILLOUGHBY. Stay—do not let us forget that little book, so much read in the fifteenth century, and praised and edited by Luther,—the *German Theology.*[6] I have read it with great

6 The theology of this remarkable with that already familiar to us in the little book is substantially the same sermons of Tauler. Luther, writing

interest. It seems to me to stand alone as an attempt to systematise the speculative element in the more orthodox mysticism of the age.

ATHERTON. We may call it a summary of Tauler's doctrine, without his fancy and vehement appeal; it is a treatise philosophic in its calmness, deservedly popular for its homely, idiomatic diction. What we were saying about Tauler applies substantially to the *Theologia Germanica*.

MRS. ATHERTON. I have been waiting to hear something about Thomas à Kempis,[7]—certainly the best known of all your mystics.

ATHERTON. Right. Who could forget the comforter of the fifteenth century? It is curious to compare the third book of his *Imitation of Christ*, with its dialogue between Christ and the disciple, and Suso's conversation, in his *Book of the Eternal Wisdom*, between Wisdom and the Servant.

GOWER. There is less genius, less *abandon*, if one may so say, about Thomas.

ATHERTON. Decidedly. That original and daring spirit which carried mysticism to such a height in the fourteenth century, could not survive in the fifteenth,—an age tending towards consolidation and equilibrium, bent on the softening down of extremes. Suso, a poet as much as an ascetic, is

---

to Spalatin, and praising Tauler's theology, sends with his letter what he calls an epitome thereof,—cujus totius velut epitomen ecce hic tibi mitto. (*Epp. De Wette*, No. xxv.) He refers, there can be little doubt, to his edition of the *Deutsche Theologie*, which came out that year.

7 See, especially, the twelfth chapter of the second book, *On the Necessity of bearing the Cross.* Compare Michelet's somewhat overdrawn picture of the effects of the *Imitation* in his *History of France*.

The *Ignitum cum Deo Soliloquium*

of Gerlacus Petrus is a contemporary treatise belonging to the same school. (Comp. capp. xxxix. and xxvi.; ed. Strange, 1849.) It is less popular, less impassioned than the *Imitation*, and more thoroughly impregnated with the spirit of mysticism. Gerlach would seem to have studied Suso: in one place he imitates his language. The cast of his imagery, as well as the prominence given to mystical phraseology, more peculiar to the Germans, shows that he addresses himself to an advanced and comparatively esoteric circle.—Comp. capp. xxii. xxiv. p. 78.

continually quitting his cell to admire nature and to mix with men. He mingles speculation borrowed from his master, Eckart, with the luxuriant play of his own inexhaustible fancy. Thomas à Kempis is exclusively the ascetic. His mysticism ranges in a narrower sphere. Hence, to a great extent, his wider influence. He abjures everything that belongs to the thought of the philosopher or the fine feeling of the artist. He appeals neither to the intellect nor to the imagination—simply to the heart. He could be understood without learning, appreciated without taste, and so thousands, in castle and in cloister, prayed and wept over his earnest page. 'See !' said he, 'this life is filled with crosses.' And multitudes, in misery, or fear of misery, made answer, 'It is true.'—'Then,' urged the comforter, 'be thyself crucified to it, and it cannot harm thee. Cease to have any care, any aim, any hope or fear, save Christ. Yield thyself, utterly passive and dead to this life, into his hands who is Lord of a better.' Then the sufferers dried their tears, and strove hard to forget time and self in contemplating Christ.

GOWER. And, let us hope, not always quite in vain.

ATHERTON. I have one more name yet upon my list, with which the mediæval mysticism reaches its conclusion. It is the great Frenchman, Chancellor Gerson.[8] His figure stands out prominently among the confusions of the time, half-way between the old age and the new. Up to a certain point, he is a reformer ; beyond it, the enemy of reform. He is active in the deposition of John XXII., yet he does not hesitate to burn John Huss. He looks on, with a smile of satisfaction, when the royal secretaries stab with their penknives the papal bulls, and the rector tears the insolent parchment into shreds. He sees, half with pity and half with triumph, the emissaries of the Pope, crowned in mockery with paper tiaras, and hung with

---

[8] 'Gerson.'—See an article by Lieb-ner (Gerson's *Mystische Theologie*) in the *Theologische Studien und Kritiken;* 1835, ii.

insulting scrolls, dragged through the streets in a scavenger's
tumbril, to be pilloried by angry Paris. But he stands aloof
in disdain when the University, deserted by the Parliament,
fraternizes with the mob to enforce reform,—when threadbare
students come down from their garrets in the Pays Latin to
join the burly butchers of St. Jacques la Boucherie,—when
grave doctors shake hands with ox-fellers, and Franciscans and
White-hoods shout together for the charter.

WILLOUGHBY. And very wrong he was, too, for those
butchers, rough as they were, were right in the main,—honest,
energetic fellows, with good heads on their shoulders. Could
they but have raised money, they would have saved France.
But Gerson would rather be plundered than pay their tax, and
had to hurry down for hiding to the vaults of Notre Dame.
I remember the story. And when the princes came back to
power, the moderates were pillaged like the rest,—and serve
them right.

ATHERTON. Yes, the reform demanded was just and moderate, and even the rioters lost none of their respect for royalty,
feeling still in their rude hearts no little of that chivalrous
loyalty which animated Gerson himself when he bent low before
the poor idiot king, and with oriental reverence exclaimed, 'O
King, live for ever!' Gerson was a radical in the Church and
a conservative in the State—the antagonist of the political
republicanism, the champion of the ecclesiastical. His
sanguine hopes of peace for his country and of reform for his
Church, were alike doomed to disappointment.

His great work on the theory and practice of mysticism was
composed during the stormy period of his public life. Imagine
how happily he forgot popes and councils, Cabochiens and
Armagnacs, during those brief intervals of quiet which he
devoted to the elaboration of a psychology that should give to
mysticism a scientific basis. Nominalist as he was, and fully

conscious of the defects of scholasticism, then tottering to its fall, he differs little in his results from Richard of St. Victor. He closes the series of those who have combined mysticism with scholasticism, and furnishes in himself a summary and critical *resumé* of all that had previously been accomplished in this direction. He was desirous at once of making mysticism definite and intelligible, and of rendering the study of theology as a science more practical, devout, and scriptural. Hence his opposition to the extravagance of Ruysbroek on the one side, and to the frigid disputation of the schools on the other. He essays to define and investigate the nature of ecstasy and rapture. He even introduces into mysticism that *reflection* which its very principle repudiates. He recommends an inductive process, which is to arrange and compare the phenomena of mysticism as manifest in the history of saintly men, and thence to determine the true and legitimate mystical experience, as opposed to the heterodox and the fantastic. He maintains that man rises to the height of abstract contemplation, neither by the intellectual machinery of Realism, nor by the flights of Imagination. If he attempts the first, he becomes a heretic; if the second, a visionary. The indispensable requisite is what he calls 'rapturous love.' Yet even this is knowledge in the truest sense, and quite compatible with a rational, though impassioned self-consciousness. His doctrine of union is so temperate and guarded as almost to exclude him from the genuine mystical fellowship. He has no visions or exaltations of his own to tell of. Resembling Richard in this respect, to whom he is so much indebted, he elaborates a system, erects a tabernacle, and leaves it to others to penetrate to the inmost sanctuary. Like Bernard, he thinks those arduous and dazzling heights of devotion are for 'the harts and climbing goats,' not for active practical men such as the Chancellor. Above all, urges this reformer both of the schoolmen and the mystics, clear your mind of phantasms —do not mistake the creations of your own imagination for objective spiritual realities. In other words, 'Be a mystic, but do not be what nine mystics out of every ten always have been.'

But now let us have a walk in the garden.

Thither all repaired. They entered the conservatory to look at the flowers.

'Which will you have, Mr. Atherton,' asked Kate, 'to represent your mystics? These stiff, apathetic cactuses and aloes, that seem to know no changes of summer and winter, or these light stemless blossoms, that send out their delicate roots into the air?'

'Those Aroideæ, do you mean?' replied Atherton. 'I think we must divide them, and let some mystics have those impassive plants of iron for their device, while others shall wear the silken filaments of these aërial flowers that are such pets of yours.'

As they came out, the sun was setting in unusual splendour, and they stood in the porch to admire it.

'I was watching it an hour ago,' said Gower. 'Then the western sky was crossed by gleaming lines of silver, with broken streaks of grey and purple between. It was the funeral pyre not yet kindled, glittering with royal robe and arms of steel, belonging to the sun-god. Now, see, he has descended, and lies upon it—the torch is applied, the glow of the great burning reaches over to the very east. The clouds, to the zenith, are wreaths of smoke, their volumes ruddily touched beneath by the flame on the horizon, and those about the sun are like ignited beams in a great conflagration, now falling in and lost in the radiance, now sending out fresh shapes of flashing fire : that is not to be painted !'

LOWESTOFFE (*starting*). The swan, I declare! How can he have got out? That scoundrel, John!

ATHERTON. Never mind. I know what he comes for. He is a messenger from Lethe, to tell us not to forget good Tauler.

LOWESTOFFE. Lethe! Nonsense.

MRS. ATHERTON. My love, how can you?

ATHERTON. The creature reminded me of an allegorical fancy recorded by Bacon,—that is all. At the end of the thread of every man's life there is a little medal containing his name. Time waits upon the shears, and as soon as the thread is cut, catches the medals, and carries them to the river of Lethe. About the bank there are many birds flying up and down, that will get the medals and carry them in their beak a little while, and then let them fall into the river. Only there are a few swans, which, if they get a name, will carry it to a temple, where it is consecrated. Let the name of Tauler find a swan!

END OF VOL. I.

PRINTED BY BALLANTYNE AND HANSON
LONDON AND EDINBURGH